D1190888

Conducting Insanity Evaluations

Conducting Insanity Evaluations

Second Edition

Richard Rogers, PhD
Daniel W. Shuman, JD

The Guilford Press
New York / London

© 2000 The Guilford Press
A Division of Guilford Publications, Inc.
72 Spring Street, New York, NY 10012
www.guilford.com

Printed in the United States of America

This book is printed on acid-free paper.

Last digit is print number: 9   8   7   6   5   4   3   2

Library of Congress Cataloging-in-Publication Data

Rogers, Richard, 1950–
    Conducting insanity evaluations / Richard Rogers and Daniel W. Shuman.—2nd ed.
        p. ; cm.
    Includes bibliographical references and indexes.
    ISBN 1-57230-521-5 (hard.).
    1. Mental illness—Diagnosis.   2. Forensic psychiatry.   I. Shuman, Daniel W.   II. Title.
    [DNLM: 1. Insanity Defense—United States—Legislation.   2. Expert Testimony—methods—Unites States—Legislation.   3. Forensic Psychiatry—methods—United States—Legislation.   4. Interview, Psychological—methods—United States—Legislation.
WM 33 AA1 R7c 2000]
RC469 . R58   2000
616.89'075—dc21
                                                                99-052484

About the Authors

Richard Rogers, PhD, ABPP, is a professor of psychology at the University of North Texas, Denton, Texas. His previous appointments included key positions at the Isaac Ray Center, Rush University, Chicago, Illinois, and Clarke Institute of Psychiatry, University of Toronto, Ontario. He received the American Psychiatric Association's Manfred S. Guttmacher Award for *Clinical Assessment of Malingering and Deception* as an outstanding contribution to forensic psychiatry. Dr. Rogers was the first recipient of the Distinguished Contributions to Forensic Psychology Award from the American Academy of Forensic Psychologists.

Dr. Rogers has written extensively on clinical and forensic practice. His previous books include *Mental Health Experts and the Criminal Courts* and *Diagnostic and Structured Interviewing*. He has also authored several psychological measures of relevance to forensic practice: the Rogers Criminal Responsibility Assessment Scales and the Structured Interview for Reported Symptoms.

Daniel W. Shuman, JD, is a professor of law at Southern Methodist University School of Law, Dallas, Texas, with adjunct appointments at the University of Texas, Southwestern Medical School, Dallas, Texas, and the University of North Texas, Denton, Texas. He is the author of *Psychiatric and Psychological Evidence*, which received the American Psychiatric Association's Manfred S. Guttmacher Award as an outstanding contribution to forensic psychiatry. Prior to joining the faculty of the Southern Methodist University School of Law, he served as assistant attorney general for the State of Arizona and as a legal services attorney in Tucson, Arizona.

Mr. Shuman is a prolific and highly regarded author on law and mental health issues. His contributions include *Law, Mental Health, and Mental Disorder; Law and Mental Health Professionals: Texas; Doing Legal Research: A Guide for Social Scientists and Mental Health Professionals;* and *The Psychotherapist-Patient Privilege.*

Preface

Substantial and far-reaching changes in the conceptualization of insanity evaluations and the legal standards that form their foundation have occurred during the last decade. The first edition of *Conducting Insanity Evaluations* was published in 1986 and outlined the essential issues for mental health professionals assessing defendants for criminal responsibility. This second edition is a fundamental revision that updates clinical methods and provides explicit standards for forensic practice. In addition, the legal context for insanity evaluations has continued to evolve both in the application of insanity standards and in the delineation of forensic practice according to standards for admissibility set forth in the Supreme Court decision in *Daubert v. Merrell Dow Pharmaceuticals* (1993).

The most significant change in the second edition is the addition of Dan Shuman as an author. His addition has improved both the sophistication of the legal analyses and the book's accessibility to a diverse readership of clinical and legal experts. Moreover, our combined efforts broaden and deepen the understanding of the insanity defense from its theoretical and conceptual roots to the immediate pragmatics of evaluations, court reports, and eventual testimony.

A vital dimension of insanity evaluations is understanding how clinical characteristics, diagnoses, and criminal behavior are assessed. A major change in the second edition is the expansion and further development of data bases. In the first edition, a descriptive data base from the Rogers Criminal Responsibility Assessment Scales (R-CRAS) was used to provide a framework for understanding the critical symptoms and their relationship to insanity constructs. In the second edition, the R-CRAS data base was enlarged through the compilation of data on 413 defendants evaluated for criminal responsibility. An additional data base was created specifically for the second edition. This data base was compiled from 23 U.S. studies on clinical, demographic, and offense characteristics on 6,479 defendants acquitted "not guilty by reason of insanity" (NGRI) in the United States. Findings from both data bases augment the relevant chapters and are summarized in Appendix A.

The second edition is a thorough rewriting and updating of *Conducting Insanity Evaluations*. The text is also expanded by the addition of two new chapters: "The Expert–Attorney Relationship" and "Communication of Findings." The common thread for both chapters is a contextualization of insanity evaluations. The first of these chapters examines front-end issues in establishing the relationship between consulting experts and attorneys. The second chapter considers back-end issues in the form of written reports and expert testimony.

Contents

PART II. CLINICAL METHODS

APPENDICES

Introduction

Overview

Conducting Insanity Evaluations provides a clear and concise outline of the clinical methods employed in the assessment of criminal responsibility. These clinical methods are framed by insanity standards and relevant case law. To achieve its goals, the book is organized into two major parts. Part I, Clinical and Legal Issues, provides a conceptual basis for understanding (1) the insanity defense and the responsibilities of involved professionals and (2) commonly encountered clinical issues (e.g., malingering and amnesia) that greatly complicate insanity evaluations. Part II, Clinical Methods, examines (1) the use of interviews, testing, and specialized procedures in insanity evaluations, and discusses (2) the integration and presentation of data to the courts. In combination, Parts I and II provide mental health professionals with a theoretical and practical framework for conducting insanity evaluations. Similarly, they provide attorneys with a foundation for evaluating the quality of insanity evaluations and challenging substandard assessments.

Forensic experts and attorneys face formidable challenges with in-

sanity cases. By definition, insanity cases involve retrospective evaluations of diagnosis and impairment that often extend months into the
past. This passage of time constrains the usefulness of many assessment
methods (see Chapters 7–10). In addition, there are reasons to suspect
malingering and other forms of deception (see Chapter 5). Memory
loss and distortion become commonplace (see Chapter 6). Beyond these
clinical challenges, the application of specific insanity standards becomes
the essential issue (see Chapter 4). Statutory language, such as "lacks
substantial capacity," becomes exceedingly difficult to operationalize
into criteria that can be tested or measured.

Professionals grapple with the challenges of insanity evaluations in
different ways based on their past training and current responsibilities.
As Rogers and Mitchell (1991) noted, substantial differences are observed even between forensic experts. Forensic psychologists are typically trained in the scientist-practitioner model, with a strong emphasis
on both clinical practice and its theoretical and empirical underpinnings. In contrast, forensic psychiatrists are generally trained in a prac-
titioner-only model, with a strong emphasis on clinical applications.
While some attorneys may have training in science or even specifically
in psychology, nothing in law school admission or course requirements
assumes exposure to any science, let alone the scientific study of human behavior. We address these fundamental differences between professionals in two chapters: Chapter 3 examines how differences in professional training affect the expert–attorney relationship, while Chapter
12 discusses the communication of expert findings to attorneys and the
courts.

Attorneys and forensic experts are often frustrated by treatises on
forensic psychology and psychiatry that have a plethora of clinical folklore and a dearth of empirical research. Attorneys want to know the
knowledge base relevant to a clinical syndrome or assessment method.
However well qualified the expert, attorneys are exasperated by the *ipse
dixit* justification for expert testimony.[1]

As mentioned in the Preface, we have assembled two data bases on
insanity evaluations and "not guilty by reason of insanity" (NGRI) patients
(see Appendix A). The first data base is composed of insanity cases collected on the Rogers Criminal Responsibility Assessment Scales (R-CRAS;
Rogers, 1984) that enables us to provide descriptive data from 413 actual insanity cases. The second data base was compiled specifically for the
purposes of this book on 6,479 individuals found NGRI. To make the information from these data bases as accessible as possible, we have presented
it in percentages.

Attorneys play an important role as gatekeepers of expert testimony, especially in light of the *Daubert v. Merrel Dow Pharmaceuticals* (hereafter referred to as *Daubert*) decision discussed in the next section of this chapter. They must ensure that testimony is both understandable and accurate. If an expert testifies that "disorganized speech is the hallmark of insanity," attorneys might use Table 7.5 to question the certitude of this statement. Likewise, an expert who testifies that memory loss is rare among insanity defendants might reference Table 6.1. Therefore, these tables serve a valuable function for both forensic experts and attorneys as a systematic check on overstated conclusions. However, we caution against misguided efforts to use these percentages to calculate probability estimates.[2]

The purpose of this chapter is threefold. First, it introduces *Daubert*, a Supreme Court decision with far-reaching effects on expert testimony in insanity trials. Second, it examines legal standards of insanity and summarizes recent developments in the post-Hinckley period. Third, it addresses issues of public perceptions of insanity affecting its general views, role as prospective jurors, and beliefs about postacquittal management of those found NGRI. Public perceptions have practical implications for how an insanity trial is conducted.

Daubert and the Parameters of Insanity Evaluations

Traditional Approaches to the Admissibility of Expert Evidence

Courts have used two fundamentally different approaches to scrutinize the admissibility of expert testimony. The "qualifications-only" approach requires the trial judge to scrutinize only the qualifications of the expert and delegates to the triers of fact the responsibility for determining the reliability of the expert's methods and procedures. The "qualifications-reliability" approach requires the trial judge to scrutinize both the expert's qualifications and the reliability of his/her methods and procedures. With the second approach, the triers of fact focus on the expert's believability. The application of these two approaches has varied over time based on considerations, such as changing assumptions about the abilities of juries and the politics of the litigation. As an example of the latter, proponents of tort reform have advocated more rigorous scrutiny of experts in personal injury litigation to advance their own agenda of reducing plaintiffs' successes. Moreover, the approach used to assess expert testimony may vary from expert to expert, even within the same jurisdiction.

In general, courts have been more likely to utilize the qualifications-only approach for clinical opinions than when the expert draws conclusions based on scientific research (Shuman & Sales, 1998). Traditionally, mental health professionals whose qualifications have satisfied the courts have been permitted to testify on the basis of their clinical assessments. Such testimony might include the defendant's mental condition and retrospective diagnoses at the time of the offense. Clinical testimony would rarely be required to meet the qualifications-reliability approach; the empirical validation of clinical methods was largely overlooked in admissibility decisions. When the offered testimony encompassed a specific syndrome (e.g., rape trauma syndrome) and its relevance to a legal issue, courts have generally imposed an additional hurdle seeking to assess the reliability of the information on which these conclusions have been reached (i.e., qualifications-reliability approach).

Within the qualifications-only approach, courts traditionally made simple distinctions based on education and discipline. For example, the legal tests for criminal nonresponsibility often use the word "disease." Because of this medical conceptualization, many courts historically limited expert testimony about criminal nonresponsibility to physicians, excluding or substantially limiting the scope of psychological testimony (Shuman, 1994). The hallmark case of *Jenkins v. United States* (1962) was important in encouraging a more pragmatic approach to the admissibility of psychologists' expertise. During the last 3 decades, both psychologists and psychiatrists have been routinely admitted as experts in insanity defense trials.

Trial courts have considerable leeway in admitting particular mental health professionals as experts. The courts often admit experts based on a minimum criteria, such as the proper training and licensure. Appellate courts generally review these decisions on the "abuse of discretion" standard, which traditionally results in great deference to the decisions of the trial judge (*General Electric Company v. Joiner*, 1997).

An important decision addressing the qualifications-reliability approach is the 1923 decision of the District of Columbia Court of Appeals, *Frye v. United States*. This case weighed the reliability of expert evidence in deciding the admissibility of a precursor to the modern polygraph. The test that the court imposed in that case envisioned science as an evolutionary process:

> Just when a scientific principle or discovery crosses the line between the experimental and demonstrable stages is difficult to define. Somewhere in this twilight zone the evidential force of the principle must be recognized, and while courts will go a long way in admitting expert testimony

deduced from a well-recognized scientific principle or discovery, the thing from which the deduction is made must be sufficiently established to have gained general acceptance in the particular field to which it belongs. (p. 1014)

The *Frye* test is based on general acceptance in a particular field of experts. Interestingly, the *Frye* test's popularity was not unanimous; critics complained that, among other things, general acceptance is a test of popularity but not necessarily of the quality of science. Against the backdrop of this debate, the Federal Rules of Evidence (FRE) were adopted in 1974. The FRE sought to codify a large body of disparate case law governing the admissibility of trial evidence in federal court. The FRE made no mention of *Frye*, leaving unclear their intention to retain or repeal it. Finally, in *Daubert*, the Supreme Court addressed the test for the admissibility of scientific expert testimony under the federal rules and clarified *Frye*'s relevance under the FRE.

Daubert Standard

Daubert was a toxic tort claim alleging that *in utero* exposure to Bendectin, an antinausea drug manufactured by Dow, caused the plaintiff's limb reduction birth defects. Interestingly, none of the 30 relevant epidemiological studies had shown a statistically significant correlation to birth defects. However, plaintiffs' experts asserted a causal relationship based on the use of animal studies, pharmacological comparison of Bendectin with known teratogens, and reanalysis of published epidemiological studies. The question before the Court was the standard that controlled the admissibility of the plaintiffs' expert opinions. The Supreme Court concluded that *Frye*'s general acceptance test had been superseded by the FRE and required the federal courts to make their own "preliminary assessment of whether the reasoning or methodology underlying the testimony is scientifically valid and of whether that reasoning or methodology properly can be applied to the facts in issue" (p. 590). Tying the scrutiny of scientific evidence to Karl Popper's (1959) notion of falsifiability, the Court suggested four considerations to assess its "scientific validity—and thus the evidentiary relevance and reliability" (p. 594):

1. "Ordinarily, a key question to be answered in determining whether a theory or technique is scientific knowledge that will assist the trier of fact will be whether it can be (and has been) tested" (i.e., falsifiability) (p. 593).
2. "Another pertinent consideration is whether the theory or

technique has been subjected to peer review and publication" (p. 594).

3. "Additionally, in the case of a particular scientific technique, the court ordinarily should consider the known or potential rate of error" (p. 594).

4. "Finally, 'general acceptance' can yet have a bearing on the inquiry. A 'reliability assessment does not require, although it does permit, explicit identification of a relevant scientific community and an express determination of a particular degree of acceptance within that community'" (p. 594).

Although *Daubert* specifically applies only to trials in federal court, many states that have adopted evidence codes patterned after the FRE have since adopted *Daubert*.

The application of *Daubert* to behavioral and social science testimony holds the potential to effect a fundamental change in the litigation landscape (Goodman-Delahunty, 1997; Richardson, Ginsburg, Gatowski, & Dobbin, 1995; Rotgers & Barrett, 1996; Zonana, 1994). If applied rigorously, *Daubert* would bar untested as well as untestable (i.e., nonfalsifiable) methods and procedures that would be an insufficient basis to support the opinion of an expert from the behavioral or social sciences. Clinical opinions that rest on experience or intuition would be barred. While some rejoice at this scenario, others fear the consequences of depriving courts of this type of evidence and seek to distinguish *Daubert*'s application to the physical or natural sciences as contrasted with the behavioral or social sciences. To advance this distinction, they argue that designing experiments on human behavior often presents different methodological and ethical problems than exist in studying natural or physical sciences. The counterargument is twofold. First, many branches of science face similar hurdles in addressing the relevant questions (e.g., methodological challenges in studying Bendectin's effect on human fetuses). Second, a rigorous application of scientific method exists exactly to avoid the risks of erroneous generalizations from untested idiosyncratic observations, from which experts are not immune.

Several Supreme Court decisions have reaffirmed the *Daubert* decision and provided guidance on its applications: *United States v. Scheffer* (1998) and *General Electric Company v. Joiner* (1997). In the latter case, the Supreme Court cautioned that judges should be vigilant for experts making unwarranted extrapolations from the data (see Grudzinskas & Appelbaum, 1998).

Some advocates, fearful of *Daubert*'s implications for psychology and psychiatry, suggest that mental health testimony might skirt its standards by claiming to be "nonscientific" but "clinical" (for a discussion, see Melton, Petrila, Poythress, & Slobogin, 1997). These advocates suggest that mental health testimony should be scrutinized under the rules of evidence not as science, but as "technical or other specialized knowledge," the standard applied to police officers, appraisers, or electricians. In response, proponents of *Daubert* note that psychology defines itself as the *scientific* study of human behavior. In particular, psychological tests, with their emphasis on reliability and validity, are based on scientific principles (Rogers, Salekin, & Sewell, 1999). Lowering the bar for admissibility of psychological evidence not only delegitimizes clinical psychology, but also demeans other areas of psychology that rest on rigorous research (e.g., experimental and cognitive psychology). Likewise, this reasoning deprecates the important advances in psychiatric research.

While decisive answers to these fundamental questions about the scope of *Daubert* have yet to be issued by the appellate courts, the impact of *Daubert* and its effect on the testimony of mental health professionals conducting insanity evaluations continues to grow. Courts now apply *Daubert* to scrutinize mental health professional testimony in criminal proceedings that explicitly invokes a scientific paradigm. Testimony on syndromes and diagnoses has come under scrutiny. Appellate courts have applied *Daubert* criteria to the admissibility of testimony on battered woman's syndrome (*United States v. Riker*, 1994), rape trauma syndrome (*State v. Alberico*, 1993), and compulsive gambling disorder (*United States v. Scholl*, 1997) to explain the mental condition of the defendant. The courts have taken this responsibility seriously. For example, in *United States v. Scholl* (1997), the court held that the expert could testify to the 10 DSM diagnostic criteria for pathological gambling, but could not elaborate on these criteria or associated features in relationship to the alleged criminal behavior.

Psychological tests have also been subjected to *Daubert* scrutiny. A sampling of these decisions are outlined below:

- In *Gier v. Educational Services Unit No. 16* (1995), use of the Child Behavior Checklist (CBCL) was deemed inadmissible because it had not been validated on the relevant population (i.e., the mentally retarded) or for a particular use (i.e., the detection of child abuse).
- In *State v. Cavaliere* (1995), use of the MMPI-2 and MCMI-II in creating profiles of sex offenders was ruled inadmissible. With considerable sophistication, the Supreme Court of New Hamp-

shire observed that the cited studies involve only admitting sex offenders, not those denying their paraphiliac behavior.

◆ In *Chapple v. Ganger* (1994), the trial court ruled on the admissibility of certain neuropsychological test batteries. The court relied heavily on the *Standards for Educational and Psychological Testing* (American Psychological Association [APA], 1985) in making its ruling.

Several observations emerge from the above cases. First, the courts appear to be focused in their determinations. For example, the general validity of the CBCL is not considered; instead, its specific application to a particular population is examined. Second, the courts appear capable of examining methodological issues with respect to generalizability.

Other issues have been subjected to *Daubert* review. For instance, testimony about the reliability of eyewitness testimony has come under *Daubert* scrutiny (*United States v. Rincon,* 1994). Other cases have addressed testimony about false confessions and the impact of mental disorders such as Munchausen's disease upon them (*United States v. Hall,* 1996; *United States v. Shay,* 1995) and the suggestibility of children (*United States v. Rouse,* 1996)

As noted above, courts have not heretofore rigorously scrutinized the reliability of clinical testimony, but that also has begun to change. For example, in the prosecution of allegations of recovered memories of childhood sexual abuse, courts have increasingly applied *Daubert* to scrutinize the claim that child victims of sexual assault can repress and then accurately recover memories of abuse (*Gier v. Educational Serv. Unit No. 16,* 1995; *Herald v. Hood,* 1993; *Isely v. Capuchin Province,* 1995; *Shahzade v. Gregory,* 1996; *State v. Hungerford,* 1995).

The Supreme Court's recent decision in *Kumho Tire Co. v. Carmichael* (1999) clarifies the application of *Daubert* in the federal courts and the state courts that apply it; according to the Court, *Daubert* applies to all expert testimony whether categorized as scientific, technical, or other specialized knowledge. Thus, courts that apply *Daubert* should apply it the testimony of psychologists, psychiatrists, and other mental health professionals offered as experts. However, the Court also made clear in *Kumho Tire* that the trial judge should be granted considerable leeway in applying the pragmatic criteria articulated in *Daubert* to assess the validity and reliability of the expert's methods and procedures.

Mental health professionals should expect to be asked to answer *Daubert* challenges. Regardless of *Daubert*'s application to behavioral and social sciences, lawyers should be prepared on two fronts: (1) to challenge opponent's experts according to these considerations, and (2) to respond to challenges of their own experts. If a court concludes that *Daubert* applies, these considerations are at the core of the decision on admissibility. However, even if these considerations are not applied consistently to the admissibility determination, they also go to the heart of the assessment of the weight or believability of the testimony. *Daubert* is symbolic of a change in attitudes about unquestioned deference to an expert's methods and procedures. Whether as a part of the admissibility determination or the assessment of believability, experts ought to be asked (1) how they know what they claim to know and (2) why we ought to believe these claims.

Standards of Criminal Responsibility

The imposition of punishment for violation of the criminal law rests on a model of behavior in which morally responsible actors exercise a choice whether to violate the law (i.e., the existence of free will; see Lipkin, 1990). Concomitantly, the law recognizes that the imposition of punishment is not appropriate on persons incapable of exercising free will (Shah, 1986). This approach to visiting criminal responsibility only on those who are deemed morally responsible for their acts requires both the commission of a proscribed act and an accompanying mental state that justifies the imposition of responsibility. Standards for assessing criminal responsibility struggle to distinguish those persons whose mental or emotional condition at the time of the offense justifies punishment from those where punishment is unwarranted. The standards attempt the separation of the truly "mad" from the merely "bad."

This section provides a brief historical overview of the insanity defense. Its purpose is to draw parallels between early cases, current insanity standards, and recent developments. The section begins with an outline of famous insanity cases prior to *M'Naghten*.

Insanity Prior to *M'Naghten*

The exemption of certain individuals from culpability can be traced to ancient times. Both in ancient Hebrew law and the Roman Justinian code of the 6th century, children and insane persons were not held responsible for their acts (Weiner, 1980). During the 17th and 18th centuries in Anglo-Saxon tradition, the definition of insanity was held to be commonsensical; it was decided by the judge and jury without the assistance of professionals. According to Coke (cited in Goldstein, 1967), an insane person is one "who completely loses his memory or understanding, a lunatic who sometimes has understanding and sometimes not, and an idiot" (p. 10). In 1265, Bracton set forth the first explicit standard, "An insane person is a person who does not know what he is doing, is lacking mind and reason, and is not far removed from brutes" (quoted in Bromberg, 1979, p. 5). According to Quen (1978), Bracton is credited with a codification of British law including the two components of crime: actus reus (i.e., the physical element or behavior) and mens rea (i.e., the mental element or purpose). Without the requisite mental state or purpose, a crime could not be committed, thus excusing infants because of their innocence and mad persons because of their lack of reason.

A brief review of pre-*M'Naghten* insanity cases is instructive in understanding the parallels between 19th-century and recent case law.

♦ *Wild beast standard.* Arnold, described as a "known lunatic," shot and wounded Lord Onslow, apparently as a result of delusional beliefs. The presiding judge articulated a strictly cognitive standard regarding knowledge and memory of the offense (Bromberg, 1979, p. 6): "It must be that a man totally deprived of his understanding and memory and doth not know what he is doing no more than an infant, brute, or a wild beast."

♦ *Delusion test.* James Hadfield suffered from the delusion that only his death would save the world. Not wanting to be damned to hell, he devised an ingenious method of saving the world without committing a mortal sin (e.g., murder or suicide). By firing in the direction of King George III, he believed he would be convicted of an attempted regicide, a capital offense (O'Reilly-Fleming, 1992; Quen, 1978). Not having committed a mortal sin, both he and the world would be saved. He was acquitted on a directed verdict based on the delusion test, that is, delusions were the source of the criminal behavior.[3]

♦ *Right–wrong test.* Charged with murder, John Bellingham was tried under the following standard: "The single question was whether, when he committed the offense, he had sufficient understanding to distinguish good from bad, right from wrong, and that the murder was a crime not only against the laws of God but against the laws of his country" (Robitscher, 1966, p. 56). Much of this language was later adopted by the authors of the *M'Naghten* standard. Incidentally, the entire case (detention, trial, sentencing, and execution) was carried out within a week and was condemned by many contemporaries as tantamount to "judicial murder" (Quen, 1978).

♦ *Delusion–volitional test.* Edward Oxford was acquitted for the attempted murder of Queen Victoria and Prince Albert. Here the delusion test was augmented by a volitional component. According to Quen

(1978, p. 239), Justice Denman issued the following opinion: "If some controlling disease was, in truth, the acting power within him which he could not resist then he will not be responsible." This volitional component presaged the later "irresistible impulse" prong of the *M'Naghten*–irresistible impulse standard.

M'Naghten Case

The modern history of the insanity defense begins with the celebrated *M'Naghten's Case* (1843). According to the trial evidence, Daniel M'Naghten attempted to kill the British prime minister. He mistakenly killed the prime minister's secretary, Edward Drummond, instead. The general consensus is that Daniel M'Naghten suffered from elaborate paranoid delusions that caused him to mistakenly hold that the British prime minister was personally responsible for his financial and personal misfortunes (Weiner, 1985). At his arraignment, M'Naghten stated: "The Tories in my native city have compelled me to do this. They followed me and persecuted me where ever I go and have entirely destroyed my peace of mind. . . . They have accused me of crimes which I am not guilty; in fact, they wish to murder me" (Quen, 1981, pp. 4–5). A minority view espoused by Moran (1981) is that M'Naghten was involved in political intrigue and his beliefs were reality-based. M'Naghten was acquitted after nine medical experts testified to his insanity (Perlin, 1994); he was subsequently committed to the Broadmoor mental institution where he spent the remainder of his life (Weiner, 1985).

Queen Victoria was openly angry and disapproving of the M'Naghten verdict, for M'Naghten was the fifth person to attempt to assassinate either British royalty or the British prime minister since 1800 (see Simon, 1983). She bitterly complained about the legal system in which defense attorneys could press for an NGRI verdict in trials such as those of Oxford and M'Naghten "whilst everybody is morally convinced that both malefactors were perfectly conscious and aware of what they did" (cited in Golding, 1983, p. 3). As a result of public and royal outrage, 15 judges from the common law courts were empaneled to respond to a series of questions regarding insanity (Simon, 1967). The judges, including Lord Chief Justice Tindel, who had presided at M'Naghten's trial, were evidently influenced in their decisions by public and private pressures as well as by other current social and political crises facing the United Kingdom (see Quen, 1978).

The *M'Naghten* standard that the 15 empaneled judges articulated, but which was never applied to M'Naghten himself, declared that juries were to be informed that the defendant was presumed to be sane, unless the defendant proved that at the time of the commission of the offense that he was "laboring under such a defect of reason, from disease of mind as not to know the nature and quality of the act he was doing; or if he did, that he did not know what he was doing was wrong" (*M'Naghten's Case*, 1843). While seeking to tighten the standard for successfully invoking the insanity defense, the commission seemed less concerned about the admissibility of expert testimony. It permitted expert testimony by medical witnesses who had not assessed the defendant near the time of the offense, but only retrospectively. It also allowed expert testimony on the ultimate issue of criminal responsibility that the fact finder was required to address.

The *M'Naghten* test proved popular in England and was quickly adopted in most U.S. jurisdictions. Despite its general popularity, lawyers and members of Parliament protested the ambiguity of the words "wrong" and "know" as an overly simplistic interpretation of criminal responsibility (Quen, 1978). The standard was further attacked by British and U.S. psychiatrists as being too narrowly defined and excluding a broader class of severely disturbed individuals who lacked the volitional capacity to avoid criminal behavior. Isaac Ray, considered the primogenitor of forensic psychiatry, maintained that the *M'Naghten* standard was the result of "only the most deplorable ignorance of mental operations of the insane" (cited in Bromberg, 1979, p. 44). Stung by this criticism, a judge in 1845 instructed the jury to disregard definitions of insanity, "especially such fantastic and shadowy definitions as in Ray" (Bromberg, 1979, p. 46).

New Hampshire Standard

The New Hampshire standard was formulated by Charles Doe, chief justice of the New Hampshire Supreme Court, with input from Isaac Ray (see Stearns, 1945). This standard, established in the trial of an ax murderer (*State v. Pike*, 1870), held that if the criminal behavior was a product of mental illness, then the individual should be exculpated (Quen, 1978). In the appeal of Pike's conviction, Justice Doe crystallized the New Hampshire rule with the following statement: "An act caused by mental illness is not a crime" (Quen, 1978, p. 243). Doe also ruled that it was within the domain of the jury to establish what constitutes insanity, and not for the judiciary to specify what that standard might be (Bromberg, 1979). The New Hampshire standard attacked what was seen as the undue narrowness of the *M'Naghten* rule with its arbitrary exclusion of severely disturbed individuals (Robitscher, 1966).

Modifying *M'Naghten:* Irresistible Impulse

The irresistible impulse test represented a broadening of the *M'Naghten* standard to include severe impairment of volition or self-control in individuals who are cognitively aware of the wrongfulness of their actions. Variations of irresistible impulse were reported contemporaneously with *M'Naghten's* trial; these trial cases include *State v. Thompson* in 1834 (cited in Simon, 1967) and *Commonwealth v. Mosler,* an 1846 Pennsylvania case (cited in Keilitz & Fulton, 1983).

Parsons v. State (1887) and *Davis v. United States* (1897) are generally regarded as the influential cases in combining the *M'Naghten* standard with a loss of volitional control. *Parsons* held that a defendant who knew right from wrong might still be acquitted based on the following two conditions: (1) "if by reason of duress of such mental disease, he had so far lost the power to choose between the right and wrong and to avoid doing the act in question, as that his free agency was at that time destroyed; (2) and if, at the same time, the alleged crime was so connected with mental disease with relation of cause and effect, as to have been the product of it solely." The federal counterpart to Parsons was *Davis v. United States,* which stated that the accused should be acquitted if "his will, by which I mean the governing power of his mind, has otherwise been voluntarily so completely destroyed that his actions are not subject to, but are beyond his control."

Standards of irresistible impulse have created much debate. It is generally accepted by jurists (see Robitscher, 1966) that this standard does not apply to individuals in states of passion—such as being blinded by anger or jealousy—since there is no direct linkage between such states and a mental disorder. Davidson (1952) argued unconvincingly that such a standard should be applied to sexual paraphilias, in which the individual is overpowered by sexual urges. This view is inconsistent with available research on large samples of sex offenders (Groth, 1979; Laws & O'Donohue, 1997).

The crux of the issue is how to distinguish between an *irresistible* impulse and an *unresisted* impulse (Gutheil & Appelbaum, 1982; Robitscher, 1966; Shapiro, 1984). One option adopted by military courts and other jurisdictions (Goldstein, 1967) is the "police at the elbow" criterion. This criterion argues that if the impulse was so overwhelming and out of control that the individual would have committed the act in the presence of a law enforcement officer, then that person should be exempt from responsibility. This approach represents a conservative approach to irresistible impulses that would likely exclude all but the most severely impaired individuals.

This standard gained some currency during the emergence of dynamic psychology in the 1920s (Bromberg, 1979). It emphasizes determinants beyond the defendant's awareness and therefore control, despite an intellectual apprehension, which is consistent with ego psychology formulations (Goldstein, 1967). A psychodynamic study of 300 murderers by Bromberg (1979) formulated a variety of unconscious motivations.

A Bold Experiment: The *Durham* Standard

The *Durham* standard (*Durham v. United States*, 1954), afforded the widest range of expert testimony regarding criminal responsibility. Writing the majority decision, Judge Bazelon argued that the then-current District of Columbia standard (i.e., *M'Naghten* plus irresistible impulse) was too circumscribed and did not take into account the advances in psychiatric knowledge (Brooks, 1974). Establishment of the *Durham* standard was based on an appeal for Monty Durham, convicted of housebreaking, who had an extensive criminal and psychiatric history.

The *Durham* standard, sometimes referred to as the "product rule," stated that, "an accused is not criminally responsible if his unlawful act was a product of a mental disease or mental defect. . . . we use 'defect' in a sense of a condition which is not considered capable of either improvement or deterioration which may be either congenital or the result of an injury, or the residual effect of a physical or mental disease" (pp. 874–875). The *Durham* standard differed in emphasis from the New Hampshire standard; the latter placed the responsibility on the jury to formulate its standard of criminal responsibility (Quen, 1978).

The *Durham* standard was heralded by several leaders in forensic psychiatry as a great advance toward humanizing archaic laws as well as an improvement for the psychiatric profession (Robitscher, 1966). This enthusiasm was not shared by those judges and prosecutors who regarded this change with skepticism and hostility, as an erosion of the current standards of culpability that might lead to mass acquittals (Brooks, 1974). Some practicing psychiatrists were ambivalent about the new standard's use of the terms "disease" and "product." The widespread enthusiasm soon waned as opposition mounted regarding the ambiguity of the standard and the problems in defining its components. Its ambiguities led Goldstein (1967) to conclude that the *Durham* standard was a "nonrule" (p. 84).

One purpose of the *Durham* standard was to encourage forensic experts to offer understandable and descriptive information regarding the defendant's mental condition in language comprehensible to the jury. From a judicial perspective, this purpose was undermined by experts testifying in arcane and conclusory terms. Bazelon, the original architect of the *Durham* standard, also masterminded its eventual repeal. He complained (cited in Huckabee, 1980, p. 17) that *Durham* did not do "nearly enough to eliminate the experts' stranglehold on the process."

During its short life of 18 years, the *Durham* standard did not gain wide acceptance in other jurisdictions. Although reviewed by 30 states and five federal courts, the *Durham* formulation was consistently rejected. Only two states, Vermont and Maine, adopted the *Durham* standard, and they restricted its use to civil cases (Simon, 1983). The fear that the liberalized *Durham* standard would result in an upsurge of insanity acquittals proved baseless. In reality, the increase was minuscule, averaging 12 more acquittals per year (see Brooks, 1974; Weiner, 1980). Thus, what was feared by many as "opening the flood gates" might better be regarded as "increasing the trickle."

Bazelon's court showed growing disenchantment with the administration of the *Durham* standard. In 1972, the grand experiment was ended. The DC Court of Appeals unanimously repealed the *Durham* standard in favor of the American Law Institute (ALI) standard in *United States v. Brawner* (1972).

An important but overlooked lesson of the *Durham* experiment is the inherently inverse relationship between ambiguity and arbitrariness. Its predecessors (i.e., *M'Naghten* and irresistible impulse) were roundly criticized for their arbitrariness in excusing only a few and finding culpable most other severely impaired individuals. In contrast, the *Durham* standard, formulated to avoid such overrefined distinctions, offered a more general (i.e., more ambiguous) formulation. The *Durham* standard, in turn, was roundly criticized for its ambiguity and lack of clear (i.e., nonarbitrary) standards. Thus, this chapter reveals the inherent tensions in formulations of criminal responsibility between arbitrariness and ambiguity.

Careful Formulation of the ALI Standard

The ALI standard, unlike other standards that were hastily constructed in response to a particular case, was the result of 10 years of dialogue from 1952 to 1962. This undertaking, underwritten by the Rockefeller Foundation, drew on the expertise of judges, law professors, behavioral scientists, and other professionals. Their meetings were dominated by Judge Learned Hand, who was venerated for his legal erudition combined with personal warmth. This group attempted to reconceptualize and redefine the cognitive and volitional elements associated with criminal responsibility. Toward this end, they offered several changes to broaden the *M'Naghten* standard's cognitive component and to redefine the irresistible impulse or volitional element (see Goldstein, 1967).

As is often the case, this new standard was heralded as a solution to the problem of providing equitable standards of criminal responsibility. As noted in *United States v. Freeman* (cited in Brooks, 1974, pp. 167–168), the ALI test is "an infinite improvement over the M'Naghten Rules. It reflects the evolution of modern psychiatry too long circumscribed 'by the outrage of a frightened queen.' " The standard (American Law Institute, 1962) articulated the following:

> A person is not responsible for criminal conduct, if at the time of such conduct as the result of a mental disease or defect, he lacks substantial capacity either to appreciate the criminality (wrongfulness) of his conduct or to conform his conduct to the requirements of law. As used in this article, the terms "mental disease or defect" do not include an abnormality manifested only by repeated criminal or otherwise antisocial conduct.

This standard was gradually adopted in the federal courts. Momentum for the adoption of the ALI standard increased with endorsements from the major professional organizations, including the American Academy of Psychiatry and Law (Pollack, 1976), the American Psychiatric Association, and the American Bar Association (ABA) (Huckabee, 1980).

The initial enthusiasm for the ALI standard was predictably tempered by growing criticism. Although the ALI standard was intended to introduce greater flexibility than *M'Naghten*, it was criticized for its "vagueness and rubber yard stick quality" (Huckabee, 1980, p. 20), a criticism echoed by others (e.g., Bromberg, 1979; Freedman, Guttmacher, & Overholser, 1961). Commenting on the interminable and unresolvable discussions of terms such as *appreciate* and *substantial capacity,* Quen (1978) described such debates as "characterized by a pathological obsessional concern, on the part of the legal and medical professionals, with the magic of words" (p. 26). A second criticism of the ALI standard was that it allowed too many defendants to be acquitted. Although it was generally believed that the ALI standard is more liberal than *M'Naghten* (i.e., easier to secure an acquittal), actual research about its impact produced mixed results (Keilitz, 1985; Rogers & Clark, 1985; Sauer & Mullens, 1976).

Hinckley and the IDRA Standard

The very unpopular acquittal of John Wanock Hinckley Jr. for the attempted assassination of a very popular president fueled intense debate over the efficacy and validity of the insanity defense. It resulted in an immediate and unprecedented congressional review of the trial, which called before a Senate subcommittee both the members of the Hinckley jury and expert witnesses (Subcommittee on Criminal Law of the U.S. Senate Judiciary Committe, 1982). Surveys of the public conducted following Hinckley's acquittal indicated strong dissatisfaction with the disposition (Hans & Slater, 1983) and widespread beliefs that the insanity standard was used too frequently and allowed defendants to escape from the responsibility of their crimes (Jeffrey & Pasewark, 1983).

Professional organizations, perhaps in response to the public condemnation of the Hinckley verdict, began to issue official statements on the insanity defense. The ABA (1983) issued its official position on the insanity defense, which argued for a curtailment of the ALI standard. The ABA advocated the elimination of the second prong of the ALI test, asserting that "there is still no accurate scientific basis for measuring one's capacity for self control or for calibrating the impairment of such capacity" (pp. 4–5). This statement is inconsistent with the empirical data finding that forensic experts were slightly *more* reliable in their application of the volitional (kappa = .80) than the cognitive (kappa = .75) prongs (Rogers, 1984). The American Psychiatric Association (1983) adopted essentially the same position as the ABA (1983). The American Bar Association also called for defining mental disease or retardation as essentially a psychosis, or a condition that "grossly and demonstrably impairs a person's perception or understanding of reality," relative to the standard of criminal responsibility (p. 12). In contrast, the American Psychological Association (1984) exercised considerable restraint in calling for empirical research on current insanity standards and their alternatives before implementing any modifications.

Federal legislative efforts culminated in the 1984 passage of the Insanity Defense Reform Act (IDRA). The standard articulated in the IDRA provided that to be found nonresponsible the defendant must prove that, "as a result of a severe mental disease or defect, he was unable to appreciate the nature and quality or wrongfulness of his act" (p. 201). This criterion combined the ALI concept of "appreciate" with the *M'Naghten* concepts of "unable" and "nature and quality." Ironically, this innovation represents only a slight shift from the original *M'Naghten* controversy (Keilitz, 1985).

States also responded to the backlash from the Hinckley acquittal. Steadman et al. (1993) found that by the end of 1990 all but eight states had made substantive changes in their insanity laws. These changes include (1) abolition of the insanity defense in three states (Utah, Montana, and Idaho), (2) adoption of more stringent insanity standards, (3) modifications in the standard and burden of proof, and (4) addition of the guilty-but-mentally-ill (GBMI) verdict (see Chapter 4). Did these changes curtail insanity acquittals? We will briefly examine Steadman et al. (1993) data on abolition, changes in proof, and GBMI.

Steadman et al. (1993) studied the effect of abolishing the insanity standard in Montana. Surprisingly, its abolition only decreased but did not stop its use. However, the most dramatic finding is what happened to markedly disturbed defendants. In examining defendants found incompetent to stand trial, they found the following outcomes:

- ◆ Prior to the abolition of the insanity defense, the outcomes were 72% NGRI, 6% guilty, 22% dismissed or deferred.
- ◆ After the abolition of the insanity defense, the outcomes were 8% NGRI, 13% guilty,[4] 79% dismissed or deferred.

In summary, Montana's abolition of the insanity defense appears to have backfired. Instead of defendants being found NGRI, nearly 4 out of 5 of these cases were dismissed or deferred.

Steadman et al. (1993) studied the effects of changing the burden of proof from the prosecution to the defense. In selected counties of New York and Georgia, they found that this modification reduced the number of insanity pleas. Despite fluctuations across states and time periods, the percentages of acquittals appeared generally comparable.

One purpose of the GBMI verdict was to reduce the frequency of insanity acquittals. In most states that have adopted the GBMI verdict, this form of verdict is given to the jury in addition to the choice of guilty, not guilty, and not guilty by reason of insanity verdicts. The GBMI verdict is generally prescribed when the defendant was mentally ill when he/she committed the offense, but does not meet the legal criteria for insanity.

Steadman et al. (1993) reviewed the available studies on how the GBMI verdict affected insanity proceedings. In examining data from Michigan, Illinois, Pennsylvania, and Georgia, they concluded that passage of the GBMI alternative did not achieve its desired effect of reducing insanity pleas or acquittals.

What lessons can be learned from this brief history of the insanity defense?

1. *Reactivity of standards.* Many changes in the insanity standards (e.g., *M'Naghten* and IDRA) are not based on legal or scientific advances. Rather, they represent highly reactive efforts to appease public outcry.

Rogers (1987b, p. 840) described the tenuous logic underlying these reactive changes: "If the verdict is wrong, then the standard is wrong."

2. *Curtailment of acquittals.* Any attempt to broaden the criteria, even slightly, generates a barrage of criticism. Every new standard is judged predominantly by the numbers that are acquitted rather than by its underlying legal theory or empirical validation.

3. *Repetition of history.* Nearly every "advance" has its parallel in pre-*M'Naghten* decisions. In the last 2 centuries, the three operative constructs remain (a) cognitive impairment (nature and quality, know, and appreciate), (b) volitional impairment (irresistible impulse and conformity of conduct), and (c) product rule (*Hadfield*, New Hampshire, and *Durham* standards). Even the language of the recently crafted IDRA standard has many parallels with the century-old Canadian standard (Rogers & Mitchell, 1991).

4. *Supremacy of cognition.* One common thread throughout the Anglo-American history of the insanity defense is that extreme deficits in cognitive abilities have always been a potential basis for an insanity acquittal. In contrast, defendants with comparably severe impairment of mood (e.g., extreme depression) are unlikely to be acquitted.

An awareness of the insanity defense's development and its historical roots is useful for attorneys and forensic experts. It provides a context for understanding the motivations for tinkering with specific standards. It also points to the often political role played by professional organizations in contributing to these tinkerings. In assuaging societal outrage, professionals have often contributed to public misperceptions of the insanity defense. The next section addresses these misperceptions.

Public Misperceptions of the Insanity Defense

The public often misperceives the insanity defense as a commonly used ploy for violent criminals to escape accountability and appropriate punishment for heinous crimes. This public outcry is not a recent phenomenon and can be traced throughout U.S. history (see Speigel & Spiegel, 1991). Media portrayals, even when presented with apparent objectivity, are prone to display lurid crimes (McCutcheon & McCutcheon, 1994) and evoke images of defendants like Jeffrey Dahmer with horrifying acts of death and destruction (Drukteinis, 1992). In selecting jurors and presenting cases, attorneys and mental health experts must be cognizant of these misperceptions and their potential influence on insanity verdicts. While the focus of research is limited to community samples, it is unlikely that judges or jurors can fully escape the effects of media presentations and pervasive public preconceptions. An unexplored issue is whether the introduction of testimony to combat these misperceptions would have the desired effect.

Silver, Cirincione, and Steadman (1994) in a multistate study of 8,953 insanity cases resulting in 2,555 acquittals confront the public myths surrounding the insanity defense and the evocative media images of the "criminally insane." In contrast to popular notions of insanity defendants committing grisly violent homicides, Silver et al. found that only 14.3% of those pleading insanity were charged with murder. In comparison, approximately twice that number (31.6%) were charged with property offenses. In examining our data base, we find that 20.5% (1,311 of 6,394) NGRI patients were acquitted of murder.[5] Interestingly, this percentage was comparable to acquittals for nonviolent crimes, at 20.0% (1,277 of 6,394). Attempted murder was relatively uncommon, at 1.6% (104 of 6,394). In contrast, various forms of assault were the most frequent, accounting for 31.8% (2,032 of 6,394) of acquittals. As observed by Leong, Silva, and Weinstock (1991), societal fears focused on those who are both "bad" and "mad" are unlikely to be abated by these estimates.

Research (e.g., Hans, 1986; Hans & Slater, 1983; Pasewark & Seidenzahl, 1979) has consistently documented the public's mistrust of the insanity defense and their belief in its prevalent use. In a college sample, Pasewark and Seidenzahl (1979) found that the public grossly misestimated the prevalence of insanity pleas (37% of all felonies) and its subsequent success rate (44%). More accurate estimates place these percentages at 1% and 26%, respectively (Silver et al., 1995). Media efforts to change these misperceptions may not produce the desired effects (McCutcheon & McCutcheon, 1994; see also Jeffrey & Pasewark, 1983).

Commentaries (Dix, 1984; Weiner, 1985) have raised important concerns of whether the image of psychiatry and other mental health professions has been sullied simply by their association with notorious insanity cases. Calls for abolition by the American Medical Association (see Keilitz & Fulton, 1983) or curtailment by the American Psychiatric Association (1983) were likely motivated by unfavorable press and intercollegial distrust. A more interesting issue is whether the public would disagree, if given the opportunity to review the same clinical data as mental health professionals. Jackson (1988) presented nonprofessionals, attorneys, and psychiatrists with two videotapes of psychiatric interviews with criminal defendants. Contrary to popular opinion, she found no differences among the groups in their ratings of criminal responsibility. Despite the modest scope of her study, it raises the tantalizing notion that the public may evidence more convergence with mental health professionals than is commonly assumed, when provided with similar data.

Other public misconceptions include:

1. *Most insanity cases are hotly contested.* Data from more than 7,000 insanity trials indicate that nearly half (42.9%) involve a formal consensus between prosecution and defense (Cirincione, 1996).

2. *Attorneys are strongly vested in the verdict.* Important survey data by Blau, McGinley, and Pasewark (1993) reveal that many attorneys (64% of prosecutors and 78% of defense attorneys) have used insanity as a means to an end. In such cases, their interests lie in a negotiated plea, often to a lesser charge.

3. *Insanity verdicts result in "getting away" with the crime.* Available data (see Pantle, Pasewark, & Steadman, 1980; Perlin, 1996; Shah, 1986) disabuse professionals and public of this fallacy; NGRI patients typically spend substantial periods of time in forensic facilities, sometimes exceeding the time that would be spent in prison if they had been found guilty of the offense.[6]

Potential Jurors for Insanity Trials

Given the rampant misperceptions regarding and abiding distrust of insanity cases, defense attorneys may wonder whether finding a jury favorable to an insanity acquittal is possible. With possibly fewer misgivings than defense counsel, prosecutors have a vested interest in selecting a jury favorably disposed to a conviction. Key findings from analogue research are presented below:

1. Cutler, Moran, and Narby (1992) found convergent results from three studies that authoritarian jurors are more likely to convict in insanity cases. Juror attitudes toward experts and the insanity defense were slightly predictive of outcome. Sample questions derived from Cutler et al. include:

   ♦ Do you believe that the testimony of experts is critical to making decisions about insanity?
   ♦ Are psychiatrists no better than anyone else in deciding whether a person is insane?
   ♦ Would you agree that a person who does a crime should do the time, whether they were mentally ill?

2. Updike and Shaw (1995) conducted a circumscribed study of public attitudes regarding the insanity defense. Within a college sample, background and sociodemographic variables were generally nonsignificant in predicting positive and negative views. However, participants' expressed religious faith and commitment was mildly predictive (beta = .21) of negative perceptions. This finding was generally supported by Tygart (1992) who concluded that religious beliefs in an afterlife, including punishment and rewards, were associated with negative views of mental illness as a legal defense.

3. Towers, McGinley, and Pasewark (1992) examined the effects jurors' and defendants' race (African American vs. Anglo American) had on insanity acquittals involving a case of postpartum depression with persecutory delusions. African American males and Anglo American females did not appear to be affected by the race of the defendant. Although African American females appeared somewhat more likely to acquit an African American than an Anglo American defendant (69% vs 61%), a strong opposite effect was found for Anglo American males, with insanity acquittals of 47% for African American and 63% for Anglo American defendants. Although limited in generalizability, the data suggest that Anglo American males may be more reluctant to support an insanity defense with an African American defendant.

Postacquittal Management of Persons Found Not Guilty by Reason of Insanity

Both professionals and the public are apt to be uninformed regarding the consequences of an insanity verdict. The absence of information may lead to faulty perceptions of post-acquittal dispositions. This section addresses two related issues: (1) disposition and placement of NGRI patients, and (2) recidivism among released NGRI patients.

Disposition and Placement of NGRI Patients

The substantial majority of NGRI patients are placed in maximum security facilities where their progress is closely monitored. McGreevy, Steadman, Dvoskin, and Dollard (1991) found that 62.5% of NGRI patients were designated as "dangerously mentally ill." When this designation occurs, hospitalizations in forensic facilities averaged more than a year (414.1 days) and were followed by much longer stays in nonforensic hospitals (917.8 days). Recent trends favor more extended hospitalizations. Linhorst and Dirks-Linhorst (1997) found that NGRI patients served substantial amounts of time prior to release; for Class A felonies, the average institutionalization was more than 6 years (75.3 months). However, more than one-half of their sample had never been released; Class A felonies continued to be hospitalized after an average of 92.3 months.

A general finding is that *the more serious the NGRI offense, the longer the institutionalization.* Baldwin, Menditto, Beck, and Smith (1993) examined length of stay for NGRI patients in a maximum security hospital. Alarmingly, severity of offense accounted for more of the variance (R^2 = .30) than all the clinical variables *combined* (R^2 = .22). One explanation is that clinicians and courts weigh more heavily the risk factors when the index offense involved violence toward others. An alternative is that the postacquittal system is covertly punishing NGRI patients under the guise of maintaining public safety (Halpern, 1992).

Jurors often worry about the consequences of an insanity acquittal and whether a dangerous person will be released untreated into the community. Many jurisdictions have developed sophisticated programs to provide systematic treatment and supervision for both inpatient and community settings (Griffin, Steadman, & Heilbrun, 1991). States with such programs include: California (Wideranders & Choate, 1994), Connecticut (Scott, Zonana, & Getz, 1990), Illinois (Cavanaugh & Wasyliw, 1985; Wettstein & Mulvey, 1988), Maryland (Cohen, Spodak, Silver, & Williams, 1988; Silver & Tellefsen, 1991), Missouri (Linhorst & Dirks-Linhorst, 1997), New York (Steadman et al., 1993), Oklahoma (Norwood, Nicholson, Enyart, & Hickey, 1991), and Oregon (Rogers & Bloom, 1982, 1985). Many programs entail multistep models to ensure effective treatment and continued monitoring. More details about several programs are presented in the next section.

One consideration is whether evidence can be introduced directly or indirectly regarding the postacquittal management of NGRI patients. Evidence can sometimes be introduced indirectly by asking an expert to describe components of his/her forensic experience that may include postacquittal assessment or treatment of NGRI patients.

Recidivism among Released NGRI Patients

The often unspoken assumptions about the "criminally insane" are interrelated and quasi-deductive: (1) "once insane, always insane," (2) "insanity is the root cause of their crimes," and thus (3) "once released and unsupervised, recidivism is only a matter of time." Are released NGRI patients likely to recidivate? Several important studies have addressed this matter directly.

Cohen, Spodak, Silver, and Williams (1988) examined rates of re-arrest for 127 male NGRI patients placed on conditional release in Maryland. They were compared to matched samples of convicted felons and mentally disordered prison transfers. They found that slightly more than one-half (54.3%) of NGRI patients were rearrested in a 5-year postrelease period; this percentage continued to increase to 65.8% when the follow-up was extended to 17 years (Silver, Cohen, & Spodak, 1989). Bogenberger, Pasewark, Gudeman, and Bieber (1987) reported similarly high recidivism rates for 107 released NGRI patients with follow-up ranging from 8 to 14 years. They found that two-thirds (67.3%) were rearrested although only 17% of rearrests involved felony offenses against persons. A very disturbing observation was the cases of homicide charges (i.e., three murders and one manslaughter). In contrast, many NGRI patients committed minor but repetitive offenses: 21.5% of the total sample were rearrested on at least six occasions.

Studies in other states have found relatively low recidivism rates. Bieber, Pasewark, Bosten, and Steadman (1988) found that only 38 of 132 (28.8%) NGRI patients in New York had recidivated, despite being released for a longer period of time than found with the patients in the Cohen et al. study.[7] Interestingly, arrests prior to the NGRI acquittal appeared highly predictive of recidivism: 16.8% without and 45.5% with prior arrests. Other data corroborate the importance of previous criminal history (e.g., severity and frequency of arrest) in predicting recidivism. More recent research from New York (McGreevy, Steadman, Dvoskin, & Dollard, 1991) found a slightly lower percentage of recidivism (22%), of which more than half (12%) occurred within 12 months of release.

Closer monitoring and intensive outpatient programming appear to produce lower recidivism rates, although this observation is based on a scattering of descriptive studies without the benefit of rigorous experimental designs. The Psychiatric Security Review Board (1991; see also Bloom, Williams, & Bigelow, 1991) in Oregon maintains statewide jurisdiction over released NGRI patients and is responsible for ensuring their effective treatment. It reports only a 15% recidivism rate for NGRI patients conditionally released between 1978 and 1986. Specific NGRI outpatient treatment programs are also likely to be successful, although systematic data are generally not forthcoming (for reviews, see Heilbrun & Griffin, 1993; Salekin & Rogers, in press). Research (Rogers, Harris, & Wasyliw, 1983; Rogers & Wettstein, 1985) on an intensive treatment program in Chicago found a very low recidivism rate, at 2.3%. More recently, a California program (Wiederanders & Choate, 1994) with a comprehensive, mandated treatment composed of weekly individual counseling, drug screening, group therapy, and monthly home visits also yielded very low recidivism rates. For 254 NGRI outpatients, close monitoring and intensive treatment resulted in 133 (52.4%) being returned to inpatient status; this aggressive management resulted in only 14 rearrested patients, for a recidivism rate of 5.5%.

Griffin, Steadman, and Heilbrun (1991) underscore several important issues in evaluating recidivism among released NGRI patients. First, rearrest rates for NGRI patients are substantially lower than for those convicted of comparable crimes.[8] Second, the large majority of rearrests occur for minor offenses. In addition, our review suggests that the intensiveness of outpatient treatment and level of monitoring are important facets of successful adjustment and decreased recidivism. In successful programs, NGRI outpatients are evaluated systematically with corroboration of their self-reporting via drug tests, home visits, and collateral data from families and significant others.

Notes

1. The underlying logic is reducible to "It is true because I say it is true."

2. Probability estimates rely on base-rates that fluctuate dramatically. Cirincione, Steadman, and McGreevy (1995) examined insanity pleas of 8,138 defendants from seven states. They found dramatic variations in acquittal rates based on the background of defendants (e.g., race, gender, and age) and the type of offense. For example, the acquittal rate for murder ranged from 14.0% to 64.7% and for nonviolent crime ranged from 10.1% to 86.6%. For further discussion, see Chapter 11.

3. O'Reilly-Fleming (1992) noted the Hadfield would have been sane under both the wild beast and right–wrong standards. Therefore, the brilliant defense by Erskine was to assert the delusion test.

4. Of the 13%, 3% were found guilty and mentally ill; they were sentenced to the same hospital used for NGRI patients.

5. Percentages of violent crime from this data base are likely to be inflated because the samples include many that remain in maximum security facilities years after their acquittals.

6. Precise estimates are difficult to calculate. If NGRI patients opted for plea bargaining to lesser offenses or reduced sentences, the time served would be reduced accordingly. To simply use NGRI patients' original offenses is to ignore the pervasive effects of plea bargaining on confinement.

7. The precise length of time is unreported. All patients were released between 1971 and 1981; the article was published in 1988.

8. Canadian research (Rice, Harris, Lang, & Bell, 1990) also confirms this finding.

PART I

CLINICAL
AND LEGAL ISSUES

Chapter 2

The Clinician's Role
in Insanity Evaluations

Agency and Professional Role

The Adversary System and the Role of the Expert

To understand the role of mental health professionals as expert witnesses in the judicial system in insanity defense evaluations, it is helpful to contrast certain features of therapeutic and forensic relationships. A central feature that distinguishes common law legal systems (e.g., those of the United States and Great Britain) from mental health systems is the legal system's use of an adversarial rather than a collaborative or inquisitorial model. The theory underlying the legal system's use of the adversarial model is that when the parties whose fate is at stake are given the opportunity and responsibility to gather and present evidence, proceedings are more likely to be fair and accurate. One feature of this model, as it has developed in the United States, is that parties are generally responsible for retaining their own experts, rather than using a single court-appointed expert.

The use of retained experts creates a host of practical and theoretical problems. Lawyers are expected to present the strongest case for their client/party's version of the facts and the law. Because lawyers choose which expert witnesses to present, lawyers engage in "comparison shopping" to find the most persuasive expert who most strongly supports their client/party's case. Knowledge of this reality creates a constant tension for ethical experts in forensic practice. In addition, because the legal system uses amateur decision makers (i.e., jurors), an expert's ability to communicate complex and confusing information clearly and simply is highly valued by lawyers (Champagne, Shuman, & Whitaker, 1991).

Another important feature is the contrasting temporal frameworks for therapeutic and forensic relationships. Although therapy is ordinarily an ongoing process in which diagnoses and treatments evolve in light of newly acquired information, judicial determinations are single cross-sectional determinations. The government and the defendant are entitled to one fair trial of the insanity defense; newly acquired, posttrial information about the defendant's mental status at the time of the offense or the accuracy of an assessment technique, for example, is unlikely to serve as grounds for a new trial.

A third feature to contrast is the nature of consent in therapeutic and forensic relationships. Patients voluntarily seeking treatment have the legal right to choose their therapist and type of therapy. Valid informed consent for therapy requires the voluntary choice of a knowledgeable, competent person. In contrast, although litigants sometimes may choose their own mental health experts, litigants who raise forensic mental health issues can avert court-ordered or opposing attorney–retained forensic examinations only by abandoning claims or defenses (Shuman, 1993). And, unlike therapy, where the therapist and the patient are both concerned about the patient's best interests, the forensic examiner and the litigant may have widely divergent goals. For example, the opinion of the state's expert on an insanity defense may result in the imposition or avoidance of serious punishment. The defendant does not choose the forensic expert or have input regarding the expert's methodology.

In the context of forensic evaluations, a key issue is whether defendants can exercise informed consent without the benefit of counsel. In a national survey of forensic program directors, Miller, Olin, Beven, and Covey (1995) found that small numbers of unrepresented defendants continue to be evaluated in close to one-half the states. More commonly, defendants are evaluated with the benefit of only nominal (i.e., no discussion of the case) representation. It is unlikely that a defendant can render an informed decision without the benefit of an attorney's input.

Thus, while U.S. society has taken a largely "free market" approach to regulating psychotherapy, U.S. courts have developed a special set of rules to assess the competence of experts to offer opinion testimony. Although these rules vary from one jurisdiction to the next, all rules include an inquiry into the expert's qualifications and the relevant knowledge possessed by members of that trade, profession, or calling. The inquiry into the expert's qualifications is much the same in most jurisdictions and requires the appropriate education, training, and experience to make a threshold claim as a well-informed expert. Most variations that exist in the scrutiny of experts involve the standard used to assess the knowledge possessed by members of that trade, profession, or calling.

Also affecting the expert's role, the Supreme Court's opinion in *Daubert v. Merrell Dow Pharmaceuticals* (1993) requires the trial judge to engage in "a preliminary assessment of whether the reasoning or methodology underlying the testimony is scientifically valid and of whether that reasoning properly can be applied to the facts at issue" (p. 590). As described in Chapter 1, the Court directed trial judges to consider the underlying reasoning or methodology on the following issues: whether it (1) has been tested, (2) withstood scrutiny by others in the field through peer review and publication, (3) tested for error rate by established standards, and (4) accepted within the relevant scientific community. *Daubert*'s application and that of its predecessors and competitors (e.g., *Frye v. United States,* 1923) to psychiatric and psychological testimony has varied widely across jurisdictions. While some courts have engaged in demanding scrutiny of the science that underlies psychiatric and psychological methods and procedures, other courts have failed to appreciate or address these issues. Generally, courts are more likely to engage in rigorous scrutiny of the methods or procedures underlying the expert's opinion when the testimony explicitly invokes the mantle of science by seeking to ground the testimony in a particular psychological test or diagnosis than where the use of science is implicit, as in clinical opinion testimony (Sales, Shuman, & O'Connor, 1994; Shuman & Sales, 1998).

The Conflict between Therapeutic and Forensic Roles

Notwithstanding the significant differences in therapy and forensic practice, many mental health professionals and lawyers gloss over these differences when therapists are employed as forensic experts. Although a superficial appeal exists for the use of therapists as expert witnesses to testify about psycholegal issues involving their patients, mental health professionals cannot do so competently or ethically because of irreconcilable professional conflicts between the therapeutic and forensic roles (Greenberg & Shuman, 1997; Heilbrun, 1995; Strasburger, Gutheil, & Brodsky, 1997). A competent forensic examiner should be skeptical, verify self-reports, integrate data gathered by different methods, and reach conclusions that are accurate and objective although not necessarily therapeutic. Conversely, a competent therapist should be empathetic and accepting. Because the information that therapists routinely gather is rarely verified, it is inadequate to provide reliable information to address the psycholegal issues presented by an insanity evaluation. Thus, therapists may appropriately testify as treating experts (subject to privilege, confidentiality, and qualifications) without risk of conflict on the history provided by the patient and treatment-related concerns: mental status and diagnosis, treatment and treatment response, prognosis, and observed clinical characteristics. These issues are not psycholegal opinions and do not raise issues of judgment, foundation, or historical truth. Therapists do not ordinarily have the requisite data base to testify appropriately about psycholegal issues of causation (i.e., the relationship of a specific act to claimant's current condition) or capacity (i.e., the relationship of diagnosis or mental status to legally defined standards of functional capacity). Issues of causation and capacity raise problematic issues for therapists concerning judgment, foundation, and historical truth (Greenberg & Shuman, 1997, p. 56). Engaging in both therapeutic and forensic roles simultaneously is discouraged in the ethical standards of numerous professional organizations, including the American Psychology–Law Society and the American Board of Forensic Psychology (see Committee on Ethical Guidelines for Forensic Psychologists, 1991), the American Academy of Psychiatry and the Law (1991, 1995), the Committee on Psychiatry and Law of the Group for the Advancement of Psychiatry (1991), and the American Psychological Association (1992, 1994).

Attitudes and Motivations of the Forensic Expert

Attitudes

Very little is known about the attitudes and motivations of forensic experts in general. Attorneys in insanity trials are very interested in the experts "baggage" (i.e., attitudes, biases, and preconceived notions) that may affect an expert's evaluation and subsequent testimony. Even more engrossing, attorneys seek to understand what motivates experts to become involved in arduous insanity trials. Given the dearth of empirical studies, this section provides our conceptualization of attitudes and motivations.

One imperfect benchmark of a forensic expert's attitudes toward the insanity defense is his/her track record with these cases. Because experts rarely have control over the sources of their referrals, the proportion of referrals from prosecution and defense provides little information by itself regarding attitudes toward the insanity defense. Rather, two indices are likely to be revealing:

♦ *Credibility index*[1] refers to the proportion of cases in which the forensic expert rendered an opinion in a report or testimony that was unlikely to be preferred by the referral source (i.e., "insane" for prosecutors, "sane" for defense counsel). One obstacle to the credibility index is that defense experts in certain jurisdictions may not be permitted by counsel to provide negative opinions.

♦ *Outlier index* considers the proportion of cases with three or more experts in which a particular expert is the *only* expert expressing a particular opinion. What is particularly telling is when these outlier cases form a consistent pattern (e.g., always "sane").

We furnish the indices for two explicit purposes. First, forensic experts should evaluate their own practices for potential biases in either being overly "helpful" to referral sources (credibility index) or strongly vested in their viewpoint (outlier index). For attorneys, these indices provide a means to question an expert's attitudes and biases about the insanity defense.

Regarding attitudes toward the insanity plea, Homant and Kennedy (1986) devised an ingenious method of addressing potential bias among mental experts. They constructed a marginal case of insanity and assessed attitudes toward the defendant's responsibility, treatability, and need for punishment. Interestingly, they found considerable variations in experts' views, although it is unclear how these views might directly influence evaluations and testimony. They also found that dispositional concerns (e.g., expressed views regarding lengthy punishment or appropriate treatment) were correlated with perceptions of insanity.

Motivation

A critical but undiscussed issue is the motivation of forensic experts to become involved in criminal cases in general and insanity cases in particular. Imagine for the moment what an honest advertisement for a typical position as a forensic expert might entail:

> *Wanted*: A doctoral-level specialist with extensive training to work (1) in adverse settings, such as jails, (2) often with violent offenders, and (3) with disturbed and frequently uncooperative defendants. The position requires the specialist to be satisfied with (4) highly variable compensation, (5) skepticism if not outright disapproval from colleagues, and (6) repeated willingness to undergo the rigors of testimony, especially cross-examination.

What motivates a forensic expert to work under these trying circumstances? Experts must ask themselves why they want to be involved in difficult evaluations that frequently eventuate in stressful and, at times, grueling courtroom testimony. Do experts see themselves as humanitarians, persons who mete out justice, or societal protectors? Like Perlin's (1994) description of law's pretextuality (its unspoken motivation) in insanity cases, we expect that experts have their own implicit motivations. Rogers and Mitchell (1991) hypothesized that motivations could be partially categorized in terms of (1) financial remuneration, (2) competitiveness (i.e., demonstrating one's own competence in a highly adversarial setting), (3) self-importance (i.e., being center stage in a real drama), and (4) academic (i.e., engaging in an intellectual pursuit). But other motivations (e.g., humanitarian interests) are likely to play a role. If attorneys can discover the expert's primary motivation for participating in insanity evaluations, their ability to use a particular expert will be augmented.

The emotional response of the forensic expert to particular crimes is worthy of self-examination. For example, if an expert is repulsed by certain crimes, he/she is precluded from offering an unbiased opinion (Madden, Lion, & Penna, 1977). Common examples of heinous crimes may include mass murder, torture, and violent assaults on children. Forensic experts should not be expected to have no negative emotional responses to particular crimes, but must be able to identify cases they find revolting or abhorrent. By excluding such cases, forensic experts acknowledge their human reactions as well as their willingness to remove themselves from potentially biased evaluations. Conversely, rare cases may occur (e.g., the homicide of an especially violent wife-battering husband) for which the expert has strong positive feelings toward the defendant's actions, thereby introducing bias into the evaluation. Rogers and Mitchell (1991) observed that defense attorneys attempt to influence emotional reactions by humanizing defendants, focusing on their backgrounds and the tragedy of their lives. In contrast, prosecutors attempt to influence emotional reactions by emphasizing the brutality of the crimes and their devastating effects on the victims and the victims' families.

A related issue is the forensic expert's attitudes toward crime. Implicit in this attitudinal set is how experts learned to deal with their own antisocial and aggressive impulses. In the first edition of this book, Rogers (1986) theorized that experts who strictly controlled their own deviant impulses may be less tolerant of the expression of these impulses by others. Conversely, it could be argued that forensic experts who developmentally were allowed a greater expression of their aggressive and antisocial impulses might be slightly more sympathetic than other experts toward criminal behavior. Some experts bristle even at minor criminal acts. Other experts are understanding, if not sympathetic, toward repetitively violent offenders because of the offenders' own apparent victimization as children.

Views of victimization are also likely to influence the outcome of forensic evaluations. As a partial analogue, the thresholds for reporting child abuse appear to be highly variable across professionals and jurisdictions (Kalichman, 1993). Some forensic experts place considerable weight on reported evidence, while others do not. In the context of insanity evaluations, some forensic experts may view the perpetrator as having been victimized through parental and social deprivation, poverty, racial and sexual discrimination, and/or personal deficits (e.g., low IQ and high impulsivity). In contrast, other experts may focus primarily on the current victims, emphasizing their reactions to the defendant's physical and emotional assaults, their suffering, and the relative permanence of the harm. Recognizing these divergent but not incompatible views, attorneys are likely to stress the type of victimization that best serves their cases. Experts may wish to resist these efforts. They have little to gain from (1) examining crime-scene pictures of stab wounds supplied by the prosecutor or (2) interviewing sympathetic childhood friends suggested by the defense counsel.

Extraneous Defendant and Victim Characteristics

The insanity evaluations and subsequent verdicts should be based on defendants' impairment and the relevance of that impairment to criminal responsibility. When marked differences are observed on extraneous characteristics (e.g., gender, race, or education), legal and mental health professionals become increasingly concerned about the potential for inappropriate influences from these variables on clinical and legal determinations. Because a successful insanity defense is the result of a multistep process (e.g., counsel raising the defense, commitment of resources to forensic experts, expert's evaluations and reports, prosecution's opposition to the defense, jury selection, and trial), differences in outcome are often challenging to explain.

Early Studies of Sociodemographic Characteristics

Early research by Rogers and his colleagues (Rogers, Cavanaugh, Seman, & Harris, 1984; Rogers, Seman, & Stampley, 1984) evaluated differences in sociodemographic backgrounds at two forensic sites (Chicago and Toledo) at two stages in this process: forensic evaluations and legal outcome. Interestingly, Rogers, Seman, and Stampley (1984) found the most pronounced difference for educational attainment. With graduation from high school as the benchmark, defendants with less education rarely were viewed as insane (18% of evaluations and 7% of verdicts). In stark contrast, more education resulted in more frequent conclusions of insanity (45% of evaluations and 43% of verdicts). For other demographic variables, differences were observed for race in clinical determinations but not in subsequent acquittals (i.e., insanity conclusions: 45% African Americans and 20% Anglo Americans). Conversely, gender differences were noted for verdicts but not for clinical evaluations (i.e., insanity verdicts: 50% female and 19% male).

Rogers, Cavanaugh, et al. (1984) expanded the sample and scope of the previous investigation.[2] Understandably, disagreements between clinical conclusions and verdicts essentially centered on persons evaluated as insane. In these cases, recommendations were less likely to be followed if the defendant was male, less educated, or unmarried. Clinically, disagreements about insanity were generally found in more marginal cases; disagreements tended to be found in cases with significantly fewer symptoms and less impairment than in cases of agreement. However, these clinical differences do not adequately explain the observed sociodemographic disparities.

Boehnert (1985) attempted to establish sociodemographic differences among three small samples: (1) those found NGRI, (2) those found guilty after raising an insanity defense, and (3) those found guilty after insanity evaluations and a subsequent plea bargaining to a stipulated conviction. Her absence of significant differences may be attributable to the similarities between the two convicted groups ("2" and "3").

Recent Research on Potential Racial Bias

Grekin, Jemelka, and Trupin (1994) conducted an important study on racial differences in the criminalization of the mentally disordered. They examined admission data for state hospitals and state prisons in Washington state. They concluded that mentally disordered minorities, especially Hispanic Americans, were more likely to be imprisoned than Anglo Americans. The inverse relationship was generally true with respect to hospitalization, with Anglo Americans being disproportionately represented. One disturbing finding was that communities with greater minority representation appeared more prone to favor imprisonment over hospitalization. While most pronounced for Hispanic Americans, similar patterns were observed for African Americans and Native Americans. Although the possibility exists that a particular ethnic group has a high proportion of the mentally disordered among those committing crimes, it seems very unlikely that this proportion would explain such systematic differences across three minority groups.

Linhorst, Hunsucker, and Parker (1998) investigated racial differences in a large-scale study of 853 insanity acquittees from Missouri. The sample was composed almost entirely (98.7%) of African American and Anglo American defendants. Their results suggested that African Americans are much less likely to receive NGRI verdicts. As a benchmark for comparison, both racial groups had roughly comparable percentages (51.4% vs. 48.2%, respectively) serving prison time. Taking into account the small differences in these percentages, Anglo Americans have approximately a 50% greater likelihood of being found NGRI.[3]

A startling discovery regarding the underrepresentation of Hispanic Americans emerged from our data base on NGRI patients. Of 4,787 NGRI acquittees for whom racial information was provided, only a negligible sample of 15 patients were identified as Hispanic Americans. This minuscule proportion (.003) of NGRI acquittees is inconsonant with the substantial numbers of Hispanic Americans charged with offenses or serving time in correctional institutions. Not all states are included in this data base. However, the absence of southwestern states would not explain such low numbers of Hispanic acquittees, especially with the inclusion of samples from California, Florida, and New York.

Do these results necessarily suggest a systematic bias on the part of mental health professionals in conducting insanity evaluations? Several alternative explanations may help to explain this alarming observation:

1. *Nonidentification of Hispanic Americans.* One possibility is that some Hispanic Americans are not accurately classified with respect to their ethnic identity in clinical and administrative records. As an illustration, an administrator of a metropolitan jail in Texas acknowledged that only Hispanic Americans with language barriers were likely to be classified correctly.

2. *Attorney bias.* Biases may occur on the part of defense attorneys in their referral of defendants for insanity evaluations. If very few Hispanic Americans are referred, then the proportion of NGRI patients may be consistent with these referral patterns.

3. *Cultural limits on forensic assessments.* Cultural differences may hamper the effectiveness of mental health professionals in performing forensic evaluations. As Fantoni-Salvador and Rogers (1997) observed, many psychological measures are assumed to be generalizable to Hispanic populations on the basis of meager normative data or are simply translated into Spanish with little consideration of their validity.

4. *Prevalence of Axis I disorders.* Hispanic Americans may manifest a much lower rate of Axis I disorders, thereby reducing the likelihood of a successful insanity defense. But data from large epidemiological studies strongly question this hypothesis. Canino et al. (1987) found similar prevalence rates for schizophrenia and mood disorders for 1,551 Puerto Rican respondents when compared to community samples from three U.S. cities (Robins et al., 1984).

5. *Biased verdict.* The triers of fact (judge or jury) may be biased against Hispanic Americans. Allied with this hypothesis, the proportion of African Americans in the NGRI samples appears lower than expected, at .35. However, the marked disparity (i.e., 15 Hispanic Americans vs. 1,800 African Americans) suggests that any cumulative bias appears directed especially toward Hispanic Americans.

Awareness that Hispanic American defendants are rarely found NGRI should sensitize mental health professionals to possible biases in their evaluations. One possible solution is the use of the Diagnostic Interview Schedule—Version III—Revised (DIS-III-R; Robins, Helzer, Cottler, & Goldring, 1989), which has been well validated with certain Hispanic populations. The DIS provides moderately reliable diagnoses for disorders frequently found among NGRI patients (e.g., schizophrenic and mood disorders).

In summary, racial biases appear to be operating for the insanity defense within the criminal justice system. They are likely to influence the process at several steps, including arrest, legal representation, decisions about prosecution, insanity evaluations and trials, and ultimately verdicts. The lack of specific accountability does not absolve forensic experts or attorneys from the weighty responsibility of ensuring that their component of the process is fair and impartial. While addressing capital sentencing, Bohm (1994) provides a penetrating analysis of racial influences (i.e., race of the defendants, victims, jurors, attorneys, and judges) on the legal outcome. For insanity evaluations, forensic experts should not be exempt from this analysis.

Recent Studies on Potential Gender Bias

Seig, Ball, and Menninger (1995) compared their data on 149 acquittees to the data in four earlier studies. The proportion of female acquittals varied markedly across different states, with a range from 6.5% to 24.8%. Although the higher percentages do not appear to be consistent with the proportion of women in incarcerated populations, no formal comparisons were undertaken.

Linhorst et al. (1998) found that gender appeared to play a role in insanity acquittals. They found that women accounted for only 5.8% of the prison population but constituted 12.5% of those found NGRI. Although women have a greater proportion of mood disorders, this finding was attenuated by racial disparities (Anglo American females, 36.5%; African American females, 19.0%; Anglo American males, 21.6%; African American males, 12.5%).

Cirincione, Steadman, and McGreevy (1995) examined insanity pleas of 8,138 defendants indicted on felonies. Across seven states, female defendants were more likely to be found NGRI than men (38.5% vs. 26.9%). While always higher, the NGRI acquittal rate fluctuated dramatically by states for both female (19.7% to 95.2%) and male (14.7% to 86.0%) defendants. Although gender appears to play a significant role, regional differences overshadow these findings.

In summary, the data suggest that women are more likely to be found NGRI than their male counterparts. The explanations for this finding are not immediately obvious, given differences in types of crimes, victims, and mental disorders. One consideration is whether forensic experts view female defendants more sympathetically. Likewise, triers of fact (judges and juries) may be more compassionate with female defendants.

Ethical Issues

Both forensic psychology and psychiatry offer general templates for ethical conduct in forensic evaluations. In this brief section, we touch on the most critical issues facing forensic experts in conducting insanity evaluations. These issues are organized by profession.

Psychologists' Professional Ethics

For psychologists, the American Psychological Association (1992) revamped its professional ethics and included a specific section on "Forensic Activities." As a secondary source for psychologists, we will also refer to the "Specialty Guidelines for Forensic Psychologists" (Committee on Ethical Guidelines, 1991). The "Specialty Guidelines" are considered a secondary source because they were intended "to be an aspirational model of desirable professional practice" (p. 656).

Key issues and comments for APA ethics as they relate to forensic practice are described below. The numbers refer to the specific ethical standards:

1.14. *Avoiding harm.* Psychologists are required to take reasonable measures to avoid harming their patients and clients. Although the results of insanity evaluations may be associated with severe consequences, most psychologists would argue that thorough and fair forensic evaluations do not *cause* harm. However, Standard 1.14 is likely to be violated by (1) biased or less-than-complete evaluations or (2) assessments conducted by inadequately trained psychologists.

1.23. *Documentation of professional and scientific work.* In Subsection (b), psychologists in legal proceedings are required "to create and maintain documentation in the kind of detail and quality that would be consistent with reasonable scrutiny" (APA, 1992, p. 4). In addition to the maintenance of test data, psychologists must keep detailed records of their clinical observations and interviews.

2.02. *Competence and appropriate use of assessments and interventions.* Subsection (b) prohibits the release of raw test results and raw data to persons not qualified to use such information. But if faced with a subpoena, psychologists are given little guidance in how to respond; Standard 1.02 requires that they "take steps to resolve the conflict in a responsible manner" (APA, 1992, p. 4). Practices within specific jurisdictions are likely to inform psychologists.

2.08. *Test scoring and interpretation services.* Subsections (b) and (c) require that psychologists take responsibility for the validity and interpretation of tests, including automated reports. Bersoff and Hofer (1991) underscored the dangers in using computerized interpretations in that the basis for these interpretations is typically unknown and proprietary. Many forensic psychologists appear to use computerized testing, even though the validity of such test interpretations are often impossible to ascertain.

5.03. *Minimizing intrusions on privacy.* In oral and written reports, psychologists are required to provide "only information germane to the purpose for which the communication is made." In insanity evaluations, potentially prejudicial information regarding family history of criminality, substance abuse, or mental disorders are irrelevant to the issue of insanity[4] and should not be included in court reports.

7.01. *Professionalism.* Forensic practice should be based on specialized knowledge and competence. Psychologists untrained in forensic assessment measures are unlikely to meet this standard.

7.02. *Forensic assessments.* Assessments must provide adequate substantiation of their conclusions. Whenever feasible, the evaluations should be based on direct evaluation of the defendant. When not allowed, psychologists should be explicit in describing how the lack of a direct examination limits their findings.

7.03. *Clarification of role.* Psychologists should avoid dual relationships under nearly all circumstances in forensic practice (see also 7.05 on Prior Relationships and the earlier chapter section on "Conflict between Therapeutic and Forensic Roles").

7.04. *Truthfulness and candor.* Psychologists are required to testify forthrightly and acknowledge the limits of their data and conclusions.

To augment these standards for forensic psychologists, Division 41 of the APA, in conjunction with the American Academy of Forensic Psychologists, developed aspirational standards. These standards specify a rigorous degree of documentation, "higher than the normative for clinical practice" (Committee on Ethical Guidelines, 1991, p. 661), and have a "special responsibility to provide the best documentation possible under the circumstances" (p. 661). Clearly, sketchy and incomplete records of forensic evaluations violate the APA ethics and breach Division 41 aspirational standards. Under the rubric of professional integrity, forensic psychologists are asked to test rival hypotheses and actively seek information in this regard.

The Division 41 (Committee on Ethical Guidelines, 1991) guidelines provide an important discussion regarding the use of hearsay evidence, especially the defendant's statements. The guidelines exhort forensic psychologists to seek "independent and personal verification" (p. 662) of hearsay statements. Especially in insanity evaluations, this expectation is often unattainable. Similar to Ethical Standard 5.03, the guidelines require forensic psychologists to refrain from disclosing hearsay or other evidence that is not directly relevant to the current legal issue. More specifically, competency evaluations should not include (1) statements by the defendant related to the index offense or (2) issues of criminal responsibility. When both competency and insanity issues are raised as referral issues, one sensible alternative is to submit two reports so that competency can be addressed independently.

A curious anomaly in the APA (1992) ethical standards is that informed consent is applied to therapy (4.02) and research (6.11) but not specifically to assessment. The Division 41 (Committee on the Ethical Guidelines, 1991) guidelines address this oversight; they require the client to be informed "of the purposes of any evaluation, of the nature of the procedures to be employed, of the intended use of any product of their services, and of the party who has employed the forensic psychologist" (p. 659). Forensic psychologists must consider whether the sharing and understanding of this information constitute informed consent.

The foundation of informed consent is whether patients understand the risks and benefits of their participation (Lidz et al., 1984). Some potential risks and benefits are best known and explained by the defense attorney. For example, considering an insanity plea may diminish the likelihood of success for other defenses. Forensic psychologists would not be in a position to estimate these risks and benefits. Another consideration is the risk–benefit analysis of evaluations conducted by specific examiners. Rogers (1987a) presented a controversial argument for "specific track records" whereby each expert would make a prospective defendant aware of how often he/she was (1) retained by the defense or prosecution and (2) offered evidence supportive of sanity or insanity. In extreme cases (e.g., when the expert was nearly always retained by and testified for the prosecution), defendants might prudently decline the forensic assessment.

Psychiatrists' Professional Ethics

For psychiatrists, the American Academy of Psychiatry and Law (AAPL; 1995) has promulgated guidelines for forensic practice. The Roman numerals refer to the specific ethical standards:

II. *Confidentiality.* Psychiatrists should protect confidentiality within the limits of the law and notify clients regarding the limits on confidentiality. The AAPL Committee on Ethics (Weinstock, 1995) issued an opinion that psychiatrists have a continued responsibility to correct any misapprehensions about their role in forensic evaluations.

III. *Informed consent.* Psychiatrists are required to obtain informed consent whenever possible. As described in the commentary, psychiatrists are prohibited from conducting forensic evaluations prior to access or availability of legal counsel.

IV. *Honesty and striving for objectivity.* Despite the adversarial process, psychiatric evaluations and opinions should reflect honesty and objectivity. The AAPL Committee on Ethics (Weinstock, 1995) issued three opinions that are relevant to insanity evaluations. First, psychiatrists should not withhold potentially damaging information from their evaluations. For a further discussion of this issue, see the next section on "Whole Truth versus Partial Truth." Second, contingency fees are unethical because of their potential influence on the objectivity of psychiatric opinion. Third, psychiatrists should make an earnest effort to evaluate defendants. When this is not possible, they should indicate this limitation in their reports and testimony.

V. *Qualifications.* Psychiatrists are mandated to accurately state their qualifications and expertise. Interestingly, the standard does not address whether psychiatrists should limit their practice to areas of expertise.

Simon and Wettstein (1997) provide an insightful commentary on forensic psychiatric ethics. Their primary focus is on examiner objectivity and neutrality. From this perspective, they argue for the avoidance of dual relationships. *Dual relationships* include prior, current, or future relationships with the examinee. They also affirm the importance of the setting for the evaluation in promoting objectivity. Impediments to objectivity may include noisy distractions, intrusions on privacy (e.g., the presence of a correctional officer), or the skewing effects of having others (e.g., a family member or attorney) present.

Appelbaum (1997) attempted to delineate the moral principles undergirding forensic psychiatry's ethical standards. He advanced two principles: truth telling and respect for persons. *Truth telling* extends beyond honesty to the open acknowledgment of limits in testimony related broadly to scientific knowledge and narrowly to a particular defendant. *Respect for persons* has several dimensions; it requires psychiatrists to (1) clarify their role in forensic evaluations, (2) honor defendants' decisions, and (3) maintain confidentiality within the limits of the law. Appelbaum also argued that the principle of nonmalificence (i.e., avoid doing harm) is problematic for forensic psychiatry.

Whole Truth versus Partial Truth

Expert witnesses, like all witnesses, are required to swear an oath to tell the truth. While this oath may have slight variations across jurisdictions, it typically includes a phrase regarding the *whole* truth. Is the purpose of this stipulation to avoid mental reservations in responding directly to questions? Conversely, is it a mandate for forensic experts to present every relevant facet of the defendant? How forensic experts interpret this requirement will be instrumental in assessing their ethical responsibility both in presenting conflicting clinical data and alternative explanations for the defendant's criminal conduct. The responsibility to tell the whole truth is unquestionable; the only question is how actively or passively the forensic expert pursues this responsibility. Should experts be satisfied with a "You don't ask, and I won't tell" tactic? Resolution of this issue presents serious risks of attorney–expert conflicts.

Forensic experts should avoid alienating attorneys in their desire to pursue a more active approach to the whole truth. For example, the witness stand is not the place to make gratuitous statements like "By the way, he told me he lied to the other psychologist." The expert's responsibility is to make the attorney for whom he/she is testifying aware of the strengths and weaknesses of the case. Major weaknesses should be presented, preferably on direct examination, in order to provide honest and balanced testimony. As argued by Rogers and Mitchell (1991), these admissions are likely to increase the expert's credibility and the persuasiveness of his/her testimony. Naturally, this argument assumes competent opposing counsel who will vigorously assail this "overlooked" material. If these admissions are only extracted by cross-examination, the expert will be seen as partisan and possibly as having something to hide.

We recommend that written reports (see Chapter 12) provide comprehensive findings, not a selective reporting of data that favors only one conclusion. In some cases, the discussion of alternative explanations for the criminal behavior may also be helpful. Comprehensive reports satisfy the requirement of making the court aware of the whole truth. Whether opposing counsel chooses to pursue data supportive of an alternative conclusion is his/her informed decision.

Certainty of Clinical Opinions

Forensic experts are asked to testify *with a reasonable degree of psychological or medical certainty*. The meaning of this certainty requirement is less than clear. At times, it appears to refer to the degree of certainty expected of experts making clinical decisions. In other instances, the courts appear to confound certainty with the standard of persuasion (Shuman, 1994).

Clinical certainty is not simply the "strength of our convictions." Most forensic experts and attorneys are self-assured and confident in their conclusions. Beyond confidence, clinical certainty should be based on several definable parameters:

♦ *Accuracy of the diagnostic methods.* Standardized methods have known reliabilities that can increase clinical certainty over the subjective "strength-of-convictions" approach. Some methods, such as the Schedule of Affective Disorders and Schizophrenia (SADS), have proven useful with retrospective diagnosis and the establishment of impairment.

♦ *Consistency of clinical data.* Highly convergent data from multiple sources (e.g., defendant, informants, and records) substantially increase the clinical certainty. As a corollary, when malingering is ruled out, then the defendant's self-report can be included in the consistency of clinical data.

♦ *Relative weakness of alternative explanations.* When alternative explanations lack merit, the clinical certainty is increased.

Attorneys in insanity trials tend to avoid questioning the clinical certainty of an expert's findings. One simple strategy would be to ask the expert to operationalize his/her meaning of "psychological" or "medical" certainty. This type of cross-examination appears eminently fair since the expert has already offered testimony relying on this standard. Responses reflecting either undue precision (e.g., "90% confident") or ambiguity (e.g., "consonant with forensic practice") are worthy of further examination.

A second strategy is to ask the forensic expert to reevaluate clinical data across the experts and how these affect his/her certainty. In complex cases, one possibility is to offer a visual presentation of clinical data and then to ask the expert to categorize them (i.e., supportive or nonsupportive) of their opinion. His/her partisanship will be readily apparent if the expert has been (1) highly selective in what data he/she used to formulate the conclusions, or (2) is exceedingly dismissive of other data.

The Ultimate Opinion Controversy

Ultimate opinions refer to those expert opinions that address either the legal standard (e.g., insanity) or components of that standard (ABA Criminal Justice and Mental Health Standards, 1989; Note, 1987). Assuming that the testimony is otherwise admissible, expert testimony embracing ultimate opinions are allowed in most jurisdictions, including the federal courts, and on nearly all issues (Shuman, 1996); the most notable exception is Federal Rules of Evidence 704(b), which excludes ultimate opinions on the issue of the defendant's mental state or condition in federal criminal proceedings. Rule 704(b) is an amendment that was passed to assuage the widespread outrage following the acquittal of John Hinckley Jr. after his assassination attempt on President Reagan. Most state courts, where nearly all insanity pleas are sought, continue to allow ultimate opinion testimony on insanity. Forensic experts typically provide ultimate opinions, at least in their court reports (Heilbrun & Collins, 1995).

Where is the controversy concerning ultimate opinion testimony? After all, the legal standards allowing ultimate opinions in most criminal cases are unambiguous. The controversy stems from a position strenuously argued by Melton and his colleagues (Melton, Petrila, Poythress, & Slobogin, 1987, 1997). They claim "near-unanimity among scholarly commentators" (Melton et al., 1997, p. 17) that "*mental health professionals ordinarily should refrain from giving expert opinions as to ultimate legal issues*" (p. 17; emphasis in the original). Their reasoning can be summarized in a simple syllogism: (1) ultimate opinions are moral decisions, not clinical judgments; (2) clinicians are not moral experts; and (3) therefore, clinicians cannot offer conclusory opinions about psycholegal questions.

Many forensic psychologists and psychiatrists uncritically accept Melton et al.'s pronouncements for the virtual prohibition of ultimate opinions. Because most courts expect ultimate opinion testimony, many experts experience intense discomfort in trying to reconcile the court's expectations with Melton et al.'s admonitions. However, Melton et al.'s reasoning is problematic. Other than in federal trials governed by 704(b), there is no cogent legal or ethical basis for experts to hesitate to offer reliable and well-substantiated testimony that speaks to the ultimate issue. An important distinction must be drawn: some experts do overstep the clinical data in rendering both ultimate and nonultimate conclusions; however, this misuse of clinical data does not rest on the ultimate/nonultimate dichotomy but instead on its substantiation.

A brief commentary on the Melton et al.'s position is outlined below. For a more comprehensive critique, please refer to Rogers and Ewing (1989).

1. *Moral decisions.* While the law expresses moral ideas, clinical data related to specific standards does not address the law's morality. In addressing competence to stand trial for a mentally retarded defendant, an expert is required to assess (1) intelligence and cognitive abilities and (2) the relevance of such abilities to the defendant's functioning in narrowly defined areas (e.g., a factual as well as a rational understanding of the legal proceedings). While the morality of convicting an incompetent retarded defendant can be debated in academic circles, it is immaterial to the competency evaluation.

2. *Unduly influence the triers of fact.* Melton et al. has speculated that ultimate opinions usurp the role of the fact finder. Two studies have addressed this issue empirically. Rogers, Bagby, Crouch, and Cutler (1990) examined the effects of ultimate opinions on an insanity case. While expert testimony was influential, ultimate opinions were not, accounting for a negligible percentage of the variance ($eta^2 = .01$). In a more elegant study, Fulero and Finkel (1991) examined diagnosis-only testimony, penultimate testimony (e.g., the defendant's understanding of the consequences of his/her conduct), and ultimate testimony. Again, the data did not support the usurpation hypothesis.

3. *Specious distinction.* Even Melton et al. (1997) acknowledged their arbitrariness in demarcating an imaginary line between ultimate and nonultimate opinions. Experts often simply substitute synonyms of excluded words and phrases. In essence, no tangible change has occurred in this exercise in semantic brinkmanship (Rogers & Ewing, 1989).

4. *Near-unanimity of scholars.* Mental health experts may be intimidated by this apparently sweeping condemnation of ultimate opinions by learned minds. However, this assertion of "near-unanimity" is simply not true. Scholars have spoken in support of selected use of ultimate opinions (Ciccone & Clements, 1987; Fulero & Finkel, 1991; Rogers, 1986; Rogers & Ewing, 1989) or have not endorsed the logic of prohibiting ultimate opinions (Shuman, 1996). Even Grisso, originally very critical of ultimate opinions (Grisso, 1986), has since moderated his position (Grisso & Appelbaum, 1992).

5. *Problems with refraining from ultimate opinions.* Demonstrating the difficulties in avoiding ultimate opinions, Melton has offered what many scholars would consider to be ultimate opinions on the morally difficult issue of adolescent abortions.[5]

If one purpose of expert testimony is to communicate without ambiguity the germane conclusions regarding the psycholegal issue, then ultimate opinions may be a useful avenue to achieve this objective. They allow the expert the opportunity to describe the relevant conclusions and the bases of these conclusions. Equally important, they provide a means to describe the limitations of the conclusions. Ironically, the prohibition of ultimate opinions sometimes obscures its limitations since the conclusions are presented less directly in an inferential rather than an explicit mode (see Rogers & Ewing, 1989). In summary, we advocate a noncoercive position enabling experts to testify or not to testify about ultimate issues, based on their data rather than arbitrary rules. Our arguments simply are intended to rebut the present moral and professional condemnation of experts offering ultimate opinion testimony.

Notes

1. We are unaware of the original source for the credibility index; our source was a personal communication with Dr. William E. Foote (June 18, 1998).

2. The sample included those reported in Rogers, Seman, et al. ($N = 115$) and data on an additional 24 participants. In addition, the study was augmented by clinical data from the R-CRAS and other sources.

3. These racial differences do not appear explainable by a lower percentage of African Americans with mental disorders. In comparison to their percentage of the whole population in census data, proportionately more African Americans received mental health services than their Anglo American counterparts.

4. Some clinicians might argue that familial history helps to establish the diagnosis. This assertion is simply not true when comprehensive assessments are conducted. Simply put, familial and genetic variables do not add incremental validity to diagnostic measures.

5. Melton, as the chief architect of the APA amicus brief in *Thornburgh v. American College of Obstetricians and Gynecologists* (1986), offered ultimate opinions concerning the capacity of adolescents to make independent decisions regarding abortions (see APA, 1986; Melton & Russo, 1987). In offering ultimate opinions, Melton extrapolated from data on appendectomies to decisions about abortions. According to APA Division 41 speciality guidelines, the preparation of amicus briefs constitutes professional forensic practice (Committee on Ethical Guidelines, 1991, p. 655).

The Expert–Attorney Relationship

Overview

A variety of different expert–attorney relationships are encountered in insanity defense evaluations. These different relationships arise from the source of the experts' involvement: (1) experts retained by the defense or the prosecution, (2) experts appointed by the court, and (3) experts employed by public or private institutions that have treated or evaluated the defendant. Given the fundamental differences in these relationships, as well as the differences in the mental health and legal professions, the achievement of successful expert–attorney relationships requires a thorough understanding of each profession's epistemology, domains of responsibility, goals and objectives, and sources of mutual distrust and agreement.

The title of this chapter, "The Expert–Attorney Relationship," is a useful place to begin examining the differences in these relationships. Ordinarily in the delivery of clinical services, the relationship between the clinician and the patient (or client) is central to the creation and definition of the clinician's roles and obligations. In stark contrast, the central relationship in forensic settings is often that between the clinician and the attorney. In any case in which an insanity defense might appropriately be considered, defendants enjoy the right to counsel (appointed, if necessary); the judge will predictably be reluctant to permit the defendant to waive this right out of concerns for fundamental unfairness and possible reversible errors. In contrast to a competent adult contacting a clinician directly for treatment, the defendant is the recipient but not the initiator of forensic services. For a variety of legal and practical reasons, the attorney plays a central role in identifying the need for a forensic consultant and arranging for the consultant's services.

Differences in these relationships not only affect the roles of experts and attorneys in insanity evaluations, they also result in different legal treatment of these relationships. In most jurisdictions, patient communications in the context of treatment are protected by some form of psychotherapist–patient privilege (e.g., physician–patient, psychiatrist–patient, or psychologist–patient). This privilege protects communications from judicially compelled disclosure, subject to waiver or exceptions to privilege. The patient is typically viewed as the holder of the relational privilege. However, communications for forensic rather than therapeutic purposes are not shielded by the psychotherapist–patient privilege. Instead, the attorney–client or work-product privilege may apply because the law regards the expert as an agent of the attorney. These privileges are not functionally equivalent; they differ with respect to exceptions and limitations.

- ◆ *Psychotherapist–patient privilege* occurs in most nonforensic, treatment-oriented clinical settings and belongs to the patient.
- ◆ *Attorney–client or work-product privilege* occurs only with forensic experts. While it technically belongs to the defendant, attorneys play a central role in its assertion.

Mental health experts must become familiar with the law of privilege within their own jurisdictions. Differences in privilege may vary by jurisdiction, type of mental health professional, and the nature of the relationship. For example, do mandatory reporting laws for child abuse apply not only to psychotherapist–patient privilege but also to work-product privilege? If so, how does a retained expert evaluate the sanity of a pedophile for his/her attorney without being required to divulge potentially incriminating information? Effective interprofessional collaboration requires an exploration of privilege and its impact on expert-attorney relationships.

Mutual Distrust and Derogation

To listen to many mental health professionals describe their initial experiences in the criminal justice system, the courts appear nightmarish. Clinicians stridently complain of being abused and tricked. They protest about being (1) kept waiting for an interminable time before testifying, (2) surprised with new facts on the witness stand, (3) prohibited from answering questions fully and telling the court what was really important, (4) forced to answer trick or incomprehensible questions, and (5) treated rudely without respect for their profession or their beneficent purposes in testifying.

To listen to many attorneys describe their initial experiences with mental health professionals in the criminal justice system, any exposure to clinicians appears nightmarish. Attorneys complain stridently of arrogance and obfuscation. They protest about (1) inaccessible clinicians who deliberately avoid contact, (2) dissembling experts who speak in riddles or hide in psychobabble, (3) narcissistic experts who expect deference and special treatment, and (4) untutored experts who do not understand the courts or the adversary system.

Readers would be naive, of course, to think that a book chapter will resolve all or even many of these problems. They reflect fundamental differences, steeped in tradition. At the turn of the century, Hugo Munsterberg (1908) in *On the Witness Stand: Essays on Psychology and Crime* arrogantly promoted what the developing science of psychology had to offer the criminal justice system on issues such as the believability of witnesses and the prevention of crime.[1] In a scathing response, John Wigmore (1909), the leading evidence scholar of the time, told Munsterberg in no uncertain terms that he and his colleagues had nothing of use to offer to the legal system and that they were not welcome. More recently, in *The Crime of Punishment*, Karl Menninger (1968) again offered to rescue the criminal justice system, in this case from its decision to punish rather than to rehabilitate criminals. After toying with Menninger's idea, the criminal justice system directly rejected Menninger's advice and moved sharply toward the retributive model and determinate sentencing.

While interprofessional relations are currently more civil, they still reflect a deep-seated mistrust and derogation. Throughout the legal system, attorneys are wary of expert testimony by mental health professionals. This wariness reflects a common concern that mental health professionals lack criteria that can be objectively verified. In many cases, their testimony is perceived as impressions based on personal values rather than as scientifically derived knowledge. Before forensic experts dismiss this viewpoint as unreasonable, they should realize that its primary source is prominent psychologists who promote this perspective: Ziskin (1995) assails most psychological and psychiatric testimony as lacking sufficient empirical foundation. Hagan (1997) denounces psychological and psychiatric experts as "whores in the courtroom." While decidedly less extreme, Melton et al. (1997) repeatedly assert their belief that mental health experts have overstepped their science. As a remedy, they have sought to severely circumscribe the scope of their expert testimony.

Mental health professionals often feel manipulated by criminal attorneys. In truth, manipulation does occur in many criminal cases. In representing their clients, attorneys are ethically obligated to "act with reasonable diligence and promptness" (Rule 1.3; ABA, 1983). In providing diligent representation, some attorneys may prepare or even coach defendants about certain tests (Lees-Haley, in press). The overriding priority is the interests of the client during the evaluation and trial. This priority may be achieved even at the expense of cordial relationships with mental health experts. A major responsibility in trials is the attorney's obligation to present evidence that casts the client in the best light. Without breaking legal ethics, attorneys may orchestrate and influence expert testimony. Mental health experts are sometimes naive in assuming that they are exempt from this critical component of trial tactics.

Attorneys should also be aware of the professional rivalries that sometimes exist between forensic psychologists and psychiatrists. Forensic psychiatrists attempted to establish their particular expertise in 1976 through board certification (Prentice, 1995). Forensic psychologists, keenly aware of professional competition, hurried to form their own board certification (Grisso, 1991). Although gestures toward professional collaboration are evident (Grisso, 1993), professional rivalries persist. Beyond competition in the marketplace, the professions differ substantially in their education: psychiatrists are predominantly trained in the practitioner model and clinical psychologists primarily in the scientist-practitioner model (see Rogers & Mitchell, 1991).

Epistemological Differences

Truth in the Adversarial System

To understand what inspires the conduct of attorneys fulfilling their professional obligations, it is helpful to consider the role that truth plays in the adversary system. From a scientific perspective, clinicians often find the adversary system an awkward vehicle to ascertain truth. For proponents of the adversary system, however, truth is a unifying concern that anchors and explains its basic structure. The adversarial pursuit of truth is grounded in the assumption that those with a stake in the outcome have the greatest incentive to discover and present relevant evidence and to scrutinize the evidence presented by the opposing party. This construct rejects the alternate assumption that investigation by disinterested parties is the best avenue to the truth, given their disengagement in the outcome. Therefore, common law embraces adversarialness as fundamental to accuracy as well as fairness.

The adversary system, indeed all legal systems, must reach a determination of truth within some reasonable, determinate time frame. Unlike science, which can and indeed must wait to make its pronouncements until adequate data have been collected and analyzed, the law must act with reasonable promptness. For example, criminal defendants cannot be confined indefinitely while an investigation proceeds. Beyond truth are other important competing goals of the adversary system, including efficiency, consistency, finality, and perceived fairness. At times, these goals may conflict, and truth must accede to another important goal. We commonly accept the validity of the precept that "justice delayed is justice denied," although we also recognize that delay may result in increased accuracy. Practical limits are readily apparent concerning the time and money that society can afford to spend on each case. Cases must have finality; eventually, the criminal justice system must reject new posttrial claims of error or newly discovered evidence. For a scientist, disregarding newly discovered data is inconceivable, irrespective of its timing. In the law, truth does not always prevail over all other values. For example, relevant information from psychotherapist–patient communications is often protected by privilege, despite its potential to assist the truth-finding process.

Forensic experts' perspectives on truth are often complex and role-dependent. Within the criminal justice system, psychologists and psychiatrists are asked to assume a multiplicity of professional roles, including scientific, evaluative, consultative, and therapeutic roles (ABA Criminal Justice Mental Health Standards, 1989, Section 7-1.1). The establishment of truth, as a matter of historical accuracy, is an important goal of legal proceedings and forensic consultations. In contrast, nonforensic treating professionals may view verification of "truth" much differently.

Historical truth plays a different role in each relationship. At least with competent adults, therapy is primarily based on information provided by the person being treated, and this information may be somewhat incomplete, grossly biased, or honestly misperceived. Even when the therapist does seek collateral information from outside therapy, for example, when treating children or incompetent adults, the purpose of the information gathering is to further treatment, not to pursue the validation of historical truth. In most instances, it is not realistic, nor is it typically the standard of care, to expect a therapist to be an investigator to validate the historical truth of what a patient discusses in therapy (Greenberg & Shuman, 1997, p. 53).

Among scientists, pursuit of truth differs fundamentally from both forensic and treatment roles. Scientists differ from both forensic consultants and treating professionals in the type of truth they are seeking. Rather than pursuing historical truth or clinical significance, scientists seek to discover and confirm the relationships among important psychological variables. Rarely are they concerned about the accuracy of specific events, whether observable (e.g., a particular defendant's report of criminal behavior) or inobservable (e.g., the same defendant's account of command hallucinations). Moreover, scientists are expected to be inconclusive (e.g., nonsignificant findings) in many of their investigations. Treating practitioners are rarely allowed this latitude. For example, some decision must be rendered about the commitment status of a specific patient. In this instance, even a "nondecision" (i.e., a postponement of the hearing) is still a decision (i.e., the patient is not hospitalized).

Haney's Commentary on Epistemological Differences

Haney's (1980) seminal work delineated the major epistemological differences between psychology and law. We outline below several critical differences that directly affect expert-attorney relationships:

♦ *Nomothetic versus idiographic.* Most research in clinical forensic psychology is based on systematic comparisons of group differences (i.e., the nomothetic approach). For example, sex offenders are compared to other offenders on standardized measures (e.g., the MMPI-2). The criminal justice system is rarely concerned with group differences. It is typically interested in the *specific* behavior of a *particular* defendant under *unique* circumstances (i.e., the idiographic approach). Attorneys often consider nomothetic data to be irrelevant because group differences do not appear to respond to case-specific questions. For instance, case-specific information may involve a specific defendant's functioning (e.g., moderate mental retardation), interpersonal conflicts (e.g., fight with a parent), substance abuse (e.g., use of marijuana on the day of the alleged offense), and special environmental circumstances (e.g., recently discharged from a supervised residential setting). By definition, nomothetic approaches cannot account for these unique combinations of characteristics.

♦ *Experimentation versus litigation.* Most psychological research is based on rigorous designs, standardized measurements, and statistical analysis. Researchers are expected to report all results, positive and negative, and to describe explicitly the limitations of their research. As previously noted, litigation is predicated on the adversarial system in which each side and their respective witnesses makes the "best case." Many experts feel genuinely conflicted between their oath (i.e., to tell the *whole* truth) and attorneys' expectations (i.e., to tell the *favorable* truth).

♦ *Probability versus certainty.* Psychologists learn to couch their conclusions in qualifying terms. Because of their scientific training, the misreporting of a positive finding is considered to be especially objectionable.[2] A prevalent method of qualifying an opinion is to state that opinion in probabilistic terms (e.g., to use "likely" or "very likely"), rather than to make a definitive statement. Occasionally, experts will attempt to make precise probabilistic statements (e.g., "an 80% likelihood"); such "precision" is rarely defensible, based on the current sophistication of our clinical-forensic research. In contrast to psychologists, attorneys prefer statements of certainty, unencumbered with qualifiers.[3]

♦ *Value-free verus value-laden.* The criminal law is unabashedly prescriptive: it delineates what values/behaviors are permissible and impermissible. Within the framework of scientific inquiry, most researchers and many psychologists perceive themselves (rightly or wrongly) as disinterested experts, uninfluenced by personal values. As acknowledged by the APA ethics (APA, 1992), personal values sometimes encroach on the objectivity of professional practice. However, attorneys should be aware why experts often take umbrage at suggestions that personal values may influence their judgment.

Competing Goals and Objectives

Neither experts nor attorneys operating within the criminal justice system are entirely free to define their goals and objectives. While they may enjoy much latitude, each profession operates within certain well-defined parameters. Within the structure of the U.S. criminal justice system, the roles of prosecutor, defense attorney, and judge are clearly defined and generally understood. Shaped by professional custom and culture, these roles ultimately are compelled by the interplay of constitutional and ethical norms. Acting outside these norms may result in a reversible error (*Kenley v. Armontrout*, 1991) or professional discipline (*Deatherage v. State*, 1997).

Criminal acts are regarded formally as a wrong against the state. The prosecutor is solely empowered to make decisions on behalf of the state about bringing charges, accepting pleas, and offering evidence in support of the charges. The prosecutor answers ultimately to the public, not to individual crime victims. In performing these roles, however, the prosecutor is ethically obligated not simply to convict, but "to seek justice" (ABA, Standards for Criminal Justice, 1993, Section 31.2). This ethical obligation is buttressed by other practical aspects of the prosecutor's role. The prosecutor not only conducts the trial but, in the event of a conviction and appeal, also defends the conviction and sentence on appeal. Thus, having decided that a case merits prosecution, the prosecutor is obligated not only to prosecute the case forcefully at trial, but also to see that the proceedings are fair and defensible on appeal.

The role of the defense attorney is to represent his or her client zealously within the bounds of the law. "Advocacy is not for the timid, the meek, or the retiring. . . . Once a case has been undertaken, a lawyer is obligated not to omit any essential lawful and ethical step in the defense, without regard to compensation or the nature of the appointment" (ABA, Standards for Criminal Justice, 1993, Section 4-1.2 commentary). But zealous advocacy nonetheless entails making strategic choices balancing a panoply of alternative risks and benefits. Consider, for example, the decision to raise an insanity defense, which is ordinarily waived if not raised in a timely fashion prior to trial. One decision involves the potential outcome: if the defense presents a successful insanity defense, the defendant is free from determinate criminal confinement but subject to indeterminate civil commitment. A second decision involves the likelihood of success: insanity defenses are usually unsuccessful (see Chapter 1, "Public Perception of the Insanity Defense") and prevent the defense from raising alternate defenses (e.g., an alibi). Unlike the prosecutor representing the state, the defense attorney has an individual client and, within the bounds of the law, is ethically obligated to follow this client's wishes. When clients are competent and understand the potential consequences of their decisions to pursue particular strategies, this requirement to follow the client's wishes works reasonably well. However, when clients have serious mental or emotional problems that limit their ability to appreciate the consequences of their choices, the attorney may be forced to make choices for the client. Especially in cases where an insanity defense is merited, defendants may lack the capacity to weigh adequately the potential risks and benefits of various defense strategies.

Judges in adversarial legal systems (e.g., the U.S. justice system) play a very different role than judges in inquisitorial legal systems. With inquisitorial systems, judges play an active role in the investigation and presentation of evidence. In adversarial systems, judges have traditionally played a less active role in these activities. They do not ordinarily investigate or present evidence. They generally rule on issues raised by the parties, but limit raising issues on their own to those that threaten the fundamental fairness of the proceedings. To some extent, this role has changed in recent years because crowded court dockets have forced judges to assume greater managerial responsibilities. However, U.S. judges in criminal cases mainly rely on the prosecuting and defense attorneys to define the issues for trial and to present issues that require a ruling to the court.

Certain tensions are apparent in our expectations concerning judges. While we expect judges to play a passive and nonintrusive role, we also hold them primarily responsible for seeing that the trial is fair. As articulated by the *ABA Model Code of Judicial Conduct* (1990, p. 1), "Our legal system is based on the principle that an independent, fair, and competent judiciary will interpret and apply the laws that govern us. The role of the judiciary is central to American concepts of justice and the rule of law." Tension results from these conflicting expectations: judges cannot be both "hands-off" and primarily accountable in criminal trials.

The goals and objectives of experts operating within the criminal justice system are also shaped by the interaction of constitutional and professional norms. Experts retained or appointed to assist the defense help to make meaningful the defendant's Sixth Amendment rights; thus their fulfillment of this role has constitutional consequences. If a psychiatrist erroneously advises the defense attorney to rely on the wrong test for insanity (e.g., the defendant is "sane"), grounds may exist to challenge a conviction based on the constitutional adequacy of the defendant's representation. Likewise, the ethical norms that govern professional practice are equally applicable in the courtroom as in clinical settings (Shuman & Greenberg, 1998). For example, psychologists are ethically obliged to recognize the limits of their expertise and only provide services (e.g., insanity evaluations) for which they are qualified (APA, 1992).

Nature of the Contractual Arrangement

The contractual agreement between the expert and the attorney will vary, depending on whether the expert is retained or appointed. *Appointed experts* are formally employed by the judge, or as an agent of the state, or an other governmental entity. The terms of these arrangements, including the rate of compensation, are typically dictated by the government. Appointed experts often have little room for negotiating core elements of the contract.

With certain limitations, *retained experts* are free to negotiate contractual arrangements that are mutually satisfactory to themselves and the retaining attorneys. One important limitation to these negotiations is the acceptance of contingency fees, which are generally regarded as unethical (see "Forensic Guidelines" in Committee on Ethical Guidelines, 1991), and in some jurisdictions are illegal (Shuman, 1994). Because damages are not awarded in criminal litigation, a contingency fee as it is conceived in civil litigation is not possible; however, payment of a different fee contingent on the result (e.g., guilty or not guilty) is conceptually possible. Not only is such a fee structure ethically precarious, it is tactically unwise because it exposes the expert's objectivity to a devastating challenge.

For a variety of different reasons, one of the challenges of criminal cases is collecting fees from clients for expert consultations. Convicted defendants may lack the means or incentive to pay their attorney or experts. Acquitted defendants are often insolvent and occasionally difficult to locate. Thus, the conventional wisdom is that experts must negotiate pretrial payment of the fee. Without a contractual arrangement, the expert may be left with no practical recourse if the client fails to pay the expert's fee. Experts may wish to consider a contractual arrangement that obligates the attorneys to pay their professional fees in cases where the defendants do not.

Domains of Professional Responsibility

This brief section outlines the professional responsibilities of attorneys and experts in two phases of insanity cases, consultation and trial. Although this section focuses on retained experts, parallel concerns often exist for appointed experts.[4]

Attorneys' Responsibilities

1. *Knowledge of the expert.* Before retaining an expert, the attorney should speak to other attorneys or experts about this expert's qualifica-

tions, reputation, and experience. In some instances, a review of reported cases in which the expert has testified is advisable. Biographical information posted on the World Wide Web can also prove useful. In the initial phone conversation, the attorney should ask candid questions about the expert's training and background. Asking delicately, the attorney should inquire whether there are any past, current, or pending (1) actions by professional organizations (e.g., ethics committees) and licensing boards or (2) litigation (e.g., malpractice claims or criminal proceedings).

2. *Case law.* The attorney should make available to the expert relevant case law, treatises, and articles on the current insanity standard. While experts should attempt to remain current, the responsibility is shared by the attorney to ensure their knowledge is up to date.

3. *Comprehensiveness of clinical and legal records.* The attorney should be proactive in making available all relevant records. Not only are expert–attorney relationships damaged by last-minute surprises, but also the effectiveness of testimony is vitiated when a less-than-complete evaluation is conducted. The attorney may also wish to inquire about the need for collateral interviews or other sources of data.

4. *Preparation of testimony.* The attorney shares the responsibility for an ill-prepared expert. When testimony is likely, ample time for preparation must be set aside. With respect to timing, the expert should not be called at the last minute under the misapprehension that adequate preparation can occur in 24 hours.

5. *Surprises and deception.* The following maxim must be considered: "A surprised expert is an ineffective expert." Major changes in direct examination without adequate preparation are, at best, unnerving. While attorneys are under no direct obligation to reveal their entire legal strategies, they should not mislead or deceive their experts. For example, small but important changes in a hypothetical question can lead to distorted testimony.

Experts' Responsibilities

The responsibilities of experts in insanity cases parallel those of attorneys. These are outlined below:

1. *Knowledge of the attorney.* Attorneys vary tremendously in personalities and style of professional interactions with experts. For example, some attorneys tend to be dominating and controlling, while others provide their experts with considerable latitude. Experts should not fault the attorney for their interpersonal or professional styles; rather, a

simple check with other forensic experts and attorneys can easily clarify this matter. As a related matter, the expert should ask the attorney about his or her experience with insanity cases.

2. *Case law.* Depending on the jurisdiction, insanity cases may be very infrequent. As a result, the attorney may not be well versed in the insanity standard or relevant case law. It is the responsibility of the expert to be knowledgeable regarding the standard, preferably with input from the attorney.[5]

3. *Comprehensiveness of the findings.* Every case has weaknesses. The expert has the responsibility of sharing with the attorney both the strengths and weaknesses of the clinical data. Weaknesses may include (1) data inconsistent with conclusions, (2) missing or unavailable data, (3) alternate conclusions, and (4) additional measures that were not administered. The attorney must be educated about the weaknesses of the case; otherwise, his/her ability to mount a successful case is likely to be compromised.

4. *Preparation for testimony.* Irrespective of funding, experts have a responsibility to know thoroughly the cases, the clinical data, and the basis of their opinions. While the attorney is ultimately responsible for direct examination, experts should play an active role in the preparation and refinement of questions. In addition, they should attempt to anticipate areas of cross-examination.

5. *Surprises and deception.* As outlined in paragraph 3, experts have a responsibility to be forthcoming about any reservations they may hold about the case, including possible weaknesses on cross-examination. An attorney must know if the case is marginal in order to make sufficient preparations and informed decisions.

Forensic Identification

Zusman and Simon (1983) coined the term "forensic identification" to describe an implicit process in the attorney–expert relationship that subtly biases experts. In a study of personal injury cases following an environmental disaster, Zusman and Simon became alarmed at the frequency with which forensic experts espoused the views of retaining attorneys. In examining the reasons for their findings, the researchers dismissed the notion that experts were "hired guns" providing manufactured testimony. Rather, they hypothesized that experts were incognizant of the attorneys' influence, which was exerted indirectly via their fact patterns. Otto (1989) conducted a preliminary study of forensic identification as it relates to insanity evaluations. Employing a case vignette approach, he was able to document the subtle influences of forensic identification.

Why does forensic identification appear to exert such far-reaching influences on forensic evaluations? The most likely answer is "primacy or anchoring bias." As described in Chapter 10, the initial or working hypothesis is likely to affect both the evaluation and its conclusions. The initial hypothesis may become a self-fulfilling prophecy, even with highly experienced clinicians (see Friedlander & Stockman, 1983). In forensic cases, attorneys persuasively present their theories or fact patterns. Experts are susceptible to forensic identification via primacy bias.[6]

In the context of the attorney–expert relationship, attorneys may wish to capitalize on forensic identification by early case conferences and selective presentation of clinical records. Recognizing their potential influence, they may wish to present their fact patterns regarding an insanity case with care and diligence. They should remember that the effectiveness of the forensic identification process is precisely because of its indirect nature. More direct efforts are likely to be seen as strong-arming tactics and may well produce a predictable backlash.

Forensic experts, valuing their independence and impartiality, will attempt to reduce the potential effects of forensic identification (Rogers & Mitchell, 1991). While not wanting to jeopardize the attorney–expert relationship, they may delay meetings with attorneys until they have had an opportunity to evaluate the defendant and review the relevant material. They may resist reviewing the first material sent by the attorney and select their own sequence of record review once the documents are fully assembled. When presented with a compelling fact pattern, experts can engage in debiasing techniques by actively seeking alternative hypotheses and challenging themselves to seek both confirming and disconfirming data.

Conclusion

When considering their colleagues in the other profession, both forensic experts and attorneys must be aware of the self-centered and naive impulse: "If *they* could only be more like *me*." The unadorned truth is that "they" cannot be "more like me." By nature of their past training and current responsibilities, attorneys and experts have different goals, ethics, and methods. Open acknowledgment of our professional differences is the critical threshold for replacing mutual distrust with mutual respect.

What do attorneys really want from their experts? Attorneys often have misplaced wishes for more accommodating experts (Rogers & Mitchell, 1991). They want "articulate, partisan experts with integrity" (Champagne, Shuman, & Whitaker, 1991, p. 387). For the following reasons, we believe that accommodating experts are *not* effective experts:

♦ *More tractable?* Criminal attorneys share with others the nearly universal desire to control their destiny and that of their clients. Within this context, a more tractable expert is immensely appealing. However, the price of tractability is credibility. Simply put, the uneven nature of the relationship is clearly observable by judges and jurors. Credibility is established precisely because the expert does not appear to be unduly influenced by outside forces, especially the attorney responsible for his/her fees.

♦ *More malleable?* Litigators are often distinguished by their considerable abilities at persuasive communication. Given these abilities, some attorneys attempt to shape the testimony of their experts and become frustrated when their efforts are unsuccessful. Besides eroding credibility, malleability is a two-edged sword. A malleable expert on direct is likely to be a malleable expert on cross-examination.

♦ *More impassioned?* Understandably, colorless and tedious testimony strikes dread into attorneys' hearts. The expert undoubtedly should be convinced and convincing in his/her testimony. However, fervency is a potent drug that denotes advocacy and zealotry. While an attorney may be gratified by this ardent display of support, irrespective of the verdict, we suspect that jurors clearly understand the incompatibility between "impassioned" and "impartial."

Attorneys in insanity trials may wish to consider issues of malleability and credibility in their selection of forensic experts. Uncompromised integrity and unmistakable impartiality are likely to augment an expert's credibility and the persuasiveness of his/her testimony.

Notes

1. Bartol and Bartol (1987) noted that Munsterberg's dismissive views of attorneys did nothing to promote cooperation.

2. The classic position in psychology is the minimization of Type I errors (i.e., reporting a nonsignificant result as significant) at the expense of Type II errors (i.e., not reporting a significant result). An enduring principle in psychology is that no finding should be interpreted unless the likelihood of a Type I error is at or below 5% (Cowles & Davis, 1982).

3. As discussed in Chapter 12, the actual effects of these qualifiers on persuasibility of testimony is unknown but assumed to be small.

4. With appointed experts, attorneys are typically limited by local arrangements and customs in their ability to form working relationships.

5. When appointed, the expert has the advantage of being able to ask both sides for relevant case law.

6. Hindsight bias may also play a role; see Chapter 11.

Addressing the Legal Standards

Overview

This chapter provides a step-by-step translation of legal standards into psychologically meaningful concepts. This process involves operationalizing insanity standards, that is, breaking the standards down into their integral parts and translating them into psychologically relevant questions. We describe this analysis for the four most prevalent insanity standards: (1) the *M'Naghten* standard, (2) the *M'Naghten*–irresistible impulse standard, (3) the American Law Institute (ALI) standard, and (4) the Insanity Defense Reform Act (IDRA) standard. In addition, we present a brief synopsis of guilty but mentally ill (GBMI) standards. This operationalization of standards is intended to provide practical guidelines about the psychological relevance of legal criteria for forensic experts to implement in their evaluations of criminal responsibility.

Ensuring that forensic experts are fully and accurately informed of the relevant legal standards is a responsibility that must be shared by attorneys and their experts. Surprisingly, fundamental misunderstandings frequently occur among mental health professionals about the relevant legal standards. For example, the results of a national survey in Canada found that more than two-thirds of Canadian mental health professionals with extensive forensic interests misunderstood the current insanity standard (Rogers & Turner, 1987; Rogers, Turner, Helfield, & Dickens, 1988). Even more disturbing, these percentages did not improve when the sample was limited to those experts with extensive forensic experience. Thus, it is imperative that attorneys ensure that their experts have an accurate understanding of the relevant legal standards prior to beginning an insanity evaluation. When attorneys are not forthcoming, experts must request this information as the conceptual basis of their evaluations. The education and updating of experts can be accomplished by primary sources (i.e., statutes and case law for the relevant jurisdiction) and general references (e.g., this text).

The forensic expert is engaged in two interrelated processes that establish (1) what the insanity standard means in psychological terms and (2) how the standard applies to a particular defendant. The first process is one of *concretization*, which entails moving from an abstract legal standard and related psychological concepts to specific observable patterns of behavior and symptoms of a mental disorder. In contrast, the second process is one of *synthesis*, which entails the incorporation of clinical data about the defendant (e.g., self-report, behavioral observations, and corroborative information), a current and retrospective diagnosis of the defendant, and the severity and degree of impairment at the time of the offense, into a conclusory opinion of how the defendant fits or does not fit the standard of criminal responsibility. This chapter addresses the first of these two processes; Chapter 11 addresses the second.

This translation process from legal standards to forensic practice is characterized by evolution and refinement (see Perlin, 1994; Roesch & Golding, 1980). Changes both in mental health and criminal justice will have concomitant effects on this multistep process. Examples of these changes are most clearly observed in the evolving diagnostic standards, as noted in the refinement of the Diagnostic and Statistical Manual of Mental Disorders (DSM—III, American Psychiatric Association, 1980; DSM—III—R, American Psychiatric Association, 1987; DSM—IV; American Psychiatric Association, 1994), and statutory and appellate changes in legal rules and procedures. It is therefore the responsibility of the forensic expert to be aware of any additional modifications of the legal standards within each jurisdiction where he/she conducts insanity evaluations.

M'Naghten Standard

As of 1997, 18 states (i.e., Arizona, California, Colorado, Florida, Iowa, Kansas, Louisiana, Minnesota, Mississippi, Nebraska, Nevada, New Jersey, North Carolina, Oklahoma, South Carolina, South Dakota, Texas, and Washington) applied *M'Naghten* as their insanity defense standard (Gee, 1997). The *M'Naghten* standard provides that for an individual to be found NGRI, he/she must be "laboring under such a defect of reason, from disease of the mind, as not to know the nature and quality of the act he was doing; or if he knew it, that he did not know he was doing what was wrong." (*M'Naghten*, 1843). This standard is best interpreted in terms of five interrelated conjunctive concepts.

Disease of the Mind

Interpretations of the meaning of *disease of the mind* have varied from a broad conceptualization including any diagnosable mental disorder (Davidson, 1965) to a more restricted position that requires severe impairment, usually in the form of a psychosis (Brooks, 1974). This stricter interpretation may have been based, in part, on the earlier diagnostic standards of DSM-II, in which any severe impairment was typically characterized as a psychosis. While psychosis appears to account for the greatest number of clinical findings of insanity (see Chapter 7), this rule of thumb (i.e., psychosis as one precondition for invocation of the insanity defense) is less relevant under the current diagnostic nomenclature. In DSM-IV (American Psychiatric Association, 1994), the term *psychosis* is limited to a specific cluster of symptoms and does not necessarily reflect the severity of the disorder. Thus, an individual with a major depressive disorder or a dissociative disorder could experience a pervasive impairment without warranting a diagnosis of psychosis. Accordingly, it is appropriate to take into account both the severity and the type of disorder in establishing the existence of a disease of the mind, utilizing the four additional concepts that make up the *M'Naghten* standard to limit its usage to those most severely impaired (see Goldstein, 1967).

Goldstein (1967) noted that the concept of disease of the mind excludes voluntary intoxication (either by alcohol or drugs) and strong emotional states. Existing legal practice uniformly limits application of this test in the case of voluntary intoxication (*State v. Solomon*, 1991). Creative attempts at the use of involuntary intoxication for criminal responsibility include the adverse effects of medication (Myers & Vondruska, 1998), drug dependence (Meloy, 1992), or drugs taken unknowingly by the defendant (e.g., "Mickey Finns"; see Goldstein,

1992b). Further, the concept of *disease* is generally construed to refer to a disorder of fixed or prolonged nature in contrast to any transitory emotional state.

Defect of Reason

Defect of reason describes the type of impairment that must result from the mental disease to exculpate the defendant. For an individual to be found nonresponsible, he/she must show marked loss in the ability to think logically and rationally. Applying a decision-making model, such an individual must show a substantial decrease in the ability to weigh alternatives, consider logical outcomes, and make a reasoned decision. A *defect of reason* involves the defendant's capacity for rational deductive thinking, predicated on the accuracy of his/her perceptions. Thus, a deluded individual, while thinking logically (e.g., "You are a monster about to injure me and others. I will kill you and thus save my life."), would still evidence a defect of reason since this thinking cannot possibly be rational, given marked distortions of the defendant's delusional beliefs (see Brooks, 1974). Another component of rational thinking is the defendant's capacity to organize and synthesize his/her thoughts. Therefore, marked deficits in the structure of thinking may well indicate a defect of reason. This deficit is likely to be manifested in disorganized thinking with clinical symptoms such as loose associations (i.e., derailment), perseveration, and markedly illogical thinking (see Othmer & Othmer, 1989; Spitzer & Endicott, 1978a).

A clinical evaluation regarding a defect of reason requires a complex judgment in evaluating an individual's ability to (1) perceive alternatives and (2) make a rational decision in analyzing and synthesizing the alternatives. There are no explicit criteria for establishing the threshold for effective reason (see Whitlock, 1963), although each element of this concept may be reviewed systematically (e.g., Rogers, 1984).

Knowing

The *knowing* component of the *M'Naghten* standard requires that the defendant not "*know* the nature and quality of the act he was doing; or if he *knew* it, that he did not *know* he was doing what was wrong." Much controversy persists on whether the word *know* refers only to a cognitive or intellectual apprehension of the nature and quality of the act or its wrongfulness, or to a more encompassing affective understanding as well (Brooks, 1974). In *People v. Wolff* (1964), the California Supreme Court defined knowing as "knowledge fused with affect." This attempt to distinguish between intellectual and emotional understanding is imprecise, since it is difficult to imagine how an individual could lose emotional awareness without concomitant loss of intellectual awareness. In a similar manner, Low, Jeffries, and Bonnie (1986) distinguish simple cognitive awareness from more affectively based appreciation of the *significance* of the actions. The term *emotional understanding* is apparently linked to the defendant's ability to recognize and respond on an emotional level to the importance of his/her actions. Thus, if homicide were equated in importance to reading a newspaper, then that defendant might qualify under this concept. The concept of emotional understanding includes an evaluation of the defendant's affective appreciation of his/her behavior.

The majority of cases using the *M'Naghten* standard are evaluated on the individual's general understanding and comprehension of his/her actions to assess the defendant's knowledge of the nature and quality of the act or its wrongfulness. As noted by Goldstein (1967), the concept of knowing refers in particular to the defendant's criminal action in contradistinction to knowing in a broader or more abstract sense. Finally, the importance of cognitive understanding is underscored by the requirement that the impairment must be based on a defect of reason.

Nature and Quality of the Act

The fourth component of the *M'Naghten* standard addresses the defendant's comprehension of the *the nature and quality* of his/her criminal conduct. *The nature of the act* is addressed to the defendant's comprehension of the physical characteristics of what he/she did and under what circumstances (Brooks, 1974; Davidson, 1965; Goldstein, 1967). Thus, if the defendant assaulted the victim (e.g., by attempting to mount the victim) while truly believing that the alleged victim was a beast of burden, then the defendant would not comprehend the nature and circumstances of that behavior. However, it is extremely rare that an individual will not understand the nature of his/her behavior (Davidson, 1965).

Comprehending *the quality of the act* is generally understood to have a broader meaning than knowing the mere physical actions that transpired. This component of the test contemplates an acknowledgment of the harmfulness of the conduct (Davidson, 1965) and its potential or actual consequences for the victim. *The threshold issue is whether the defendant was able to recognize what was the likely outcome of his/her conduct.* An example of a defendant who should satisfy this requirement of *M'Naghten* would be a delusional woman who, while attempting to baptize the devil out of her baby, accidentally drowned the child without a clear awareness of the potential harmfulness of her actions. The Wisconsin Supreme Court addressed the concept of *the quality of the act* in *State v. Esser* (1962), noting that the defendant must have a clear realization of his/her behavior and ruling that a vague awareness without real insight was insufficient knowing the quality of the act to impose criminal responsibility.

Wrongfulness

As delineated by Brooks (1974, p. 145), comprehension of the *wrongfulness* may be conceptualized as "(1) that which is illegal or contrary to law; (2) that which is contrary to public morality; (3) that which is contrary to the actor's private morality." Courts typically define the requirement that the defendant not know the wrongfulness of his/her conduct in terms of the defendant's incapacity to recognize illegal behavior or behavior that is contrary to law or private morals and delusionally based (i.e., definitions 1 and 3). In an often-quoted opinion, Judge Cardozo of the New York Court of Appeals reasoned that the term "wrong" includes moral as well as legal wrongs:

> The [*M'Naghten*] judges expressly held that a defendant who knew nothing of the law would none the less be responsible if he knew that the act was wrong, by which, therefore, they must have meant, if he knew that it was morally wrong. Whether he would also be responsible if he knew that it was against the law, but did not know it to be morally wrong, is a question that was not considered. In most cases, of course, knowledge that an act is illegal will justify the inference of knowledge that it is wrong. But none the less it is the knowledge of wrong, conceived of as moral wrong, that seems to have been established by that decision as the controlling test. That must certainly have been the test under the older law when the capacity to distinguish between right and wrong imported a capacity to distinguish between good and evil as abstract qualities. (*People v. Schmidt*, 1915, p. 957)

Thus, while the original *M'Naghten* decision defined wrongfulness as "acting contrary to law" (cited in Goldstein, 1967, p. 51), this definition has been broadened in most jurisdictions to include moral wrongfulness.

In analyzing the term *wrongfulness* under the *M'Naghten* standard, Davidson (1965) suggested a careful investigation of the defendant's behavior prior to and following the criminal actions. He advised that postarrest behaviors (e.g., turning oneself in, making statements of remorse, and attempting to avoid prosecution) may be evidence of the defendant's knowledge regarding the wrongfulness of his/her acts. Similarly, he indicated that preparatory behavior for the criminal act and behavior that was intended to avoid subsequent arrest should be considered as evidence of knowledge of its wrongfulness. Examination of these factors may be helpful in the majority of cases. A major exception involves the defendant whose delusional beliefs include the government and law enforcement personnel. For example, if the defendant believes that police are really masquerading terrorists, then attempts to evade them would not address the wrongfulness of his/her actions.

Several potential problems emerge in the implementation of the wrongfulness component. Wrongfulness can be examined on two parameters: (1) the clarity and unequivocalness of the defendant's intentions and behavior, and (2) the perceived seriousness of a wrongful behavior. For an example of the latter, a manic investor may be fully aware of the wrongfulness of his/her business transactions but convinced of their inconsequentiality (e.g., "just a technicality"). In addition, the defendant may have strong conflicting beliefs regarding the wrongfulness of his/her actions. For instance, a defendant may hold rigidly to a code of honor that justifies vengeance against anyone who disgraces his/her family. The primary determinant in this case is the basis of this code of honor and whether it and subsequent actions are derived from mental illness. Psychotic symptoms might include a gross misapprehension of who the defendant is (e.g., a chivalrous knight), a gross misperception of another's conduct (e.g., a friendly wink is interpreted as irrefutable proof of a romantic liaison), or a gross misconstruction of the significance of a situation (e.g., a harmless joke is misread as malicious and devastating humiliation). Such determinations are greatly complicated by defendants' subsequent needs, intentional and unintentional, to provide psychological justification for their criminal actions.

The Group for the Advancement of Psychiatry (1983) has raised a related issue on wrongfulness: Do psychotic defendants appreciate wrongfulness if they deliberately carry out criminal behavior so that they will be punished? For example, a delusional male defendant may mistakenly believe he has committed unspeakable crimes and seek methods of securing what he regards as justified punishment (e.g., by deliberately assaulting a police officer). A defendant who commits an act in order to be punished obviously understands the illegality of the punishable behavior. The more debatable issue is moral wrongfulness. While the criminal act may be morally repugnant, it may also serve a "greater good" (Appelbaum, 1990). In most cases, however, the self-destructive behavior is neither as clear-cut nor as directly related to delusional thinking; in these cases, defendants would not likely qualify with respect to the wrongfulness component of the *M'Naghten* standard.

M'Naghten–Irresistible Impulse Standard

The combined *M'Naghten*–irresistible impulse standard has fallen into disfavor and is used, as of 1997, only in New Mexico and Virginia (Gee, 1997). The addition of irresistible impulse was intended to broaden the *M'Naghten* standard so that individuals who had failed its cognitive component (i.e., they knew the nature and quality of their act and knew that it was wrong), but who, on the basis of a mental disorder, had lost the capacity to control their behavior would be adjudged nonresponsible. One of the most influential cases establishing the combined *M'Naghten*–irresistible impulse rule was *Parsons v. State* (1887), which articulated that, in addition to the *M'Naghten* rule, a defendant should be found not criminally responsible when "(1) if, by reason of the duress of such mental disease, he had so far lost the power to choose between the right and wrong, and to avoid doing the act in question, as that his free agency was at the time destroyed; (2) and if at the time, the alleged crime was so connected with much mental disease, in the relation of cause and effect, as to have caused the product of it solely" (pp. 866–867). This standard includes three important conjunctive components that require that, based on a mental disease, the defendant has: (1) lost the power to choose (2) between right and wrong and (3) lost the ability to avoid doing the act. While there is considerable variation in the language of existing standards, all standards address these three components. The following sections examine the implementation of the three primary criteria for the irresistible impulse standard.

Loss of Power to Choose

The loss of volitional–behavioral capacity is the pivotal issue in meeting the requirement for proof of an irresistible impulse. It has been described variously as the absence/incapacity of free agency, will, willpower, and mental power (in Goldstein, 1967; Keilitz & Fulton, 1983). To satisfy the irresistible impulse test, the *loss of power to choose* must be the result of a mental disease or defect and not be merely a strong emotional reaction. Thus, an emotional state flowing from moments of rage would not satisfy this component of the test (Goldstein, 1967).

The fundamental issue in the determination of *loss of power to choose* is the distinction between *irresistible* and *unresisted* impulse (American

Psychiatric Association, 1983; Shapiro, 1984). Many defendants experience at least some ambivalence and conflict about engaging in a criminal activity. Standing by itself, this ambivalence/conflict is insufficient to satisfy the *loss of power to choose*. Instead, the "power to choose" must be assessed on two parameters: First, does the defendant want to resist the criminal act? Second, does the defendant have the capacity to resist? Thus, even the severest compulsions do not necessarily preclude the intention/desire of an individual to engage in criminal behavior.

The loss of power to choose must reflect some internal imperative to carry out behavior that is forbidden both on a societal and a personal basis. This internal imperative may be experienced symptomatically as an overriding compulsion (i.e., a pattern of repetitive behaviors that the defendant is incapable of resisting), although this is a fairly rare occurrence. One such example is a male defendant with a compulsion to explore others' personal possessions. The defendant is apprehended by a female homeowner who awoke to find the defendant in her bedroom looking through her family photos. More commonly, the loss of volitional capacity is experienced as an internal and nonnegotiable demand. This internal demand must meet the following criteria:

♦ *Must be unable to be satisfied by other available alternatives.* In the preceding example the defendant must have an internal need to enter this home and then to see these particular family portraits or other possessions that would not be satisfied by browsing in a bookstore.

♦ *Must be incapable of any extended delay.* Although the loss of volitional capacity does not have to be sudden (see Goldstein, 1967), it cannot be delayed indefinitely if it is irresistible. The individual's capacity to resist an impulse and his/her coping methods for resisting may indicate adequate behavioral control. This observation may not hold true where there has been a sudden loss of a coping method (e.g., the death of a spouse).

♦ *Must experience this loss of volitional capacity with a sustained negative effect on the individual's day-to-day functioning.* If this loss is based on a mental illness (see Davidson, 1965), it should have a disinhibiting and/or disorganizing effect on the individual's overall functioning.

Thus, a pattern of mental illness and problems of behavioral control should be identifiable. In assessing the defendant's mental disorder, the forensic clinician should ascertain the defendant's overall psychological impairment, capacity to be choiceful and purposeful in major areas of life, and capability of resisting impulses forbidden both personally and legally.

Right and Wrong

The "loss of power to choose" of the irresistible impulse standard refers to the capacity of defendants to choose between right and wrong. Wrongfulness has been previously defined as a component of the *M'Naghten* standard; *rightfulness,* by extrapolation, is behavior that is either legally or morally correct. The forensic expert must assess the basis on which the defendant perceived his/her behavior as right or wrong, since the clarity of this distinction is closely related to the individual's capacity to resist. For example, a mentally retarded male defendant may not resist his angry impulses toward a sibling because his only awareness of wrongfulness is his parents' displeasure. If based on incapacity rather than ignorance, this defendant has less volitional control than if he realized the gravity of societal/criminal sanctions. The forensic expert must address how, on this occasion, the knowledge of right and wrong does not allow the individual to resist criminal behavior. One formulation considered in several jurisdictions (see Goldstein, 1967) is the *policeman-at-the-elbow rule.* This formulation asks whether the immediate presence of a law enforcement officer would inhibit or substantially modify the criminal behavior. While this may be useful as a general guideline, an important consideration is that for those individuals struggling for behavioral control, the presence of any authority figure might result in a temporary avoidance of criminal activity. In the previous example, the mentally retarded defendant may not have injured his sibling had his parents been present. However, this external constraint (parents' presence) does not necessarily indicate an adequate understanding of right and wrong.

Avoid Doing the Act

This component, focusing on the "loss of power" to refrain from the criminal act, addresses the inevitability of the behavior and its uncontrollability, as observed in the language of the irresistible impulse standard (Goldstein, 1967): "acts beyond his control," being "overwhelmed," and "unable to control his actions or impulses." The forensic expert must address whether, at the time of the offense, the criminal behavior became an inevitable and psychologically necessary expression of the mental illness. The following clinical issues must be addressed:

1. The clinician must establish the determinants of the uncontrollable behavior and whether it is based on a mental disorder. This

complex judgment includes the role of situational variables, temporary emotional states, and substance abuse in affecting the loss of behavioral control.

2. The clinician must ascertain the extent to which the defendant was able to foresee his/her vulnerability in a particular situation and thereby avoid it. For example, if a male pedophile were to babysit for a particularly attractive child, he may knowingly be placing himself in a situation where his behavior will become uncontrollable. In other words, how preventable was this behavior?

3. The forensic expert must assess how the defendant attempted to resist or avoid the criminal actions. The clinician must carefully assess the defendant's various motivations in establishing the defendant's intentions and the uncontrollability of his/her behavior.

An area of controversy in forensic psychology and psychiatry is the role of the unconscious in criminal behavior. One classic explanation for criminal behavior is that it represents the unconscious expression of repressed aggressive and sexual impulses. According to this formulation (see, e.g., Bromberg, 1979; Tanay, 1978), since the determinants of behavior are unconscious, the crime is uncontrollable. Deviant behavior would therefore be construed as superego lacunae, or impulses beyond the individual's ability to control or sublimate. Further, such loss of control is construed as evidence of a mental disorder. Such reasoning may become tautological: "You act out because you are mentally ill; you are mentally ill because you act out." The conclusion is not that the unconscious plays no role in the production of criminal behavior; rather, it suggests that the forensic expert begin first with the defendant's mental functioning, carefully evaluating severity and degree of impairment and its impact on the criminal behavior. To begin with the criminal behavior and to attempt to formulate psychological explanations for such behavior is untenable, given the criteria of criminal responsibility standards.

ALI Standard

As of 1997 Connecticut, Hawaii, Kentucky, Maryland, Massachusetts, Michigan, Oregon, Rhode Island, Tennessee, Vermont, West Virginia, Wisconsin, and Wyoming followed the American Law Institute's (ALI) Model Penal Code standard (Gee, 1997). The ALI standard (American Law Institute, 1962) states that a defendant is not culpable if "as a result of a mental disease or defect, he lacks substantial capacity either to appreciate the criminality (wrongfulness) of his conduct or to conform his conduct to the requirements of law." This standard specifically excludes "any abnormality manifested by repeated criminal or otherwise antisocial conduct." It includes five operative conjunctive concepts that must be addressed (Brooks, 1974): (1) mental disease or defect, (2) lack of substantial capacity, (3) appreciation, (4) criminality or wrongfulness, and (5) conformity of conduct to the requirements of law (Fig. 2.3). A number of states have adopted the ALI standard with some modifications. For example, Arkansas follows the ALI test but requires a lack of capacity to appreciate the criminality of the conduct rather than a lack of substantial capacity to appreciate its wrongfulness.

Mental Disease or Defect

This criterion, while paralleling mental disease in the *M'Naghten* standard, typically includes both functional and organic disorders. In defining this concept, most ALI jurisdictions have followed *McDonald v. United States* (1962), which defines mental disease as "any abnormal condition of the mind which substantially affects mental or emotional processes and substantially impairs behavior controls." This definition continues to be applied in most states that use the ALI test (Weiner, 1985). An unresolved issue is what diagnoses constitute a "disease or defect." One viewpoint is that any mental disorder with the possible exception of antisocial personality disorders would be sufficient to qualify, if that diagnosis is found in a current diagnostic nomenclature, such as DSM-IV (American Psychiatric Association, 1994). Others have discouraged the utilization of personality disorders, arguing that they are insufficient to exculpate criminal responsibility (e.g., Rachlin, Halpern, & Portnow, 1984). Rogers (1984) suggested that no class of disorders should be summarily excluded, although it is improbable that some disorders would ever meet the insanity standard (e.g., psychosexual dysfunctions, simple phobias, most somatoform disorders, and several personality disorders). As with the *M'Naghten* standard, it is the responsibility of the forensic expert to examine any severe disorder and utilize the subsequent criteria for establishing the defendant's criminal responsibility. The American Psychiatric Association (Insanity Defense Work Group, 1983, p. 685) suggested that disorders leading to exculpation typically be of "the severity (if not always the quality) of conditions that psychiatrists diagnose as psychoses." This emphasis is correctly placed on the severity of the disorder.

Additional debate has centered on the inclusion/exclusion of antisocial personality disorders (APD). The original ALI standard explicitly excluded any disorder manifested only by repeated criminal or otherwise antisocial conduct. The rough translation of this concept as a definition of APD has been questioned both on legal (e.g., *United States v. Currens*, 1961) and psychiatric (Overholser, 1962) grounds. To meet the current diagnostic criteria for APD, the individual must manifest a developmental pattern of maladjustment with impairment at home, at school, and in interpersonal spheres. In addition, as an adult, the individual must evidence impairment beyond antisocial behavior in not meeting social expectations or having a satisfactory work history (American Psychiatric Association, 1994). It is very unlikely that an individual meeting these diagnostic criteria would have symptoms limited to antisocial or criminal behavior; such behavior would be more consistent with a nonpsychiatric or V diagnosis of adult antisocial behavior. In summary, the APD diagnosis is not systematically excluded by the ALI standard.

The data base on insanity acquittals (see Appendix A) has demonstrated that "mental disease" is not limited to psychotic and mood disorders. Interestingly, Axis II disorders (see Chapter 7, Table 7.2) were observed as the primary diagnosis in 12.0% of NGRI patients. Twelve percent may be an overestimate (i.e., some NGRI patients may have had an Axis I disorder at the time of the offense that is now in remission). Still, the breadth of disorders clearly extends beyond Axis I diagnoses. Systematic comparisons between NGRI aquittals and guilty verdicts does emphasize psychotic disorders without substance abuse (Howard & Clark, 1985; Rice & Harris, 1990; Rogers, Cavanaugh, et al., 1984; Rogers, Seman, & Stampley, 1984).

Lack of Substantial Capacity

To satisfy the ALI test, the presence of a mental disease or defect must result in a lack of substantial capacity. The concept *lack of substantial capacity* was adopted by the framers of the ALI standard to include severe but not necessarily complete impairment of the defendant's cognitive and volitional abilities at the time of the offense. To quote the drafters of the ALI test (in Huckabee, 1980, p. 20), the term *substantial* is utilized to "support the weight of the judgment; if capacity is greatly impaired, that presumably should be sufficient." The concept of substantial capacity is intended to avoid the use of absolutes (see Brooks, 1974) in making a judgment about major interference or impairment with respect to the twin prongs (wrongfulness and conformity of conduct) of the ALI standard. Given the imprecision of terms, the forensic expert must address the threshold question: were the defendant's cognitive–volitional abilities disrupted in a major way during the commission of the offense? Would the offense have occurred without such impairment?

The loss of substantial capacity may result from an interruption, disorganization, or gross distortion of the individual's psychological functioning because of a mental disorder:

1. *Interruption.* Most problematic is the determination of a loss of substantial capacity in individuals whose functioning appears to be well integrated except for discrete episodes. Such interruptions are difficult to assess because of their variable nature and the typical absence of such episodes during subsequent assessments in institutional settings. Thus, an individual experiencing a severe bipolar disorder may have a discrete manic episode that severely disrupts his/her cognitive and volitional abilities for relatively brief periods.

2. *Disorganization.* Blatantly psychotic individuals may not be able to process their situation adequately, because they grossly misperceive environmental stimuli, and they may lack the capacity to integrate such stimuli in a meaningful and rational manner. Such individuals, because of their disorganization (e.g., schizophrenic or organic impairment) cannot cognitively appreciate their immediate situation and sufficiently control their subsequent conduct.

3. *Distortion.* Individuals may respond to their environment in a coherent and internally logical manner yet severely misconstrue the meaning of others' verbalizations and/or actions. Such misapprehension of meaning based on psychopathology constitutes more of a distorted than a disorganized process. Thus, an individual with a paranoid disorder may have intact intellectual functions, with the notable exception of circumscribed persecutory delusions.

Appreciate

To meet the first prong of the ALI test, the mental disorder or defect must impair the defendant's appreciation. The term *appreciate* was incorporated into the ALI standard to broaden the earlier concept of knowing beyond just intellectual apprehension (see Introduction). The intent of the change was also to assess the defendant's emotional understanding—that is, his/her ability to understand and recognize the significance of his/her conduct. The term *appreciate*, therefore, covers not only a rudimentary awareness of the inappropriateness of actions, but also the magnitude of this inappropriateness. As noted in *Wion v. United States* (1964, p. 430), the term *appreciate* is defined as "mentally capable of knowing what he was doing and mentally capable of know-ing that it was wrong."

The forensic expert must assess the defendant's cognitive abilities in understanding his/her physical actions, the likely or expected out-come of such actions, and the significance of these actions. This under-standing includes an awareness of what happened and was expected to happen both to the defendant, as the perpetrator of criminal activity (e.g., arrest and possible conviction), and to the victim(s) of his/her activities (e.g., the potentially devastating effects of being raped). Cer-tainly, a mentally retarded individual who did not understand the irre-versibility of death would be grossly impaired in his/her comprehen-sion of the results of excessively dunking a younger sibling in the tub and the legal consequences of such behavior. The individual's activi-ties, either in preparation for the criminal activity or in an attempt to avoid prosecution (e.g., avoidance of identification, concealment of evidence, and/or evasion of police), often provide relevant evidence of the defendant's ability to appreciate.

The assessment of emotional understanding, or the significance of the defendant's criminal activity, is frequently more difficult. The defendant's ability to recall his/her perceptions of the importance of the behavior and his/her affective arousal are typically more difficult to assess than his/her memories of the actual events and his/her overt actions. The forensic expert may wish to address just how bad the de-fendant perceived the criminal behavior to be. This perception should be probed thoroughly based on both what happened and relevant hy-pothetical situations. Examples of hypothetical situations include:

1. How would the defendant respond if he/she were the recipient or victim rather than the perpetrator of the crime?
2. What would have been the defendant's emotional response and actions if such criminal behavior were carried out against a loved one?
3. What was the victim's emotional response to the criminal be-havior? Was it understandable—that is, did the defendant know why the victim cried or was angry or upset?
4. What was the defendant's reaction to the victim's expressed emo-tions?

In summary, the forensic expert must assess the defendant's recog-nition of his/her behavior, understanding of the likely consequences of that behavior, and awareness of its significance. This evaluation pri-marily addresses the individual's cognitive abilities but also includes an assessment of the emotional understanding of the importance of that person's criminal conduct to him/herself and the victims (see Rogers, 1984).

Criminality or Wrongfulness

To meet the first prong of the ALI test, the lack of substantial capacity must affect the defendant's appreciation of criminality. States using the ALI test have adopted either the original term, *criminality*, or its alternative, *wrongfulness* (Keilitz & Fulton, 1983). *Criminality* refers to any conduct for which societal sanctions are imposed to prohibit that conduct for the protection of the community. Criminal behavior is statutorily defined by federal and state law. Defendants are not expected to know the precise wording of the relevant criminal statutes or the specific penalties that may be imposed; rather, this prong of the test requires that defendants understand that the behavior is criminal and have some awareness of the magnitude of the offense. To meet this component of the ALI standard, the lack of comprehension of criminal behavior must be the result of a mental disease or defect. Nonpsychopathological reasons (e.g., cultural isolation) are not sufficient to qualify for this criterion.

The alternative term, *wrongfulness,* has been adopted in many jurisdictions as being slightly more inclusive than criminality. Wrongfulness augments the concept of criminality by including those defendants who recognized that their conduct was criminal but, on the basis of a delusion, believed it was morally justified (Rogers, 1984). This reasoning is articulated in *United States v. Freeman* (1966) and parallels the *M'Naghten* standard in its definition of wrongfulness.

Conformity of Conduct to the Requirements of the Law

The phrase "conformity of conduct" represents the volitional–behavioral prong of the ALI standard. The term *conformity of conduct* supplanted the earlier *irresistible impulse* and refers to any marked loss in self-determined purposive behavior at the time of the offense. *Conformity of conduct* addresses the defendant's ability to choose and to withhold important behavior preceding and including the crime in question. A loss of cognitive control is frequently paralleled by a concomitant loss of volitional–behavioral control. However, Rotter and Goodman (1993) observed that criminal defendants with obsessive-compulsive disorders may have insight (i.e., cognitive awareness) into their compulsive behavior, yet be unable to control it.

Several dimensions must be considered in examining the conformity of conduct criterion:

1. The standard refers to the capacity to conform and whether the defendant exercised this capacity; reckless or impulsive behavior may not necessarily reflect on the individual's capabilities but only on his/her choice.
2. The ability to conform refers only to criminal behavior (i.e., the requirements of law); deficits in volitional–behavioral control unrelated to criminal behavior do not qualify under this criterion.
3. Assessment of the choicefulness of the criminal behavior (see Halleck, 1992) involves a careful examination of the individual's perceived options and decision-making abilities. As with the *M'Naghten*–irresistible impulse standard, the forensic expert must evaluate the deliberateness of the defendant's actions, choices available to the defendant, and the point, if it does exist, when criminal actions became inevitable.

Given the retrospective nature of insanity evaluations, the clinical determination of conformity of conduct is frequently challenging. For a variety of reasons, the defendant may wish to portray his/her behavior as uncontrollable and therefore exonerable. For this reason, the forensic expert may wish to separate the defendant's reported volitional control from clinically assessed control (see Rogers, 1984). Such division allows the clinician to focus on all corroborative sources of clinical information in reaching a decision about the lack of volition. Further, the forensic expert is cautioned not to confuse *ineptness* with *uncontrollability*; bungling of criminal behavior with a high probability of arrest is not necessarily related to either mental illness or criminal responsibility. Similarly, ritualistic behavior may or may not be symptomatic of mental illness and should be carefully evaluated for its relevance to volitional abilities. For example, some defendants with sexual paraphilias may intentionally use ritualistic behavior to heighten their sexual pleasure; these behaviors (dependent, of course, on the impairment) are unlikely to represent uncontrollable behavior. A final dimension of volitional control is the defendant's capacity to foresee and thus avoid potentially explosive situations. If the defendant deliberately places him/herself in a situation where violence is likely to occur, then this factor of avoidability must also be assessed within the spectrum of volitional–behavioral control.

IDRA Standard

The Insanity Defense Reform Act (IDRA) of 1984, passed in response to negative public reaction to John Hinckley's successful insanity defense following his attempted assassination of President Reagan, changed both the substantive and the procedural law governing the use of the insanity defense in federal criminal prosecutions. Procedurally, the act places the burden on the defendant to prove, by clear and convincing evidence, that he/she meets the substantive elements of the test. In addition, the act amends Federal Rule of Evidence 704, to limit the ultimate issue testimony of an expert in an insanity defense case that would otherwise have been permissible:

> (b) No expert witness testifying with respect to the mental state or condition of a defendant in a criminal case may state an opinion or inference as to whether the defendant did or did not have the mental state or condition constituting an element of the crime charged or of a defense thereto. Such ultimate issues are matters for the trier of fact alone.

Substantively, the act moves the standard for the insanity defense to federal criminal prosecutions from one that relied heavily on the ALI test to one that relies heavily on *M'Naghten*:

> It is an affirmative defense to a prosecution under any Federal statute that, at the time of the commission of the acts constituting the offense, the defendant, as a result of a severe mental disease or defect, was unable to appreciate the nature and quality or the wrongfulness of his acts. Mental disease or defect does not otherwise constitute a defense.

The act eliminates the ALI volitional prong from the federal test and exculpates only in the case of cognitive impairments. In addition to elimination of the volitional prong of the ALI standard previously applied in most federal courts, the modifier *severe* was added to clarify that a pattern of antisocial tendencies, "inadequate personality," "immature personality," and other nonpsychotic behavior was not intended to be included within the defense (*United States v. Salava*, 1992). Finally, the act changes the ALI test's cognitive requirement of "lacks substantial capacity either to appreciate . . . or to conform" to "unable to appreciate the nature and quality or the wrongfulness." In the application of this hybrid standard, the forensic expert is referred to the appropriate components of the respective standards.

Guilty But Mentally Ill Standard

Responding to a number of cases of horrific highly publicized crimes committed by individuals who had been only briefly confined after an insanity acquittal, beginning with Michigan in 1975, a number of states enacted guilty but mentally ill (GBMI) legislation (Maeder, 1985; Smith & Hall, 1982). GBMI proponents had a number of different agendas: some GBMI proponents sought to decrease the overall incidence of insanity acquittals; some sought to decrease the incidence of inappropriate insanity acquittals; and, some sought to ensure treatment for mentally disordered offenders. Although this legislation has been subject to much criticism (Slobogin, 1985), including criticism by the ABA Standards for Criminal Justice (1993), it has proliferated.

The general pattern of this legislation is to leave in place the existing verdict forms given to the fact finder—guilty, not guilty, not guilty by reason of insanity—but to add the GBMI verdict. The GBMI verdict generally applies when the fact finder concludes that the defendant committed the act charged and is mentally ill, but does not meet the requirements for the NGRI verdict. Defendants found GBMI are subject to the same sentences as defendants who have been found guilty of that offense, but their place of confinement or the treatment they are afforded may vary from that offered other prisoners. While some states inform juries of the consequences of a GBMI verdict (*Bell v. Evatt*, 1995), other do not (*Neely v. Newton*, 1998). The courts have not found that the Constitution requires juries to be informed of the consequences of a GBMI verdict.

This section focuses on the implementation of the Michigan-based GBMI standard because it was the first GBMI scheme and served as the model for many other states (Michigan Stat. Ann., 1979; see Robey, 1978). This standard includes three conjunctive requirements: first, the defendant committed the offense; second, that the defendant experienced a legally defined mental illness at the time of the offense; and third, that the defendant did not meet the state's insanity defense standard. For the purposes of this decision model, deciding whether the defendant committed the offense is strictly within the purview of the fact finder. This leaves the forensic expert with two tasks: (1) to assess whether the defendant meets the insanity defense standard and (2), if not, whether the defendant meets the criteria of mental illness defined under the GBMI standard. Thus, in any assessment of GBMI criteria, the forensic expert must first complete a thorough insanity defense standard evaluation prior to addressing the GBMI definition of mental illness.

The Michigan standard for the GBMI verdict incorporates its Mental Health Code's definition of mental illness, which is defined as "a substantial disorder of thought or mood which significantly impairs judgment, behavior, capacity to recognize reality, or ability to cope with the ordinary demands of life" (Michigan Stat. Ann., 1979). As of 1998, this standard has been adopted with some variations in thirteen states: Alaska, Delaware, Georgia, Illinois, Indiana, Kentucky, Michigan, Nevada, New Mexico, Pennsylvania, South Dakota, and Utah. Pennsylvania and South Carolina have retained the *M'Naghten* test as their insanity defense standard but have adopted the ALI criteria for their GBMI standards (Pennsylvania, 1997). Thus, forensic experts in these jurisdictions must examine the criteria included in the ALI formulation when conducting their GBMI evaluations.

The GBMI standard consists of three operative concepts: (1) that the defendant does not qualify for an NGRI finding, (2) that the defendant has a substantial disorder, and (3) that the defendant has significant impairment in one or more areas as a result of that disorder. Each concept is delineated in the subsequent subsections.

Does Not Qualify for the NGRI Standard

This component of the GBMI standard requires an evaluation of the defendant on the issue of insanity, as defined in the state's NGRI standard, prior to any determinations of GBMI. Thus, a forensic expert should never conduct a GBMI evaluation in these jurisdictions without a prior insanity defense evaluation. An additional problem is posed when the forensic expert is unable to reach an opinion regarding the insanity defense assessment with a reasonable degree of medical or scientific certainty. Under these circumstances, the forensic expert should make clear his/her uncertainty regarding the issues of sanity and then proceed to address the GBMI standard (see Rogers, 1984). Such an approach would not deprive the triers of fact of valuable information on the broader context of criminal responsibility since the GBMI and NGRI standards are addressed concurrently.

Substantial Disorder of Thought or Mood

This component includes two important criteria: explication of the term *substantial* and delineation of *disorders of thought and mood.* The requirement that the disorder be *substantial* is an attempt to limit the disorders considered under this standard. Clarification is necessary to determine whether the word *substantial* refers to the severity of the disorder (e.g., moderate vs. mild depression), the type of disorder (e.g., dysthymic disorder vs. adjustment disorder with a depressed mood), or both. From a clinical perspective, it would be most logical to apply the term *substantial* to the severity of disorder since the type of disorder is not necessarily related to overall impairment. For example, a severe obsessive-compulsive disorder may be as disabling as any schizophrenic disorder.

The clinical determination of substantialness involves a careful investigation both of the severity and extensiveness of the symptoms and of their potential impact on the individual's day-to-day functioning. The severity of symptoms may be assessed on several indices, including the frequency and duration of the symptoms during the period of the alleged offense, the avoidability of the symptoms (i.e., Can the defendant ignore or alleviate the symptoms?), and the psychological discomfort and disruption experienced by the individual as a result of the symptoms. The impact of the disorder on day-to-day functioning is considered under the third component, significant impairment. The severity of the disorder may be assessed with respect to individual symptoms and overall severity. Two rudimentary measures of severity are the Global Assessment Scale (GAS) found with the SADS (see Chapter 7) and the derivative Global Assessment of Functioning (GAF) included in DSM-IV (American Psychiatric Association, 1994).

The types of mental disorders considered under the GBMI standard are very similar to those considered with the insanity defense standard (Keilitz, 1984). The Center for Forensic Psychiatry (1974) considered "disorders of thought" to be schizophrenic and other psychotic disorders and "disorders of mood" to be major mood disorders. This formulation is unnecessarily narrow. For example, severe anxiety disorders may clearly show a major mood disturbance, and certain dissociative disorders may manifest disturbances of thought. Other disorders (e.g., borderline personality disorder and paranoid personality disorder) must be carefully reviewed on a selective basis regarding disturbances of mood and/or thought. Thus, the clinician is cautioned against summarily dismissing a disorder on the basis of type without careful consideration of its substantialness and its impairment of thought or mood.

Significant Impairment

Significant impairment, while suffering from definitional ambiguity, refers to a mental disorder that disrupts or disorganizes the individual's day-to-day functioning. This impairment must result from a mental disorder and involve ongoing impairment. It must be observed within the context of day-to-day functioning and not be limited to the criminal behavior. In contrast, many criminals show extraordinarily poor judgment, but this is not conclusive evidence of either a mental illness or impairment of judgment as a result of that mental illness. In addition, this criterion specifies that the significant impairment must be in one or more of the following areas: judgment, behavior, capacity to recognize reality, and/or ability to cope with the ordinary demands of life.

Judgment refers to the defendant's ability to perceive and accurately weigh alternatives, assess benefits and risks, and make reasoned decisions (Rogers, 1984). The issue in each case is the capacity and not whether this capacity is utilized. Finally, the impaired judgment must be the result of a mental disorder and must significantly impair the individual's decision-making capacity. In contradistinction, many intoxicated individuals lack a substantial capacity to judge adequately the ramifications of their behavior, yet this intoxication would not qualify under the GBMI definition of mental disorder.

Impairment of behavior refers to ongoing disturbances in the defendant's actions. These behavioral disturbances must be symptomatic of mental disorder. For example, any individual may engage in what appears to be ritualistic behavior; the behavior becomes symptomatic of mental disorder when it is a result of a diagnosable disorder with some loss of voluntary control. For example, what distinguishes an obsessive-compulsive disorder from normal behavior is the individual's inability to resist the behavior. Other disturbances of behavior might include phobic responses, perseveration, and actions as a result of a manic syndrome.

Capacity to recognize reality refers to the intactness of the individual's perception of external stimuli and his/her integration of these perceptions in a consensually validated manner. Impaired reality testing may be the result of distortion and/or disorganization of the individual's perceptual process. This impairment may range from being transient and peripheral (i.e., momentary feelings of depersonalization), which would not qualify as GBMI, to blatantly psychotic symptoms, which would qualify. A severe impairment of reality testing would likely produce impaired judgment as well and should alert the forensic expert to reevaluate the defendant's sanity. In examining the R-CRAS data base, we found that lack of reality testing evidenced a high correlation ($r = .90$) with ALI insanity.

Ability to cope with the ordinary demands of life refers to the defendant's ability to secure and maintain basic physical and emotional needs. To satisfy this test, an inability to meet basic self-care needs must be the result of mental disorder, not the adoption of an alternate lifestyle (e.g., hobo-type existence) or economic misfortune (e.g., failure of social welfare agencies to provide adequate support). This capacity for self-care is typically measured in the individual's psychological ability to maintain personal hygiene, provide him/herself with food and shelter, and display minimally adequate social skills. Further, it is likely that an individual who, because of a mental disorder, is not capable of purposeful or goal-oriented activities (e.g., work, hobbies, and day treatment program) would also qualify as one who lacks the capacity for self-care.

"Marked deficits in judgment" are the most commonly found criterion of the GBMI standard among noninsane defendants. Table 4.1 summarizes the percentage of GBMI defendants meeting the four criteria of significant impairment. Excluding those assessed as clinically insane, the percentage of defendants manifesting moderate impairment on GBMI criteria average 5.4%. Of these criteria, impaired judgment (8.7%) was the most common, indicating either (1) the ability to weigh the risks/benefits of different alternatives or (2) substantial interference with the capacity to recognize important problems and follow through on a decision. While each criterion of the GBMI standard requires evaluation, these data suggest that a thorough examination of impaired judgment is likely to be critical. The majority of defendants that meet other GBMI criteria also meet the impaired judgment criterion.

Other Standards

Several states utilize standards of insanity not addressed in the preceding formulations. New Hampshire continues to use the New Hampshire "product" standard that, with minor modifications, has been its standard since 1870 (*State v. Pike*, 1870). The jury is instructed that the defendant is not criminally responsible if the defendant's behavior was the product or offspring of a mental disease, although neither mental

TABLE 4.1. GBMI Criteria on 104 Noninsane Defendants Evaluated for Insanity

GBMI criteria	Moderate impairment	Severe impairment
Impaired judgment	8.7%	0.0%
Impaired behavior	2.9%	0.0%
Impaired reality testing	4.8%	1.0%
Impaired capacity for self-care	5.0%	0.0%

Note. In accordance with the GBMI standard, defendants evaluated as insane were excluded.

disease or the concept of "product" or "offspring" is defined (*State v. Plummer,* 1977) . This rule places the responsibility for determining these issues as questions of fact on the jury. The forensic expert, under such a system, offers information regarding diagnosis and subsequent impairment but is not asked to address explicitly either legal criteria or psychological constructs regarding criminal responsibility (Emery & Emery, 1984).

Idaho, Montana, and Utah have legislatively eliminated an insanity defense (Steadman et al., 1993). They have opted for an approach that places all consideration of the defendant's mental condition under the label of "mens rea" assessing whether the defendant has the requisite state of mind, which is an element of the offense, but does not separately consider the question of insanity. The statutes in these states permit the defendant to present evidence of mental illness to rebut the state's evidence that the defendant had the requisite state of mind, but not separately to support an insanity defense (*State v. Searcy,* 1990). Because it is not an affirmative defense, but rather simply a challenge to the state's proof that the defendant meets the requisite mens rea or specific intent requirement, there are no explicit criteria available for its implementation (see Keilitz & Fulton, 1983).

Do Different Standards Make a Difference?

The continued tinkering with specific insanity standards is based on the underlying premise that different standards will result in different outcomes. Rogers, Seman, and Clark (1986) conducted the first systematic study of the *M'Naghten* and ALI standards on 125 insanity referrals to established forensic centers in Illinois, Ohio, and Michigan. They found that defendants qualifying for insanity under one standard were likely to qualify under both standards. The *M'Naghten* was slightly more restrictive than the ALI standard, with 13.6% versus 16.0% evaluated as insane.

Wettstein, Mulvey, and Rogers (1991) utilized the expert opinions of four experienced psychiatrists on 164 defendants clinically evaluated as insane. They examined four standards: *M'Naghten,* ALI cognitive prong, ALI volitional prong, and the American Psychiatric Association proposal (i.e., "Because of mental disease or mental retardation, was the defendant unable to appreciate the criminality of his conduct at the time of his offense?"; Wettstein et al., 1991, p. 23). The majority of cases (62.8%) qualified under each of the four standards. Surprisingly, nearly one-fourth qualified under the ALI volitional prong only; these results are at variance with other research (see Rogers & Clark,

1985; Silver & Spodak, 1983). Also of interest, these forensic psychiatrists were more confident in their judgments about the ALI volitional prong than about the other three standards (81.6% vs. 75.3%).

Steadman et al. (1993) considered how changes in California's insanity standard from the ALI to a restricted *M'Naghten* standard would affect insanity pleas and acquittals. Unlike the original *M'Naghten*, the California statute imposes an additional requirement that defendants meet both the "nature and quality" and "wrongfulness" components in order to be acquitted. In a study of seven counties, they found a downward trend in the frequency of insanity pleas that started prior to the new legislation and continued after its passage. Despite this tightening of the standard itself, the acquittal rates remained unaffected.

Other researchers have examined whether different insanity standards have an appreciable effect on prospective jurors. In her seminal work, Simon (1967) compared the *M'Naghten* and *Durham* standards and found no significant differences in a housebreaking case, although differences were observed in an incest case. In addition, Finkel and his colleagues studied exhaustively the effects of insanity standards on mock jurors. Finkel, Shaw, Bercaw, and Koch (1985; see also Finkel & Handel, 1988) found that both existing (e.g., *M'Naghten*, *M'Naghten* plus irresistible impulse, ALI) and prior (wild beast and *Durham*) insanity standards did not affect the outcome in five different cases. Similarly, the application of the Insanity Defense Reform Act (IDRA) did not affect acquittal rates (Finkel, 1989; Finkel & Slobogin, 1995; Ogloff, 1991).

Research on prospective jurors in analogue studies does suggest that the presence of a third alternative, such as GBMI, is likely to reduce the number of acquittals. Results by Roberts, Golding, and Fincham (1987) suggest that the GBMI verdict may be viewed inaccurately as a "compromise" between NGRI and guilty verdicts.[1] Subsequent research by Finkel (1991) confirms this suspicion. Across four representative cases, the presence of GBMI instructions reduced recommendations for insanity from 50.0% to 36.1%.

Conclusion

In summary, this chapter has reviewed the relevant legal and psychological literature with respect to specific standards of insanity. Progress has been made over the last several decades in articulating the insanity standards more systematically. However, legal criteria for criminal responsibility have always been and are likely to continue to be inexact definitions relating culpability to psychological impairment. As empirical research on standards of criminal responsibility continues, it will be the responsibility of forensic psychology and psychiatry to offer more explicit models for the courts to consider in their refinement of criminal responsibility.

Note

1. The GBMI is hardly a compromise. Defendants with GBMI verdicts typically receive similar sentences to those found guilty; indeed, they often receive only the same minimal treatment that would have been available to them with a guilty verdict.

Chapter 5

Malingering and Deception

Overview
Explanatory Models of Malingering
Feigned Psychopathology
Feigned Cognitive and Neuropsychological Assessment
Conclusion

Overview

The clinical assessment of criminal responsibility must address the quality and accuracy of information provided by the defendant, including any intentional distortions. Without a thorough investigation of malingering and other response styles, conclusions regarding impairment and responsibility are necessarily suspect. This chapter provides a critical distillation of theory and research that informs forensic practice; for a more comprehensive coverage, the standard reference is Rogers (1997). Within the domain of psychological impairment, defendants may feign psychopathology (e.g., schizophrenia), cognitive impairment (e.g., mental retardation), or both. As outlined in subsequent sections, measures and detection strategies are often not generalizable across these categories: feigned psychopathology and cognitive impairment require their own measures and strategies. For feigned psychopathology, defendants must create a plausible array of psychiatric symptoms and associated features. For feigned cognitive impairment, defendants must simply make more errors while portraying a sincere effort. Because of these dissimilarities in feigning presentation, specific strategies are required to assess feigned psychopathology versus feigned cognitive impairment.

The chapter begins with a brief overview of explanatory models of malingering. This section is important to both attorneys and clinicians, because *forensic experts' beliefs about why persons malinger may affect their assessment of malingering*. The next two sections examine the clinical strategies for the detection of malingered mental disorders and feigned cognitive impairment. The final section examines how these data are integrated in the formulation of an opinion about malingering.

As an introduction for attorneys and a review for forensic experts, key terms and phrases are here summarized:

♦ *Malingering.* The accepted definition of malingering is the deliberate fabrication or gross exaggeration of psychological or physical symptoms to achieve a recognized external goal (American Psychiatric Association, 1994).

♦ *Defensiveness.* Defensiveness is the polar opposite of malingering; it involves the intentional denial or gross minimization of psychological or physical symptoms.

♦ *Irrelevant or random responding.* Some defendants do not become involved meaningfully in the assessment, which produces highly inconsistent results. For example, an individual may complete an inventory, such as the MMPI-2, without reading the items. Irrelevant responding is sometimes mistaken for malingered profiles.

♦ *Secondary gain.* This term is often abused and typically based on unwarranted inferences. Some clinicians apply the term whenever a person benefits or potentially benefits from their disorder. As delineated by Rogers and Reinhardt (1998), the term has several distinct meanings: involuntary psychic defenses (psychodynamic perspective), reinforced illness behavior (behavioral perspective), or postulated external incentives (forensic perspective). Because of its highly inferential nature and continued controversies over its meaning and etiology, we recommend that forensic experts avoid this term in insanity evaluations.

Explanatory Models of Malingering

Rogers (1990a, 1990b) described the three current explanatory models for understanding the motivation to malinger: pathogenic, criminologic, and adaptational. The first two models are based on monistic ideas of malingering; they assume that it is motivated either by illness (pathogenic) or badness (criminogenic). In contrast, the adaptational model makes no trait-based suppositions about malingering. Rather, the adaptational model considers malingering to be a decision based on adversarial circumstances and often resulting from cost–benefit analysis of different alternatives. While these three models are predominately applied to malingering, they also have implications for other response styles (Rogers & Dickey, 1991).

The *pathogenic model* posits an intrapsychic mechanism (see Eissler, 1979/1986; Jung, 1903/1957) to explain malingering in which feigning is an attempt to control underlying psychopathology by consciously producing the symptoms. The model postulates that consciously produced symptoms of malingering will be replaced eventually by involuntary symptoms of the underlying disorder. Beyond the controversy over compensation neurosis (Miller, 1961; for a commentary, see Resnick, 1997), attorneys have observed the "curative power" of financial settlements on seemingly intractable disorders. While such accounts are likely overblown, a deteriorative pattern of involuntary symptoms has not been generally observed among malingerers.

Rogers and his colleagues (Rogers, Sewell, & Goldstein, 1994; Rogers, Salekin, Sewell, Goldstein, & Leonard, 1998) conducted several prototypical analyses[1] that considered the relative representativeness and salience of explanatory models, including the pathogenic model. In general, the pathogenic model was much lower prototypicality irrespective of gender, the setting (forensic or nonforensic), or the malingered presentation (mental disorder, cognitive impairment, or medical syndrome). However, individual cases occasionally may occur for which the pathogenic model is compelling.

The *criminologic model* was embraced by the DSM-III and subsequent versions, although the logic of this espousal has yet to be explicated. Admittedly, antisocial motivation (i.e., securing unearned or unwarranted benefits at the expense of others) provides an obstensibly reasonable explanation of malingering. With most clinical forensic research undertaken with criminal populations, the putative link between criminality and malingering is understandable, although it may reflect an illusory correlation. In any event, the presence of criminality/psychopathy is not a specific explanation of malingering: the vast majority of antisocial persons do not engage in malingering (Rogers & Cruise, 1998).

Rogers, Salekin, et al. (1998) found that experienced forensic psychologists rated malingerers with moderate prototypicality for the criminological model. The notable exception was female malingerers in nonforensic settings, who rated comparatively low in prototypicality. Interestingly, no differences were observed in the prototypical ratings for the criminological model regarding the type of malingered presentation (i.e., medical syndromes, cognitive impairment, or mental disorders).

The *adaptational model* was developed by Rogers (1990a, 1990b) to provide a more encompassing and less pejorative paradigm for malingering than the existing pathogenic and criminological explanations. It is composed of two dimensions: (1) an appreciation of the adversarial context, namely, that mental health professionals' objectives may be at cross-purposes with the examinee's goals, and (2) by weighing of alternatives, the examinee selects malingering as a potential method of achieving his/her goals. The model is considered "adaptational" from the examinee's perspective as an effort to further his or her goals; importantly, this term does not suggest that this response style is either socially sanctioned or psychologically healthy.

Rogers, Sewell, and Goldstein (1994) examined the prototypicality of the adaptational model by asking 320 forensic experts to render ratings, based on their professional experiences with malingerers. The adaptational model proved to be the most prototypical. In a second prototypical analysis, 220 forensic experts were asked to select two cases (one forensic and one nonforensic) that were the most prototypical malingerers that they had ever evaluated. In this case, the results were less clear, with the adaptational and criminological models being approximately equal in protypicality. In summary, two observations emerge. First, the adaptational model appears to be the most relevant in explaining why malingerers feign (Rogers, Sewell, & Goldstein, 1994). Second, the clearest examples of malingerers tend to be rated highly on characteristics associated with both the adaptational and the criminological models (Rogers, Salekin, et al., 1998).

Feigned Psychopathology

A pivotal issue for most insanity evaluations is establishing the authenticity of reported psychopathology. By definition, many symptoms are not directly observable. Sometimes forensic reports will make unwarranted inferences regarding the veridicality of symptoms based on the absence of certain clinical features. For example, with psychotic symptoms, some patients with auditory hallucinations will stare into space and will appear to be listening, if not responding, to nonexistent voices. Many hallucinating patients will have no observable indicators; therefore, inferences of feigned hallucinations are unwarranted. For attorneys involved in insanity cases, a critical distinction must be made between the presence and absence of these clinical features:

♦ The *presence* of certain clinical features may provide indirect corroboration of a symptom's authenticity. In the current example,
inpatient observations of behavior consistent with hallucinations
provide useful data.

♦ The *absence* of certain clinical features typically provides no information. In the current example, a bona fide patient may have
no outward manifestations of auditory hallucinations.

The underlying reason for not making inferences is the highly
heterogeneous nature of symptoms and clinical features. No recognizable patterns can be discerned to define behavior associated with a genuine disorder. As noted, attorneys must be alert for unwarranted inferences regarding the absence of clinical features. Unfortunately, many
forensic reports make impermissible leaps between the absence of certain features and the likelihood of malingering. However, this type of
unwarranted inferences about clinical features must be distinguished
from blatant contradictions (e.g., observations of animated conversa-
tions from a patient reporting extreme social withdrawal); the latter
may be evidence of feigning.

This section provides a useful overview of detection strategies for
the assessment of feigned psychopathology. For more comprehensive
coverage, the standard reference is *Clinical Assessment of Malingering and
Deception* (Rogers, 1997). To assist in its clinical applicability, the section is organized into three sections: interview-based methods, structured interviews, and psychometric measures.

Interview-Based Methods

The blessing and bane of traditional clinical interviews for the detection of malingering are their versatility. This versatility provides an un-
paralleled opportunity to explore a patient's unique presentation of
symptoms and to investigate the authenticity of particular symptoms
via clinical probes. But this same versatility militates against standardization. Forensic experts relying on traditional interviews are very limited in their ability to render systematic comparisons between genuine
and feigning patients. As a standard for forensic practice, we recommend the following: *no determination of malingering should rest solely on
traditional interviews.* Conversely, all determinations of malingering
should include traditional interviews for the purpose of accessing important case-specific information.

Interview-based strategies have been established for more than a
decade (Rogers, 1988, 1997) and are well known by most forensic ex-

perts. Therefore, this section will focus on providing legal professionals with a straightforward distillation of these strategies. How might attorneys make use of these strategies? One use is to ensure that the forensic expert has (1) an adequate understanding of the detection strategies, and (2) has carefully applied them to the current insanity case. As a practical example, an expert may testify that the defendant was malingering but not elaborate on how validated strategies were used in this determination. The attorney may wish to query the expert on these validated strategies. For example, one strategy involves an excessive number of "rare symptoms" (i.e., symptoms that occur rarely in clinical populations). General questions to ask the forensic expert about rare symptoms might include the following:

1. Please define for the court what is meant by "rare symptoms" (i.e., a specific strategy for the identification of malingerers)?
2. What are specific examples of "rare symptoms" that you personally observed in your evaluation of the defendant?
3. What conclusions can be drawn regarding the presence (or absence) of "rare symptoms"?

This format can be utilized consecutively for each of the interview-based strategies. Obviously, the presence of many convincing examples is likely to be compelling, while the absence of such examples casts doubt on the expert's certitude. The greatest danger to malingering testimony is sweeping conclusions based primarily on experience, judgment, or intuition. The purpose of these questions is to avoid potentially devastating testimony that is unlinked to clinical knowledge and is unabashedly subjective. Such impressionistic testimony is captured in the phrase "I know a malingerer when I see one."

Six detection strategies have been empirically tested across multiple studies. These are defined below:

♦ *Rare symptoms* refers to symptoms and other features indicative of impairment that are observed only infrequently in clinical populations. The presence of several symptoms is not likely to be significant to the determination of malingering. However, a more extensive endorsement of rare symptoms is very unusual for genuine patients and is likely evidence of feigning.

♦ *Improbable and absurd symptoms* reflect preposterous symptoms and features that are unlikely to be endorsed by clinical or normal populations. Given the outlandish nature of these inquiries (e.g., "Does your liver have magical powers?"), it is crucial that the patient is psychologically engaged in the process and is not responding in a flippant manner.

♦ *Indiscriminant symptom endorsement* describes the individual who is endorsing a high proportion of symptoms beyond what is typically seen in clinical populations. For this strategy to be successful, the interview must cover a very wide range of psychopathology. Otherwise, a high proportion of symptom endorsement is often genuine (e.g., a severely depressed person is likely to endorse most depressive symptoms).

♦ *Symptom combinations* is an ingenious strategy based on certain symptoms that are unlikely to occur together. By inspecting pairs of symptoms, clinicians are sometimes able to detect unlikely patterns. Although applicable to traditional interviews, this strategy is best used with structured interviews where the likelihood of certain symptom pairs co-occuring has already been established.

♦ *Contradictory symptoms* refers to those malingerers who endorse incompatible symptoms. These contradictory symptoms typically center on mood syndromes, especially the simultaneous endorsement of symptoms of depression and mania. Care must be taken, however, because some rapidly cycling patients (swift alterations of mood) may also endorse apparently contradictory symptoms.

♦ *Symptom severity* refers to the patient's reported intensity of various symptoms. While many genuine patients have reported a dozen or more symptoms to be severe or very severe, the endorsement of most symptoms in this extreme range is very unlikely among genuine patients. For this strategy to be successful, the clinician must document an extensive list of symptoms and specifically designate which symptoms were endorsed as extreme or unbearable.

In summary, legal professionals should be alert for unsubstantiated testimony that is not defined by detection strategies and not corroborated by specific examples. It is also important to observe what doesn't work. Concerning feigned mental disorders, some forensic experts rely on "inconsistency of presentation"; based on empirical studies, this is *not* an acceptable detection strategy. Inconsistency of presentation does not reliably differentiate malingerers and genuine patients. Although some malingerers are inconsistent, a substantial minority of genuine patients are also highly variable in their clinical presentation and symptom endorsement.

Structured Interviews

Traditional interviews, as discussed in the previous section, are limited by their lack of standardization. To address this limitation, structured interviews were developed, beginning in the 1970s, to systematize the assessment process (see Rogers, 1995a, and Chapter 9). With respect to feigning, two structured interviews are available: the Structured Interview of Reported Symptoms (SIRS; Rogers, 1992; Rogers, Bagby, & Dickens, 1992) and the Schedule of Affective Disorders and Schizophrenia (SADS; Spitzer & Endicott, 1978a). The SIRS was developed as a specialized measure of feigning and related response styles, while the SADS is an Axis I diagnostic interview on which indices of potential feigning were developed.

SIRS

The SIRS is a 172-item structured interview that is composed of eight primary scales for the assessment of feigning. As a structured interview, the format is standardized for the questions, sequencing of questions, and rating of responses. This standardization allows for systematic comparison across feigners (simulators and suspected malingerers) and honest responders (genuine patients and nonpatient controls). Table 5.1 provides a distillation of psychometric data[2] on reliability, effect sizes, and cut scores. Although the availability of the SIRS test manual (Rogers et al., 1992) is restricted to mental health professionals with sufficient training, updated summaries of its validation are readily available (see Rogers, 1995a, 1997) to all clinical and legal pro-

TABLE 5.1. Psychometric Characteristics and Cut Scores for SIRS Primary Scales

Primary scales	Scale characteristics			Cut scores	
	Alpha	Reliability	Effect size	Probable	Definite
Rare Symptoms	.85	.98	2.07	≥5	≥9
Symptom Combinations	.83	.97	1.58	≥7	≥12
Improbable/ Absurd Symptoms	.89	.96	1.40	=6	≥7
Blatant Symptoms	.92	.95	2.08	≥11	≥24
Subtle Symptoms	.92	.96	1.60	≥16	≥26
Selectivity of Symptoms	na	1.00	1.79	≥18	≥32
Severity of Symptoms	na	1.00	1.80	≥10	≥17
Reported versus Observed Symptoms	.77	.91	1.74	≥7	≥12

Note. Alpha and interrater reliabilities were derived from Rogers et al. (1992). "Effect size" is the unweighted mean for Cohen's *d* combining (1) suspected malingerers and clinical samples and (2) simulators and clinical samples. "Probable" and "Definite" reflect the established cut scores for feigning. Please note that many genuine patients have one or two scales in the probable range.

fessionals. Because of limitations of space, this section is devoted to the SIRS's clinical applicability, especially within forensic settings.

Attorneys and mental health professionals not versed in psychometric theory often have important questions about the SIRS and its clinical applicability. These questions typically involve (1) its reliability, (2) the breadth of its validation studies, (3) the accuracy of its feigning classification, and (4) its usefulness in forensic evaluations. These issues are addressed below.

Reliability. As a structured interview, clinical inquiries and their concomitant ratings are highly standardized. As a result, a high degree of interrater reliability is achieved. More specifically, the reliability coefficients of the primary scales generally exceed .90, with median reliabilities ranging from .95 to 1.00 (Lindblad, 1994; Rogers et al., 1992). In practical terms, this finding means that different clinicians produce highly similar results in their administrations of the SIRS.

Breadth of Validation Studies. Most measures of malingering rely solely on simulation research (i.e., analogue research in which participants "play the role" of feigners) but do not test their results with known or suspected malingerers. Research (see Rogers, 1997) has demonstrated that simulation-only validation is likely to produce spurious results. To address this critical issue, the SIRS validation combines both simulation and known-groups (i.e., suspected malingerers). Altogether, research studies on the SIRS have a combined total of more than 1,100 participants.

Accuracy of Feigning Classification. Group differences on psychological measures between feigners and genuine patients are relatively easy to achieve but have very little practical significance. The sine qua non of malingering evaluations is the effectiveness of a measure to accurately classify individual persons. When categorized as feigning on the SIRS, very few errors are made (i.e., less than 1% in the validation studies). An important distinction between the SIRS and most other measures of feigned psychopathology is that the SIRS employs uniform cut scores to distinguish feigned and genuine presentations. Thus forensic experts do not need to worry about whether they are applying the "correct" cut scores.

Usefulness in Forensic Evaluations. Research studies have examined the effectiveness of the SIRS with pretrial defendants, residents in a treatment-oriented correctional setting, prison inmates, psychiatric patients, and forensic patients. Comparisons across correctional and noncorrectional settings (see Rogers et al., 1992) produce comparable results. In summary, the SIRS appears to be well suited for forensic evaluations.

Summary. The SIRS appears to be the best validated measure of feigned psychopathology and is widely used in forensic assessments. In addition, the SIRS appears to meet the *Daubert* standard: (1) its results are empirically testable (i.e., falsifiable); (2) its error rate for feigning is known and very low; and (3) its validity is generally accepted with publications in peer-reviewed journals. We recommend that the SIRS be a component of any insanity evaluation in which malingering is suspected. Any determinations of feigned psychopathology that do not include the SIRS are vulnerable to vigorous cross-examination.

R-SIRS and CT-SIRS. Goodness (1999) attempted several modifications of the SIRS for the retrospective evaluation of insanity defendants. The simpler modification was the Retrospective SIRS (R-SIRS) in which the focus of SIRS items was shifted from the current time to the time of the offense. The second modification was a Concurrent Time SIRS (CT-SIRS) that combines the R-SIRS (i.e., time of the offense) with the SIRS (i.e., current time). The interreliability of both versions remained uniformly high for the R-SIRS and CT-SIRS primary scales (all $rs = 1.00$).

Goodness's research involved forensic patients residing in a maximum security hospital who were asked to complete versions of the SIRS on honest and feigning conditions. With 25 R-SIRS and 26 CT-SIRS defendants, the original SIRS scoring correctly classified 68.0% of feigning and 84.0% of honest conditions of the R-SIRS and 73.0% of feigning and 81.0% of honest conditions of the CT-SIRS.

Simple modifications to the scoring of the R-SIRS and CT-SIRS suggested that higher rates of classification are likely; however, these modifications require cross-validation. Because of its simplicity, we recommend the use of the R-SIRS with the original SIRS scoring. Defendants in the feigning range have a moderate likelihood of malingering (PPP = .72), while defendants determined to be nonfeigning (i.e., ≥ 6 scales in honest range and ≤ 1 scale in the probable range) had a moderately high likelihood of responding honestly (NPP = .81)

SADS

The applicability of the SADS to insanity evaluations is summarized in Chapter 9. This brief section summarizes the available data on its use for the assessment of suspected malingering. For more detailed information about the SADS feigning scales, their validity, and item composition, refer to Rogers (1997).

Rogers (1988, 1997) rationally constructed five SADS scales for the detection of possible feigning. These scales were based on two sources: (1) normative data from forensic and chronic psychiatric samples (combined N = 254), and (2) a known-groups comparison of 22 suspected malingerers (Ustad, 1996). Cut scores were established for four scales: Contradictory Symptoms, Symptom Combinations, Severe Symptoms (episode and last week), and Indiscriminant Symptom Endorsement. However, these cut scores should only be used for screening purposes, that is, to decide whether feigning should be comprehensively assessed. They lack the necessary cross-validation to be used in the actual determination of malingering or factitious disorders.

An important feature of these scales is that they incorporate symptoms from both the past (e.g., time of the offense) and the current time. Therefore, a person attempting to feign past symptomatology grossly may exceed these cut scores even if his/her current presentation is not feigned. Therefore, the SADS is strongly recommended in cases where the defendant is reporting severe psychopathology at the time of the offense and comparatively little psychological impairment for the current time.

Psychometric Measures

Inapplicable Measures

Many criminal attorneys and even many forensic experts are surprised to learn that most psychological tests provide insufficient data for determinations of malingering. This section provides a succinct overview of psychological tests used for the assessment of psychopathology. While this section is intended to provide a basic overview, the application of multiple strategies to complex cases requires a sophisticated understanding. In such cases, many experts and attorneys will need to consult experts on malingering.

Before beginning the overview, it is useful to consider what tests should *not* be used in the determination of malingering:

♦ *Projective tests, such as the Rorschach, TAT, Sentence Completion Tests, and Human Figure Drawings.* Schretlen (1997) provides an authoritative review of projective measures and feigning. He concludes that the evidence on the Rorschach indicates (1) that it is vulnerable to feigning, and (2) that methods for the detection of feigning are inadequate. Other projective measures lack sufficient research on feigning and have no systematic methods for its detection. Projective methods should not be interpreted in cases where feigning is likely or suspected.

♦ *The Millon Clinical Multiaxial Inventory (MCMI; Millon, 1983, 1987, 1994) and its subsequent revisions.* Very few studies were conducted on the MCMI and MCMI-II, and these yielded at best only moderate classifications of response styles. No research is available on the MCMI-III and response styles. Moreover, the usefulness of the Debasement Scale for the evaluation of feigning is strongly questioned. In the normative sample composed of apparently genuine patients, several clinical scales were highly correlated with the Debasement Scale (see Millon, 1994, Appendix G): C (Borderline) = .80, SS (Thought Disorder) = .82, D (Dysthymia) = .85, and CC (major depression) = .85. With correlations of this magnitude, it is unclear whether the Debasement Scale is a measure of feigning or genuine impairment.

Unlike most psychological tests, two multiscale inventories have been studied extensively with respect to fake-bad or malingered profiles: the Minnesota Multiphasic Personality Inventory (MMPI and MMPI-2) and the Personality Assessment Inventory (PAI). These two inventories will be examined in detail with respect to feigning. Please see Chapter 8 for an extensive description of their validation and forensic applications.

MMPI-2

We caution forensic experts against the use of the original MMPI for the detection of feigning; many of the validation studies lack the sophistication of more recent research (see the meta-analysis by Berry, Baer, & Harris, 1991). For this section on the MMPI-2, we rely upon two major sources: the Rogers, Sewell, and Salekin (1994) meta-analysis and Greene's (1997) normative data. A common theme from both sources is the marked variability in validity indicators among both clinical populations and feigners. Because of this variability, forensic experts must apply stringent criteria or run the serious risk of false-positives (i.e., misclassifying a genuine patient as a malingerer).

As an important caution, MMPI-2 profiles must be scored for random or inconsistent responding *before* any determination of feigning can be rendered. A patient randomly completing the MMPI-2 is likely to endorse 50% of the items on most validity indicators. A 50% level of endorsement results in extremely elevated indicators that may be mistaken for malingering. Common reasons for inconsistent responding include (1) not reading the MMPI-2 questions, (2) lack of comprehension, (3) psychotic interference, and (4) oppositionality. Scores on the Variable Response Inconsistency (VRIN) scale of greater than 14 are the best indicator of inconsistent responding (see Berry et al., 1991). In nearly all cases,[3] *no determinations of malingering can be rendered with inconsistent profiles.* Therefore, it is incumbent for attorneys to ask questions about response consistency.

Table 5.2 summarizes validity indicators of feigning from two perspectives: (1) the range of scores typically found in clinical populations (i.e., 15th to 85th percentiles) and (2) the upper range of optimum scores for the detection of feigning. If one focuses on the upper range, the likelihood of false-positives is substantially reduced. As can be readily observed, clinical elevations on these scales are typically found in patient populations. Therefore, only extreme elevations should be viewed as evidence of feigning. For example, raw scores on the F scale exceeding 30 would be interpreted as evidence of feigning. Even with extreme elevations, however, additional corroboration with other clinical methods is needed before any determination of malingering is possible.

An important clinical question is whether these validity indicators are largely redundant. In other words, would one indicator (e.g., the F scale) be just as effective as multiple measures? Proponents of the single-indicator approach point to (1) high interscale correlations across va-

TABLE 5.2. MMPI-2 Validity Indicators for Clinical Samples and Feigners

Indicator	Commonly found in clinical samples	Likelihood of feigning
F	3 to 21	>30
Fb	NA	>25
F–K	−15 to 12	>25
O–S	−15 to 211	>190[a]
L–W	17 to 65	>67
Ds	7 to 30	NA
Dsr	NA	>28

Note. The category "Commonly found in clinical samples" represents the range from 15% to 85% for Greene's (1997) normative data on 3,475 patients. The category "Likelihood of feigning" represents the upper range of optimum cutting scores in Rogers et al. (1994). F = Infrequency scale; Fb = Infrequency–Back scale; F–K = Gough (1950) Dissimulation index; O–S = total *T* score difference between the Obvious and Subtle subscales (Wiener, 1948); L–W = critical items for Lachar and Wrobel (1979); Ds = Gough (1954) Dissimulation scale; Dsr = Dissimulation scale—revised; NA = not available.

[a]Given the overlap with clinical populations, forensic experts may wish to employ the more stringent cut score of >211.

lidity indicators and (2) the lack of demonstrated incremental validity for using multiple indicators in specific samples (Bagby, Buis, & Nicholson, 1995). On the matter of intercorrelations, Greene (1997) found moderate correlations (*r*s in the .60–.80 range) for nonclinical samples and high correlations (*r*s > .80) for clinical samples. However, these correlations leave unanswered the critical question, "Are these indicators highly correlated in feigners?" Rogers, Sewell, and Ustad (1995) examined these intercorrelations for simulators and found a median *r* of .74, indicating that these indicators share slightly more than 50% of the variance. Obviously, these indicators cannot be viewed as equivalent in assessing response styles for feigners. Moreover, research suggests that (1) different indicators may be more effective, depending on the type of feigned condition (Rogers, Bagby, & Chakraborty, 1993) and (2) multiple indicators may have incremental validity (Arbisi & Ben-Porath, 1998). Therefore, we strongly recommend the use of multiple measures.

PAI

For overreporting symptoms on the PAI, Morey (1991) developed the Negative Impression (NIM) scale and suggested that individuals with elevations (i.e., NIM > 77*T*) were likely feigning. As the large-scale study of the PAI and feigning, Rogers, Sewell, Morey, and Ustad (1996) examined PAI protocols for 60 sophisticated simulators (doctoral students with 1 week preparation), 116 unsophisticated simulators, 221 genuine patients, and 50 controls. Use of the NIM cutting score (>77*T*) identified approximately two-thirds (65.1%) of unsophisticated simulators but was largely unsuccessful (i.e., 24.7%) with sophisticated simulators. In addition, nearly one-fourth (24.4%) of schizophrenic patients were misclassified as feigning. Rogers et al. (1996) developed and cross-validated a discriminant function that appeared to be highly effective at detecting potential feigners (i.e., calibration sample = 92.2%; cross-validation sample = 80.4%). Morey (1996) described this function as the "Rogers index."

Several more recent studies have shed further light on the PAI and the detection of feigning. Morey and Lanier (1998) performed a series of ROC analyses on 44 simulators and 45 patients with dramatic differences on NIM, the Rogers index, and an empirically derived "malingering index." Of these, the Rogers index appeared to be the most effective; a cut score of >.99 yielded a sensitivity of .84 and a specificity of 1.00. However, caution must be exercised in light of the modest sample size and relative absence (i.e., <10.0%) of psychotic patients in the clinical comparison group. A second study was conducted by Rogers, Sewell, Cruise, Wang, and Ustad (1998) that addressed the applicability of PAI malingering indicators to forensic-correctional populations. The Rogers, Sewell, et al. (1998) research combined data from previous studies (Rogers, Ustad, et al., 1998; Wang et al., 1997) to create a known-groups design with 57 suspected malingerers and 58 genuine patients. They found that the Rogers index was relatively ineffective with forensic populations, but that extreme elevations on NIM or the malingering index appeared to be very effective.

Combining results from the three recent studies (Rogers, Sewell, et al., 1998; Rogers, Ustad, et al., 1998; Wang et al., 1997), several convergent findings were observed. The key findings are summarized:

- *Low likelihood of malingering* indicates when the PAI profile can be interpreted without substantial concerns that feigning will distort the clinical profile. Cut score for "low likelihood" is NIM < 77 T.
- *Substantial likelihood of malingering* indicates extreme scores typically associated with feigning; these require independent confirmation. Cut scores for "substantial likelihood" are NIM > 110 T or Malingering index > 5.

MMPI-2 versus PAI

In conducting forensic evaluations, clinicians are frequently concerned with administering the best multiscale inventory for the assessment of feigning. In this case, either the MMPI-2 or the PAI could be justified. The main advantage of the MMPI-2 is the extensive body of research on feigning; its principal limitation is lack of consensus regarding effective cut scores. The primary advantages of the PAI include (1) a general consensus on the use of NIM and the Malingering index, and (2) validation with both simulation and known-groups comparison. Its principal limitation is the breadth of feigning research across different settings.

Feigned Cognitive
and Neuropsychological Assessment

The assessment of feigned cognitive deficits is directly applicable to only a very small proportion of insanity cases. More specifically, defendants occasionally purport to have mental retardation or brain damage that impaired their comprehension or behavioral control at the time of the offense. In the great majority of cases, however, the pivotal issue involves psychotic and other symptoms rather than cognitive impairment per se. In such cases, assessment of feigned cognitive impairment plays a peripheral role in insanity evaluations.

Many attorneys will likely wonder, "Why not use feigned cognitive impairment to assess feigned psychopathology?" The reasons are three-fold:

1. Feigned psychopathology requires the creation and gross exaggeration of plausible symptoms with associated features. By contrast, feigned cognitive impairment simply requires poor effort or guessing. The detection strategies are entirely different across the two domains.

2. Detection strategies for feigned cognitive impairment generally lack the same level of validation as those employed for feigned psychopathology. The use of less-validated strategies is unwarranted in forensic evaluations.

3. Most importantly, detection strategies for feigned cognitive impairment generally have not been tested on patients with Axis I disorders. Therefore, a genuine patient with schizophrenia might be misclassified as feigning on cognitive-based strategies.

This section will focus on feigned cognitive impairment, especially on neuropsychological measures. The feigning of mental retardation will be deemphasized; school records and past achievement tests often provide important corroborative data about spurious reports of mental retardation. In addition, such pervasive feigning of cognitive abilities is likely to be detected on more specialized measures that focus on bogus memory deficits. This section is organized into two components: (1) a discussion of detection strategies and (2) a summary of the application of detection strategies to neuropsychological measures.

Detection Strategies for Feigned Cognitive Impairment

Rogers, Harrell, and Liff (1993) described six potential strategies for the detection of feigned neuropsychological deficits: floor effect, symptom validity testing (SVT), performance curve, magnitude of error, atypical presentation, and psychological sequelae. In addition, other investigators have employed several additional strategies that include (1) violations of learning principles (Cercey, Schretlen, & Brandt, 1997), (2) consistency across parallel items (Frederick & Foster, 1991), (3) forced choice testing (Pankratz & Binder, 1997), and (4) response time (Beetar & Williams, 1995). Brief descriptions of these strategies are provided:

♦ *Floor effect.* This strategy involves the identification of test items on which nearly everyone is successful. These items are identified by testing cognitively impaired samples, which excluding untestable cases of pervasive cognitive impairment (e.g., delirium or severe dementia). A minority of malingerers are often indiscriminant in their poor performances and may "fail" at these very simple items.

♦ *Symptom validity testing (SVT).* This strategy involves classification of feigning based on a failure rate that exceeds chance probabilities. When items are presented in a multiple-choice format (typically two choices), the likely performance of a person with no ability (i.e., chance performance) can be calculated. Persons who substantially exceed this failure rate are classified as feigning, based on the logic that such poor performance is only achievable by recognizing and discarding the correct choice. The successfulness of this strategy is often limited by the methodology (i.e., only two choices on relatively easy material).

♦ *Forced choice testing (FCT).* Sometimes confused with SVT, this strategy is based on poorer than expected performance. More specifically, the underlying premise of FCT is that normative data can be reliably established for cognitively impaired patients. Subperformance based on normative data is viewed as feigning. Unlike the probabilistic estimates of SVT, FCT is vulnerable to misclassifications of genuine patients who deviate from the normative patterns.

♦ *Performance curve.* This strategy involves multiple comparisons of success rates with increasing item difficulty. Item difficulty is generally established by administration of items to large clinical samples. Feigners are often unaware of the need to modify their performance to match item difficulty. An advantage of this strategy is that cognitively impaired persons are likely to show similar decrements based on item difficulty, irrespective of their abilities.

♦ *Magnitude of error.* This strategy assumes that feigners will have difficulty in selecting plausible "wrong" answers. By examining clinical samples, predictable errors are likely to be identified. Patterns of atypical errors (e.g., "near misses" or "gross mistakes") may signal an attempt at feigning. Initial research (Martin, Franzen, & Orey, 1998) found promising results for the magnitude of error in detecting feigned memory deficits.

♦ *Atypical presentation.* Unlike previously described strategies, this strategy is based on clinical judgment rather than numerical scoring. Practitioners consider whether the pattern of cognitive impairment "makes neuropsychological sense" (Hartlage, 1998). As noted by Pankratz (1988), unusual patterns are commonly observed among genuinely impaired patients. As a nonstandardized strategy, the empirical support for this approach cannot be demonstrated.

♦ *Consistency across parallel items.* Not to be confused with the configural approach of atypical presentation, this strategy systematically evaluates performance on pairs of items with nearly identical difficulty. This strategy assumes that feigners may not recognize the similarity of items and be detectable by their variability. In extended testing, clinicians must take into account the potential effects of fatigue on producing variable performance.

♦ *Psychological sequelae.* This strategy is premised on the assumption that cognitive impairment will be accompanied by psychological signs and symptoms. This strategy remains largely uninvestigated, although naive persons appear to have an intuitive understanding of symptoms concomitant with postconcussion syndrome (Mittenberg, D'Attilio, Gage, & Bass, 1990; Mittenberg, DiGiulio, Perrin, & Bass, 1989) and mild brain injury (Lees-Haley & Dunn, 1994).

♦ *Violations of learning principles.* Established patterns in the process of learning new information have been observed. Given lists of new information, nonimpaired persons tend to learn both the beginning (primacy effect) and end (recency effect) of the list better than the middle of the list. This strategy is based on the notion that feigners will not be aware of these effects on their performance. According to Cercey et al. (1997), attention to primacy and recency effects has yielded mixed results. A commonly used learning principle is increased performance on recognition tasks or cued material in comparison to direct recall (Lezak, 1995).

♦ *Response time.* This strategy is based on the assumption that feigners will "expend" more effort (i.e., have slow response times) in completing cognitive measures (J. M. Williams, 1998). Rogers and Sewell (1998) have recommended that response time should be measured in relationship to item difficulty. As a secondary measure of the performance curve, genuine patients are likely to need more time to succeed at difficult items than at easier items. It is postulated that feigners will find this multifaceted task (i.e., assessing item difficulty, deciding on the appropriate error rate, and determining the response time) to be daunting. Because of the demands for item timing, response time is essentially limited to the use of computerized testing.

What is the relevance of these strategies to forensic evaluations? Why should attorneys involved in insanity cases be knowledgeable of these strategies?

1. Many forensic experts are not well versed in the underlying strategies. Because any determination of malingering is likely to preclude an insanity acquittal, these determinations should be based on sound knowledge, not uncertain inference.

2. Some strategies, such as floor effect and FCT, are vulnerable to misclassifications, especially if large-scale normative data are not available. With the assistance from their own consultants, attorneys need to vigorously question results based on strategies that are susceptible to misclassifications.

3. Many strategies for feigned cognitive deficits measure *incomplete effort* or *carelessness*. However, many genuine patients with severe mental disorders have difficulty sustaining effort and become careless. Because the validation of most strategies did not include genuine patients with schizophrenia or major depression, serious errors in classification are likely. Conclusions regarding incomplete effort or carelessness may be discredited if the forensic expert cannot rule out the effects of an Axis I disorder.

Survey of Neuropsychological Measures for Feigned Cognitive Impairment

The purpose of this subsection is to provide a brief overview of neuropsychological measures used for the detection of feigned cognitive impairment. A host of specialized measures have emerged during the last 2 decades; these are summarized in Table 5.3 and accompanied by a brief commentary. In addition, test batteries have been examined for the purposes of detecting unlikely patterns across subtests.

Specialized Measures

Specialized measures of cognitive feigning form two clusters: traditional and proprietary measures. Championed by Lezak (1995), *traditional measures* involve relatively simple materials that were developed by clinicians for the assessment of motivation and malingering. In contrast, *proprietary measures* are often more elaborate and were typically developed expressly for commercial purposes. Interestingly, both traditional and proprietary measures typically have several important features in common:

♦ *Short-term memory.* Nearly all the specialized measures address short-term memory and provide indirect evidence of attention. Other domains of cognitive functioning are typically neglected.

TABLE 5.3. Specialized Measures of Feigned Cognitive Impairment

Specialized measure	Description and validation
Rey 15 Item	A very brief screen for feigned memory deficits; studies have produced variable results (see Rogers et al., 1993). *Strategy:* Floor effect. *Caution:* Patients are sometimes misled by false instructions regarding the difficulty of the task.
21 Item Memory	A brief screen of verbal memory (7 rhyming word pairs; 7 semantically similar word pairs; 7 semantically unrelated word pairs) with recall and recognition tasks. *Strategies:* SVT and FCT. Several studies by Iverson and Franzen (1996; Iverson, Franzen, & McCracken, 1991, 1994) suggest promise for the FCT.
Dot Counting	A screen of feigned deficits in attention and concentration that measures time and accuracy in counting 12 arrays of dots (6 grouped; 6 scattered). *Strategy:* Violation of a learning principle. Regarding validation, use of various scoring indices limit clinical usefulness.
Portland Digit Recognition Test (PDRT)	A test of feigned memory deficits (Binder, 1990) based on the two-choice recognition of 5-digit numbers at different time intervals with a distractor (i.e., counting backwards). *Strategies:* SVT and FCT. Although many simulators do not achieve below-chance performance, SVT provides very strong evidence of feigning. Validation studies with FCT are open to criticism because of their reliance of differential prevalence design.
Test of Memory Malingering (TOMM)	A test of feigned visual memory (Tombaugh, 1997) involving two learning trials each with the same 50 pictures that are followed by two-choice a recognition trial and a retention trial 20 minutes later. *Strategies:* Floor effect, SVT, and violation of a learning principle. Validation studies (see Rees, Tombaugh, Gansler, & Moczynski, 1998) suggest that the floor effect may distinguish simulators from others. Research is needed with more diverse normative samples.
Validity Indicator Profile (VIP)	A test of feigned cognitive impairment that is composed of a forced-choice format (2 alternatives) on two scales: a 78-item verbal test and a 100 item nonverbal test. *Strategies:* SVT, multiple measures of performance curve and response consistency. According to the elaborate classification rules, most simulators and nearly one-half of malingerers are labeled as putting forth suboptimal effort. The results are tempered by two findings: (1) only 6% of simulators and 0% of malingerers were actually classified as "malingering" and (2) more than half of the mentally retarded sample were miscategorized as putting forth suboptimal effort.

(cont.)

TABLE 5.3 (cont.)

Specialized measure	Description and validation
Computerized Assessment of Response Bias (CARB)	A modified version of the PDRT that is computerized (Allen, Conder, Green, & Cox, 1997). *Strategy:* SVT and floor effect (i.e., persons with severe brain injuries generally succeed with ≥90% accuracy). An important concern is that a substantial minority of persons with depression or other disorders are likely to "fail" the CARB.
Word Memory Test (WMT)	The WMT is a verbal test of immediate and delayed (30 minutes) memory for 20 word pairs in a variety of recognition and recall tasks. *Strategies:* floor effect, response consistency, performance curve, and learning principle. Current studies (see Green, Astner, & Allen, 1996) are difficult to interpret, given the lack of clarity in establishing criterion groups. However, their preliminary results appear very promising as a screening measure.
Structured Inventory of Malingered Symptomatology (SIMS)	The SIMS is a 75-item true–false test with several scales to address feigned cognitive impairment: low intelligence, neurologic impairment, and amnesia. Although group differences were found for persons simulating these conditions (see Smith, 1997), its application to feigned cognitive deficits is compromised by the lack of normative data on truly impaired (e.g., persons with neuropsychological impairment or mental retardation). The SIMS is best construed as a general screen for potential malingering rather than a specific screen for feigned cognitive deficits.
Test of Cognitive Abilities (TOCA)	The TOCA (Rogers & Sewell, 1998) is an 112-item sequencing task for which clients must select from four alternatives the correct response for the beginning and end of the sequence (e.g., _, 2, 3, 4, 5, _). *Strategies:* SVT, magnitude of error, floor effect, performance curve, and response time. Currently under development, initial research produces promising results. An important feature is that all participants are warned about purpose of the test and its various strategies, thereby obviating concerns about coaching and examiner deception.

Note. SVT = symptom validity testing; FCT = forced choice testing.

♦ *Single strategy.* Most specialized measures rely on a single strategy. Even when more than one strategy is identified, often one strategy predominates. For example, the TOMM employs both floor effect and SVT, but classifications are based essentially on the floor effect.

♦ *Reliance on simulation design.* Nearly all the research relies on simulation design, often without studying the effects of coaching. Given the reliance on a single, easily understood strategy, any coaching (e.g., a simple admonition not to miss the easy items) is likely to thwart the effectiveness of these measures. In addition, the similarities between simulators and suspected malingerers must be tested and not simply assumed. Therefore, studies without known-groups comparisons are limited in their real-world applications.

Table 5.3 summarizes 10 different measures for assessing feigned cognitive deficits. The first 3 measures (Rey 15 Item, 21 Item Memory, and Dot Counting) are traditional methods found in the clinical literature. The remaining 7 measures exist either as proprietary efforts (PDRT, TOMM, VIP, CARB, and WMT) or research editions (SIMS and TOCA). As previously noted, nearly all measures address immediate and short-term memory. The notable exceptions are the VIP, SIMS, and TOCA.

Most atypical responses on these measures alert forensic experts to the need for a thorough evaluation of feigned cognitive impairment. Please note that the essential function of these measures is to screen for possible feigning, not to determine of malingering itself. With the exceptions noted below, the validation of cognitive measures is insufficient to render a classification of malingering. Attorneys should be alert to the potential overinterpretation of atypical findings as firm evidence of malingering.

The most robust strategy of cognitive feigning is SVT; highly deviant SVT results can be used to make a determination of feigned cognitive deficits. With sufficient trials and below-chance performance, forensic experts can establish with a high level of probability that a person is feigning. The limitations of SVT are twofold: most measures (1) utilize the simplest format (i.e., two choices), which is easy to thwart; and (2) rely on very rudimentary items that appear to be too easy to fail. Importantly, these limitations are not fundamental flaws with SVT but are drawbacks in its current applications. Because of these limitations, many malingerers are not identified by SVT. However, below-chance performance yields virtually no false-positives. If identified by below-chance performance, an individual's likelihood of feigning is very high.

Specialized Measures of Criminal Responsibility: The MRT

Hiscock, Rustemier, and Hiscock (1993) devised two forced-choice measures for potential use in assessments of criminal responsibility. Employing SVT for two alternatives, Hiscock et al. created (1) a 72-item General Knowledge Test for assessing simple information, and (2) a 72-item Moral Reasoning Test (MRT) for distinguishing between right and wrong moral actions. Simulators were asked to complete the measures as if they did not know the difference between right and wrong. The MRT was the more successful of the two measures. Using SVT detection strategy, the MRT correctly identified 60.6% of naive simulators, 33.8% of coached simulators, and 100% of the normal controls. The current validation lacks clinical comparison samples, including mentally disordered defendants and brain-injured patients. Clearly, further research on the MRT with actual insanity cases is warranted.

Test Batteries

Trueblood and Binder (1997) provided 86 experienced neuropsychologists with test data from extensive test batteries. The investigators found that these neuropsychologists were highly accurate at their classification of genuine cases (23 of 26 cases, or 88.5%). In contrast, they were less accurate with malingered cases (43 of 60 cases, or 71.7%). Interestingly, the presence of SVT data improved neuropsychologists' confidence in their decisions but did not substantially affect their accuracy.

The following subsections address the ability of the Halstead–Reitan and Luria–Nebraska to classify feigned and genuine protocols. In many studies, the neuropsychological batteries extended beyond these measures and included other neuropsychological measures and the WAIS-R. Additional studies focused on the WAIS-R and the Wechsler Memory Scale—Revised (WMS-R; Wechsler, 1987) are also distilled.[4]

Halstead–Reitan

Heaton, Smith, Lehman, and Vogt (1978) conducted the classic study on the Halstead–Reitan, WAIS, and MMPI with 10 neuropsychologists. Their results were troubling in that accuracy ranged from chance to 20% above chance for differentiating feigned and nonfeigned batteries. Goebel (1983) examined Halstead–Reitan data on 52 brain-injured and 202 unimpaired participants with a high level of accuracy at detecting feigned protocols. Unfortunately, constraints in the methodology limit the usefulness of these results. While proposing discriminant models, these studies evaluate neuropsychologists' composite judgments on feigning rather than the validation of specific indices of malingering.

Several recent studies have addressed feigning on the Halstead–Reitan. Trueblood and Schmidt (1993) evaluated the performance on the Halstead–Reitan, the WAIS-R, and several memory tests with a known-groups comparison. Their groups were composed of 8 malingerers (below-chance performance of SVT), 8 patients with questionable motivation, and 16 patients with genuine impairment. They found statistically significant group differences for overall impairment on the General Neuropsychological Deficit Scale and selected Halstead–Reitan subtests. However, malingered protocols often exhibited similar ranges as brain-injured controls, thereby limiting the clinical usefulness of these findings. Perhaps an unintended conclusion from the Trueblood and Schmidt study is that patterns on the Halstead–Reitan and WAIS-R are likely to be inconclusive in the determination of malingering. In contrast, Mittenberg, Rotholc, Russell, and Heilbronner (1996) employed a simulation design to compare test performance on the Halstead–Reitan for simulators and brain-injured persons. With 10 predictor variables, they achieved high classification rates for a cross-validated discriminant function (88.8%). The discriminant function was also tested against a small number of actual malingerers from this and earlier research; it proved to be highly successful.

Reitan and Wolfson (1996, 1998) proposed specific indices with the Halstead–Reitan for the detection of dissimulation. They evaluated response consistency, through the readministration of the Halstead–Reitan and WAIS-R; they found significant differences between 20 nonlitigating and 20 litigating head-injured patients. We dispute their conclusions that the "dissimulation index" is a measure of feigning for two reasons: First, the effectiveness of a measure cannot be established with simply a differential prevalence design. Second, the very modest clinical sample is unlikely to be representative of brain-injured patients. In addition, the design is very labor-intensive and unlikely to be affordable in most clinical settings.

Luria–Nebraska

Relatively little research has examined the usefulness of test patterns on the Luria–Nebraska for the identification of malingered protocols. Mensch and Woods (1986) conducted a modest study of the Luria–Nebraska and feigning. Unfortunately, they compared test performances of unimpaired individuals under honest and faking instructions. The critical question of whether the Luria–Nebraska could differentiate accurately between brain-injured and feigned protocols was not addressed.

Golden and Grier (1998) cited unpublished research by the first author in which 20 normal participants were asked to feign brain injury. A subsample asked to avoid detection tended to produce unimpaired test results on the Luria–Nebraska. In a subsample not given this instruction, 6 of 10 produced abnormal findings, with 4 of the 6 being detected by an experienced neuropsychologist. As Golden and Grier readily acknowledged, however, 10–20% of brain-injured patients also produce "normal" patterns on the Luria–Nebraska. In summarizing across the two studies, no reliable cut scores or indices have been established to address feigning on the Luria–Nebraska.

WAIS-R and WMS-R Patterns

In reviewing analogue studies on feigned intelligence and memory, a critical issue is whether simulators follow the instructions to feign. Conversely, simulators may feel challenged by the tests and put forth considerable effort, irrespective of the instructions. Consider the following two studies:

- In the Heaton et al. (1978) study, simulators had average WAIS IQs of 96.2 while faking "severe disabilities" arising from brain injuries.
- In the Mittenberg, Theroux-Fichera, Zielinski, and Heilbronner (1995) study, simulators had average WAIS-R IQs of 90.16.

Simulators in other studies (e.g., Trueblood & Schmidt, 1993) do evidence impaired intellectual functioning on the WAIS-R, although some participants continue to attain average IQ estimates. Overall intellectual functioning (Verbal IQ, Performance IQ, and Full Scale IQ) is generally a poor discriminator between feigned and brain-injured protocols. Performance subtests, such as Digit Span, have yielded group differences in several studies. In summary, WAIS and WAIS-R test data are not effective at the detection of malingering.

Several studies have investigated the WMS-R and its usefulness with feigned brain injury. For example, Bernard (1990) found group differences between simulators and brain-injured patients on most WMS-R scales, although the overlap of scores militated against specific cut scores. A discriminant analysis produced only modest results on cross-validation with substantial false-positives. More recently, Mittenberg, Azrin, Millsaps, and Heilbronner (1993) found that simulators performed more poorly than expected on the Attention/Concentration index. While brain-injured patients tended to have *higher* scores ($M = 10.64$) on the Attention/Concentration index in comparison to their General Memory Index, the opposite was true for simulators. More specifically, simulators had *lower* scores ($M = 14.38$) on the Attention/Concentration index when compared to the General Memory Index. In conclusion, the WMS-R should not be used to discriminate feigned from bona fide protocols. However, a very low Attention/Concentration index in relationship to General Memory Index should signal the need for a comprehensive assessment of cognitive feigning.[5]

Conclusions on Test Batteries

Despite the positive results by Trueblood and Binder (1997) regarding neuropsychologists' capacity to use test batteries for feigning, researchers have yet to establish empirically based rules. Two parallel problems thwart this effort. First, the heterogeneity of brain injuries and the resulting deficits dramatically reduce the likelihood of a reliable "feigned test pattern." Second, the heterogeneity of malingerers simply compounds the "feigned test pattern" strategy and diminishes the likelihood of success. Important exceptions are (1) discriminant functions cross-validated on multiple samples and (2) specialized indices that take into account detection strategies.

General recommendations offered for forensic practice follow:

1. The Mittenberg et al. (1996) Halstead–Reitan discriminant function may provide evidence of feigning with its excellent classification rate (88.8%); corroboration is critical, given its false-positive rate of 16.2%. No other conclusions from the Halstead–Reitan or Luria–Nebraska should be cited as evidence for or against malingering. Atypical findings should simply signal the need for a more comprehensive assessment.

2. Likewise, WAIS-R or WMS-R results do not provide clear evidence of feigning. Although some simulators are likely to have lower than expected scores on Digit Span, a similar pattern may be found for those with anxiety disorders. Please note that the WAIS-III and WMS-III have not been evaluated with respect to cognitive feigning.

3. Decrements in the WMS-R Concentration/Attention Index (e.g., ≥ 19 points lower than the General Memory Index) are highly atypical and should signal the need for a full assessment of malingering.

4. When malingering is a potential issue, specialized measures of cognitive feigning will likely be needed.

Conclusion

Rogers (1997) compiled threshold and decision models for the assessment of malingering. Germane to our discussion of insanity evaluations, we offer the following conclusions about the classification of malingering. For purposes of clarity, we define *retrospective* malingering to refer to malingering of past episodes. In contrast, *current* malingering refers to malingering of present episodes. In insanity cases, defendants may engage in retrospective malingering but claim that their symptoms are greatly lessened at the present time. In such cases, an assessment of current malingering would likely overlook a critical issue in insanity cases: retrospective malingering.

Because of fundamental differences between feigned psychopathology and feigned cognitive impairment, the respective detection methods are summarized separately. For easy reference, Table 5.4 distills detection methods for current and retrospective malingering of mental disorders.

Retrospective Malingering of Psychopathology

Two structured interviews, the SADS and the SIRS, appear to provide the most relevant information regarding the feigning of a past episode (e.g., the time of the offense). As described in Chapter 9, the SADS provides a superb structure for examining a defendant's self-reporting at the time of the offense. Comparisons are possible between (1) the defendant's unstructured account and SADS ratings, (2) the defendant's and an informant's SADS ratings, and (3) the defendant's SADS ratings administered at separate times. As previously discussed, data are avail-

---

TABLE 5.4. Determinations of Feigned Mental Disorders in Insanity Evaluations

Measures of current feigning

   SIRS
   Extreme scores on the PAI or MMPI-2
   Highly atypical SADS results

Measures of past feigning

   Retrospective SIRS (R-SIRS)
   Highly atypical SADS results

Note. "Current feigning" assumes that the defendant's presentation *has not* varied substantially between the time of the offense and the time of the assessment. This presentation could be construed as a single episode. "Past feigning" assumes that the defendant's presentation *has* varied substantially between the time of the offense and the time of the assessment. In this case, the evaluation of malingering is entirely retrospective.

able on the SADS with forensic patients so that anomalous results can be evaluated more closely. In this regard, Ustad (1996) and Rogers (1997) provide detection strategies and cut scores for potential feigning.

The SIRS was developed as a current measure of feigning. However, Goodness (1999) tested the effectiveness of two variations (R-SIRS and CT-SIRS). Importantly, her research evaluated forensic patients for their retrospective account of their past offenses. Utilizing the standard SIRS cut scores, the R-SIRS and CT-SIRS appear to be moderately effective, although they may produce false-positives (preliminary estimates < 20%).

Current Malingering of Psychopathology

Current malingering is highly relevant in many insanity cases because either (1) the forensic assessment is conducted soon after the alleged offense, or (2) the defendant's reported psychopathology has remained relatively constant from the time of the offense to the time of the evaluation. In other cases, current malingering may provide indirect evidence of feigning. Clearly, the establishment of feigning at the current time calls into question the veracity of the defendant's account for the time of the offense. However, it does not preclude the possibility of genuine impairment. In one insanity case, a male defendant responded to treatment at a forensic hospital. With his psychotic symptoms largely resolved, he was concerned that his present adjustment was incompatible with an NGRI verdict. As exemplified by this case, current malingering does not equate to retrospective malingering.

Forensic experts should rely on multiple sources of data in establishing current malingering. Key findings from the chapter are distilled in the following outline:

♦ *SIRS.* Exceeding the cut scores provides the strongest evidence of feigning with very few false-positive rates. An important caution is whether the defendant was untestable. If the defendant is unable to respond meaningfully to the SIRS inquiries, then the SIRS should not be administered (see Rogers et al., 1992).

♦ *MMPI-2.* Extreme elevations on the MMPI-2 validity indicators provide moderate evidence of feigning. Three cautions must be borne in mind: First, profiles completed inconsistently (e.g., randomly answered without reading items) also produce extreme elevations. Scoring for VRIN can minimize this problem by excluding inconsistent profiles. Second, most computerized reports and practitioner books advocate the use of moderate elevations. Such use results in unacceptably high false-positives. Third, some defendants fudge on self-report measures but respond forthrightly on interview-based methods. Because insanity evaluations are largely dependent on interview-based information, forensic experts should confirm their MMPI-2 findings with the SIRS.

◆ *PAI.* Extreme elevations on PAI validity indicators provide moderate evidence of feigning. The PAI has an advantage over the MMPI-2 because of its validation with suspected malingerers from correctional-forensic settings. The three cautions that apply to the MMPI-2 also apply to the PAI.

◆ *MCMI-III.* Validity indicators are insufficiently validated. Attorneys should fight vigorously for the exclusion of any MCMI-III data related to feigning.

◆ *Projective methods.* No standardized validity indicators are available. As with the MCMI-III, attorneys should fight vigorously for their exclusion with reference to the issue of feigning.

Retrospective Malingering of Cognitive Impairment

No methods have been validated for retrospective malingering of mental retardation or compromised cognitive abilities.

Current Malingering of Cognitive Impairment

Most measures of cognitive feigning perform a valuable *screening* function: they raise the index of suspicion that a patient or defendant might be feigning. However, they do not address the critical question, Is this defendant malingering? Measures that perform a screening function lack the ability to classify specific individuals at a sufficient level of accuracy.

An important distinction must be underscored between *malingering* and *incomplete effort.* As previously described, many defendants may put forth an incomplete effort for a range of reasons. One largely unexplored reason is the presence of an Axis I disorder that interferes with motivation or concentration. In direct contrast to incomplete effort, malingering requires a sustained effort to fabricate or grossly exaggerate cognitive impairment.

Key findings of the chapter are distilled below in an outline format:

◆ *SVT.* Regardless of the specific method, the SVT provides the strongest evidence of feigning. This method is unique in that below-chance probabilities can be calculated. Its primary drawback is an over-reliance on a two-alternative design that is transparent for some simulators.

♦ *Floor effect.* These methods often produce relatively low false-positives and should be included in assessments of feigned cognitive impairment. Three cautions must be considered. First, many malingerers do not wish to appear extremely impaired. Second, coaching is very easy to accomplish because of the strategy's simplicity. Third, patients with severe Axis I disorders may have difficulty with repetitive designs (e.g., TOMM) which could produce false-positives.

♦ *FCT.* This strategy is based on group comparisons. In the absence of large normative samples drawn from heterogenous clinical and forensic settings, this strategy should not be used in the classification of forensic patients as malingerers.

♦ *Performance curve.* This strategy is probably the most sophisticated and difficult to feign successfully. At present, however, the methods lack extensive research, with the exception of the VIP. Therefore, this strategy should only be used in conjunction with other strategies.

♦ *Discriminant models.* From a purely empirical perspective, atypical patterns of scales can be used to determine feigned protocols.[6] In this regard, the Mittenberg et al. (1996) Halstead–Reitan discriminant function appears to be effective, although further corroboration is clearly necessary.

Other strategies continue to be in the developmental stages. The determination of cognitive feigning is based on two considerations: First, does SVT provide convincing evidence of malingering? Second, if not, does a combination of other strategies provide convergent evidence of malingering?

Malingering and Insanity

The courts often view the genuineness of insanity pleas with suspicion. Any expert evidence about malingering, however unsubstantiated, is likely to have a chilling effect on NGRI verdicts. Therefore, forensic experts must exercise care and caution in making determinations of malingering.

In concluding this chapter, we would like to raise an important *Daubert* issue. The capacity of forensic experts to determine malingering based solely on "clinical judgment" and "clinical experience" has yet to be established. Such unstandardized testimony does not have known error rates and is not likely to be falsifiable. However, cases do occur for which experts could make the argument that gross inconsistencies with documented evidence (e.g., reported suicide attempts requiring hospitalization vs. documentation that refutes these reports) would justify such expert testimony. Therefore, we offer two specific recommendations about unstandardized testimony:

1. Testimony on malingering without standardized measures probably does not meet the *Daubert* standard and generally should be avoided.
2. When data on standardized measures do *not* indicate feigning, forensic experts should not conclude or imply that their clinical judgment supersedes validated measures of malingering. This position is insupportable on *Daubert* or ethical grounds.[7]

Notes

1. Prototypical analysis has been used with diagnostic issues by asking experts to rate the most representative characteristics of a disorder or response style. Ratings of prototypicality address the relative importance of certain characteristics to a construct, such as the pathogenic model.

2. Key issues include interrater reliability (Will different experts agree?) and effect sizes (Do the scales really differentiate between feigned and genuine disorders?).

3. Rogers and Nussbaum (1991) demonstrated that occasional cases of malingering can be detected in apparently inconsistent profiles when the probability of achieving extreme scores on validity indicators substantially exceeds random responding (i.e., 50%).

4. No studies of feigning are yet published on the most recent versions of these tests (WAIS-III and WMS-III).

5. The underlying strategy appears to be the performance curve. According to Mittenberg et al. (1993), differences ≥ 20 represent an 80% likelihood of feigning, and of ≥ 35 a 99% likelihood of feigning. Given the sample size ($N = 78$), these percentages should be viewed as general benchmarks.

6. J. M. Williams (1998) underscored some of the dangers in applying discriminant functions to malingering on the basis of conventional scoring. Conventional scoring generally ignores detection strategies and runs the risk of being more an index of impairment than a measurement of feigning.

7. For example, APA ethics (1992) require that forensic evaluations (1) be based on sufficient methods and data to substantiate findings and (2) acknowledge limitations of conclusions. To disregard standardized data and to overstate the relative validity of one's own conclusions would be a flagrant disregard of APA ethics.

Chapter 6

Amnesia and Dissociation

Overview
Dissociative versus Organic Amnesia
Specific Organic Syndromes
Malingered Amnesia
Dissociative Disorders and Criminal Responsibility
Automatism and Criminal Responsibility
Memory Loss and Distortion
Conclusion

Overview

Schacter (1986a) found in his classic review that amnesia is commonly reported among offenders charged with violent crimes (see also Herman, 1995). In many cases, defendants experience an alcoholic blackout in which they simply do not register (i.e., encode the memory) the criminal activity. Other offenders, traumatized by the event or injured during the arrest or subsequent detention, experience amnestic syndromes. Still other defendants feign their memory loss, attributing it either to an alcoholic blackout or to an amnestic disorder. Utilizing the R-CRAS data base, Table 6.1 summarizes the percentages of amnesia among insanity cases with and without intoxication.

As reported in Table 6.1, the severity and prevalence of memory loss is comparable between sane and insane defendants for the time of the offense. The coding of R-CRAS data did not allow us to examine amnestic syndromes by themselves with alcoholic blackouts excluded. As a partial solution, we excluded cases with moderate or greater levels of intoxication that might be associated with alcoholic blackouts. When these intoxicated defendants are removed, the percentages of sane de-

TABLE 6.1. Memory Loss for the Time of the Offense with and without Intoxication

Memory loss	% Sane		% Insane		% Undetermined	
	Total	Not intoxicated	Total	Not intoxicated	Total	Not intoxicated
Moderate	7.6	2.4	8.4	6.3	13.3	3.3
Severe	4.5	1.0	6.3	4.2	13.3	13.3
Extreme	5.2	1.4	5.3	4.2	16.7	3.3

Note. Defendants are classified by court reports as sane, insane, or undetermined (i.e., "no opinion"). Total = the complete group; Not intoxicated = the group with intoxicated defendants removed. For levels of memory loss, Moderate = forgot major portions of the crime; Severe = forgot most of the crime but remembers enough to believe it happened; Extreme = no memory of the crime.

fendants with severe or extreme amnesia plummet, while percentages for insane defendants remain relatively constant. However, the most interesting finding involved cases in which forensic experts could not reach an opinion. In these undetermined cases, amnesia was commonly observed (i.e., 43.3% of the time) and continued to play a significant role even when the potential role of intoxication was eliminated (i.e., 19.9%). The lack of a defendant's account definitely complicates the determination of criminal responsibility.

Hermann (1986) presented an insightful overview of the complex relationship between amnesia and criminal culpability. With insanity evaluations, it is important to distinguish (1) amnesia at the time of the offense from (2) amnesia at the time of the trial. If amnesia originated at the time of the offense, it is potentially relevant to the insanity defense. If amnesia arose subsequent to the crime, then it is not germane to insanity, but may be relevant to competence to stand trial. Because of this critical distinction, forensic experts are faced with several diagnostic challenges:

- Does the defendant have a bona fide dissociative or organic amnesia?
- If so, was this amnesia present at the time of the crime?
- If so, how did this amnesia at the time of the crime affect his/her criminal responsibility?

In light of these diagnostic challenges, this chapter is organized into six sections. The first three sections address types of amnesias (i.e., dissociative vs. organic amnesias and organic syndromes) and their genuineness (i.e., evaluation of malingered amnesia). The next two sections examine the relationship between amnestic syndromes and the legal constructs of insanity and automatism. Beyond these challenges, forensic experts must grapple with memory distortions common in insanity trials. The final section offers several conclusions toward integrating the complex literature of amnesia and criminal responsibility.

Dissociative versus Organic Amnesia

In a classic review, Kopelman (1987) underscored both the definitional simplicity and the diagnostic complexity in establishing psychogenic and organic amnesias. With the publication of DSM-IV (American Psychiatric Association, 1994), the traditional term "psychogenic amnesia" was replaced with the current descriptor, "dissociative amnesia." With respect to etiology, *organic amnesias* have a known biological cause, while *dissociative amnesias* are assumed to have functional (i.e., nonbiological) origins. This diagnostic dichotomy based on etiology is problematic, given the difficulties in establishing or excluding the biological bases of amnesia (Cercey et al., 1997).

Controversies Regarding Dissociative Amnesia

In the context of recovered memory, claims of dissociative amnesia have created significant controversies. At the heart of the debate, researchers and clinicians are polarized regarding the phenomenon of dissociation: Can life events substantively alter consciousness, memory, and identity? If so, can these alterations and their effects on behavior be reliably measured? Ross (1998) outlined the historical trends regarding the understanding of dissociation:

- ♦ In the 19th century, dissociation was viewed as a loss of ego strength and a core element in the pathogenic process, resulting in a wide range of psychopathology.
- ♦ For most of the 20th century, with its questioning of analytic constructs and the meteoric rise of behaviorism, dissociation was generally discarded.
- ♦ During the 1980s, a resurgence of interest was fueled by reports of dissociative identity disorder and traumatized Vietnam veterans.

The history of dissociation is important to our understanding of the current controversies. Both the type of training (e.g., behavioral or dynamic) and the timing of training (e.g., prior to 1980) are likely to affect practitioners' receptivity to dissociation and dissociative disorders.

Pope, Hudson, Bodkin, and Oliva (1998) assailed the validity of dissociative amnesia by examining 12 prospective studies. In adult studies, Pope et al. (1998) concluded that subjects uniformly remembered the traumatic events. Before credulously accepting this conclusion, we must consider several issues. First, some of the traumatic events were well publicized (e.g., the *Challenger* explosion), thereby potentially contaminating original memories with repeated media presentations. Second, perpetrators of crime (e.g., murderers) were systematically excluded. Third, and most importantly, research participants were asked direct questions about their memory of the trauma; such direct questioning is likely to produce an expectancy effect and possible memory distortion. For example, a research participant may be asked, "Do you remember the *Challenger* explosion?" This questioning may both signal the researcher's expectations of an affirmative response and stimulate a remembrance of forgotten material.[1] Brewin (1998) offered a further critique of the Pope et al. (1998) review and its potential biases.

Research documenting dissociative amnesia is very difficult to conduct. Williams (1994) interviewed 129 women with documented sexual abuse. Forty-nine (38.0%) reported that they did not recall the sexual abuse, although many did report other embarrassing information, including other instances of abuse. Pope et al. (1998) reanalyzed the Williams data and (1) removed 5 women who were too young to remember (<3 years old at the time of the abuse), and (2) suggested that cases without physical evidence of penetration should be excluded because genital fondling "might not be particularly memorable to a young child" (p. 212). They dismissed the remaining cases as potentially explainable by other factors "without a need to invoke dissociative amnesia" (p. 212).

The polarization of professional views regarding dissociative amnesia provides a surplus of rhetoric and a shortage of empiricism. The dichotomized views are further complicated by controversies over the veridicality of "recovered" memories, especially in the realm of sexual abuse (see Pendergast, 1995; Piper, 1993; Terr, 1994). The truth probably lies between the polarities. Studies, such as Williams (1994), probably *overestimate* the prevalence of dissociative amnesia. Reviews, such as Pope et al. (1998) that categorically dismiss any positive findings, probably *underestimate* the prevalence of dissociative amnesia.

Attorneys should be alert for zealotry among forensic experts. Experts who commonly find dissociative amnesia should be tested with vigorous cross-examination regarding the merits of their findings in both current and past cases. Likewise, attorneys should be alert for experts who invoke the following flawed logic: "Dissociative amnesia doesn't exist, therefore this defendant could not possibly be experiencing it." Given the marked lack of consensus, an expert would be imprudent to summarily dismiss this DSM-IV diagnosis. Any experts who categorically repudiate dissociative amnesia are vulnerable to questions regarding their self-proclaimed authority in an area of diagnostic controversy.

A final issue is whether dissociative amnesia and other dissociative disorders are very uncommon and thus rarely applicable to insanity cases. Applying the DSM-III-R criteria to a nonclinical population, Ross (1991) interviewed 454 community participants and found a lifetime prevalence rate of 11.2% for dissociative disorders. According to Ross (1998), clinical studies report substantial percentages (i.e., 15–20%) of dissociative disorders when standardized assessments are employed. Because DSM-IV applies more stringent criteria,[2] these percentages are likely to be overestimates. Still, the available data strongly indicate that dissociative amnesia cannot be neglected because of either (1) the controversy surrounding the diagnosis or (2) its prevalence.

Assessment of Dissociative versus Organic Amnesia

Lowenstein (1998) characterized dissociative amnesia as the impairment of memory for personal experience within four domains: First, large groups of memories and associated affect are not remembered. Second, lost memories often relate to day-to-day information. Third, learning of new information is generally intact. Fourth, dissociated memories are often expressed indirectly (e.g., through visual images, nightmares, or somatoform symptoms). From a diagnostic perspective, Cardena and Spiegel (1998) provide an excellent overview of dissociative amnesia and its evolution from DSM-III-R to DSM-IV. For example, loss of personal memory was required to be "sudden" in DSM-III-R; that requirement was eliminated in DSM-IV because some cases of dissociative amnesia with a gradual insidious course are reported.

Elliot (1987) and Rubinsky and Brandt (1986) provided thorough overviews of the differences in clinical presentation between dissociative and organic amnesias. As summarized in Table 6.2, dissociative amnesias tend to focus on specific personal memory related to a traumatic or highly stressful event. In contrast, organic amnesias tend to be much less specific, with impairment of both personal and nonpersonal memory. Other important differences have been documented. Dissociative amnesias have a fairly characteristic pattern, with a sudden onset

TABLE 6.2. Symptoms and Associated Features of Dissociative and Organic Amnesias

Symptoms or features	Dissociative amnesia	Organic amnesia
Precipitating event	Psychic trauma	Brain injury or disease
Memory domain	Personal memory	Both personal and nonpersonal memory
Permanence	Reversible impairment	Irreversible impairment
Type of memory loss	Posttrauma memory loss	Both pre- and posttrauma memory loss
Onset	Sudden[a]	Sudden with brain injury, otherwise depends on specific organic syndrome
Capacity to learn	Often unimpaired	Often compromised
Confabulation	Not typical	Depends on specific organic syndrome
Hypnotizability	Often high	Unknown[b]
Response to amytal	Often improvement	Worsening

Note. A distillation of clinical reviews, including American Psychiatric Association (1994), Elliot (1987), Kopelman (1987), Rubinsky and Brandt (1986), and Squire and Shimamura (1988).

[a]Although more common, DSM-IV does not require a sudden onset (Cardena & Spiegel, 1998).

[b]Assumed to be normally distributed among patients with intact attentionality and concentration.

and a partial, if not complete, eventual resolution of the memory loss. In comparison, organic amnesias are more variable in their onset and memory loss is generally permanent. One hallmark of dissociative amnesia is the capacity of patients to learn new information; this capacity is often compromised in patients with organic amnesia.

Preliminary efforts to distinguish dissociative and organic amnesias have yielded promising results on two clinical methods: assessment of drug-assisted interviews and hypnotizability (see Chapter 10). Many patients with dissociative amnesias have recovered memories with sodium amytal (see Rogers & Wettstein, 1997). In contrast, amytal interviews administered to patients with organic amnesias are reported to produce drowsiness, less responsiveness, and no memory recoveries (Cercey et al., 1997). Chapter 10 provides a review of drug-assisted interviews, including their limitations in forensic evaluations. Less data are available about hypnotizability scales as a potential identifier of dissociative amnesia. While reported as a "laboratory finding" (American Psychiatric Association, 1994), the stability and fakability of these scales is very open to question (see Miller & Stava, 1997; see also Chapter 10).

Diagnoses of organic amnesias are sometimes missed, with the memory loss erroneously attributed to dissociative amnesia. Kopelman, Green, Guinan, Lewis, and Stanhope (1994) reported a case study in which a male embezzler claimed amnesia for his criminal acts. He had a prior history of two apparent fugue states and depression. CT scans and neuropsychological testing at the time of his trial revealed no major abnormalities. However, further testing on MRI and PET scans (see Chapter 10) following his conviction revealed multiple infarcts in the left temporal lobe. Since it was discovered after the trial, the relevance of this organic amnesia to criminal charges was not formally assessed.

Cercey et al. (1997) raised an interesting diagnostic consideration. While they affirm the merits of diagnosing organic amnesias, Cercey et al. suggested that (1) the intentionality underlying dissociative amnesia is difficult to assess and (2) its differentiation from feigned amnesia is likely to be problematic. From a different viewpoint, we contend that intentionality is problematic for most amnesias, whether organic or dissociative. Except for pervasive cognitive disorders (e.g., severe dementias), the relationship of brain dysfunction to intentionality is challenging to assess. While documented brain pathology may add credence to claims of amnesia, its existence does not bar the fabrication or gross exaggeration of tested and reported amnesia. As further support for our perspective, we submit that feigned dissociative amnesia may be easier to detect than feigned organic amnesia because most memory tests for malingering address the capacity to learn new information.[3]

Several specialized measures have been proposed for the diagnosis of dissociative amnesias:

1. Koppelman, Wilson, and Baddeley (1989, 1990) developed the Autobiographical Memory Interview (AMI) to measure autobiographical memories from childhood, early adulthood, and recent years. Reported memories must be verified by relatives and significant others. The AMI appears to be best suited for patients with extensive losses of personal memory. The original validation (Koppelman et al., 1989) compared 23 amnestic patients to 16 healthy controls and established good interscorer reliability ($r = .83$). More recent research has focused on case studies and clinical differences among criterion groups (e.g., individuals with multiple sclerosis and patients treated with ECT).

2. Ross, Heber, Norton, Anderson, Anderson, and Barchet (1989) created the Dissociative Disorders Interview Schedule (DDIS). Its initial

validation was based on relatively small numbers ($N = 80$; 20 patients with dissociative identity disorder). The DDIS has a moderate interrater reliability ($r = .68$; see Ross, 1991). More recently, Ross (1998) reported very promising results with interrater reliability and diagnostic validity but cautioned that further validation is needed.

3. Steinberg (1993) constructed the Structured Clinical Interview for DSM-IV Dissociative Disorders (SCID-D). The SCID-D appears to have good reliability for its symptoms scales (see Rogers, 1995a) and is linked with DSM-IV disorders. Although its items are face-valid, it provides a standardized method of assessing dissociative amnesia and other dissociative disorders.

Organic amnesias are typically screened by their clinical features (see Table 6.2) and confirmed by brain scans and neuropsychological testing. An important study by Kopelman and Stanhope (1997) stressed the importance of establishing specific lesions in relationship to amnesia. As measured by the Wechsler Memory Scale—Revised, substantial differences in general and delayed memory were found for front lobe, diencephalic, and temporal lobe lesions. Equally interesting was the wide dispersion of scores within each lesion group (SDs ranged from 14.0 to 21.0). Several issues deserve brief comment. First, the research addressed anterograde amnesia (acquisition of new information). Second, even state-of-the-art assessments of specific lesions (e.g., via CT, MRI, and PET scans) cannot be equated with specific memory losses, because of the variability within lesion groups.

Specific Organic Syndromes

Cercey et al. (1997) organized organic amnesias into four general categories that are often identifiable by phenomenology and etiology. These categories are summarized below:

1. *Chronic global amnesia* is characterized by permanent and severe anterograde amnesia. The etiology of chronic global amnesia can involve diverse disease processes that include Korsakoff syndrome (i.e., alcohol amnestic disorder), strokes, and cerebral hypoxia. In chronic cases, Korsakoff syndrome results in both anterograde and retrograde amnesia. For retrograde amnesia, earlier memories tend to be more intact than those close to the onset of amnesia (Sackeim & Stern, 1997).

2. *Material-specific amnesia* is defined by chronic anterograde amne-

sia that is circumscribed to either verbal or nonverbal memory. Again, the etiology is diverse; lesions are often associated with trauma, tumors, or strokes.

3. *Transient global amnesia* is distinguished by sudden onset of anterograde amnesia with limited retrograde amnesia. This rare condition is brief in duration and typically results from transient ischemic attacks (TIAs), although other medical conditions may be implicated (Sackeim & Stern, 1997). Transient global amnesia is typically unrelated to stress and rarely involves personal identity (Kaplan & Sadock, 1988). Examining 114 cases, Hodges and Warlow (1990) found chief complaints of disorientation to time and repetitive questioning; recurrence was comparatively rare and estimated at 3% per year.

4. *Focal retrograde amnesia* is typified by isolated yet permanent loss of autobiographical memory with mild impairment of anterograde memory. This very rare condition is associated with brain abnormalities in brain imaging studies and abnormal EEGs in the temporal lobes.

Weisberg, Strub, and Garcia (1993) provided a useful template for differentiating types of organic amnesias and other forms of memory impairment based on presentation. Their decision tree is composed of three main branches:

1. Isolated memory loss with normal mental status
   a. If confused and unable to learn during episode, consider transient global amnesia, seizures, and posttraumatic brain injury.
   b. If able to learn and acting normally, consider dissociative amnesia or dissociative fugue.
2. Gradual memory loss in an alert patient
   a. If difficulty with recent memory and other cognitive impairment, consider dementia.
   b. If no other cognitive difficulties, consider "functional disorders."
3. Heavy alcohol use
   a. If memory loss only while intoxicated, consider alcoholic blackout.
   b. If gradual memory loss with mild cognitive impairment, consider dementia or subdural hematoma.
   c. If severe recent memory loss but other functions spared (especially with delirium tremens or Wernicke's encephalopathy), consider alcohol-induced persisting amnestic disorder (i.e., Korsakoff syndrome).

Applying the Weisberg et al. (1993) template to forensic cases is likely to facilitate decision making about what types of memory impairment need to be investigated. Chronic global amnesia and material-specific amnesia should be considered separately because they do not correspond to Weisberg et al. typology. Fortunately, these presentations are dramatic in their memory loss and are unlikely to be overlooked. In commenting on this template, Strub and Wise (1997) suggested that epidemiological and historical data could be used to augment this decision model. For example, younger age and history of mental disorders might increase the likelihood of a dissociative rather than an organic amnesia.

Alcoholic blackouts deserve a brief discussion, given their frequency in offender populations (Rogers & Mitchell, 1991). Most commonly, intoxication results in alcoholic blackouts in which the offenders fail to register the memory. This failure in memory registration does not imply that reasoning and higher cognitive functions were not intact at the time of the offense. More specifically, the mere presence of blackouts does not signify cognitive or volitional incapacity at the time of the alleged crime (Mitchell, 1988).

Blackouts typically occur after a period of heavy drinking (Ewing, 1988), although their onset and frequency appears to be highly variable. The formerly held belief that blackouts represent end-stage alcoholism is now questioned. In a longitudinal study of 12,686 participants, Jennsion and Johnson (1994) found that (1) blackouts were common among young adults (ages 19–26) but (2) remission occurred in approximately two-thirds of the cases when assessed 4 years later. Campbell and Hodgins (1993) found that blackouts were very common (86%) in substance abuse patients. These blackouts were typically very circumscribed, lasting at most a few hours; in contrast, blackouts for a day or more were atypical (6.5%) and not found in patients with an isolated blackout. Interestingly, blackouts were often associated with shakes (77%) and DTs (60%). The rapid ingestion of alcohol in the presence of drug use or head injury is suspected to contribute to alcoholic blackouts (Cunnien, 1986).

The challenge in assessing blackouts is that they are entirely dependent on the defendants' retrospective self-report. The simulation of a blackout requires no elaborate account of symptoms or realistic portrayal of cognitive abilities. Rather, the defendant merely reports heavy drinking and asserts an inability to remember the offense. For both organic and dissociative amnesias, a critical issue is whether the reported memory loss is genuine. The next section addresses the detection of feigned amnesia.

Malingered Amnesia

Iverson (1995) combined data from four studies to examine closely the different strategies employed by simulators attempting to feign memory impairment. Although all participants were asked to simulate a situation[4] involving civil litigation, the results are instructive for all forensic evaluations. With respect to memory complaints, participants were divided as to whether they were asked to feign complete or partial amnesia. During the assessment, common strategies used by the participants were (1) "going blank" (i.e., forgetting presented material), (2) becoming confused about the directions, (3) having poor attention/concentration, and (4) manifesting aggravation, frustration, or emotional upset. Both forensic experts and attorneys sometimes may be misled by presentational style to believe the amnesia is genuine. On this point, Schacter (1986a, 1986b) found that mental health professionals were routinely fooled by amnestic simulators who appeared to try hard or become frustrated with their memory problems. In summary, forensic experts should not be persuaded that amnesia is genuine by any of the following:

- ◆ Memory and concentration problems at the time of the testing
- ◆ The amount of apparent effort expended by the defendant "trying" to remember
- ◆ The emotional response of the defendant to his/her memory loss (e.g., frustration or emotional upset).

The purpose of this introduction is to question the role of clinical intuition in the determination of feigned memory deficits. The clinical judgment that the defendant "seems genuine in his/her efforts to recall" is likely to capitalize on variables commonly feigned by simulators. We hypothesize that the opposite clinical judgment, "Does not appear to be genuine in his/her efforts to recall," is also fraught with misclassifications. In this regard, Schacter (1986a) found that experts' certainty regarding their judgments of feigned amnesia bore no relationship to their accuracy.

The focus of this chapter is on retrograde amnesia (i.e., prearrest behavior including the index offense). Although defendants may feign anterograde amnesia (i.e., capacity to learn new information), this feigning has only indirect relevance to insanity evaluations. In cases where reported amnesia is questioned, an investigation of anterograde amnesia may provide insight into the authenticity of the purported memory loss. For anterograde amnesia, please refer to Chapter 5 and the discussion of feigned cognitive impairment.

This section is organized into four segments for the detection of malingered amnesia. We begin with an examination of Schacter's (1986a) "feeling-of-knowing" (FOK) beliefs that is based on amnestic simulators' beliefs among their amnesias. The next two segments address malingered amnesia per se: (1) SVT for episodic memory (SVT-EM; Frederick, Carter, & Powel, 1995) and (2) indirect memory tests. The final section summarizes additional methods with references to laboratory procedures discussed in Chapter 10.

Feeling-of-Knowing (FOK) Beliefs

Schacter (1986b) devised the FOK format, in which individuals were queried by an interviewer about the recoverability of their memory loss for prior personal events. To test the FOK, simulators of amnesia were asked to make three ratings regarding likelihood of remembering "forgotten" material, if they were given (1) more time, (2) a hint, and (3) a recognition task. Simulators tended to have lower FOK ratings than participants with genuine memory loss. In other words, they expressed doubt that any of these strategies (i.e., more time, hints, or a multiple-choice format) would help them recover "lost" memories. Several enduring problems militate against the forensic application of FOK ratings:

- ♦ As observed by Cercey et al. (1997), FOK ratings have not been conducted with amnestic patients. Therefore, the meaning of low ratings remains obscure.
- ♦ The magnitude of difference between simulators and persons with memory loss in the Schacter (1986b) study was very modest for FOK ratings, thereby calling into question their clinical utility.
- ♦ Coaching amnestic simulators to foil the FOK ratings is extremely simple. FOK ratings can be easily defeated by simply making an optimistic appraisal of one's capacity to remember with additional assistance.

SVT for Episodic Memory (SVT-EM)

Frederick, Carter, and Powel (1995) pioneered the use of SVT-EM to study episodic memory in criminal defendants. When faced with a questionable amnestic syndrome, Frederick et al. constructed a two-alternative multiple-choice task (written or presented orally) based on specific details of the defendant's crime. Individuals whose performance is significantly below chance are likely recognizing the correct response and selecting the incorrect response (see the discussion of SVT in Chapter 5). Frederick et al. reported two cases in which defendants claimed amnesia and performed at substantially less-than-chance levels (i.e., 35.5% and 23.2%).

One potential danger of the SVT-EM is its assumption that different alternatives are equiprobable. When asked the hair color of the victim, a genuinely amnestic person might be more likely to guess "black" than "blond," based on prevalence, racial bias, or other unknown factors. To address this issue, Denney (1996) recommended that the questions be administered to a representative sample that has no knowledge of the crime. In his case studies, several participants scored at below-chance levels. However, this problem could likely be corrected via the elimination of skewed items.

In summary, the SVT-EM appears to be a highly effective tool for detecting feigned amnesia. For defendants with partial memories, testing them for "residual memory" by making their best estimate of nonremembered items would circumvent problems attaining below-chance probabilities. An untested but logical alternative would be to ask defendants to rank-order the likelihood of multiple alternatives (e.g., What day of the week did the crime occur? Approximately how much money was taken?). Complex probabilities could be computed regarding the proportion of incorrect responses before the correct response is given. The rank-order alternative would also require testing on individuals unfamiliar with the crime. Its potential advantage is that defendants would have great difficulty computing multiple probabilities.

Indirect Memory Tests

Horton, Smith, Barghout, and Connolly (1992) conducted a series of experiments with university samples that has implications for forensic evaluations. They utilized "indirect memory tests" that make no reference to the recall of prior events (e.g., a crime) but simply ask the person to complete tasks that implicitly rely on this knowledge. Because previous research had demonstrated that amnestic patients perform in the normal range on indirect memory tasks, Horton et al. (1992) hypothesized that simulators could be detected. Tasks included completion of words in which several letters are provided. They found that simulators tended to avoid the target words (e.g., *kn_ _ _* for *knife*) and speculated that this methodology might be applied to forensic assessments. To parallel these studies, criminal defendants would first be asked their complete recall for the time of the offense. Then they would be asked to complete indirect memory tests with key details cued.

This methodology faces several daunting challenges in its application to feigned amnesia by insanity evaluatees. Beyond gathering highly specific information about the crime, the following issues must be considered:

♦ Defendants must be supplied with "forgotten" information analogous to the research participants. However, providing such information blurs the distinction between retrograde and anterograde amnesia.

♦ A comparison group must be used and must be given identical information as the defendant in order to test the significance of any finding. For example, if presented with "40 Del _ _ _ _ _ St.," does anyone respond with the address (e.g., 40 Delaware St.) where the homicide occurred?

♦ Certainty in the results is likely to be constrained by the lack of specific data on genuine amnesias, particularly dissociative amnesias.[5]

In conclusion, the potential for indirect memory tests in assessing malingered amnesia has yet to be realized. Indirect memory tests provide a means to study the deliberate suppression of memory (Cercey, 1997). However, the challenges of creating a case-specific test with sufficient data on comparison samples is likely to militate against its application in all but the most problematic insanity cases. In such cases, indirect memory tests provide a potentially less-transparent method than SVT-EM; however, their results are more vulnerable to alternative explanations.

Other Methods

Other methods utilized in the assessment of retrograde amnesia typically involve specialized procedures, such as hypnosis, polygraph, and drug-assisted interviews. These procedures are summarized in Chapter 10, which also includes a description of their efficacy and a discussion of their relevance to criminal responsibility. In this segment, we offer a distillation of the findings that relate to retrograde amnesia.

Lynch and Bradford (1980) examined 22 defendants claiming amnesia with polygraph examinations. Using the polygraph for external validation, they categorized the reported amnesia for the time of the offense as either genuine, indeterminate, or deceptive. They used the control question technique (CQT; see Chapter 10) for the polygraph. Because the CQT has not been systematically tested with Axis I patients, it is unclear whether some mentally disordered defendants were accurately classified as deceptive. Moreover, the use of the CQT for differentiating feigned from genuine amnesia has not been sufficiently tested. In contrast, the guilty knowledge test (GKT) would appear especially adaptive to the evaluation of feigned amnesia.[6] As described in Chapter 10, with the GKT information known only to the perpetrator is presented in a multiple-choice format. When extensive information is available about the crime, several dozen questions could be created. Persons with "guilty knowledge" (i.e., memory of their criminal involvement) should evidence greater arousal to the correct alternatives, regardless of their verbal responses.

Both forensic hypnosis and drug-assisted interviews have been used to assess the accuracy of defendants' accounts regarding the time of the offense. As described in Chapter 10, both procedures have severe limitations on their usefulness in forensic assessments. While more information may be elicited from some defendants, the meaning of this further information is obscure. First, both persons with genuine dissociative amnesia and those feigning amnesia may report additional data with either hypnosis or drug-assisted interviews. Second, these procedures are likely to produce memory distortions (i.e., pseudomemories) that further complicate the assessment. As outlined in Chapter 10, the use of these procedures is generally discouraged in insanity evaluations.

A final method of examining feigned amnesia at the time of the offense is the inspection of MMPI profiles. Parwatikar, Holcomb, and Menninger (1985) compared 24 homicidal defendants who claimed amnesia to 50 homicidal defendants who confessed to their crimes. They found higher elevations for MMPI Scales 1, 2, and 3 for those claiming amnesia than for those confessing. As noted by Schacter (1986a), Parwatikar et al. made the tenuous assumption that individuals misclassified by a discriminant function were feigning amnesia. For this assumption to be true, the discriminant function would have to be a perfect measure of amnesia. In a sample of purportedly amnestic sex offenders, Bourget and Bradford (1995) failed to find MMPI differences when the amnestic offenders were compared to admitting and nonadmitting sex offenders. Given MMPI problems with discriminant validity (see Rogers & McKee, 1995), it is doubtful that a replicable pattern for circumscribed feigned amnesia could ever be established.

Dissociative Disorders and Criminal Responsibility

Legal and mental health commentators are deeply divided on whether dissociative disorders might warrant an acquittal in an insanity defense

(Perr, 1991). Because the dissension is crystallized with dissociative identity disorder (DID), the following discussion focuses on this controversial disorder. The basic argument for application of the insanity defense to the case of DID is that the defendant did not have an integrated person. Rather, coexisting within the same individual are both criminally responsible and nonresponsible personalities (Saks, 1997).

As an introduction for attorneys, DID, formerly known as multiple personality disorder, is characterized by two or more identities or personality states that recurrently govern behavior (American Psychiatric Association, 1994). Amnesia for personal information plays a critical role in allowing the relative independence of separate identities. The diagnosis of DID remains controversial. Historically, DID was considered to be extremely rare, with approximately 200 cases reported in the world literature (Gilmore & Kaufman, 1988). In stark contrast, Ross (1998) reported that he treats more than 200 cases *per year* in his own facility. Mental health professionals are divided as to whether (1) original reports on the prevalence of DID represented a startling *under-diagnosis* or (2) the popularity of dissociative treatment units has heralded a dramatic *overdiagnosis* of DID.

The controversy over the DID diagnosis (see Cardena & Spiegel, 1998) has contributed to the continued debates over the role of DID in criminal responsibility. In the following two sections, we examine the arguments for and against DID and its relevance to the NGRI verdict. We conclude with general guidelines for evaluating DID cases in the context of insanity evaluations.

The Equating of DID with Insanity

French and Shechmeister (1983) presented an argument for an "unconscious" defense for DID defendants. They argue that if the dominant personality is completely unaware (i.e., "unconscious") of a second personality and its criminal actions, then the dominant personality should not be held responsible. Utilizing the language of the ALI standard, French and Shechmeister argued that both the "ability to appreciate criminality" (cognitive prong) and to "conform his conduct" (volitional prong) may well be compromised in defendants with DID.

Saks (1995, 1997) offers a thoughtful and provocative view of DID and insanity. She considers three different conceptualizations of DID as (1) different people, (2) different personalities, and (3) components of a deeply divided personality. Irrespective of the conceptualization, Saks argues that nearly every DID NGRI case should result in an acquittal. For instance, she argues that innocent personalities under the "different people" conceptualization should not be punished because of a single perpetrating alter. With both different personalities and a divided personality, she maintains, the person likely lacks knowledge of the criminal act and cannot be held culpable.

DID and Skepticism

Radwin (1991) described the public and legal backlash at successful insanity defenses for DID defendants. Strong public outrage about DID as a basis for an insanity acquittal followed the highly publicized acquittal of Billy Milligan and his 24 personalities for repetitive acts of rape. Several courts have made clear that a DID diagnosis does not require an insanity acquittal (*Kirby v. State*, 1991; *State v. Rodrigues*, 1984).

Several commentators have questioned the advisability of dividing personality into separate entities for the purposes of criminal responsibility. In questioning the wisdom of distinct entities, Slovenko (1993) speculated whether this approach would require each personality to receive his/her own *Miranda* warnings and his/her own legal counsel. Appelbaum and Greer (1994) argued that DSM-IV has softened its emphasis on discrete personalities, which may have a concomitant effect on the courts. Opposed to the distinct entities, Behnke (1997) is the strongest advocate for the mental state of the person at the time irrespective of the DID diagnosis. According to Behnke, the thinking and behavior at the time of the offense is the critical issue. As an example from federal court, he observes that if the person or "personality" at the time of the offense was "able to appreciate the nature and quality or the wrongfulness of his acts," then the defendant should be found culpable.

General Guidelines for DID and Insanity

Appelbaum and Greer (1994) concluded that, despite the fanfare about DID, it is infrequently asserted and rarely successful in insanity cases. Citing unpublished data, they found that DID was the diagnosis in only 15 of 7,689 insanity cases, for a negligible rate of .002. Whether rare or not, however, forensic experts must carefully consider DID in cases where dissociative symptoms are present.

We have organized this subsection into four components that address: (1) potential bias, (2) authenticity of DID diagnosis, (3) legal approaches, and (4) clinical issues. These components provide a general framework for conceptualizing DID with reference to insanity evaluations.

Potential Bias

Lewis and Bard (1991) convincingly argued that DID is likely to be underdiagnosed in forensic cases because of experts' unwillingness to even consider the diagnosis. If an expert does not believe in the existence of the diagnosis, then his/her impartiality is brought into question. Even acknowledging the controversy surrounding the diagnosis, any categorical discounting of DID is problematic. Attorneys may wish to probe for potential bias with systematic inquiries. Examples of such inquiries include:

1. Have you ever diagnosed DID in your professional career? Have you ever consulted on or even observed a genuine case of DID?
2. [If "no" to question 1] Given your inexperience with DID, did you consult with an expert on DID in conducting your insanity evaluation of the defendant?
3. [If "no" to question 1] Do you believe that the diagnosis of DID occurs in clinical practice? What data would you need before you could testify unequivocally that a defendant has DID? Please tell me in detail about his/her clinical presentation.

Experts with a strong bias against the DID diagnosis are unable to be impartial in insanity cases where prominent dissociative symptoms are observed. The presence of such bias addresses directly the credibility of the forensic expert.

We are also concerned about experts in DID who have diagnosed hundreds of cases. While it is true that these experts are sought out by other health care professionals, the issue of advocacy must be addressed. In one instance, a highly touted DID expert suggested that the use of several nicknames was indicative of DID. Although DID patients may have used more than one nickname, this variable is unlikely to represent different identities per se. Rather, the incautious use of such ambiguous, non-DSM indices is likely to reflect its own bias. In this regard, attorneys may wish to question experts about diagnostic disagreements. We are left to wonder about the objectivity of a DID expert who has never disputed a DID diagnosis rendered by others.

Authenticity of DID Diagnosis

A critical consideration in the assessment of DID is the authenticity of the diagnosis. Authenticity is affected by four interrelated issues: (1) reliance of hypnosis, (2) iatrogenic (i.e., medically created) presentations, (3) malingering, and (4) other deception.

1. *Hypnosis.* Because nonhost personalities rarely occur during the assessment, examiners often rely on hypnosis. As described by Lewis and Bard (1991), controversy surrounds the use of hypnosis and its usefulness for diagnostic and forensic purposes (see Chapter 10). In addition, hypnosis may contribute to iatrogenic presentations via hypersuggestibility, and it is also vulnerable to malingering.

2. *Iatrogenic presentation.* Clinicians can reify dissociated personality fragments that can lead to "an escalating spiral of symptomatic distress, destructive behavior, and regressive unraveling of the personality" (Beahrs, 1994, p. 225). When patients with severe borderline personality disorders and traumatic histories are subjected to multiple hours of hypnosis several times per week, the likelihood of iatrogenic DID increases substantially. As an example of iatrogenic DID, one author (Rogers) was involved in an insanity case in which a highly publicized DID expert asserted a diagnosis of DID with more than 50 personalities. When intensive hypnosis and education regarding her "personalities" ceased, the patient's borderline personality disorder clearly emerged. Despite close scrutiny, no other personalities were observed during several years of outpatient treatment.

3. *Malingering.* As discussed in Chapter 10, defendants can both feign being in a hypnotic trance and feign while in a trance. The convenience of the DID "It wasn't me" defense greatly concerns both the courts and experts; the defendant does not need to create a long-standing disorder (e.g., schizophrenia) but asserts that the symptoms are typically *not* present. Rather, a submerged (i.e., inobservable and uncontrollable) personality subverts the defendant's intentions and overrides his/her will. The duping of mental health professionals in the Bianchi case (i.e., the Hillsdale strangler) and their subsequent embarrassment has made forensic experts especially sensitive to feigned DID (Miller & Stava, 1997).

4. *Other deception.* Lewis and Bard (1991) underscore an overlooked issue regarding deception among identities. Given the deeply conflictual nature of DID, some personalities may lie to each other and to the examiner. One purpose may be to attack the host personality and his/her credibility or culpability. According to Lewis and Bard (1991, p. 746), it is even possible for one personality to masquerade as a second personality. The unverifiability of personalities' statements and even their identities obviously magnifies the problems of credibility.

Legal Approaches

Behnke (1997) provides a succinct analysis of three different legal approaches used in the assessing of criminal responsibility among DID defendants: alter-in-control, each-alter, and host-alter. These legal approaches are outlined here:

1. *Alter-in-control.* The key issue is what alter (personality) was in control at the time of the offense and whether he/she met the insanity standard. The alter-in-control is the prevailing approach in state courts (Owens, 1997).

2. *Each-alter.* The key issue is whether each personality meets the insanity standard. The courts do not make clear the legal outcome in divided opinions (i.e., some personalities are responsible while others are not). Saks (1997) argues that all alters should be exculpated if any deserve an insanity acquittal.

3. *Host-alter.* The key issue is whether the dominant or primary personality met the insanity standard (see *United States v. Shaffer,* 1993).

From a clinical perspective, the alter-in-control would appear to be the most compelling in assessing the defendant's retrospective functioning at the time of the offense. As a rough comparison, a defendant with a bipolar disorder is assessed specifically for his/her functioning (e.g., depressed, hypomanic, or manic mood) at the time of the offense. However, forensic experts must clarify in the early stages of insanity evaluations which legal approach is to be utilized and applied in the relevant case law (Steinberg, Bancroft, & Buchanan, 1993).

Clinical Issues

The DSM criteria for DID have evolved during the last 2 decades (Slovenko, 1993). The emphasis in DSM-IV (American Psychiatric Association, 1994, p. 487) is on the presence of two or more identities or personality states that recurrently take control of the person's behavior. What constitutes a separate identity or personality state? According to DSM-IV, an identity or personality state is composed of "its own relatively enduring pattern of perceiving, relating to, and thinking about the environment and self" (American Psychiatric Association, 1994, p. 487). The most observable (ergo, verifiable) component of this complex definition is "relating to the environment."

One commonsensical approach to "relating to the environment" is whether persons in continued contact (e.g., spouses and members of immediate family) observe different identities that are not explainable by substance abuse. Notice that the emphasis is on *identity;* many persons act very differently with diverse reference groups (e.g., visiting with inlaws vs. socializing with high school friends). The key question is whether the person perceives him/herself as fundamentally different and assumes a new name and identity.

DSM-IV (American Psychiatric Association, 1994) reintroduced amnesia as a critical component of DID. Persons in close contact with the defendant should be able to document significant periods of memory loss, again not explainable by substance abuse. DID amnesia is very complex because some identities may vary widely in memory loss. In examining the genuineness of dissociative amnesia for different identities, the SVT-EM would appear to have merit. However, any extended use of hypnosis is likely to obscure data regarding the potential feigning of amnesia.

The unanticipated *de novo* discovery of DID during an insanity evaluation brings into question the convenience of the discovery and possibly heightens the ever-present possibility of feigning. Nevertheless, forensic experts cannot discard consideration of the diagnosis in such cases. As noted by Cardena and Spiegel (1998), the great majority of DID cases remain undiagnosed in their initial evaluations by mental health professionals. Especially with *de novo* insanity cases, forensic experts may wish to consult with DID specialists prior to making their diagnosis.

Other clinical considerations include the following:

1. The use of the SCID-D (see Steinberg, Bancroft, & Buchanan, 1993) and the DDIS may provide useful ancillary data. Although we advocated structured interviews for most differential diagnosis, the nature of self-report data is fundamentally different for cases in which DID is suspected. Depending on the identity, dissimilar and potentially contradictory information can be elicited. Therefore, the SCID-D and DDIS should not be used as the primary basis for the DID diagnosis.

2. Extensive use of hypnosis is likely to erode diagnostic certainty in DID diagnosis. The introduction of pseudomemories and the potential for iatrogenic DID complicate the clinical presentation and subsequent diagnosis.

Automatism and Criminal Responsibility

Automatism refers to an unconscious state, such as somnambulism, in which the person carries out nonvolitional behavior. Because defendants with automatism often experience amnesia, we have included automatism in this chapter. In this section, we briefly describe the different types of automatism and discuss their relevance to criminal responsibility.

Fenwick (1990) delineated the main types of automatism: sleep automatism, epileptoid automatism, alcohol and drug automatism, hypoglycemic automatism, and psychogenic automatisms. These types are described below:

1. *Sleep automatism.* Sleep automatism or somnambulism are typically subsumed under sleep-walking disorders. According to DSM-IV (American Psychiatric Association, 1994), sleep-walking disorders are characterized by (a) unresponsiveness to others, (b) great difficulty in awakening, and (c) amnesia for the episode. Most behaviors that occur in this state are routine with low complexity, although exceptions do occur. According to Fenwick (1987), somnambulism rarely has its onset in adulthood and typically occurs in the first 2 hours of sleep. With criminal acts, Fenwick (1987) noted that attempts to conceal the crime are very rare.

2. *Epileptoid automatism.* The relationship of epilepsy to crime is discussed in more detail in Chapter 10 in the section "The EEG and Diagnostic Imaging." Here we wish to stress the extreme rarity of aggressive behavior during seizures and its brevity, averaging 29 seconds (Delgardo-Esceuta et al., 1981). According to Fenwick (1990), persons with epileptoid automatisms should manifest (a) no premeditation or concealment, (b) appear confused and disoriented, and (c) be amnestic to the episode. Fenwick also cautioned that memory prior to seizure should be intact; reports of memory loss just prior to the seizure can be used to disconfirm the diagnosis.

3. *Alcohol and drug automatism.* The existence of this type of automatism is debatable. As outlined in Chapter 10 (see "Measures of Alcohol and Drug Abuse"), intoxication may lead to blackouts with a failure to register memories. However, blackouts should not be confused with automatism (Rogers & Mitchell, 1991). The crucial difference is that most alcoholics experiencing blackouts were aware of their behavior at the time of alcohol ingestion. Therefore, their behaviors were not automatistic. Voluntary intoxication does not typically exculpate defendants from responsibility; however, in some states it may negate the mens rea requirement of certain crimes (Dressler, 1995). Its alternative, involuntary intoxication, is both rare and difficult to establish (Goldstein, 1992b). Automatism based on substance abuse appears nearly impossible to establish unless highly atypical reactions to prescribed medications can be documented.

4. *Hypoglycemic automatism.* Diabetics may experience hypoglycemia because of low blood sugar. Although confusion is common, a state of unconsciousness is very rare. In addition, most diabetics have control

over hypoglycemia through diet and medication. Their unwillingness to exercise control would negate automatism (Fenwick, 1990; Melton et al., 1997).

    5. *Psychogenic automatism.* Current thinking about dissociative disorders is not aligned with automatism. In the prior section on DID, we noted that separate identities or personality states are sometimes aware of their actions.

    Melton et al. (1997) in their review report that the automatism defense is rarely raised in criminal cases and when raised is unlikely to be successful. The convenience of asserting a single external factor (e.g., sleepwalking or low blood sugar) as wholly responsible for the index crime is likely to stretch the credibility of many jurors, especially when other alternative explanations (e.g., prior conflicts) are available. As noted by Melton et al. (1997), an additional issue is the controllability of the automatistic behavior. As delineated by Rogers and Mitchell (1991), if the defendant could foresee the possibility of automatistic behavior (e.g., seizures), he/she should take precautions both in terms of treatment (e.g., adhere to drug regimen) and risks to others (e.g., avoid target shooting).

    The defense of automatism differs from insanity on several significant points. First, the automatism defense is not predicated on a mental disorder. Second, an acquittal for automatism does not carry the postacquittal requirements (e.g., civil commitment) found with an insanity acquittal. Most courts have viewed automatism as a separate defense, although a minority have regarded it as a specialized insanity defense (see Schopp, 1991).

Memory Loss and Distortion

Under the rubric of eyewitness testimony, extensive reviews (e.g., Loftus, 1979; Penrod, Fulero, & Cutler, 1995; Wells, 1987) have summarized the vast literature on memory loss and distortion following involvement as an observer of a violent crime. The purpose of this section is not to provide an in-depth examination of variables affecting the accuracy of recall. Rather, this section presents an overview of memory as a reconstructive process. Its twin purposes are to provide experts and attorneys with (1) information on how memory distortion may affect defendant's recall in insanity evaluations, and (2) clinical guidelines on how experts may minimize memory distortion.

    Yuille and Daylen (1998) reported that patterns of recall vary markedly across persons involved in traumatic events. They identified seven distinct patterns that may affect posttrauma recall. In addition to these previously discussed (e.g., dissociative amnesia), several patterns emerged that distort memory: (1) normal forgetting, (2) active forgetting (i.e., conscious avoidance of the memory), and (3) script memory (i.e., recall of specific events becomes blended together). While most research has focused on normal forgetting, these other patterns also exert influences on the memory of traumatic events.

A Fundamental Misassumption about Defendant's Recall

Many attorneys and forensic experts intensely scrutinize variations in the defendant's recall at the time of the crime. Variations in the defendant's detailed account are sometimes taken as evidence that the defendant is attempting to manipulate the process, possibly even malinger.[7] What is the underlying assumption of scrutinized inconsistencies? The implicit assumption appears to be the existence of so-called flashbulb memories. Simply put, *flashbulb memories* assume that unique and highly emotional events will be remembered with great detail and accuracy. However, the validity of flashbulb memories has been called into question. McCloskey, Wible, and Cohen (1988) found that flashbulb memories are similar to ordinary memories; they suffer from the same problems with accuracy and completeness.

The danger of flashbulb-memories misassumption is their intuitive appeal. Most mental health and legal professionals are fully aware that memory can never be equated with a videotape, yet their memories after an emotionally evoking event often appear especially vivid and real. However, these perceptions of vividness do not translate into a cameralike accuracy.

Memory as a Reconstructive Process

Goodman and Hahn (1987) described the basic reconstructive process of memory. In the *acquisition phase*, individuals cannot possibly process all information occurring. Therefore, they selectively encode what is salient and novel to them. In the *retention phase*, some details are readily forgotten or distorted. Information provided by others (e.g., police or defense attorney) may alter memories. In the *retrieval phase*, the type of questions and other environmental conditions will further distort memories.

What are the implications of reconstructed memory? Simply this: *Even the most cooperative, self-disclosing, and forthright defendants will have inaccuracies and distortions in their accounts of the index crimes.* By themselves, variations in memory details are nothing more than that. They occur in every defendant, forensic expert, and criminal attorney.

Buckhout (1974) is responsible for discovering a fundamental paradox in memory recall: with the passage of time, individuals become *less* accurate in their recall, but *more* certain in their accuracy. When applied to insanity evaluations, Buckhout's paradox suggests that defendants may become more adamant in stating the accuracy of their recall of the offenses, while at the same time their accuracy is actually decreasing. Forensic experts should not confuse a defendant's certainty with his/her accuracy (see also Deffenbacher, Bothwell, & Brigham, 1986).

Loftus (1979) clearly delineated the malleability of memory to external events. Memory is subordinate to meaning. In asking research participants to complete a questionnaire following a film of a car accident, she discovered that changing a single word in the question could substantially affect recall.[8] Wells (1987) reviewed the literature on the effects of questioning on witnesses' recall of a simulated crime. The following results are germane to insanity evaluations:

+ Unstructured accounts produced the greatest accuracy.
+ Open-ended questions also evidenced a high degree of accuracy.
+ Leading questions had substantially lower accuracy.
+ Multiple-choice questions had very low accuracy.

Leading questions can lead to subsequent distortions in memory. When research participants are given false information in the form of a question, that false information is encoded as part of the original memory (Loftus, Miller, & Burns, 1987). Applying this finding to insanity evaluations suggests that misinformation can produce distorted results. For example, suppose the defendant is asked: "When she made a threatening gesture with the knife, what did you do?" Let's assume the female victim was simply holding the knife. Thus this leading question could produce a pseudomemory regarding the "threatening gesture." With the passage of time, pseudomemories become easier to produce (Loftus, 1992).

The defendant's self-perceptions may also influence the reconstructive process. Beyond any attempt to influence others, defendants are likely to engage in a self-justifying recollection of events. Criminal defendants, like other persons, attempt to make sense of their actions. Defendants are likely to find different answers to the question, "What kind of person would have done this crime?" As we noted previously, the *meaning* that defendants ascribe to their criminal actions is likely to affect their recall of the crime.

The reconstructive process is likely to be further distorted by the presence of psychotic symptoms at the time of the alleged offense or in subsequent months. Experts need to be alert to how memory reconstruction may serve either psychotic or nonpsychotic explanations. A special concern is a psychotic defendant who has been successfully treated. In this case, the defendant may seek rational, nonpsychotic explanations for his/her behavior.

Minimizing Memory Distortion: Clinical Guidelines

Given the vulnerability of the defendant's memory, forensic experts must be sensitive to avoiding further memory distortions. Toward this end, we offer the following guidelines for clinical inquiries during insanity evaluations:

1. The forensic expert should use general nondirectional questions, particularly in the initial evaluative phase. This format allows the defendant to recall to the best of his/her ability what occurred and what the defendant remembers about his/her internal processes. After the defendant gives a complete and unstructured account, the forensic expert will likely ask more specific questions regarding the self-report. However, there is no need for these questions to be leading. A general question (e.g., "What were you feeling at the time ___ happened?") is clearly superior to a leading question (e.g., "Were you really enraged at the time ___ happened?").

2. The sequencing of the defendant's self-report should be kept chronological during the initial assessment because the *order* of recall may influence the *extent* of recall. Thus, a chronological self-report allows for less structuring and potential contamination of the defendant's memory.

3. The forensic expert should avoid the *loaded premise*. This type of inquiry involves the use of dependent clauses with which the defendant may or may not agree. For example, "After Mr. ___ ridiculed you, what did you do?" may be loaded both factually and emotionally, thereby distorting the defendant's recall. Particularly in the case of emotionally loaded questions, the forensic expert may antagonize the defendant into disregarding his or her memory and responding with defensiveness or defiance. As an egregious example, consider the following: "How did you let such a little punk get the best of you?"

4. The forensic expert should minimize explanatory-type questions (i.e., "Why?") interspersed with the defendant's report. Such questions interposed with recall may unnecessarily distort the defendant's memory

of his/her thinking and motivation. More acceptable are questions about *what* the defendant was feeling and thinking.

5. The forensic expert should minimize the use of speculative questions. Examples of such questions include: (a) "What do you imagine would happen?" (b) "What was the victim thinking?" and (c) "What was likely to happen if you hadn't acted?" Given the indistinct boundary between memory and nonmemory, such speculations may be added unwittingly to the defendant's memory, thereby contaminating further recall.

Conclusion

The retrospective nature of insanity evaluations makes the reliance on memory an essential element of the process. The etiology of memory loss is complex and multidetermined. Although relatively infrequent, specific organic amnesias may substantially affect the recall of personal and episodic memory. More commonly, dissociative amnesias are reported in which dissociation must be differentiated from the desire to forget. With all reported amnesias, the genuineness of the memory loss must be addressed.

The relationship of dissociation to criminal responsibility must be addressed. Despite the fanfare regarding DID, the diagnosis does exist and may serve as a basis for an insanity acquittal. As a cautionary note, we ask that attorneys and forensic experts be aware of the professional polarization regarding DID and not succumb to it. Automatisms with their concomitant memory losses may be considered in conjunction with assessments of criminal responsibility. Very rare cases occur (e.g., driving away from the scene of an accident with a postconcussion syndrome) in which automatisms must be considered in relation to criminal behavior.

Memory loss and memory distortion are frequently overlooked by forensic experts. Of critical importance, memory inconsistencies and inaccuracies are inevitable in insanity evaluations. To minimize further memory distortions, we provide forensic experts with guidelines for conducting insanity evaluations. These guidelines may also provide the basis for rigorous cross-examination of experts when memory inconsistencies are used in formulating opinions regarding the defendant's veracity.

Notes

1. Consider the following example: When asked, "Do you remember Mr. *X* from high school?", the individual may reply affirmatively, although the memory was only activated by the question.

2. For dissociative disorders, DSM-IV requires additional criteria not found in DSM-III-R: (1) symptoms result in substantial distress or impairment, and (2) additional disorders must be excluded.

3. Capacity to learn new information is generally intact with dissociative amnesia but often compromised with organic amnesia. Therefore, it is reasonable to hypothesize that tests of malingered memory would be particularly effective with dissociative amnesia.

4. As analogue studies, all participants attributed their memory loss to traumatic brain injuries (i.e., automobile accidents) and were involved in personal injury suits.

5. Studies of indirect memory tests have focused on organic amnesias.

6. Although not formally tested on mentally disordered offenders, the type of questions are unlikely to be affected systematically by the defendants' mental state. For example, "Was the victim wearing a green dress? . . . a blue dress? . . . a yellow dress? . . . a red dress?" Also, the use of many questions militates against any single response biasing the outcome.

7. Ironically, overly consistent accounts are sometimes described as having a rehearsed quality, which may also be described as an attempt to manipulate the process.

8. In questioning the speed of colliding cars, the word "smashed" produced reliably higher speeds than the word "hit" (Loftus & Palmer, 1974).

PART II

CLINICAL METHODS

Chapter 7

Clinical Interviews

Overview
Goals
Diagnostic Issues
Content Issues
Corroborative Clinical Interviews
Conclusion

Overview

Clinical interviews represent both the cornerstone and the keystone of insanity evaluations. Clinical interviews constitute the cornerstone of insanity evaluations because they serve as the foundation for gathering data specific to each case. *The greatest challenge for insanity evaluations is the assessment of a unique defendant under singular circumstances.* Only clinical interviews have the versatility for systematically collecting background data and information about the offense itself. Likewise, clinical interviews serve as the keystone of insanity evaluations. Despite the great value of standardized methods (structured interviews and testing), clinical interviews are critical for integrating clinical data and acquiring essential information about the crucial relationships between psychopathology and criminal behavior. In the next section, we emphasize the constraints on clinical interviews when utilized without structured interviews.

Impediments to Interview-Based Assessments

The versatility of clinical interviews, which allow the full exploration of case-specific information, is achieved at the expense of standardization.

Particularly when interviews are not coupled with structured interviews, the potential for biased evaluations increases. Borum, Otto, and Golding (1993) provide a succinct yet balanced review regarding potential constraints on the usefulness of clinical data in forensic assessments. In keeping with Borum et al. (1993), we outline four relevant dimensions as they relate to insanity evaluations:

1. *Confirmatory bias.* Experts tend to (a) seek and overvalue data that is consistent with their hypothesis, and (b) disregard or undervalue data that are inconsistent with their hypothesis. For example, an expert may assume that the defendant in a sexual assault had nonpsychotic motivations for the crime; this bias may result in an emphasis of antisocial/paraphiliac symptoms and a deemphasis of psychotic symptoms. Systematic application of structured interviews (e.g., SADS) is likely to minimize this bias.

2. *Anchoring or primacy bias.* Consistent with hypothesis-testing models of assessment (Rogers, 1986), initial ideas and formulations are difficult to discard. For example, hearing an attorney's theory about the defendant at the onset of an evaluation may cause an expert to form initial hypotheses that prove difficult to abandon. Potential solutions include (a) use of systematic data gathering (e.g., structured interviewing), (b) avoidance of forensic identification (e.g., refraining from lengthy preevaluation interviews with attorneys; see Chapter 3), and (c) rigorous consideration of alternative hypotheses. In the case of John Wayne Gacy, the notorious serial murderer, several nonforensic colleagues exemplified the primacy bias in advancing their initial formulation: "Gacy had to be crazy to do what he did."[1]

3. *Hindsight bias.* Because they already know the outcome, forensic experts may overvalue "logical" antecedents in explaining the crime. For example, their knowledge that a violent murder occurred without any apparent rational explanation may lead experts to overvalue antecedent information (e.g., setbacks in the defendant's recent past). One possible solution (Fischoff, 1982) is to require experts to produce countervailing evidence (i.e., information that supports other conclusions) to deliberately address the possibility of hindsight bias. In the above example, the expert would marshal evidence of rational thinking (e.g., planning for the crime) before drawing any conclusions about whether the motivation for the crime was rational or irrational. This approach has had some success in reducing overconfidence in diagnoses (Arkes, Faust, Guilmette, & Hart, 1988).

4. *Overreliance on unique data.* Exotic symptoms and behaviors tend to command greater attention. Described in the literature as "salience

bias" (Taylor, 1982), highly distinctive stimuli are likely to unduly influence subsequent judgments. In the Jeffrey Dahmer case, bizarre sexual acts and cannibalism may have diverted attention from diagnostically relevant material. Again, the use of standardized assessment methods tends to minimize the importance accorded to exotic symptoms and extreme behaviors.

Goals

The goals of an insanity evaluation differ both qualitatively and quantitatively from those of nonforensic evaluations. In addition to a careful appraisal of the defendant's believability, the assessment of criminal responsibility requires a thorough and thoughtful examination for two discrete periods: (1) the time of the offense, for determining criminal responsibility; and (2) the current time, for comparison purposes. This section of the chapter is organized into five segments, addressing the defendant's (1) credibility, (2) experience of the offense, (3) motivation for the crime and its relationship to psychopathology, (4) awareness of criminality, and (5) control over criminal behavior.

Establishing the Defendant's Credibility

A major purpose of clinical interviews is the appraisal of the defendant's believability in his/her account of index offenses and his/her own behavior. Since forensic experts cannot directly observe many symptoms and associated features, they must assess the accuracy of the defendant's reports. A combination of extensive clinical and collateral interviews, buttressed by the SADS (see Chapter 9) and corroborative records, often comprises the best data base for making this important decision.

An important admonition in assessing a defendant's believability is to *avoid implicit allegations of secondary gain.* Rogers and Reinhardt (1998) examined secondary gain and its use/misuse in professional practice; they found that mental health professionals conceptualize secondary gain differently depending on the context. In clinical practice, psychologists and psychiatrists are likely to construe secondary gain as either (1) the gratification of intrapsychic needs (psychodynamic perspective) or (2) the psychosocial reinforcement of maladaptive behaviors for avoiding negative stimuli (behavioral perspective). In contrast, forensic experts often view the basic motivation as the deliberate acquisition of a highly desired legal objective (e.g., an insanity acquittal). Unfortunately, some forensic experts mistakenly equate the *potential* for secondary gain with the *assessment* of secondary gain. Although an insanity acquittal may spare a defendant a lengthy incarceration or even free him/her from the threat of execution, experts can make no assumptions about a particular defendant's motivation. As an analogue, simply because many forensic experts may have the potential to claim unearned financial gain (e.g., by overcalculating their professional time), we should never presume that a specific forensic expert is engaged in this unethical and illegal behavior. Based on the conceptual and clinical problems with secondary gain (see Rogers & Reinhardt, 1998), we strongly recommend against the use of secondary gain as a construct in forensic settings.

A defendant's credibility may be affected by both intentional and unintentional distortions in self-reporting. Intentional distortions are discussed at length in Chapter 5. Unintentional distortions may arise from (1) the malleability of memory (e.g., reconstructions of traumatic events), and (2) the influences of external events (e.g., interrogations). The malleability of memory (see Chapter 6) may affect the accuracy of recall in a defendant who believes in the accuracy of his/her account. Moreover, police investigations and prior evaluations are likely to exert an often subtle influence on the defendant's memory of events and the significance attached to them.

Credibility is not the touchstone of objectivity; no sources of data are shielded from subjective factors. However, extended interviews with the defendant are likely to assist the forensic expert in reaching conclusions about the defendant's presentation and its plausibility. In this regard, we prefer a detailed rather than an intuitive approach to plausibility:

♦ *Detailed approach.* The forensic expert relies on a systematic review of details provided by the defendant, including comparisons of narrative descriptions to specific responses. From this perspective, the goal is the painstaking assembling of specific information to evaluate its plausibility.

♦ *Intuitive approach.* The forensic expert relies on a broad appraisal of believability (e.g., "Is this defendant on the level?"). Our concern with the intuitive approach is that it tends to underutilize empirical data (e.g., consistency of symptoms across interviews) and often involves a vague matching (e.g., "This defendant seems like other defendants that were believable"; see Kahneman & Tversky, 1982). This intuitive process is thwarted by a lack of information regarding the actual classification (believable vs. nonbelievable); therefore, this matching may simply be a perpetuation of inaccurate perceptions (see Dawes, 1989).

Credibility should not be confused with consistency. The defendant's impairment at both the time of the offense and the current time may affect his/her consistency. Very disorganized patients are often inconsistent within the same interview. In establishing credibility, *patterns* of inconsistency are much more important than the mere *presence* of inconsistency. When the inconsistencies *only* involve the addition of potentially exculpatory information (e.g., sudden remembrance of a command hallucination that compels the criminal act), this is relevant to the defendant's believability. More random or indiscriminant inconsistencies raise questions about the accuracy of self-reporting but do not necessarily address the defendant's sincerity. In such cases, collateral sources will be critical in establishing the defendant's symptoms and behavior.

The issue of consistency has been used occasionally as a two-edged sword against claims of insanity. Whether the defendant is consistent or inconsistent is employed as evidence of sanity. The specious logic follows two propositions:

♦ If the defendant is consistent in his/her retrospective account, then this consistency indicates a high level of functioning. Ergo, the defendant is sane.

♦ If the defendant is inconsistent in his/her retrospective account, then this inconsistency indicates a strong likelihood of feigning, but not severe impairment. Ergo, the defendant is sane.

An important consideration in establishing the defendant's credibility is whether the defendant admits to committing the criminal behavior in question. Defendants who deny their participation in the criminal act or report amnesia for the offense pose a daunting challenge to forensic experts. Without the defendant's own account of the criminal behavior, insanity is very difficult to establish. However, cases are found in which either denial or amnesia becomes the central issue. With respect to the former, the plausibility of the defendant's account can often be ascertained. For example, when several disinterested witnesses report behavior directly contradicting the defendant's account (e.g., "I wasn't even there" or "I didn't have a weapon"), this information is germane to the defendant's believability. More often, the defendant's version is less verifiable, requiring inferences from multiple data sources. Similar issues exist with reported amnesia, except with amnesia claims the forensic expert has an opportunity to evaluate the genuineness of memory loss and its apparent etiology (see Chapter 6).

Phenomenological Issues in Establishing the Defendant's Experience

The defendant's account of his/her emotions, thoughts, and behavior preceding, during, and following the offense forms the essential framework for the evaluation of criminal responsibility. For this purpose, defining the "time of the offense" involves three phases: (1) preparatory actions, (2) the crime itself, and (3) immediate postoffense behavior. In other words, the crime must be understood within its context. Both preceding and ensuing behavior are vital to understanding the defendant's awareness of criminality and the controllability of his/her behavior.

The forensic expert should make an effort to understand the defendant's phenomenological framework. To do so, the following issues should be addressed:

1. What is the relationship between the defendant's thoughts and reported emotions?
2. Similarly, what is the relationship between (a) the defendant's thoughts and emotions and (b) his/her subsequent behavior?
3. Were there any describable changes in the defendant's sensations or perceptions?
4. If so, were these changes in perceptions related to the defendant's thoughts, emotions, or behavior?

The goal of understanding the defendant's phenomenological framework is an uninterrupted account in as much detail as possible of what occurred one or more days prior to the crime, during the crime, and immediately following the crime. It is important to let the defendant know that the forensic expert wants to know every salient detail about his/her thoughts, emotions, and behavior. Prompts during this time should be very general and open-ended:

- What happened next? (Behavior)
- What were you aware of? (Perceptions)
- What were you thinking? (Cognitions)
- What were you feeling? (Emotions)

One objective of this detailed account and inquiry is to test the limits of the defendant's recall. The defendant will not recall many thoughts, emotions, and perceptions. However, the more salient elements of the defendant's experience are likely to be retained. Subsequent questions may explore the relationships between thoughts and other elements of the defendant's experience. This thorough and un-hurried examination of the defendant's phenomenological experiences forms the baseline for more focused inquiries.

The Defendant's Motivation

A major goal in criminal responsibility assessments is to address the defendant's past and current life goals. During the period prior to and including the criminal behavior, what did the defendant want to accomplish? The appraisal of this goal is achieved by both the defendant's account and inferences from his/her behavior:

1. During the period prior to the offense, what were the defendant's stated goals?
2. How did the defendant's life circumstances, at that period of time, fulfill these goals?
3. What was accomplished by the crime in relationship to the defendant's goals?
4. If the defendant was to be assessed solely on his/her behavior, what are the likely purposes served by the criminal behavior? To what extent was the criminal behavior successful or unsuccessful in reaching its goals?
5. What motivated the defendant during the period of the crime to seek this alternative over other choices?
6. In considering these motivational issues, what is the most parsimonious and demonstrable explanation for the defendant's criminal behavior?

An important factor in ascertaining the defendant's motivation is the degree of planning and preparation observed in the criminal behavior. A well-planned and executed crime may suggest a different motivational structure than an unplanned or random offense. Table 7.1 contrasts the degree of planning and preparation for sane and insane defendants. An important observation illustrated in Table 7.1 is that detailed planning is relatively uncommon among all defendants but especially infrequent among those considered insane (i.e., 4.3%). Equally important is the quality of planning/preparation. For example, a woman with systematic delusions may have very involved ideas about how to stop enemy agents from hurting her; however, the irrationality of her plans (e.g., use of an umbrella to protect against gamma rays) is germane to the assessment of her criminal responsibility.

TABLE 7.1. Planning and Preparation for the Crime

Degree of planning and preparation	Sane defendants	Insane defendants
Elaborate planning and preparation extending over a week	0.3%	0.0%
Detailed planning and considerable preparation extending over at least several days	2.8%	1.1%
Detailed planning with some general preparation	10.4%	3.2%
Some general planning; little or no preparation	22.6%	9.5%
Thoughts about the crime; no real planning or preparation	27.8%	21.1%
Unplanned; no forethought or preparation	36.1%	65.3%

The Defendant's Diagnosis

On occasion, diagnoses are improperly equated with criminal responsibility. Defendants with schizophrenia are assumed to lack the requisite abilities to comprehend the criminality of their actions. More commonly, diagnoses (e.g., personality disorders) are inappropriately equated with sanity. The underlying logic (e.g., "not psychotic, therefore not insane") is indefensible. Although most nonpsychotic defendants are sane, each defendant deserves a thorough and fair evaluation.

Despite the previous analysis, certain disorders may be precluded as the sole basis for an insanity defense. For example, Oregon amended its statutes to preclude defendants with only Axis II diagnoses from being found NGRI (Oregon Revised Statute 161.295, 1996); for rationale, see Reichlin, Bloom, and Williams (1993). The ALI standard excludes defendants whose disorder is "manifested only by repeated criminal or otherwise antisocial behavior." While intended to disallow persons with antisocial personality disorder (APD), this provision fell short of its expectations. Because APD is a broader category than antisocial behavior with developmental, familial, and genetic characteristics (Bursten, 1982; Dinwiddle, 1996), it is not prohibited by the ALI standard.

What diagnoses have resulted in successful insanity verdicts? In the insanity data base (see Appendix A), we compiled data on the primary diagnoses for 5,000 acquittees (see Table 7.2). These numbers should be viewed as approximations because (1) some studies used postacquittal diagnoses and (2) very infrequent diagnoses were not incorporated into this data base.

As noted in Table 7.2, schizophrenic disorders accounted for the majority (62.2%) of the defendants acquitted as NGRI. This finding incorporates large-scale research on characteristics of successful insanity defenses (Bloom et al., 1991; Silver et al., 1994). For example, Rice and Harris (1990) found that psychotic disorders, especially schizophrenia, were implicated in 75% of insanity acquittals. Moreover, the courts are more likely to agree with experts' recommendations when psychotic

TABLE 7.2. Postverdict Diagnoses among NGRI Patients from Forensic Data Base

Diagnostic category	Mental disorder	Total	Percentage
Psychosis		3,280	65.6
	Schizophrenia	3,112	62.2
	Schizoaffective	30	0.6
	Other psychoses	26	0.5
	Psychosis (ungrouped)	112	2.2
Mood disorders		251	5.0
	Major mood disorder	228	4.6
	Major depression[a]	8	0.2
	Bipolar disorder	15	0.3
Organic disorders and mental retardation		290	5.8
	Organic	103	2.1
	Mental retardation	187	3.7
Personality disorders		601	12.0
	Axis II disorders[b]	601	12.0
	Antisocial personality	252	5.0
Other disorders or conditions		578	11.6
	Substance abuse	559	11.2
	Malingering[c]	19	0.4
Total sample with primary diagnoses		5,000[d]	100.0

Note. Percentages are only approximations because they do not take into account very infrequent diagnoses (e.g., dissociative identity disorder) reported in the forensic literature.

[a]Probably an underestimate because depressed patients with mood-incongruent psychotic features were classified historically as psychotic.

[b]Personality disorders include antisocial personality disorder.

[c]Problematic patients were diagnosed by hospital staff at one maximum security hospital without use of standardized measures.

[d]An additional 573 NGRI patients either had diagnoses that did not conform to the above categories or had their diagnoses deferred.

diagnoses are presented (Howard & Clark, 1985; Rogers, Cavanaugh, et al., 1984).

Beadoin, Hodgins, and Lavoie (1993) compared two groups of patients with schizophrenia who were involved in homicides: 14 NGRI patients and 12 convicted offenders. Perhaps the most revealing observation was that 10 additional NGRI patients were too impaired to participate in the study. Interestingly, substance abuse was common among both schizophrenic groups, but NGRI patients were unlikely to have been intoxicated at the time of the offense.

Mood disorders were underrepresented in the data base, accounting for only 5.0% of the NGRI patients. Possible explanations for this percentage include the following:

1. The cognitive emphasis of insanity standards weighs against mood disorders where the awareness of criminality is not likely to be completely impaired. For insanity standards that do not include a volitional prong, severe manic episodes may not sufficiently compromise cognitive functioning to warrant an NGRI verdict.
2. Diagnostic imprecision, especially in early studies, may lead to a disproportionate number of NGRI patients being diagnosed as psychotic.
3. Some studies included NGRI patients with diagnoses more than 5 years following their acquittals. Because mood disorders appear to be less chronic than schizophrenic disorders, post-acquittal assessments may underestimate their prevalence at the time of the offense.

Distilling earlier research on mood disorders, Teplin and Voit (1996) found a substantial incidence of mood disorders among male and especially female detainees. While diagnosis of depression and bipolar disorders are clearly relevant to criminal responsibility, the likelihood of such disorders compromising cognitive abilities is significantly lower than psychotic disorders. One possible exception is cases of intrafamilial violence (Kunjukrishnan & Varan, 1992), primarily those cases that involve a gross misappraisal of circumstances (e.g., killing one's own children to save them from the pains of living).

Anxiety disorders appear to be very infrequently the primary diagnosis among defendants evaluated for insanity. The main exception appears to be post-traumatic stress disorders (PTSD) in which flashbacks are sometimes asserted as impairing cognitive or volitional capacity. However, even PTSD appears to be rarely asserted as the primary diagnosis in insanity cases. In this regard, Appelbaum et al. (1993) found that PTSD was rarely diagnosed (28 of 8,135 cases, or .003) in insanity cases and less likely than other disorders to be successful (i.e., NGRI verdicts: 28.6% for PTSD vs. 41.5% for other disorders).

The data base also yielded several surprises with respect to the prevalence of Axis II and substance abuse disorders. Axis II disorders appeared to be the primary diagnosis in 12.0% of NGRI patients; interestingly, APD was represented in 5.0% of the acquittals. Substance abuse disorders composed the primary diagnosis in 11.2% of the cases. These estimates underscore the point that primary diagnoses of personality and substance abuse disorders, ipso facto, should not be used as curtail the insanity evaluation. Instead, the impairment stemming from any mental disorder is the most important consideration.

The Defendant's Awareness of Criminality

The determination of criminal responsibility requires an assessment of the defendant's knowledge of his/her alleged criminal behavior and understanding of criminal responsibility. Of particular interest is (1) how the defendant conceptualized his/her behavior at the time of the offense and (2) how this conceptualization is similar or dissimilar to the conceptualization at the current time.

1. Did the defendant view his/her behavior as criminal? Moreover, did this person view it as morally justified?
2. What were the defendant's expectations of the legal system if apprehended for the alleged crime?
3. What did the defendant believe would be a fair and just resolution of the current legal situation?

Sane and insane defendants vary widely in their awareness of the criminality of their actions. As presented in Table 7.3, the great majority of those defendants clinically evaluated as insane evidenced either vague (35.8%) or no awareness (45.3%) of the criminal nature of their behavior. In contrast, lack of awareness was very rare in sane defendants and was associated with severe intoxication. In its clinical determination, lack of awareness must amount to more than simply ignorance or a misconstruing of the criminal code (e.g., "My home is my castle; therefore, I should kill any trespassers"). The lack of awareness must stem from a mental disorder. Typically, the defendant's delusional or disorganized beliefs, if they were true, would legally justify his/her actions.

TABLE 7.3. Degree of Awareness for the Crime

Degree of awareness	Sane defendants	Insane defendants
Relative complete awareness of the criminality; general understanding of penalties	67.4%	11.5%
Awareness of criminality and penalties; lack of appreciation of the severity of the crime	27.4%	7.4%
Vague awareness of the criminality and wrongfulness	3.5%[a]	35.8%
No awareness of criminality or wrongfulness	1.7%[b]	45.3%

[a]When cases of severe intoxication are removed, this estimate is 0.8%.
[b]When cases of severe intoxication are removed, this estimate is 0.0%.

The Defendant's Self-Control

This goal of the insanity evaluation addresses the defendant's perceptions of his/her actions and the degree of control over them. This is a particularly complex issue that involves establishing what it means for the defendant to be "in control" or "out of control." *Control is best conceptualized as a chronologically based continuum.* Many defendants may experience diminished control of their behavior at the end-stages of an emotionally charged crime. For example, a defendant may report, "After attacking the victim, I couldn't stop stabbing him." For issues of insanity, the initiation of the criminal behavior is a critical point in establishing self-control.

Four critical issues must be addressed:

1. What did the defendant perceive to be his/her choices at the time of the criminal behavior? Can these choices be understood in terms of the defendant's goals?
2. To what extent were these choices forced on the defendant, as opposed to being experienced as options?
3. What was the defendant's capacity to withhold or discontinue the criminal behavior?
4. Although the defendant may have acted in an explosive or violently unrestrained manner, to what extent did the defendant make choices prior to this behavior with the knowledge that such behavior is likely to occur? This final issue addresses the defendant who may know that his/her presence and/or actions in a particular situation may lead to violence and yet deliberately chooses to be in a situation in which the likelihood is greatly increased.

Many defendants report that they lost control of their behavior during the offense. Sometimes the defendants' underlying logic is understandable although not compelling. If the behavior is highly atypical (e.g., murder), irrational (e.g., homicide as a method of dissolving a contentious marriage), and has devastating consequences (e.g., life imprisonment), a defendant might argue he/she is not in control of his/her behavior. After all, persons in control of their behavior would not engage in such unrestrained actions to their own extreme detriment. This logic is not compelling: the focus centers on the choicefulness at the time of the offense, not a post-hoc analysis of the irrationality of a strong emotional state (e.g., rage). Otherwise, large numbers of criminals could argue, "I didn't reasonably foresee the consequences of my actions [including arrest], therefore, I should not be held culpable."

In research from the R-CRAS data base, we found it helpful to differentiate the defendant's reported loss of control from the expert's estimate of the defendant's loss of control. Please note that this issue extends far beyond malingering and deception. Many defendants simply cannot make sense of their own criminal behavior and consequently attribute their actions to a loss of control. Table 7.4 summarizes loss of control from both the defendant's perspective and the expert's conclusion. It demonstrates from the expert's perspective substantial misappraisals from both sane (i.e., tending to overestimate) and insane (i.e., tending to underestimate) the loss of control. Even among defendants clinically evaluated as insane, the majority do not experience a total loss of control over their behavior.

TABLE 7.4. Loss of Behavioral Control: Defendant's Reported Account versus Expert's Estimation

Loss of behavioral control	Sane defendants		Insane defendants	
	Reported	Expert	Reported	Expert
No impairment	35.5%	48.6%	21.7%	6.3%
Slight impairment (incidental details)	12.8%	20.0%	10.8%	3.2%
Mild impairment (impulsive)	15.8%	21.1%	8.4%	9.5%
Moderate impairment (initiated but lost control later)	12.8%	7.1%	7.2%	10.5%
Severe impairment (lost control for significant portion)	16.7%	3.2%[a]	37.3%	48.4%
Extreme impairment (complete loss of control)	6.4%	0.0%	14.5%	22.1%

[a]When cases of severe intoxication are removed, this estimate is 1.4%.

The Assessment Process

The individual style and temperament of the forensic expert as well as the particular needs of the defendant place great demands on the assessment process. Recognizing the individual differences, each expert must provide a thorough and comprehensive evaluation of criminal responsibility, tailored to the specific case. This section summarizes components of the assessment process that are essential to evaluating the defendant's self-report. Forensic experts must consider their own interpersonal presentation and its effect on the defendant's cooperativeness.

The expert's relationship to the defendant should be respectful and professional. No attempts should be made to act as a friend, advocate, or protector (Shuman, 1995). These roles may inappropriately minimize the importance of the evaluation and its potentially negative consequences for the defendant. Conversely, the expert should be respectful of the defendant's rights: (1) not to respond to specific questions and (2) not to participate in the evaluation. The forensic expert must avoid at all costs assuming a nonclinical role and employing inquisitorial or cross-examination questioning.

The assessment process progresses more smoothly if the forensic expert moves from general nondirectional questions to specific directed inquiries during the clinical interviews. This progression may assist the expert in establishing rapport with the defendant and gathering the defendant's uninterrupted account. This approach may also assist the expert in avoiding preconceptions or missing valuable data that would be otherwise overlooked. Importantly, this general account serves as a reference point in subsequent clinical interviews in evaluating the defendant's consistency and veracity. The forensic expert should avoid challenging the defendant's statements during early interviews. Any confrontations, if necessary, should be delayed to later interviews so that (1) rapport will likely be established and (2) the complete evaluation will not be jeopardized.

In complex insanity cases, the forensic expert must be willing to be involved in extensive clinical interviews over multiple time periods. Ideally, separating the defendant's accounts by a week's interval will minimize his/her memory of previous responses. This format also affords the expert time to prioritize psychological difficulties/symptoms and their relative importance to the issue of criminal responsibility. In probing the self-account, it is often useful to ask for details and specific examples of symptoms or problems experienced by the defendant. Understanding how the defendant typically addressed these problems will highlight the similarities or distinctiveness of his/her behavior at the time of the offense.

A recurring problem in insanity evaluations is that defendants sometimes appear to give self-reports that have a rehearsed quality. Any hasty conclusions that this rehearsed quality is evidence of deception is unwarranted. Although deception might be implicated, the practice effects of repetitively recounting the offense may also lead to this rehearsed quality. In addition, some defendants dissociate from their emotional experiences of the crime. The result is a relatively emotionless account that may even appear contrived. Some experts ask defendants to tell them more about a particular incident to erode this rote quality. Others attempt to intensify the immediacy of the report by asking the defendant to reexperience his/her feelings at the time of the offense. Occasionally experts will ask defendants about a critical event in reverse chronological order: for example, "What happened just before you pulled the knife from the kitchen drawer?" . . . "What happened before that?" This technique, though sometimes useful, is also potentially confusing for the defendant.

In later stages of the evaluation, comparative questioning may be useful. The defendant might be asked to compare his/her reported symptoms at the time of the offense with those experienced at the present time. This type of inquiry allows the expert to calibrate his/her observations with the reported impairment at the current time. This comparison provides a benchmark for understanding past reporting of symptoms and associated features. Beyond any efforts to distort self-reporting, patients in general vary in the intensity with which they experience similar symptoms. Comparative questioning assists the expert in understanding the defendant on this important dimension.

Confrontational methods should be used parsimoniously and only where the clinical data are necessary for completing the forensic assessment. For example, the expert may respectfully question inconsistencies in self-reporting. One possibility is that the defendant is able to reconcile apparently incompatible accounts. The expert may present him/herself as unconvinced (if this is actually the case) by components of the self-reporting in an attempt to elicit more information. The expert may entertain other explanations and ask for the defendant's input.

An often troublesome issue is the assessment of a defendant's formulation of his/her motivation with respect to the criminal behavior. Attempts to have the defendant make connections between his/her emotional and cognitive experiences and their relationship to the alleged offense is sometimes helpful. At times the expert may choose to use additional information, such as police investigative reports or laboratory studies, to question the defendant's account. We present several examples.

♦ "I am having trouble understanding this. You told me you were screaming threats at Ms. *X*, yet she meant nothing to you. . . . Could you help me with this?"

♦ "You told me that you never met Mr. *X* before, but there are three witnesses that saw the two of you arguing the week before. . . . How do you explain this?"

♦ "I reviewed the drug tests; I don't think you were entirely 'straight' (or 'forthcoming') with me about what you were using."

A controversial issue is whether the defendant should be confronted directly regarding his/her deceptions or malingering. In case conferences, we have heard experts defend this practice as providing the defendants with an opportunity to deny to admit their inveracity. First, we contend that *it would be unethical for a forensic expert to attempt to elicit a "confession" or admission on the basis of inconclusive data.* This gambit would represent a deliberate misrepresentation of the findings and would violate the professional relationship. If the expert has conclusive data, then the question becomes, "What would be achieved by such a confrontation?" How would any relevant information be elicited? Cases in which new information would be obtained are likely to be rare. The extracting of an admission is unnecessary in the light of conclusive data and is fraught with potential role conflicts. A crucial distinction must be underscored between confrontations during the evaluation and simply informing a defendant about general conclusions after the evaluation is complete.

Diagnostic Issues

Specific mental disorders should not be equated with a loss of criminal responsibility. Instead, the focus centers on prominent symptomatology and its effect on the defendant's functioning. Of particular importance is the consideration of psychotic symptoms, namely, hallucinations, delusions, and gross disorganization of thinking and/or behavior. Because of the importance of assessing both the presence and the impact of psychotic symptoms on behavior, these symptoms will be examined individually.

Hallucinations

Hallucinations refer to the misperception of external stimuli without the stimulation of the appropriate sense receptors. Patients with schizophrenia frequently experience auditory hallucinations but rarely have olfactory or tactile hallucinations. The duration of hallucinations vary widely but typically involves only a small portion of the day. Many patients develop some coping strategies for managing or controlling their hallucinatory activity; these strategies include physical activity, increased interpersonal contact, or changes in environment stimulation. Although the first edition reported that command hallucinations were relatively infrequent, more recent research, detailed below, indicates that command hallucinations are much more common than once thought.

Hallucinations, by their nature, are not directly observable. A thorough examination of the defendant's self-report is imperative; so too is the collection of corroborative data. Witnesses or individuals living with the defendant will sometimes observe indirect evidence of hallucinations (e.g., the defendant apparently attending or responding to nonexistent stimuli). In addition, persons with hallucinations occasionally may check the veracity of their perceptions with significant others. However, many individuals are so convinced in the reality of their hallucinations as to obviate the need for any confirmation.

Forensic experts must differentiate between "alien thoughts" (i.e., ideas the defendant wishes to disown) and true auditory hallucinations. The following indicators are useful in making this critical distinction:

1. Hallucinations have a definite auditory quality permitting the defendant to identify the tone, volume, rate, and speech qualities as well as other characteristics of the speaker (e.g., age, sex, race, and emotional state).
2. Hallucinations are typically experienced as originating from outside of the person. Occasionally, hallucinations are perceived from body parts (e.g. a person's limb) often outside of the head.
3. Hallucinations commonly ask for or elicit an interaction, which does not occur with alien thoughts.

Clinical data on hallucinations demonstrate their marked effect on defendant's functioning. As reported in Table 7.5, approximately one-third of insane defendants experience hallucinations at the time of the offense that either contribute to or determine the criminal behavior. In contrast, genuine hallucinations among defendants assessed as sane are comparatively rare (1.1%) and appear unrelated to the criminal behavior.

A detailed examination of the types of hallucinations is available through unpublished SADS data on criminal responsibility (Rogers, Thatcher, & Cavanaugh, 1984). These data on 78 defendants suggested the presence at the time of the offense of the following hallucinations

**TABLE 7.5. Relationship of Psychotic Symptoms
to Sanity/Insanity Determinations**

Psychotic symptoms	Group	Relationship to the offense		
		Unrelated	Contributed	Determined
Hallucinations	Sane	1.1%	0.0%	0.0%
	Insane	4.4%	14.4%	21.1%
Delusions	Sane	1.4%	1.4%	0.0%
	Insane	2.2%	13.0%	61.9%

for insane defendants: auditory (42%), visual (16%), olfactory (4%), and somatic or tactile (7%).

For the purposes of this section, we conducted a supplementary analysis of data by Rogers, Gillis, Turner, and Frise-Smith (1990) regarding the hallucinations of 45 psychotic pretrial defendants. With reference to speech characteristics, we found most patients heard voices that were typically either soft or average volume and were spoken at an average rate. The typical duration of auditory hallucinations varied widely. Although the typical duration was very brief ($\leq$15 seconds) for approximately one-half of the sample, a small number reported very extended hallucinations ($\geq$15 minutes). With respect to laterality, most heard auditory hallucinations in both ears (76.1%), with small numbers hearing them predominantly in the left ear (8.7%) or in the right ear (15.2%). In all cases, the speech was either partially (26.7%) or completely (73.3%) understandable and almost always spoken in the patient's preferred language (97.8%).

The forensic expert must appraise the impact of the hallucinations on the defendant's day-to-day functioning, especially at the time of the offense. This appraisal entails a comprehensive assessment of the content and occurrence of hallucinations and the patient's response to them. It includes an examination of the patient's volitional capacity in selecting a behavioral response, if any, to the hallucinations. Finally, the forensic expert must distinguish between command hallucinations that deliver direct orders and other intrusive hallucinations that may elicit responses from the patient.

Thompson, Stuart, and Holden (1992) examined the role of command hallucinations for a random sample of 124 defendants found legally insane. The insanity cases were divided into three groups: command hallucinations (34, or 27.4%), noncommand hallucinations (45, or 36.3%), and no hallucinations (45, or 36.3%). Importantly, a direct relationship was observed in 62% of the cases between the command hallucinations and the index criminal behavior. Nearly all acquittees with hallucinations (85.3% command and 91.1% noncommand) were diagnosed with a schizophrenic disorder.

Kasper, Rogers, and Adams (1996) examined psychotic patients with command hallucinations ($n = 27$), other hallucinations ($n = 27$), and no hallucinations ($n = 30$). Among 25 patients that could provide detailed information about their command hallucinations, alarming percentages had heard violent commands in the last month: 48.0% commanding violence toward self and 36.0% violence toward others. Even more alarming, the majority had obeyed at least some of these violent commands.

A recent review by Hersh and Borum (1998) emphasized the relationship between command hallucinations and delusions. They concluded that the delusional material consistent with the hallucinatory command substantially increased the risk of compliance. Their summary of previous studies underscored the previous conclusions about the substantial frequency with which violent commands are obeyed.

The following questions (see also Rogers, Nussbaum, & Gillis, 1988) may assist the forensic expert in determining the relevance of the hallucinations to criminal responsibility.

1. To what extent do hallucinations intrude on or impede the patient's day-to-day functioning?
2. What coping behaviors has the patient developed in response to these hallucinations?
3. Did the patient experience command hallucinations? From the patient's perspective, what makes these hallucinations "command hallucinations"?
4. How much authority does the patient place in these hallucinations? What is the nature and extent of the patient's relationship to the command hallucinations? How has it changed over time?
5. Assuming that command hallucinations were not isolated to the period of the alleged criminal behavior, what made the difference for the patient in deciding either to follow or not follow commands on this occasion?
6. To what extent was the content of the command hallucinations consistent with the patient's wishes? If so, were the commands secondary or incidental to the decision to commit the offense?
7. How specific were these command hallucinations and to what extent were they open, from the patient's perspective, to multiple interpretations? For example, an auditory hallucination stating "End it all" might signify a wide range of activities.

8. If the criminal behavior was either preceded by preparation or followed by actions designed to avoid arrest, what is the relationship of such behavior to the intrusive or command hallucinations? Did the defendant expect to "get away with the crime"? Was this because of his/her actions, or because of promises made by the command hallucinations?
9. When arrested, were the reported command hallucinations volunteered only after more rational accounts of the criminal behavior had been offered by the defendant?

Delusions

Delusions are patently false beliefs about external reality that are firmly held, despite what constitutes obvious and incontrovertible proof to the contrary (American Psychiatric Association, 1994). In evaluating delusions, the forensic expert must be sensitive to different subcultures and the heterogeneity of religious tenets. Beliefs should not be considered delusional if they are shared by other members of the person's religion or subculture, even if they appear to defy well-established mainstream actualities.

Delusions must be distinguished from overvalued ideas. As noted, delusions are patently false beliefs that are frequently manifested with unshakable conviction and are commonly unavailable for reexamination. *Overvalued ideas* are characterized by the patient's overinvestment in misbeliefs. Overvalued ideas generally differ from delusions in two fundamental ways (see Othmer & Othmer, 1989): (1) the inaccuracy of the belief is more open to question and (2) the conviction in the belief is not necessarily unwavering.

The prevalence of delusional beliefs in defendants evaluated for criminal responsibility is summarized in Table 7.5. As observed, delusions constitute the most critical category of symptoms for sanity evaluations. Of those evaluated clinically as insane, delusions played a *contributing* role in 13.0% and a *determining* role in 61.9% of evaluated cases. Unpublished data from Rogers, Thatcher, and Cavanaugh (1984) found that insane defendants typically had the following types of delusions: paranoid (53%), ideas of reference (36%), control (22%), grandiosity (20%), and thought insertion (9%).

The clinical guidelines for establishing the present and potential impact of delusional beliefs on criminal behavior parallel those considered with hallucinations. Establishing retrospectively the presence of delusions involves a detailed inquiry over multiple interviews to confirm the existence of the beliefs and the patient's conviction in these beliefs.

The evaluation of the patient's convictions is frequently complex, given that defendants often have difficulty in differentiating their current certitude from their beliefs at the time of the crime.

The clinical guidelines for the evaluation of delusions include the following assessment inquiries:

1. What makes these beliefs delusional? More specifically, to what extent is the forensic expert convinced of the patient's acceptance of insupportable beliefs in the absence of consensually validated support for these beliefs (i.e., within the society as a whole, a religious denomination, or a recognized subculture)?
2. What is the basis or rationale for the belief or belief systems in question? Is the underlying logic tenuous or frankly bizarre?
3. How does the defendant differentiate fanciful ideas from beliefs that carry a strong conviction?
4. How does the defendant respond to a critical questioning of his/her beliefs now and at the time of the crime?
5. Did the defendant, at the time of the crime, recognize that these beliefs were very different from those of most other people? If this awareness of differences did exist, how did the defendant explain it?
6. How permanent were these delusional beliefs at the time of the crime? It is essential that the forensic expert establish, as closely as possible, when specific delusional beliefs were first recognized and when (if at all) they were subsequently questioned or disregarded. There is no consensus in the literature of a minimal time for which delusional beliefs must exist; however, very transient misbeliefs or misapprehensions, existing for less than several days, rarely reach the diagnostic criterion for a delusion.
7. What influence, if any, did the delusions have on the criminal behavior?
8. To what extent were these influences capable of being resisted?
9. How explicit were the delusional beliefs in relationship to the criminal behavior? If in fact the delusional beliefs were only general (e.g., "I am to serve the will of God"), then how did the defendant reason from such a general statement to the specific criminal behavior?
10. To what extent did the delusion suggest, instruct, demand, or impel the defendant to carry out specific criminal behavior?
11. Did the defendant recognize his/her behavior as criminal? If so, what effect did this recognition have on the behavior?
12. What factors were considered by the defendant, including de-

lusional beliefs, in deciding to engage in the criminal behavior in question?

13. To what extent was the criminal behavior congruent with other nondelusional wishes of the individual?

14. If the delusional beliefs were chronic, how did the defendant select this particular time to engage in the criminal behavior?

Impaired Understandability of Speech

Gross impairment of understandable speech was traditionally referred to as *incoherence* (Spitzer & Endicott, 1978a); it reflects a marked deficit, because of psychopathology, in an individual's ability to communicate meaningfully. This lack of comprehensibility involves a disorganization or incompleteness in the individual's speech patterns. Impaired comprehension is often the result of formal thought disorders. *Formal thought disorders* are defined by disturbances in the structure and sequencing of speech. They include derailment (loosening of associations), illogical thinking, and neologisms (i.e., invention of new words or definitions often with the expectation that they will be readily understood by others). Incoherence and formal thought disorders are rarely experienced without other psychotic symptoms (i.e., delusions and hallucinations).

Based on the R-CRAS data base, moderate to severe impairment of verbal coherence was commonly found among insane defendants with definite delusions (77.8%) or suspected/definite hallucinations (80.8%). As noted in Table 7.6, impaired understandability is rarely severe, even among insane defendants. Moderate to severe impairment was found with approximately one-fourth of insane defendants (27.1%), while even mild impairment was uncommon among sane defendants (5.8%).

TABLE 7.6. Severity of Impairment in Sanity/Insanity Determinations

		Severity of impairment		
Dimension	Group	Mild	Moderate	Severe
Speech	Sane	5.8%	0.0%	0.0%
	Insane	18.9%	20.3%	6.8%
Self-care	Sane	8.6%	2.2%	0.0%
	Insane	31.6%	26.3%	15.8%
Social behavior	Sane	26.3%	23.7%	5.4%[a]
	Insane	10.2%	37.5%	48.9%

[a]When cases of severe intoxication are removed, this estimate is 0.0%

Bizarre and Disorganized Behavior

Bizarre behavior calls attention to itself because of its unusualness and social inappropriateness. Because of its subjective determination, which is partially contextual, bizarre behavior must be distinguished from behavior reflecting (1) a particular subculture or religion or (2) a lack of training or knowledge of prevailing customs. Bizarre behavior goes beyond idiosyncratic behavior in its gross violation of social norms without any logical or understandable reasons. For example, an individual who puts on a chicken costume and struts about making clucking sounds would not necessarily be considered bizarre if the act was performed for the opening of a family restaurant, but would clearly be considered bizarre if the individual was attending a spouse's funeral. Therefore, any judgment regarding bizarreness must take into account both the defendant's background and the context of the behavior.

An important consideration in assessing abnormal behavior is whether it should be considered bizarre. For example, are the ritualistic acts of cutting and torturing, sometimes found with sadistic rape, considered bizarre? While alien and probably abhorrent to the larger community, these sadistic acts may be understandable in the framework of the defendant's paraphiliac behavior. A crucial issue is whether the bizarre behavior is the result of bizarre thinking. Therefore, an assessment of the defendant's thoughts and intentions is critical to this assessment. In inspecting the R-CRAS data base, we found that very few defendants (1.4%) evaluated as sane evidence any bizarre behavior at the time of the offense. In contrast, more than one-half (56.1%) of defendants evaluated as insane evidenced several or more examples of bizarre behavior.

The following questions may be helpful in evaluating a defendant's bizarre behavior:

1. Does the defendant see his/her behavior as bizarre (i.e., "strange," or "out of character")? If so, on what basis?
2. How does the bizarre behavior serve or not serve the defendant's purposes?
3. What is the relationship of the bizarre behavior to the defendant's perceptions, thinking, and emotions?
4. Under what circumstances does the bizarre behavior usually occur?
5. Is the bizarre behavior limited only to this or other criminal acts? If so, how much control does the defendant have over the bizarre behavior?
6. Where in the sequence of criminal behavior does the bizarre behavior occur?

7. What effects, if any, did the defendant observe as a result of his/her bizarre behavior? Did the bizarre behavior facilitate or impede the criminal behavior?
8. Was the bizarre behavior observed by anyone else? If so, what was the effect of the bizarre behavior on those observing it?

Disordered behavior, reflecting difficulties in accomplishing purposeful actions and the satisfaction of self-care needs, is often comparatively easy to assess (see Table 7.6). Impairment is most often observed in the disruption of goal-oriented behaviors in which the individual has difficulty either in tracking (i.e., staying with and completing relatively simple tasks) or through psychomotor agitation or retardation that impedes purposeful behavior. To warrant the determination of disorganized behavior, the defendant must have manifested ineffectual attempts to carry out day-to-day activities that are not the result of voluntary intoxication. Corroborative information is often essential because such defendants frequently have gross memory impairment.

A closely related issue is the absence of responsible behavior within the major spheres of the individual's daily life. Care must be taken to distinguish incapacity secondary to severe psychopathology from antisocially based irresponsibility. Regarding Axis I disorders, a defendant's capacity to engage in work or school, and to establish responsible and reciprocal relations constitute an important benchmark of psychological functioning. As reported in Table 7.6, the R-CRAS data base reveals that approximately one-half (49.8%) of insane defendants experienced major impairment in both work and social relationships. In contrast, very few insane defendants (5.4%) have severe impairment of social behavior; it appears to be associated with severe intoxication.

The expert may use the defendant's capacity to work as one of many important indicators of overall psychological functioning. As previously noted, the key issue is *capacity* rather than *choice*. Therefore, an antisocial individual who chooses not to be employed or a religious person who selects a solitary existence would not necessarily be considered for this category.

Depressive Symptoms

Depressive symptoms by themselves are rarely sufficient to satisfy the legal standard of insanity. The task is complicated by the fact that many defendants, evaluated for insanity, were dysphoric[2] at the time of the offense. Still other defendants become dysphoric following their arrest and detention. Nonexclusive causes of dysphoria include guilt about the crime, frustration at being caught, depression about detention, and apprehension about the pending trial. Therefore, experts must distinguish the affect at the time of the offense from the defendant's mood following his/her arrest.

Defendants are frequently vague and confused when describing their negative emotions. As found on the SADS, the use of nonleading and open-ended questions—such as "How were you feeling?" and "What was your mood like?"—are often more helpful than specific questions, such as "Were you depressed?" Asking the defendant to describe the day of the crime, and possibly the preceding days, may be useful in eliciting specific emotions and indirect evidence of his/her intensity. If necessary, general inquiries can be followed with specific inquiries that are anchored to events: "What where you feeling when you locked the doors?" Such anchoring increases the likelihood of a recollection rather than a speculation based on plausibility.

The severity of the depressed mood is critical to determining criminal responsibility. Through careful inquiry, the expert can often establish the duration of the depressed mood, its onset, course, and severity. Severity is measured in terms of pervasiveness, hopelessness, suicidal ideation, and impairment in day-to-day functioning. In the absence of psychotic symptoms, severe depression poses a challenge to forensic experts conducting insanity evaluations. What degree of depression warrants exculpation? Does a severely depressed woman who intends to kill herself and her children as an act of altruism qualify clinically as insane? What if she fully realizes the criminality of her actions but believes there is no alternative to the unremitting horror of continued living? A decisive factor should be the level of her conviction in these beliefs. If she is unable to separate her own excruciations from her children's comparatively normal life, then her reality testing is grossly impaired. The specific legal standard plays a determining role in whether this case might be found insane; this particular example reflects more volitional than cognitive incapacity.

In the R-CRAS data base (see Table 7.7), the prevalence of moderate depression was comparable across sane (10.8%) and insane (11.2%) defendants. Differences were observed at severe and extreme levels. Sane defendants essentially did not achieve these levels (0.8% severe and 0.0% extreme), but a small proportion of insane defendants had either severe (11.2%) or extreme (5.6%) depression.

Manic Symptoms

Defendants with manic episodes are likely to report a distinct and remarkable change in their mood, level of activity, and thinking:

TABLE 7.7. Severity of Mood Symptoms in Sanity/Insanity Determinations

Mood symptom	Group	Severity of impairment		
		Moderate	Severe	Extreme
Depressed	Sane	10.8%	0.8%	0.0%
	Insane	11.2%	11.2%	5.6%
Elevated/euphoric	Sane	0.4%	0.4%	0.0%
	Insane	2.3%	8.0%	0.0%
Anxiety	Sane	17.6%	5.2%	1.4%
	Insane	26.6%	24.1%	6.3%

- ♦ elevated or euphoric mood that is overly positive, given the person's circumstances
- ♦ hyperactivity with marked changes in speed and quantity of activities
- ♦ accelerated thinking with pressured thoughts and consistent with elevated mood

Grandiosity, accelerated thinking, and marked deficits in judgment are relevant to the assessments of criminal responsibility. *Grandiosity* encompasses an inflated and unrealistically positive assessment of an individual's abilities and attributes. Grandiosity becomes delusional when this self-appraisal involves unchallengeable and unwarranted convictions in one's importance or special abilities. As an example, a successful male stockbroker became convinced during a manic episode that he could control the entire cattle industry. In a euphoric mood, he grossly overestimated his worth and abilities and was eventually arrested for violating federal banking regulations. If he had been able to reflect on his actions, he would have realized that they were blatantly irrational and obviously illegal. The crux of the assessment was his ability to exercise judgment and introspection during the months that these illegal activities transpired. In this particular case, he appeared utterly unconcerned by the dismay of his wife and friends over his manic behavior (e.g., frenzied trades) and appeared incapacitated with respect to his own grandiose thinking.

Accelerated thinking and poor judgment are difficult to assess in the absence of grandiose delusions. Many individuals in severe manic episodes are cognitively aware of their thoughts and actions, but simply do not appear to care. Accelerated thinking must be considered on a continuum; at its extreme, patients sometimes become incoherent because of their pressured speech and thinking. However, as a retrospective evaluation, they may appear in relative control of their thinking when recounting events surrounding their alleged crime. Collateral interviews may be critical to establishing the degree of impairment due to accelerated thinking. Impaired judgment is easier to assess when its goals appear to be markedly illogical. For instance, when a woman without children buys several hundred diapers for no apparent reason, the illogicality of this purchase is relatively obvious. In contrast, when a male stranger with bipolar disorder exposes himself to a woman to signal his romantic interests, other nonmanic motivations must be evaluated.

Inspection of the R-CRAS data base indicates that elevated or euphoric moods are relatively uncommon among insanity defendants (see Table 7.7). Among those evaluated as clinically insane, a severe manic mood with a major influence on criminal behavior was observed in 8% of the cases. Interestingly, no extreme cases were observed in which the euphoric mood and manic symptoms were so intense as to interrupt or abort the criminal act. The relatively low number of cases substantially affected by a manic mood likely reflects the small proportion of mood disorders, especially bipolar disorders, referred for insanity evaluations (see Table 7.2).

As a practical guideline, a manic episode must be established with convincing examples of elevated or euphoric mood and concomitant symptoms. Often manic behavior is highly intrusive on significant others and can be easily corroborated. Elevated and euphoric mood in the absence of highly positive events is often memorable to friends and co-workers. Manic symptoms must be differentiated from reckless behavior and drug use. In the former case, high-risk behavior may be motivated by sensation-seeking but lack the persistently elevated mood and hyperactivity. In the latter case, manic-like symptoms are circumscribed to periods of drug use.

Anxiety Features

Anxiety disorders are very rare as the primary diagnosis of persons found insane. However, many defendants experience some symptoms of anxiety during the commission of the offense. This anxiety is often situationally based and focused on the criminal behavior. As noted in Table 7.7, nearly one-third (29.2%) of sane and the majority (57.0%) of insane defendants experienced moderate to pervasive anxiety at the time of offense. Some experts may be surprised at the percentage of insane defendants with marked anxiety, surmising that anxiety is often associated with knowledge of the offense and fear of arrest. A more accurate perspective may be that insane defendants typically perceive themselves in a crisis that warrants urgent, if not extreme, measures. Therefore, the anxiety may result from the perceived exigencies of the situation rather than from any specific expectations of arrest.

Dissociation and Depersonalization

Dissociative episodes, including dissociative identity disorders, were covered in detail in the previous chapter. Please refer to Chapter 6 for a review of dissociative and amnestic symptoms.

Defendants, regardless of impairment, may experience momentary or brief experiences of depersonalization (e.g., "This could not possibly be me" "I feel unreal") or derealization (e.g., "This isn't really happening") during the criminal behavior. These feelings may occur more frequently in an individual's retrospective attempt to make sense of what occurred. It is relatively common for defendants to look back on their criminal actions as a nightmare or something unreal from the past. In contrast, defendants rarely experience a depersonalization disorder that extends throughout the time of the offense. Simply because a person feels unreal would not be sufficient to meet the standards of criminal nonresponsibility.

Content Issues

Content issues address the topics investigated through clinical interviews with a focus on what occurred at the time of the offense and the defendant's background. This outline includes the instant offense, psychiatric, criminal, and social history.

1. *Informed consent.* A *Miranda*-type warning is required in capital cases when testimony is anticipated at a subsequent capital sentencing hearing by a court-ordered examiner (*Estelle v. Smith*, 1980). In addition, some states require that defendants be informed that their examination is not privileged to avoid rendering these communications privileged (Shuman, 1993). In addition, mental health professionals are required by professional ethics to inform the person being examined of the purpose of the evaluation, the referral source (i.e., judge, defense counsel, or prosecutor), and the limits of confidentiality. Regarding the purpose of the evaluation, the defendant must be provided with a rudimentary understanding of the insanity plea and its ramifications. The defendant should understand his/her choice to participate in the as-

sessment. Experts are divided over whether an exhaustive review of risks/ benefits is ethically mandated. As a practical matter, forensic experts are unlikely to know the risks and benefits of the plea in a particular case.[3] Experts should be aware of the modest study by Elliot et al. (1993) that found retrospectively that 16 of 20 NGRI acquittees were likely incapable of consenting to the insanity plea.

2. *Time of the offense.* The defendant's account of his/her behavior preceding, during, and following the criminal behavior is the sine qua non of an insanity evaluation. The time framework will vary from case to case. As a general guideline, it is often helpful to examine the week preceding the criminal behavior and to gather as much clinical data as possible about the 24-hour period following the alleged offense. The defendant's account is best gathered in an unstructured manner by simply asking the defendant to report as much as possible about what he or she was feeling, thinking, and doing on each day. A systematic approach yields valuable information about the limits of the defendant's memory and establishes a baseline of the defendant's functioning. It is often helpful to discuss the day of the offense in detail, focusing on each hour and testing the limits of the defendant's memory. This exhaustive approach is also helpful for the detection of malingering because defendants often have difficulty supplying plausible details and not presenting gross inconsistencies on subsequent interviews.

3. *Review of smptoms.* A systematic review of psychological symptoms, based on the defendant's account, is invaluable. Use of structured Axis I interviews, especially the SADS (see Chapter 9), is strongly recommended. Cross-comparisons of retrospective symptoms with current symptoms is useful in understanding the severity of reported symptoms.

4. *Psychiatric history.* A detailed review of past psychiatric history is essential. The focus should not only include prior episodes but also specific symptoms and their severity. In establishing the validity of a disorder, data on the course of the disorder (e.g., a chronic and deteriorating course) and earlier symptoms provides a diagnostic comprehensive picture. Clinical records are especially useful for corroborating the patient's self reporting.

5. *School and work history.* School and work history are indirectly applicable to determining criminal responsibility. In understanding prior episodes and functioning at the time of the offense, a defendant's inability to work or to maintain social relationships provides evidence of his/her level of impairment. Of course, the expert must differentiate impairment due to a major mental disorder from antisocial personality characteristics. This distinction is often straightforward, based on developmental (i.e., conduct symptoms) and adult APD criteria.

Developmental Background

A brief review of significant events is often useful in understanding the defendant. This review may provide data on conduct-disordered symptoms, cognitive deficits, or periods of maladjustment. As a caution, some experts attempt to explain complex adult behaviors on the basis of childhood events; such longitudinal abstractions, however plausible, are unlikely to meet the *Daubert* standard of admissibility.[4]

Family History

A brief review of family history is sometimes helpful in understanding the defendant. However, its relevance to criminal responsibility is typically marginal. In addition, family history does not typically assist with diagnosis. Even in cases with extensive histories, genetic markers rarely exceed 50% and never improve on the diagnostic methods (e.g., structured interviews) that should be used in most insanity evaluations.

Corroborative Clinical Interviews

Corroborative interviews are typically coordinated with attorneys for retained experts and with the courts for appointed experts. These interviews provide important clinical data about the defendant's functioning. In many cases, use of corroborative interviews should be established as the *standard of practice* for insanity evaluations. Such interviews may provide new perspectives on the antecedents and determinants of the criminal behavior. Victims, often inaccessible to the expert because of the nature of the crime or the reluctance of attorneys, have a unique perspective on the defendant's criminal behavior from their direct observations of the defendant's speech and actions. Witnesses may also provide firsthand accounts of the defendant. With both victims and witnesses, it is important to establish their attitudes toward the defendant and its potentially biasing effect on their recall.

Friends and family with whom the defendant was living may provide specific information about symptoms and impairment at the time of the offense. With well-defined episodes of Axis I disorders, this verification can be invaluable. As with witnesses, we have consulted on cases in which cohabitants attempted to "help" as well as "punish" the defendant. Their motivation must be a part of the evaluative process. Finally, the arresting officers are sometimes useful in providing additional information about the defendant's speech and behavior. Depending on the jurisdiction, arrest reports vary in the degree that they address aberrant behavior or impaired speech. We caution experts simply not to equate the absence of reported findings in arrest reports with the absence of such anomalous behavior.

The content of corroborative interviews is likely to address the aforementioned topics, beginning with an unstructured format ("Tell me about . . .") and then focusing on critical issues. It is important to realize that no one providing corroborative interviews is on trial and that these individuals must be treated with considerable respect, both in discussing the interviewee's actions and honoring their decision to participate in a corroborative interview. As a tragic example, questions to a female rape victim may implicitly shift the blame for the sex assault to her (Fischhoff, 1992).

Corroborative interviews may provide additional clinical information about the defendant and his/her actions. In violent cases, such as homicide or rape, witnesses may have difficulty being objective about their observations. In general, experts should maintain a professional relationship with interviewees and be appropriately supportive of witnesses who have already experienced a highly stressful and emotionally upsetting situation.

Given the subjectivity of psychiatric symptoms, experts should not accept any corroborative version as a quasi-objective basis for discounting the defendant's self-reporting. However, disconfirming information from a relatively unbiased observer may constitute an important element in the overall determination of the defendant's sincerity and response style. As with every other aspect of the insanity evaluation, the goal is to collect clinical data relevant to the case and to assess the credibility of each data source.

Conclusion

Interviews for the assessment of criminal responsibility are clinically demanding and time-consuming. The forensic expert must be prepared to conduct extensive interviews, typically several hours in length, to develop a full understanding of the defendant's retrospective functioning. The interview process requires detailed notes on the content and manner of the defendant's account. Some notation regarding the type of inquiry (e.g., open-ended vs. highly detailed question) may also provide a context to understand apparent inconsistencies. Documentation of interviews should also include direct quotes from the defendant on pivotal issues. Clinical observations are also important to report systematically for subsequent preparation of the court report and subsequent testimony (see Chapters 11 and 12).

Integration of the interview data requires planning and organization of the assessment process. The forensic expert may wish to consider his/her goals and the types of interviews (i.e., unstructured and structured) conducted at each contact with the defendant and corroborative sources. A careful review of interview material prior to the completion of the assessment will assure that areas of ambiguity or clinical uncertainty are thoroughly addressed.

Notes

1. Rogers later testified for the prosecution regarding Gacy's sanity.

2. Encompassing depression, *dysphoria* is a broad term to describe subjectively unpleasant feelings (e.g., depression, worrying, and frustration).

3. Little is known about the consequences of a failed insanity defense (see Silver, 1995).

4. Given the complexity of human development and the diverse reactions to childhood trauma, post hoc extrapolations are vulnerable to hindsight bias and do not meet the *Daubert* criterion of falsifiability.

Chapter 8

Psychological Testing

Overview
Projective Methods
Multiscale Inventories
Intellectual and Neuropsychological Testing
Conclusion

Overview

Psychological testing is a standardized measure of specific behaviors that is administered according to uniform procedures with an objective form of measurement (Anastasi, 1988). As a quick primer for attorneys, the following concepts are critical to the understanding of psychological testing:

♦ *Reliability* is an estimate of a measure's consistency. Namely, does the measure produce similar results when administered at different times (i.e., test–retest reliability) or rated by different psychologists observing the same interview/procedure (i.e., interrater-reliability)?
♦ *Validity* is an estimate of a measure's ability to assess what it was designed to assess. In clinical assessment, validity is most often conceptualized in terms of group differences (e.g., sane vs. insane defendants). For the measures covered in this chapter, primary considerations are whether the measure can be checked against an independent external criteria (i.e., criterion-related validity) or whether it measures predicted differences based on theory (i.e., construct validity).

Test validation may appear to be the exclusive realm or *acanum acanorum* of psychologists, inaccessible to other mental health professionals, let alone attorneys. While the language and methodology may

183

appear esoteric, the underlying concepts of consistent (reliable) and accurate (valid) measurement are easily understood (Heilbrun, 1992). An additional concept is generalizability, namely, can the test be applied to different populations (e.g., minorities) in different settings (e.g., hospitals and court clinics).

Daubert and Psychological Testing

In *Daubert v. Merrell Dow Pharmaceuticals, Inc.* (1993), the Supreme Court recognized the differences between scientific and legal conceptualizations of validity. While acknowledging that science uses "reliability" and "validity," the Court noted that the legal standard for the admissibility of scientific knowledge is "evidentiary reliability." *Evidentiary reliability* refers to the trustworthiness of the data. Reassuringly for forensic experts, the Court held that "in a case involving scientific evidence, *evidentiary reliability* will be based upon *scientific validity*" (p. 2795, footnote 9, emphases in the original). Because validity cannot occur without reliability, a logical interpretation of the *Daubert* standard is that as a condition of admissibility each psychological test should be required to demonstrate its reliability and validity.

The *Daubert* standard, discussed in Chapter 1, deserves a brief comment concerning relationship to psychological testing. Many psychological tests are employed in insanity evaluations, which have only indirect relevance to criminal responsibility. For example, the use of intelligence tests is entirely proper for ruling out the potential effect of mental retardation on the commission of a crime. In contrast, any attempt to equate poor performance on the Comprehension subtest of the Wechsler Adult Intelligence Scale—Third Edition (WAIS-III; Wechsler, 1997) with poor comprehension of the criminal act lacks any scientific basis.

Important considerations in the application of *Daubert* to psychological testing are included:

1. *Validity for a designated purpose.* Paralleling psychological tests, the Court held that validity should not be considered an encompassing concept, but must be considered in relationship to specific issues relevant to the case (p. 2796). While forensic psychologists and psychiatrists may take exception to vigorous cross-examination probing a test's validity, the validity of most tests is focused and may not be applicable to current case.

2. *Threshold of relevant evidence.* The Court in *Daubert* recognized

the important role of the Federal Rules of Evidence (Rule 403), which permits the exclusion of whose relevance evidence that is substantially exceeded by its dangers to the trial process. In deciding the admissibility of evidence, courts can exclude expert evidence if its probative value is substantially outweighed by the risk that it will mislead the jury (*Daubert v. Merrell Dow Pharmaceuticals, Inc.*, 1993, p. 2798). How should this criterion apply to psychological testing? We submit that when conclusions are offered with a "reasonable degree of psychological certainty," yet the empirical data suggests that the likelihood that these conclusions are true is less than 50%, then they pose a serious risk that jurors are likely to be misled.

This minimalistic threshold (i.e., a conclusion is at least 50% likely to be true) can be tested formally by applying utility estimates. The likelihood that an elevated score signifies a disorder is technically known as positive predictive power (PPP). If the PPP is less than .50, then the use of this indicator has less then an even chance of representing an accurate determination.[1] Put simply, if an interpretation is more likely to be wrong than right, then jurors are likely to be misled regarding what a test or procedure proves. Because experts are often required to testify to a reasonable degree of psychological or medical certainty, jurors should have every expectation that certainty exceeds the "flip of a coin."

Incremental Validity and Psychological Testing

Many psychologists still subscribe to the use of test batteries in assessing psychological impairment. An alternative, described in greater detail in Chapter 11, is the selective use of tests with a focus on incremental validity. *Incremental validity* refers to whether the combination of tests leads to greater accuracy then the application of a single measure. Sechrest (1963) presented compelling evidence that the single best-validated measure is often diagnostically superior to multiple measures. More recently, Gallucci (1990) reviewed traditional psychological testing and reached a similar conclusion: *most studies suggest that the use of multiple measures does not result in incremental validity*. As an example with forensic populations, Kurtz and Meyer (1994) found that the SIRS was more accurate in the assessment of malingering than either the MMPI-2 alone or the combination of the SIRS/MMPI-2. In other words, the MMPI-2 did not add incremental validity to the SIRS but rather decreased the overall accuracy of classification. Attorneys should not overlook incremental validity in evaluating forensic reports and expert testimony:

1. What is the best-validated measure of the relevant issue (e.g., symptom, diagnosis, or psycholegal construct)?
2. Do any studies indicate the improved accuracy (incremental validity) of adding other less-validated measures?

Some psychologists trained in the classic "test battery" model of psychological assessment (see Ziskin, 1995) are likely to have trouble separating their personal convictions about the usefulness of test batteries from the empirical evidence. While being sympathetic to such personal convictions, attorneys need to focus on the best-validated measure and any evidence of incremental validity. In summary, incremental validity must be proven, not merely asserted.

Projective Methods

Human Figure Drawings

Overview

The undergirding assumptions of human figure drawings are threefold: (1) the drawings represent important and stable personality characteristics, (2) the interpretation of these personality characteristics is consistent across persons and background, and (3) projected material is not readily accessible to the patient and cannot be easily manipulated. With figure drawings hundreds of interpretations are possible, reflecting a myriad of possibilities ranging from ego defenses to sexual deviations and diagnoses. For example, Gilbert (1978) offers approximately 500 specific interpretations with innumerable combinations.

Machover (1949) developed the first systematic interpretation of human figure drawings with their important symbolic representations of psychopathology. But in his seminal work Swenson (1957, 1968) failed to find empirical support for most Machover interpretations and concluded that interrater reliabilities were likely too modest for most clinical applications. Roback (1968) examined individual interpretations and found empirical support for an unacceptably low 10% (i.e., 3 of 31) of interpretations.

This conflict over the merits of the Draw-A-Person (DAP) is not completely settled. Extrapolating from 21 indices of anxiety, Riethmiller and Handler (1998) concluded that the data supported the use of the DAP, although an inspection of their Table 1 (p. 465) reveals that only one-half of the findings (11, or 52.4%) have a preponderance of positive findings. In rebuttal, Joiner and Schimdt (1998) conclude that

Riethmiller and Handler are construing their compiled data too optimistically and the level of overall agreement is negligible (kappa = .18). Despite potential extrapolations, this more recent debate is relatively circumscribed to the assessment of anxiety. Notwithstanding pleas to the contrary, the DAP lacks the necessary criterion-related validity for general use in clinical and forensic assessment.

Mitchell, Trent, and McArthur (1993) developed a new scoring system for what they termed the Human Figure Drawing Test (HFDT) which is composed of the patient's "best representation of two human figures (one of each gender)" (p. 1). Dimensional scores are generated based on a continuum from unimpaired to severe cognitive impairment.

Forensic Applications

The psychometric limitations of the HFDT militate against its usefulness in forensic practice. These limitations are outlined below:

1. *Interrater reliability.* Estimates of interrater reliability appear circumscribed with the use of two raters on 80 protocols. In addition, estimates of agreement (i.e., kappa coefficients) are relatively modest at .73 and .44.

2. *Criterion groups.* The nonclinical normative sample was composed entirely of hospital staff, many of whom had specific training in the treatment of persons with mental disorders. In addition to being nonrepresentative of unimpaired populations, they differed markedly from the clinical groups used in the HFDT validation. The nonclinical group was older (38 vs. 33 years old), better educated (13 vs. 10 years), with proportionately more females (51% vs. 35%) and fewer minorities (10% vs. 47%). Therefore, any differences between clinical and nonclinical samples cannot simply be attributable to psychological impairment.

3. *Validity.* Overall impairment scores tend not to discriminate clinical groups (see Mitchell et al., 1993, p. 164). For example, clinical groups with depression and antisocial personality disorder have virtually the same impairment scores. Likewise, bipolar and paranoid disorders are indistinguishable. Even more concerning for forensic evaluations, a discriminant analysis misclassified 80% of nonclinical participants as patients with mental disorders.

Daubert Standard

Human figure drawings do not appear to meet the standards set out in *Daubert* on three grounds. Regarding *falsifiability*, the sheer number of interpretations and combination of interpretations make the original human figure drawings virtually untestable. In this regard, the HFDT does appear falsifiable; it simplifies interpretations to 74 criteria, some of which are mutually exclusive (e.g., dominant female vs. dominant male). The most serious criticism of human figure drawings, including the HFDT, is the *known error rate*. Although not fully tested, interpretations of human figure drawings are much more likely to be wrong than right. Moreover, interpretations are seriously contaminated by artistic ability (Cressen, 1975). Finally, the *general acceptance* of human figure drawings, at least in forensic practice, has not been achieved. Recent surveys of forensic experts indicate that human figure drawings play a negligible role in competency and insanity evaluations (Borum & Grisso, 1995).

A summary of human figure drawings in relationship to *Daubert* is uniformly negative:

1. *Human figure drawings and insanity*: not supported.
2. *Human figure drawings and diagnosis*: not supported.
3. *Human figure drawings and clinical interpretation*: not supported.

Rorschach

Overview

No single measure in psychometric history has stirred as much controversy as the Rorschach Inkblots. In 1911, Hermann Rorschach, a young psychiatrist, created as many as 40 cards to study psychodiagnostics in patient populations. Unfortunately, the publisher's unwillingness to reproduce more than 10 plates and Rorschach's early death influenced the scope and direction of the Rorschach (Exner, 1969). Since Rorschach's death, six major systems of scoring and interpretation have been implemented: Beck, Hertz, Klopfer, Piotrowski, Rapaport–Schafer, and Exner. As summarized in Exner's (1969) seminal work, marked differences are apparent among the systems.

How does the Rorschach relate to personality functioning? As summarized by Erdberg (1990), two frameworks have been proposed: *stimulus-to-fantasy* and *perceptual-cognitive*. The stimulus-to-fantasy framework posits the symbolic projection of need states onto the blots. In contrast, the perceptual-cognitive framework examines how the person organizes ambiguous materials. The crucial difference is that the stimulus-to-fantasy framework postulates that inkblot responses are symbolic of important internal dynamics, while the perceptual-cognitive framework postulates that the responses are stable representations of how the person approaches other real-world situations.

Does the Rorschach constitute a psychometric measure? Weiner (1995) articulated both *subjective* and *objective* perspectives of the Rorschach. From the first perspective, the Rorschach is "an entirely subjective measure involving ambiguous stimuli and an unstructured task" (Weiner, 1995, p. 330). From the second perspective, psychometric properties of individual scores and indices can be computed. In line with the subjective stance, Weiner advocates the declassification of the Rorschach as a test. For legal professionals evaluating forensic reports, this distinction between subjective and objective is crucial:

♦ *Subjective* emphasizes the generation of hypotheses with comparatively little attention to the undergirding psychometrics. Many psychologists, who do not rigorously administer or score the Rorschach by standard procedures, presumably endorse the subjective perspective. Often, psychiatrists utilizing consultant's reports on the Rorschach are unaware that a subjective perspective was employed.

♦ *Objective* emphasizes the use of standardized administration and scoring procedures. Reports typically focus on those interpretations with established external validity. Two hallmarks of an objective stance are (1) explicit reference to empirical findings and (2) explicit delimitations of interpretation where empirical data are not forthcoming.

Surprisingly many time-honored interpretations do not achieve the objective perspective. For example, responses to color have been interpreted as reflecting emotional states. But in a classic review of more than 150 studies spanning the different Rorschach systems, Frank (1976) found that nomothetic interpretations of color were likely suspect. Although color appeared to have some relationship to affect, the variability of responses vitiated against empirically based interpretations.

Exner (1974, 1986, 1991, 1993) is largely responsible for saving the Rorschach from spirited attacks during the 1980s that predicted its final demise. Through his efforts, the Comprehensive System was cobbled together from the five existing Rorschach systems and extensively tested. With considerable candor, Exner (1991) described the steps and missteps in creating the Comprehensive System. More recently, reviews (Exner, 1997; Weiner, 1997) have extolled is current validity and continued vitality.

Despite the many accomplishments of Exner, the Rorschach continues to engender controversy. Wood, Nezworski, and Stejskal (1996a, 1996b) levied strong criticisms at the Comprehensive System, raising important questions about its reliability and validity. Exner (1996) responded to some of these criticisms, while Meyer (1997a, 1997b) launched an acerbic attack of Wood et al.'s analysis of the Rorschach's interrater reliability. Wood, Nezworski, and Stejskal (1997) responded acrimoniously to Meyer's critique.[2] Given the richness and complexity of Rorschach interpretation, we wonder whether this debate misses a potentially larger issue: Instead of attending to interscorer agreement, where the data are mixed (see also McDowell & Acklin, 1996; Ziskin, 1995), defenders and critics alike should be addressing the more critical issue of inter-interpretation agreement. Simply put, do identically scored profiles yield similar interpretations? The panoply of possible interpretations is both the boon and bane of the Rorschach. If highly experienced clinicians reach discordant conclusions based on identical data, then inter-interpretation agreement is suspect.

Exner (1991) emphasized the use of configural interpretations and introduced indices of special interest to diagnosis: the schizophrenia index (SCZI) and the depression index (DEPI). Regarding Exner's own normative data, schizophrenic inpatients typically score ≥ 4 on the SCZI (81.6%), although substantial numbers (18.8%) of depressed patients have similar scores. Likewise, depressed inpatients often scored ≥ 5 on DEPI (75.2%) with relatively few seen in schizophrenic inpatients (10.2%). Ganellen (1996) calculated the diagnostic efficiency of Exner's data on the SCZI and DEPI with very positive results (i.e., sensitivity and PPP $\geq .79$). Two points are worthy of comment. First, detractors might observe that the use of inpatients represents an extreme sample and is a less-than-stringent test of diagnostic efficiency.[3] Second, diagnoses were apparently rendered without the benefit of structured interviews with their own established reliability.

A nagging problem with configural interpretations is the unknown interrelations among 91 unique variables and 64 ratios and derivations. As an example with SCZI, if several of its 10 variables are highly correlated, then the resulting discriminant function is confounded. A potential avenue for further research on the Rorschach is the reduction of variables and unnecessary intercorrelations through the use of factor analytic models (Floyd & Widamen, 1995). A rigorous examination by Anderson and Dixon (1993) with adolescent inpatients lends support to the use of factor structure for both empirical validation and clinical interpretation.

Forensic Applications

Several studies have examined the admissibility of the Rorschach in criminal and civil cases. Weiner, Exner, and Sciara (1996) concluded that the Rorschach's use in forensic cases is widely accepted, reporting only rare challenges to its admissibility in 7,934 recent cases. They acknowledged that their data might be skewed (1) by the exclusive use of

Rorschach clinicians who attend their workshops and (2) their small sample ($N = 93$). An additional concern is the unreported return rate, which constrains the interpretability of these data. Meloy, Hanson, and Weiner (1997) reviewed legal citations for the Rorschach and found only seven recent cases (1985–1995) that addressed its reliability and validity. The authors concluded that "based on our empirical findings, the Rorschach has authority, or weight, in higher courts of appeal throughout the United States" (p. 61). We respectfully differ with this sweeping conclusion. Based on Meloy et al.'s own analysis of recent cases, the admissibility of the Rorschach was affirmed in two cases and ruled inadmissible in four cases.

Borum and Grisso (1995) surveyed forensic psychologists and psychiatrists on the use of psychological measures for insanity evaluations. They found that only approximately one-third of forensic psychologists (32%) and psychiatrists (30%) *ever* employed the Rorschach in insanity evaluations. The frequency of use varied markedly. Of those employing projective methods, relatively few (weighted $M = 13.6\%$) considered any projectives as a standard component (i.e., > 80% use) of their insanity assessments.

Surprisingly few recent studies have examined the Rorschach's usefulness in criminal forensic populations. Beyond an abundance of case studies, most forensic research can be divided into components: (1) feigning on the Rorschach and (2) early comparative studies between different types of offenders. The effectiveness of the Rorschach in the detection of malingering is summarized in Chapter 5. However, Schretlen's (1997) comprehensive review suggests two inescapable conclusions: (1) motivated persons can successfully simulate severe psychopathology and (2) consistent indicators of malingering have yet to be established.

Rorschach studies have attempted to distinguish offenders on the basis of psychopathy and violence. For example, Meloy and Gacono (1992) examined aggressive indices for moderate and severe psychopaths and found a significant group difference for one of four indices. Using the Comprehensive System, Coram (1995) found significant differences on seven variables in extreme comparisons between violent murderers and nonviolent offenders. Prandoni and Swartz (1978) attempted to establish normative differences for offenders with psychotic and organic disorders.

Boehnert (1985) conducted a study of defendants adjudicated sane and insane on 90 Rorschach protocols. She did not report which Rorschach system was used on these protocols administered in 1978. The only significant difference she found concerned Sum C, with insane defendants ($M = 2.73$; $SD = 2.39$) scoring lower than those found sane ($M = 5.93$; $SD = 3.73$) or not raising the insanity defense ($M = 4.90$; $SD = 4.04$). When combined with Extended F+ %, the resulting discriminant analysis had a very modest classification rate of 51.6%.

Daubert Standard

Our guidelines, based on the *Daubert* standard, for the use of the Rorschach in insanity evaluations are delineated:

1. *Rorschach and insanity:* not supported. Available data are very sparse and not positive for the use of the Rorschach to differentiate between sane and insane defendants.

2. *Rorschach and malingering:* not supported. Studies (Schretlen, 1997; see Chapter 5) demonstrate convincingly that the Rorschach can be successfully feigned and that reliable indicators of malingering have yet to be established.

3. *Rorschach and diagnosis:* partial support in very selected cases. When any evidence of possible feigning is present during the evaluation, the Rorschach should *not* be used (see #2). The SCZI and DEPI, in the absence of feigning, may offer corroborative data of severe schizophrenia or depression, but should not be equated with diagnosis (Exner, 1997). A circumscribed but potential use of the Rorschach is with disordered defendants who deny symptomatology. In such cases, these indices may prove valuable as indirect means of assessing severe psychopathology in cases where more direct methods are ineffective.

4. *Rorschach and psychopathology:* very limited support. The Rorschach emphasizes perceptual style and organization. While certain indices may reflect psychopathology, these indices are not necessarily specific to psychopathology but encompass personality functioning more generally.

Holtzman Inkblot Technique

Overview

The Holtzman Inkblot Technique (HIT) represents a major research effort to integrate the qualitatively rich projective interpretations with more empirically based psychometric methods. The HIT is the result of an extensive investigation of 4,500 original inkblots that, through a series of preliminary studies, were refined to two equivalent sets of 45 inkblots that evoke a wide range of responses on HIT determinants. The HIT offers several psychometric advantages over the Rorschach: (1) the number of responses is standardized; (2) all research is based on a single scoring system; (3) most interpretations avoid complex indices; and (4) two parallel forms allow for retesting.

Reliability and Validity

A major limitation of the HIT is that the majority of recent studies are published in international journals and are not readily available in English. This section is limited in its scope to earlier studies based on American populations.

The HIT has demonstrated a high degree of reliability with respect to interscorer reliability, split-half reliability, test–retest reliability, and the equivalence for Forms A and B (see Holtzman, 1984a). Interscorer agreement for individual determinants is very high (rs from .89 to .99). Test–retest reliability is much more variable and dependent on the interval before retesting (Holtzman, 1984b). As with the Rorschach, much more attention has been paid to interscorer agreement than to agreement of clinical interpretations.

Swartz, Reinehr, and Holtzman (1983) summarize the HIT validity studies. The large majority of studies report positive findings with respect to personality variables. Like the Rorschach, the picture is mixed with respect to diagnostic findings. With respect to malingering, Schretlen (1997) concluded that the data were insufficient regarding whether the HIT could be successfully feigned. An interesting option for the detection of feigning would be a systematic comparison of the defendant's responses on Forms A and B. Given the time expenditure for two HIT administrations, use of nonprojective methods is recommended.

Daubert Standard

At present, the great majority of recent HIT studies are published in languages other than English. Based on earlier research, the HIT would appear to have several important psychometric advantages over the Rorschach for the assessment of personality variables. For malingering and issues of criminal responsibility, earlier studies do not provide sufficient support in terms of peer-reviewed research or known-error rates to satisfy the *Daubert* standard.

Thematic Apperception Test

Overview

The Thematic Apperception Test (TAT) was developed by Henry Murray (1943) in the late 1930s; the first published version became available in

1943. The TAT was developed as a method of exploring personality dimensions focusing on the patient's needs, presses (i.e., internal states in response to external forces), and thema (i.e., need–press combinations reflecting the individual's motivational trends). Since this early development, attempts have been made to utilize the TAT as a basis for psychodynamic formulations, as a diagnostic tool, and as a measure of fantasy and motivational patterns. More recently, empirical investigations have focused predominantly on variations in personality functioning and less on the TAT's usefulness in intrapsychic formulations and differential diagnosis.

The TAT is composed of 20 cards for each gender, with 11 cards shared by both males and females and 9 cards specific to each gender. According to the original format, 20 cards were administered to each testee in two separate sessions. However, this format is rarely followed today, when typically 10 or fewer cards are administered in a single session (Anastasi, 1988). The marked variations in the administration of the TAT may be viewed either as flexibility or as a psychometric nightmare. Needless to say, the reliability of the TAT is severely constrained by the absence of standardized administration, ordering and presentation of cards, and interpretive system. Despite cogent arguments during the development of the TAT (e.g., Murstein, 1965), for a single standardized procedure, its administration and interpretation remain highly individualistic. The obvious question remains: "Are any generalized estimates of reliability possible when different clinicians use different numbers of cards, different cards, different sequencing, and different scoring systems?"

Borum and Grisso's (1995) survey found that the TAT was rarely used in insanity evaluations by forensic psychologists (8%) and psychiatrists (10%). As noted previously, projective measures in general were rarely used (20% of psychologists and 3% of psychiatrists) as a standard component (i.e., >80% of evaluations) of insanity assessments.

Multiscale Inventories

MMPI and MMPI-2

Overview

The Minnesota Multiphasic Personality Inventory (MMPI; Hathaway & McKinley, 1951) and its revised version, the MMPI-2 (Butcher, Dahlstrom, Graham, Tellegen, & Kaemmer, 1989) remains the predominant multiscale inventory in forensic evaluations. More specifically, Borum and Grisso (1995) found that either the MMPI or the MMPI-2 were employed by 94% of forensic psychologists and 80% of forensic psychiatrists.

For mental health and legal professionals not versed in psychometrics, the most obvious question is "What is the MMPI-2?" The MMPI-2 is composed of 567 true–false questions written to "assess a number of major patterns of personality and emotional disorders" (Butcher et al., 1989, p. 1). Most MMPI-2 items are not unique to a particular scale but may be scored on several scales, a system that affects the MMPI-2's discriminant validity. The MMPI-2 scales are organized into general categories:

1. *Clinical Scales* were first developed for differential diagnosis and named accordingly (e.g., Depression and Schizophrenia). Because this endeavor was unsuccessful, the focus has evolved to clinical and behavioral characteristics associated with scale elevations or a constellation of elevations (i.e., codetypes).

2. *Validity Scales* were composed originally of three scales (i.e., L, F, and K) to test whether patients were underreporting or overreporting their psychopathology. These three scales have been augmented with approximately a dozen additional scales and indicators of response styles.

3. *Content Scales* consist of 15 scales that are simply organized by relevant clinical constructs. For example, the "Fears" content scale contains 23 items related to specific fears.

4. *Supplementary and Special Scales* are residual categories with hundreds of specific scales. A handful have been well validated for clinical purposes; however, most of these scales were developed for specific aims with narrowly defined populations.

The MMPI-2 requires an 8th-grade reading level which is an important concern with many offenders. Klinge and Dorsey (1993) examined the reading levels of 350 forensic patients and produced several findings especially relevant to the MMPI-2. First, the median reading level for patients was 7.1, with 43.1% performing at or below grade 6. Second, educational attainment could not be used to screen forensic patients for their reading levels; their median grades completed was 11.0.

This brief overview underscores a critical point, namely, that the complexity of MMPI scales and their interpretation requires specialized training. Please note the following caution: *Insanity evaluations are the worst place to learn the MMPI-2*. Mental health professionals not versed in psychometrics and not trained in the MMPI-2 should consult with well-qualified psychologists. Moreover, reliance on computer interpretations is a false comfort; these reports tend to vastly overinterpret MMPI-

2 protocols and do not describe their limitations. Likewise, attorneys need their own consultants. Available texts for attorneys on the MMPI-2 preparation and testimony are either devastatingly negative (Ziskin, 1995) or unduly optimistic (Pope, Butcher, & Seelen, 1993).

The remainder of this MMPI-2 section assumes that the reader has some expertise with the MMPI-2. Listed below are common pitfalls that we have often observed in forensic reports.

1. *Within-normal-limits profiles.* Profiles without clinical elevations are sometimes interpreted incorrectly as a "lack of psychological impairment" or "absence of an Axis I disorder." According to Greene (1991), these profiles are common and often represent severe chronic disorders or a person whose impairment is not captured by the MMPI-2.

2. *Diagnostic conclusions.* Although many patients have clinical elevations on the relevant scales, clinical elevations or codetypes cannot be equated with a diagnosis. The reason is that many patients with different diagnoses have similar elevations. Cornell (1996) found that diagnoses based on clinical scales (e.g., Scale 2 or Depression) would likely be wrong at least two out of three times.

3. *Content scales improve clinical classification.* Ben-Porath, Butcher, and Graham (1991) and Munley, Busby, and Jaynes (1997) found that two content scales improved the diagnosis of depression and schizophrenia. However, large-scale research (Archer, Aiduk, Griffin, & Elkins, 1996) found that content scales contributed very little to clinical interpretation and were likely confounded by social desirability (Jackson, Fraboni, & Helmes, 1997). Augmenting clinical scales with corresponding content scales is methodologically suspect, given the substantial overlap (e.g., 34.7% of the items on the Bizzare Mentation content scale are also on the Schizophrenia clinical scale).

4. *Reliance on traditional scales for defensiveness.* Many forensic experts rely solely on traditional indicators (i.e., L, K, and F-K) in detecting defensiveness. A meta-analysis by Baer, Wetter, and Berry (1992) indicated that two specialized scales are more effective in detecting those minimizing psychopathology: Wiggins's social desirability (Wsd) and the positive malingering (Mp) scales. In addition, Wsd appears to be relatively effective even with individuals coached on how to foil the MMPI-2 (Baer, Wetter, & Berry, 1995).

5. *Equating MMPI and MMPI-2 interpretation.* Although forensic clinicians have been reassured about the comparability of the MMPI and the MMPI-2 (e.g., Pope et al., 1993), major differences are observed in codetypes, both in the MMPI-2 normative data (Butcher, Williams, Graham, Tellegen, & Kaemmen, 1989) and in subsequent research

(Dahlstrom, 1992; Edwards, Morrison, & Weissman, 1993). The assertion of comparability is difficult to defend for codetypes when the MMPI to MMPI-2 correspondence is less than 50%.

Forensic Applications

Despite thousands of research studies on the MMPI and several hundred on the MMPI-2, very little attention has been paid to their usefulness in insanity evaluations. As previously noted, insanity evaluations pose unique challenges because of their retrospective nature and the application of a specific psycholegal standard of criminal responsibility. The following two questions are critical in evaluating the value of the MMPI-2 to insanity evaluations:

1. Do MMPI-2 clinical profiles differentiate between those determined to be sane and those determined to be insane?
2. Do the MMPI-2 validity indicators facilitate the determination of malingering that might otherwise threaten the integrity of insanity evaluations?

Three early studies compared differences in MMPI elevations based on the sanity of the defendants. Kurlychek and Jordan (1980) found no significant differences in MMPI elevations; their attempt to assess two-point codetypes was compromised by the small sample size. Rogers and Seman (1983) examined MMPI differences for 52 defendants charged with murder. The only difference they observed between sane and insane evaluatees was on Scale 5, which offered very little relevant information. Boehnert (1987, 1988) examined MMPI profiles for NGRI patients compared to evaluatees not found NGRI, nonforensic inpatients, and nonclinical inmates. Although statistics are not available, inspection of modal MMPI profiles suggested that NGRI patients tended to have *lower* clinical scale elevations than either sane (*M* difference = 7 points) or nonforensic clinical groups (*M* difference = 14 points). Taken together, these results are strongly consistent: the MMPI does not document more severe impairment for insane versus sane defendants.

Two additional studies examined the usefulness of the MMPI in insanity evaluations. Daniel, Beck, Herath, Schmitz, and Menninger (1984) examined MMPI correlates with clinical recommendations of sanity/insanity. With zero-order correlations, they found no significant correlates (*median r* = −.05) with clinical recommendations. A study by Heilbrun and Heilbrun (1989) yielded expected differences with 55 male NGRI patients tending to score higher on Scales 6, 7, and 8 than

207 prisoners assessed for parole. However, interpretation of these results is difficult for three reasons: (1) potential parolees tend to minimize psychopathology (see Walters, 1988) and are therefore inappropriate as a comparison group; (2) differences were reported based on local norms and not standard T scores[4]; and (3) individual scale differences are not available.

The usefulness of the MMPI-2 for insanity evaluations has received even less attention than the usefulness of the original MMPI. Rogers and McKee (1995) conducted a major descriptive study of the MMPI-2 in South Carolina with four criterion groups based on clinical determinations: (1) NGRI (n = 18) based on the *M'Naghten* standard, (2) GBMI (n = 21) in which the South Carolina standard parallels the language of the ALI standard except for its verdict, (3) sane with a major mental illness (n = 42); and (4) sane without a major mental illness (n = 136). Although the insane group evidenced its highest elevations on Scales 6 and 8, these scales were indistinguishable from the other groups'.[5] The GBMI group substantially overlapped with both sane and insane groups.

The validity scales of the MMPI-2 also deserve our consideration. Fink (1995) in a small study of 16 NGRI patients found a slight elevation of Scale F (approximate T of 62.8) with scores on F-K and O-S in the normal range. In contrast, Rogers and McKee (1995) found that Scale F was elevated for all groups with the following averages: insane (79), GBMI (79), sane with major mental illness (89), and sane without major mental illness (74). In summary, mild to moderate elevations of Scale F are very common among those evaluated as either sane or insane.

Daubert Standard

The MMPI-2 has found general acceptance as a psychological test and is well regarded in peer-reviewed journals. However, *Daubert* requires an analysis not only of scientific validity but of "fit" as well, that is, "whether that reasoning or methodology properly can be applied to the facts in issue" (p. 590). Insofar as "fit" is concerned, we provide the following guidelines on MMPI-2 conclusions in insanity evaluations:

1. *MMPI-2 and insanity*: not supported. An example is "This MMPI-2 profile is consistent with defendants evaluated as not criminally responsible" [or any substitution of nonultimate language]. Research has failed to establish any consistent patterns between those evaluated as sane or insane.[6]

2. *MMPI-2 and diagnosis*: not supported. An example is "This MMPI-2 profile is consistent with ____ diagnosis." Codetypes and clinical el-

evations do not signify a particular disorder, but are consistently found with a range of diagnoses.

3. *MMPI-2 and malingering*: partially supported. An example is "This MMPI-2 profile is consistent with malingering." In the case of extreme elevations (e.g., Scale F > 30; see Chapter 5; also see Rogers, Sewell, & Salekin, 1994), this statement likely meets the *Daubert* standard. However, moderate elevations are common among NGRI patients, other forensic evaluatees, and psychiatric inpatients. In such cases, malingering is indistinguishable from genuine impairment.

4. *MMPI-2 and clinical correlates*: partially supported. An example is "This MMPI-2 profile is consistent with the following clinical correlates. . . ." Some clinical characteristics are well established, but many evidence only modest correlations ($rs < .40$) with clinical data.

Addendum to the MMPI-2: A Synopsis of the MMPI-A

The MMPI-2 is intended for the clinical assessment of older adolescents (≥18 years) and adults (Butcher & Williams, 1992). In rare cases, defendants are evaluated for insanity who are younger than 18 years. A logical question is whether the MMPI for Adolescents (MMPI-A; Butcher et al., 1992) can be substituted for the MMPI-2. Despite superficial similarities (e.g., validity and clinical scales with identical names), the MMPI-A is substantially different than the MMPI-2 based on its item content and length. Current interpretation is based not on the convergence between the MMPI-A and the MMPI-2, but on correlates derived from the original MMPI (see Archer, 1992).

Recent research suggests several cautions for any forensic application of the MMPI-A:

♦ Cashel, Rogers, Sewell, and Holliman (1998) completed an external validity study of the MMPI-A with male adolescent offenders. They found clinical correlates that were very discrepant from the MMPI-based interpretations of the MMPI-A. The clinical correlates found in Archer (1992) are generally *not supported* for use with adolescent offenders.

♦ Rogers, Hinds, and Sewell (1996) found that recommended cut scores for feigning were not effective among dually diagnosed adolescent offenders. Instead, they found the F-K > 20 appeared to be promising as a screen for potential feigning. With a nonoffender sample, Stein, Graham, and Williams (1995) found positive results supporting the use of F-K > 19 as well as elevations on Scale F (≥23). Given these mixed findings, F-K > 20 appears to be the best indicator for adolescent offenders.

Programmatic research for establishing clinical correlates for the MMPI-A appears to be slowly emerging. However, the present status of clinical research would discommend the MMPI-A for any applications to insanity evaluations.

MCMI-II and MCMI-III

Overview

The Millon Clinical Multiaxial Inventory (MCMI; Millon, 1983, 1987, 1994) is a 175-item multiscale inventory that was developed as a brief, theory-driven diagnostic measure that was coordinated directly with DSM (Millon, 1983). Originally the MCMI was composed of 20 scales: 11 personality disorder scales and 9 clinical syndrome scales. Item overlap is substantial; on average, each item loads on 3.68 scales. Fundamental changes were introduced in the subsequent revisions. The second edition (i.e., MCMI-II) replaced 45 items (27.5%), added five new scales, and introduced a weighted scoring. The item overlap is very substantial, with each item averaging 5.44 scales. The third edition (i.e., MCMI-III) replaced 95 items (54.3%) and further modified the scoring system. Most significantly, scales and scale composition changed markedly. On the MCMI-II, scales average 41.08 items in length; on MCMI-III, the numbers dwindled to just 16.30 items per scale. While improving the item overlap (each item averaged only 2.51 scales), the MCMI-III shares little in common with its predecessors. Therefore, an often overlooked yet inescapable conclusion remains: *Validity studies for MCMI and MCMI-II cannot be applied to the MCMI-III.*

The most contentious element of the MCMI-III and its predecessors is the claim of its consonance with DSM-IV. As articulated by Millon (1994, p. 3), "Few currently available diagnostic instruments are as consonant as the MCMI-III not only with the nosological format and conceptual terminology of the DSM-IV but also with its diagnostic criteria." Millon also claimed that "individual scale cut-off scores on the MCMI-III can be used to make decisions concerning primary behavior disorders or syndrome diagnoses" (p. 4). However, Millon's own data does not support this assertion; the basic research for the validation of the MCMI-III produced meager results when compared to experienced clinicians' diagnostic ratings.[7] For Axis II disorders, the average correlation was a paltry .22, which accounted for less than 5% of the variance. Axis I disorders fared even worse, with a mean correlation of .14, accounting for a minuscule 2% of the variance.

Several key issues regarding the clinical use of the MCMI and its revisions (MCMI-II and MCMI-III) are summarized below.

1. The MCMI was never intended to differentiate clinical and nonclinical populations. The MCMI was developed to assess disorders and syndromes in mentally disordered persons. Therefore, any use of the MCMI to establish a mental disorder in a nonclinical population (e.g., criminal defendants without psychiatric histories) should be avoided. Millon does not offer a scintilla of data supporting the use of the MCMI-III for nonclinical forensic purposes.[8]

2. The MCMI-III interpretation is confounded by patient placement. The identical responses are interpreted differently for an outpatient or an acute inpatient. In many jail settings, defendants, who might otherwise be hospitalized, are treated in the secure environment of the jail. MCMI-III score-adjustment rules make no allowance for this eventuality.

3. The MCMI is distinguished from other multiscale inventories by its attention to Axis II disorders. Can clinicians rely on the MCMI for the assessment of Axis II disorders? Rogers, Salekin, and Sewell (1999) conducted a meta-analysis of 31 MCMI Axis-II studies. For MCMI-II, they found substantial construct validity for 3 of 13 scales, those assessing avoidant, schizotypal, and borderline personality disorders. In contrast, the MCMI-III had poor construct validity; not only did designated scales correlate poorly with the corresponding diagnosis ($Mr = .22$), but other scales correlated higher than the designated scales in 64% of the cases.

4. Computer-generated reports are not intended to replace clinical expertise and psychometric training. Millon (1994) is very clear in the MCMI-III test manual that computer-generated reports are not the finished product. Rather, they represent "a series of tentative judgments rather than a set of definitive statements" (p. 4) that "should be evaluated in conjunction with additional clinical data" (p. 4). Furthermore, clinicians are advised that sociodemographic data may independently influence computer-generated reports. An explicit admonishment is given: "the clinician should carefully consider the impact of important demographics, not only to compensate for their effects but for the insights they may furnish and for their ability to individualize and enrich the meaning of MCMI-III clinical data" (p. 4). Unfortunately, no guidance is given on how to fulfill this onerous obligation.

Forensic Applications

McCann and Dyer (1996) devote a full volume to forensic uses of the MCMI and its adolescent counterpart, the Millon Adolescent Clinical Inventory (MACI; Millon, 1993). The explicit purpose of McCann and Dyer's book is to promote the use of the MCMI in forensic contexts. In spite of this perspective, McCann and Dyer caution against the use of the MCMI-III in court, warning about its lack of empirical validation.

McCann and Dyer (1996) found virtually no research on the MCMI-II or the MCMI-III and their application to criminal forensic issues. Instead, they attempted to extrapolate from a handful of original MCMI studies of sex offenders and perpetrators of domestic violence. As previously noted, marked differences are evident between the three versions that makes such an enterprise highly speculative. We have not found in our own review any studies of the MCMI-II or the MCMI-III and the assessment of criminal responsibility.

We categorically disagree with McCann and Dyer's (1996, p. 84) assertions regarding the relevance of the MCMI-II for insanity evaluations. Their contentions that the MCMI-II can be used to assess the relationship of delusional systems and the role of alcohol and drugs in criminal behavior is unfounded. Given the marginal utility of MCMI-II scales,[9] even for diagnostic purposes, any attempt to go beyond diagnostic data to explore their complex relationship to specific criminal acts is patently meritless. McCann and Dyer (1996, Table 4.2) further claim that the MCMI-II is useful for the assessment of malingering via scale elevations. While promising, the empirical data are not sufficient to substantiate this claim.[10]

Daubert Standard

The MCMI-II has circumscribed applications under the *Daubert* standard. Key issues are summarized below:

1. *MCMI-III and insanity*: not supported. The MCMI-III should not be used in insanity evaluations based on its diagnostic invalidity. Its inadequacy as a diagnostic measure was clearly demonstrated by Retzlaff (1996). For Axis II disorders, elevation of a designated scale as evidence of the corresponding disorder is likely to be wrong 82% of the time. The numbers are not much better for Axis I disorders, for which a designated scale is wrong 69% of the time. These levels of inaccuracy are below the threshold for the admissibility of relevant testimony.

2. *MCMI-II and Axis II diagnosis*: partly supported. Although not a substitute for diagnosis, the MCMI-II can be used for corroborative data concerning avoidant, schizotypal, and borderline personality disorders. MCMI-II shows only modest construct validity for other Axis II disorders.

3. *MCMI-II and forensic conclusions*: not supported. Most forensic studies were completed with the original MCMI and cannot be generalized to the MCMI-II. Clinicians have virtually no clinical data on the use

of the MCMI-II in forensic populations. Without research data, the MCMI-II does not meet general acceptance for forensic conclusions.

Personality Assessment Inventory

Overview

The Personality Assessment Inventory (PAI; Morey, 1991) is a new-generation multiscale inventory designed for the systematic assessment of psychopathology and treatment considerations. The PAI is composed of 11 clinical scales and 5 treatment scales with additional scales for the assessment of response styles and interpersonal dimensions. The PAI represents an important departure from previous multiscale inventories both in its structure and in its clinical interpretation. Because many forensic experts and most attorneys are unaware of the PAI, we enumerate its distinguishing features:

1. *Reading comprehension.* Recognizing that low literacy levels among the mentally ill is often an obstacle to psychological testing, Morey (1991) designed the PAI to maximize comprehension. The PAI requires no more than a grade 4 reading level.

2. *Item overlap.* Unlike the MMPI-2 and MCMI-III, the PAI has selected items that measure only one scale (e.g., Borderline Features). Item overlap militates against discriminant validity[11] and confounds clinical interpretation.

3. *Gradations of response.* Instead of the traditional true–false format, patients are afforded a greater range of responses from false, to slightly true, mainly true, and very true. Gradational responses capture the quantitative aspects of an item response, which are entirely missing in the true–false format.

4. *Subscale interpretation.* Unlike the MMPI-2, the subscales were developed as an integral component of the PAI and its clinical interpretation. PAI subscales assess unitary constructs; the median alpha for subscales is a robust .83 for clinical samples. In addition, subscales are carefully constructed to facilitate interpretation. For example, Depression is divided into Cognitive, Affective, and Physiological subscales.

The PAI has excellent normative data comprised of a census-matched study of 1,000 community participants and a representative clinical sample of 1,265 patients from 69 clinical facilities. Validity studies are largely based on convergent validity coefficients with other psychometric scales (see Morey, 1991, Tables 9.5–9.16). As expected, these correlations are moderate in magnitude, often in the .40 to .50 range.

No effort was expended to match the clinical syndromes measured by the PAI scales with DSM diagnosis. However, Morey (1996) describes common PAI elevations with common disorders. Results of LOGIT analyses are described but the accuracy of the resulting functions is not provided. As acknowledged by Morey (1996, p. 146), the reported patterns should be viewed as "a useful starting point in identifying particular disorders."

Forensic Applications

Forensic research has investigated the usefulness of the PAI with respect to diagnostic validity and response styles. To date, no PAI studies have been reported that directly address insanity evaluations.

Three studies have addressed the PAI's convergent validity with mentally disordered offenders. Rogers, Sewell, Ustad, Reinhardt, and Edwards (1995) evaluated the usefulness of the PAI as a measure of schizophrenia and mood disorders with disordered jail detainees housed on a special mental health unit. The PAI, while useful as a screen for severe psychopathology, was limited in its discriminant validity (i.e., ability to distinguish among diagnostic groups) by the intercorrelations of the designated scales.[12] More recently, Rogers, Ustad, and Salekin (1998) compared PAI scales to corresponding symptom constellations on the Schedule of Affective Disorders and Schizophrenia (SADS; Spitzer & Endicott, 1978a). They found moderate convergent validity ($r = .50$) but modest evidence of discriminant validity. Encouragingly, they found good evidence of convergent validity between the PAI suicide scale and (1) SADS suicidal symptoms ($r = .63$) and (2) the Suicide Scale ($r = .74$) of the Suicidal Probability Scales. Wang et al. (1997) reported convergent validity for the PAI in the evaluation of problematic behaviors (malingering, suicide risk, and aggression) for inmates in a forensic hospital.

PAI studies of malingering are summarized in Chapter 5. Of particular relevance, Rogers, Sewell, Cruise, Wang, Ustad (1998) found that the Rogers Discriminant Function (RDF; Rogers, Sewell, Morey, & Ustad, 1996) should not be employed in forensic settings. Based on known-groups comparison with forensic malingerers and patients, they recommended that (1) elevations of the NIM scale ($\geq 77T$) be used as a screen for possible malingering and (2) that extreme elevations on NIM ($\geq 110T$) or the Malingering Index (≥ 5; Morey, 1996) offer strong corroborative data of feigning.

Daubert Standard

Because of its format, reading ease, and well-validated scales, the PAI holds considerable promise for the future. At present, we provide the following guidelines on the PAI conclusions in insanity evaluations:

1. *PAI and insanity*: not supported. No data are available on its usefulness in discriminating sane and insane defendants.
2. *PAI and diagnosis*: not supported. Morey (1996) explored the relationship of the PAI and diagnosis. However, this preliminary investigation is not a substitute for diagnosis.
3. *PAI and malingering*: partially supported. Extreme scores (NIM $\geq 110T$ and Malingering Index ≥ 5) offer strong corroborative data on malingering.
4. *PAI and clinical correlates*: partially supported. Most scales and subscales provide correlates of moderate magnitude regarding psychopathology and clinical syndromes.

Basic Personality Inventory

Overview

Jackson (1987) originally published the Basic Personality Inventory (BPI) to assess broad facets of personality and psychopathology in a variety of professional settings. The BPI is a 240-item, true–false inventory requiring approximately a 5th-grade vocabulary (Schinka & Borum, 1993). It is composed of 12 scales addressing difficulties with socialization/impulse control, mood/emotional adjustment, thought disorders, self-perception/sociability, and response styles. Importantly, the clinical scales are composed of nonoverlapping items which augment the BPI's discriminant validity. Unlike other multiscale inventories (e.g., MMPI-2 and MCMI-III), normative data are available for both adult and adolescent populations.

Many psychologists and most psychiatrists are unlikely to be aware of the BPI and its psychometric properties. We believe this inattention reflects more on commercialism than on empiricism. Despite its prestigious author, the BPI has not received the massive advertising efforts of its competitors. Given its substantial validation with offender populations, forensic experts should be aware of the BPI and its potential usefulness, especially with adolescent populations.

Forensic Applications

Austin, Leschied, Jaffe, and Sas (1986) evaluated the BPI's validity for a very large sample ($N = 1,232$) adolescent offenders. In examining its factor structure with principal components analysis and varimax rotation, they accounted for 65.7% of the variance with three factors: Psychiatric Symptomatology, Depression, and Social Symptomatology. Social Symptomatology (i.e., comprised of Alienation, Interpersonal Problems, and Impulse Expression scales) clearly differentiated those with and without extensive delinquent histories. This factor may be useful in evaluating the antisocial backgrounds of adolescent offenders.

Bonynge (1994) performed a cluster analysis of 213 adolescent inpatients and identified three clusters of disordered adolescents based on psychiatric problems, interpersonal difficulties, and rebellious behavior. Bonynge found modest convergent validity when these clusters were examined in relationship to the SCL-90-R and diagnosis. However, the lack of psychotic inpatients limits the applicability of this research to adolescent insanity evaluations.

Kroner and Reddon (1996) addressed the BPI factor structure for 486 incarcerated offenders. They found that most of the individual clinical scales appeared to be unidimensional when subjected individually to principal components analysis. Overall, the BPI's clinical scales yielded two dimensions in a confirmatory factor analysis: general psychopathology/adjustment and antisocial orientation. These data suggest that the BPI may be valuable with offender populations for establishing important correlates; however, data on pretrial defendants would be more germane.

The BPI appears to produce reliable results among incarcerated offenders. Kroner, Reddon, and Beckett (1991) found adequate estimates of internal reliability (median alpha = .72) and good test–retest reliabilities at a 1-month interval (median r = .71). These estimates would likely be higher if those offenders who had responded irrelevantly or with a specific response style had been removed from the analysis.

Several studies have examined the usefulness of the BPI for the assessment of malingering and dissimulation. The BPI has several methods for examining feigned profiles: (1) a Deviation scale that measures diverse forms of psychopathology, and (2) several social desirability scales that are typically very low among those feigning a mental disorder. Bagby, Gillis, and Dickens (1990) compared the BPI protocols of 31 simulators to 32 nonclinical controls. As predicted, simulators had markedly high scores on the Deviation scale and low scores on Balanced Desirability. In the absence of a clinical sample, these data have limited interpretability. In a more extensive study, Helmes and Holden (1986) compared 60 simulators to 404 psychiatric inpatients. Results of a discriminant analysis revealed 87–90% accuracy in identifying potential malingerers.

Daubert Standard

Although less publicized than other multiscale inventories, the BPI is based on sound validation and has been used extensively with offender populations. It utilizes accepted methodology and validation has been subjected to peer review. In line with the *Daubert* standard, we offer the following guidelines:

1. *BPI and insanity*: not supported. No data are available on its usefulness for insanity evaluations.
2. *BPI and response styles*: partially supported. Preliminary data suggest the usefulness of Deviation and Balanced Desirability. However, the BPI may be more useful in the rare cases where the defendant in an insanity case is minimizing his or her symptomatology (see Bagby et al., 1990). The BPI includes multiple and sophisticated indices of defensive responding.
3. *BPI and clinical correlates*: partially supported. Most clinical scales appear to be unidimensional in their assessment of clinical correlates. The BPI would appear to be the measure of choice for the assessment of clinical correlates among adolescent offenders.

Intellectual and Neuropsychological Testing

Martell (1992) presented cogent arguments explaining why neuropsychological impairment should be considered in selected insanity cases. Despite continued advances in neuroimaging methods (e.g., CT and PET scans), these techniques primarily address brain pathology and not its crucial linkage to behavioral impairment. In contrast, the strength of neuropsychological measures is the standardized assessment of cognitive and behavioral dysfunction.

What constitutes an adequate neuropsychological evaluation? Neuropsychologists are divided about what constitutes an adequate test battery; some favor "fixed batteries" such as the Halstead–Reitan, while others advocate more flexible approaches (Reed, 1996; A. D. Williams, 1998). Among fixed batteries, many neuropsychologists evidence considerable allegiance to a particular test battery (e.g., Luria–Nebraska).

The vast array of neuropsychological batteries currently employed by clinical psychologists militates against any straightforward evaluation of their validity. Therefore, this section will focus on two measures of intellectual functioning (i.e., WAIS-III; Wechsler, 1997; and Stanford–Binet-IV; Thorndike, Hagen, & Sattler, 1986) and two neuropsychological test batteries (i.e., Halstead–Reitan; Reitan & Wolfson, 1993; and Luria–Nebraska Neuropsychological Battery [LNNB]; Golden, Purisch, & Hammeke, 1985). Prior to their review, several screening models will be examined.

The Relationship of Intellectual and Neuropsychological Impairment to Criminal Responsibility

The linking of neuropsychological data from a particular defendant to a specific crime is a complex and daunting task. As outlined by Hall and McNinch (1988), the interaction of organic conditions with discrete cognitive abilities and response styles provides a formidable array of possible variations. Because neuropsychological deficits are generally stable, the interaction of environmental events with these deficits must be explicated. Organic mental disorders are rarely observed as the primary diagnosis among NGRI patients. From the data base on insanity acquittees, only 103 of 5,573 (1.8%) NGRI patients were diagnosed with organic mental disorders. Similarly, the R-CRAS data base yielded very low percentages. As summarized in Table 8.1, only 4.3% of insane and 1.4% of sane defendants had definite organic damage. With only one insanity defendant (1.1%) did this organicity grossly impair functioning (intentionality and behavioral control). What accounts for such small percentages? The following issues must be considered:

1. Severe organic cases may be excluded from criminal prosecution or plea-bargained to a treatment alternative. For example, persons with severe dementia may assault others but are unlikely to be brought to trial. Less severe cases are unlikely to meet the insanity standards (Menniger, 1986).

2. Organic impairment is likely to be underdiagnosed either because of the lack of resources or the presence of prominent Axis I symptomatology. In the latter case, Axis I disorders may result in marked deficits on neuropsychological measures (see Adams, Meloy, & Moritz, 1990) that is difficult to differentiate from organic mental disorders per se.

3. Neuropsychological correlates with violent behavior tend to be nonspecific and lack demonstrated classificatory accuracy. These correlates are common in incarcerated populations, suggesting poor

TABLE 8.1. Severity of Organic Symptoms and Mental Retardation in Sanity/Insanity Determinations

	Clinical determinations	
	Sane	Insane
Severity of organicity		
Suspected	4.2%	1.1%
Definite	1.4%	3.2%
Definite and pervasive	0.0%	1.1%
Severity of retardation		
Mild	9.4%	4.2%
Moderate	0.3%	0.0%
Severe or profound	0.0%	0.0%

discriminability between sane and insane defendants. In a recent review, Martell (1996) found that very high percentages (>80%) of violent offenders had abnormal test results on the Halstead–Reitan Neuropsychological Battery.

4. The ecological validity of neuropsychological tests (Henrichs, 1990), especially as applied to criminal behavior, has yet to be established. In forensic settings, neuropsychologists increasingly are questioned about the real-world applications of their test results (Long & Collins, 1997).

Neuropsychological Screens for Offender Populations

Iverson, Franzen, Demarest, and Hammond (1993) recommended that offenders in correctional settings be systematically screened for signs of brain dysfunction and its concomitant impairment and possible etiology. They suggested the use of selected Halstead–Reitan tests for motor and sensory skills, scales from Luria–Nebraska and subtests of WAIS-III for language skills, subtests of the Wechsler Memory Scale for memory functions, the Wisconsin Card Sorting Test or Category Test for abstraction and problem-solving skills, and the MMPI-2 and specialized measures for assessment of possible malingering. As acknowledged by the authors, this "screening" process is labor-intensive and may not be feasible in many settings.

Fowles (1988) suggested several streamlined approaches to screening offender populations for neuropsychological impairment. One alternative is the use of the Mental Status Examination in Neurology (Strub

& Black, 1985), a qualitative assessment that requires extensive knowledge of neurocognitive functions. A second alternative is the Wysocki–Sweet Screening Battery (Wysocki & Sweet, 1985) that is composed of seven brief measures. Fowles (1998) recommended that both alternatives be augmented with a brief screen of verbal intelligence, the Shipley Institute of Living Scale (Zachary, 1986).

Wechsler Adult Intelligence Scale—Third Edition

Overview

The Wechsler Adult Intelligence Scale—Third Edition (WAIS-III; Wechsler, 1997) represents a recent revision of the WAIS-R that was widely accepted as the standard for intellectual assessment. Like its predecessors, the WAIS-III is organized into two domains: verbal and performance abilities. However, substantial changes (different items, administration, and scoring) have been made in the subtests. Despite these substantial changes, the WAIS-III results correspond closely to those for the WAIS-R: .94 for Verbal IQ (i.e., VIQ), .86 for Performance IQ (i.e., PIQ), and .93 for Full Scale IQ.

The WAIS-III was completely restandardized on a national sample of 2,450 adults with oversampling for ethnicity and educational levels (see Psychological Corporation, 1997). As is true with earlier versions, the reliability of WAIS-III scales is (1) consistently high for most scales with the exception of several performance subtests (Symbol Search, Picture Arrangement, and Object Assembly) and (2) exceptionally high for IQ estimates (i.e., VIQ = .97; PIQ = .94; Full Scale IQ = .98). Initial studies (Psychological Corporation, 1997) have produced very positive results with respect to external criteria (e.g., specific cognitive measures and diagnostic groups). In summary, the WAIS-III appears to be a highly reliable and well-validated measure of intellectual functioning.

As an important caution, psychologists often overinterpret test data regarding intellectual abilities. As a common example, Matarazzo (1990) observed that marked discrepancies between Verbal and Performance IQ (i.e., VIQ vs. PIQ) are prevalent among unimpaired populations. While based on the WAIS-R, this observation holds true for the WAIS-III. Although a difference between VIQ and PIQ of 8.76 is "statistically significant" (see Table B.1 in Wechsler, 1997), its clinical relevance is questionable. As reported in Table B.2 (Wechsler, 1997), 17.6% of the normative sample has VIQ-PIQ differences of 15 or more. Moreover, 7.3% had difference of 20 or more. Likewise, great care must be taken when interpreting "differences" between various WAIS-III indexes; dif-

ferences between indexes of 15 or more points are very common (23.1–
32.4% of normative samples).

Forensic Applications

The validity of the WAIS-III as a measure of intellectual functioning is
well established. However, clinicians are cautioned not to equate IQ
scores with specific capacities. As observed by Long and Collins (1997),
IQ scores are often unlikely to capture an individual's ability. Therefore, the WAIS-III is extremely valuable at documenting intellectual
deficits. Except at the extremes, it has only indirect bearing on issues
related to criminal responsibility (see Nestor & Haycock, 1997).

Stanford–Binet—4th Edition

Overview

Thorndike et al. (1986) authored the most recent edition of the
Stanford–Binet—4th edition (SB-4). With its addition of 15 subtests,
the SB-4 is a radical change from earlier editions. It now measures four
general domains: Verbal Reasoning, Abstract/Visual Reasoning, Quantitative Reasoning, and Short-Term Memory. Summaries of its test validity have noted problems with its standardization and construct validity (Lindmann & Matarazzo, 1990; Perlman & Kaufman, 1990). Preliminary data do suggest a high correlation between the WAIS-III and
the Stanford–Binet, at least with persons of above-average intelligence
(Wechsler, 1997).

   The SB-4, unlike earlier editions, was designed primarily for use
with children. An examination of its normative sample reveals that it
was standardized for ages 2 through 24. Close inspection (see Thorndike
et al., 1986, p. 23) reveals a less-than-adequate representation for young
adults. For the inclusive ages of 18 to 24, only 194 participants were
used in its standardization.

Forensic Applications

The Stanford–Binet is rarely used in forensic cases; instead the WAIS-R
and WAIS-III appear to have been adopted as the standard measure for
assessing intelligence. More specifically, Lees-Haley (1992) found that
the Stanford–Binet was employed infrequently by forensic psychologists. With respect to insanity evaluations, Borum and Grisso (1995)
concluded that the WAIS-R was the predominant measure:

- Among forensic psychologists, 78% use the WAIS-R versus 2% the Stanford–Binet.
- Among forensic psychiatrists, 57% use the WAIS-R versus 0% the Stanford–Binet.

Forensic experts likely wonder if the SB-4 should ever be employed in insanity evaluations, given the psychometric advantages of the WAIS-III. One important but circumscribed use of the SB-4 is to establish very low IQs, which is not possible with the WAIS-III.[13] Given the problems with the SB-4 standardization, this use is best limited to adolescents (ages 13–17) on which adequate norms are available.

Halstead–Reitan Battery

Overview

The Halstead–Reitan Battery (HRB; Reitan & Wolfson, 1993) is a collection of neuropsychological measures. The HRB is typically comprised of the five core tests: Category Test, Tactual Performance Test, Speech Perception Test, Seashore Rhythm Test, and Finger Tapping Test. An impairment index is derived by the number of test scores in the impaired range. In addition to these five tests, the HRB battery typically includes the WAIS-R or WAIS-III, the Trail Making Test, and the Aphasia Screening Test. Neuropsychologists often add additional tests (see Goldstein, 1990), including the Klove Grooved Pegboard, Klove Roughness Discrimination Test, Visual Field Examination, and the MMPI-2. Although the HRB is described as a "fixed battery," this designation is not completely accurate because of the numerous variations employed in neuropsychological practice.

Lezak (1995) provides a balanced critique of the HRB. As she observed, one of the challenges in reviewing the HRB is that its lengthy test manual does not include sufficient data on the psychometric properties of the HRB.[14] Because the original normative data were inadequate, Heaton, Grant, and Mathews (1991) compiled new norms that took into account age, education, and gender. However, care must be taken in using these norms because the "normal" group had relatively high intelligence (M IQ = 113.8), thereby confounding interpretation (A. D. Williams, 1998). Lezak (1995) reviewed studies on the reliability of the HRB Impairment Index and found highly variable results. She also examined its diagnostic validity with different clinical populations. She found that it generally discriminated organic patients from normal controls However, Lezak raised the critical issue of whether the HRB provided incremental validity over the use of WAIS. In summary, she questioned its diagnostic usefulness with specific syndromes while affirming its ability to make global distinctions (i.e., impaired vs. normal).

Goldstein (1990) raises additional concerns about the HRB, including its neglect of memory and its inability to distinguish brain damage from schizophrenia. With respect to the latter, Goldstein noted that some patients with chronic schizophrenia have documented atrophy on brain scans; therefore, the lack of differentiation may be justified. This conclusion appears premature; systematic research comparing the relevant groups (i.e., schizophrenics with and without atrophy) still need to be conducted.

Forensic Applications

Williams (1997), in considering its use in forensic practice, described the HRB in very positive terms: "No other battery is as well validated with such a variety of neurological and psychiatric disorders. This is invaluable in making differential diagnoses" (p. 60). Similarly, Barth, Ryan, and Hawk (1992) support the HRB's use in forensic practice. This opinion is not universally shared, however. Faust (1995), while acknowledging Reitan's contributions to the field, questions the HRB's propensity for overdiagnosis and its limitations in ecological validity. In addition, Lezak's review, noted above, cannot be dismissed. As an important caution, Wedding (1983) found, based on HRB and WAIS results, that the *neuropsychologists' confidence was inversely related to their accuracy*. One alternative is to utilize the HRB to assess discrete abilities and to deemphasize its role in differential diagnosis. For the purposes of insanity evaluations, the severity of cognitive deficits is considerably more relevant than diagnostic categorization in establishing criminal responsibility.

Borum and Grisso (1995) addressed the frequency of neuropsychological tests in insanity evaluations. They found that the HRB was employed by 8% of forensic psychologists and 3% of forensic psychiatrists. These data leave unanswered the question of what is preferred by forensic neuropsychologists. Lees-Haley, Smith, Williams, and Dunn (1995) addressed this question, at least as it applies to personal injury evaluations. In a survey of 100 experts, they found that core HRB tests were administered from 21% (Speech Sounds Perception Test) to 38% (Finger Tapping Test) of the time. Two observations are salient. First, the majority of forensic neuropsychologists did not employ the HRB. Second, those who did often deviated from the standardized administration.

In summary, neuropsychologists are divided on the value of the HRB for differential diagnosis and likely disagree about its ecological validity. Most experts accept that its individual tests may be valuable at assessing specific deficits. As a cautionary note, the HRB is vulnerable to feigning (see Chapter 5). Without the use of a discriminant function, neuropsychologists are unlikely to be effective at detecting feigned protocols.

Luria–Nebraska Neuropsychological Battery

Overview

With the Luria–Nebraska Neuropsychological Battery (LNNB), Golden et al. (1985) operationalized the qualitative tasks developed by Luria with the goal of assessing a wide range of neurological deficits. The LNNB is composed of 269 items organized into 11 summary scales. Regarding its validation, Anastasi (1988) wrote approvingly about the LNNB's success in screening for brain damage and its potential usefulness in localizing damaged areas.

Lezak (1995) summarized the validation studies of the LNNB. While the split-half reliabilities appeared excellent, she questioned the wisdom of this approach, given the highly diverse items. She concluded that the LNNB was effective at making global distinctions (impaired vs. unimpaired) but found major diagnostic problems in studies that attempted to replicate original findings. She expressed concern that studies by the authors of the LNNB resulted in very positive findings that were not shared by other investigators. Similarly, Goldstein (1990) observed that professional opinions about the validity of the LNNB are highly polarized.

Forensic Applications

In stark contrast to his opinions about the HRB, Williams (1997) dismisses the LNNB for forensic practice in a single sentence. This lack of attention is shared by Doerr and Carlin's (1991) review of forensic neuropsychology. Faust (1995) wondered whether the LNNB is "a battery whose time never came and has since gone" (p. 996). He noted (1) the intense controversy about both its conceptualization and its validation and (2) its general lack of adoption by neuropsychologists.

Borum and Grisso (1995) found that the LNNB was rarely used (2% of forensic psychologists and 0% of forensic psychiatrists) in insanity evaluations. In surveying forensic neuropsychologists, Lees-Haley et al. (1995) found only 10% who used partial or full administrations of the LNNB. It appears to be rarely used in criminal forensic assessments (see Lees-Haley, 1992).

In summary, forensic experts are likely to avoid the use of the LNNB because of controversy and very mixed research findings. Even as a measure of neuropsychological deficits, the polarized views of its conceptual underpinnings and continued problems in replication militate against its use in insanity evaluations. In terms of *Daubert*, problems in establishing known-error rates and achieving even a modest level of acceptance among neuropsychologists would argue against its acceptability.

Conclusion

Psychological testing, despite its specialized terminology and complicated statistics, is based on very simple concepts of reliability and validity. Often with minimal assistance, professionals with no psychometric training can appreciate both the value and the limitations of testing. Consistent with both the standards for psychological testing and the *Daubert* standard, the most critical question remains, "Valid for what purpose?"

Notes

1. Test data are typically used to establish a clinical construct (e.g., symptoms or response style). When used to exclude a clinical construct, then the likelihood of a low score signifying the absence of that construct (i.e., negative predictive power) would be relevant.

2. While sidestepping this caustic debate, Wood et al. (1997) do have a valid point that kappa coefficients cannot be computed on estimates derived from other studies.

3. Ganellen's main point is that the Rorschach is more accurate than the MMPI and the MCMI-II at identifying schizophrenia and depression. However, his analysis is biased in favor of the Rorschach. For example, his Rorschach studies include only inpatients with major depression; his studies of other measures include (a) outpatients and (b) persons not qualifying for major depression (e.g., dysthymia and adjustment disorders).

4. As a benchmark, the scales do not appear to be particularly elevated for NGRI patients across Scales 6, 7, and 8; the composite M scale elevation was 54.3.

5. One exception was observed for Scale 8; contrary to expectations, the Sane with major mental illness group ($M = 89$) scored higher than the NGRI group.

6. Please note that experts in all studies had access to MMPI and MMPI-2 data; this knowledge of MMPI/MMPI-2 findings would likely bias the results *in favor of significant findings.*

7. Although the validation research had many shortcomings (Retzlaff, 1996), including the lack of formal diagnostic interview, these limitations are the responsibility of its developer.

8. Millon (1994, p. 5) asserts that the MCMI-III is appropriate for forensic purposes, "owing to the presence of many such cases in the MCMI-III norma- tive sample." We are left with several unappealing alternatives. If many cases are nonclinical (i.e., not impaired by a mental disorder) forensic cases, then the normative sample is contaminated. If few cases are nonclinical forensic cases, then this assertion is baseless. Simply because the normative sample includes many *clinical* forensic cases provides no evidence of its usefulness with *nonclinical* forensic cases.

9. Regarding substance abuse, see the summary by Rogers and Kelly (1997).

10. Bagby, Gillis, and Dickens (1990) and Retzlaff, Sheehan, and Fiel (1991) were moderately effective in detecting malingered MCMI-II profiles.

11. For an example with the MMPI-2, approximately 25% of the items on Scale F also appear on Scale 8. Do these shared items measure malingering or severe psychopathology?

12. Because clients were not limited to a single diagnosis, some intercorrelations were expected. However, the magnitude of these correlations far exceeded the convergent validity coefficients.

13. The lower bound for IQs on the WAIS-III is 45.

14. Although the comment was directed at the 1985 version, it is equally applicable to Reitan and Wolfson (1993).

Chapter 9

Structured Approaches
to Insanity Evaluations

Schedule of Affective Disorders and Schizophrenia
Mental State at the Time of the Offense Screening Evaluation
Rogers Criminal Responsibility Assessment Scales
Conclusion

Schedule of Affective Disorders and Schizophrenia

Overview

Structured interviews have established new and more stringent standards for diagnostic reliability and validity. Especially for Axis I diagnoses (e.g., psychotic and mood disorders), semistructured diagnostic interviews provide highly reliable, standardized data on both symptoms and syndromes. Rogers (1995a) provides a comprehensive coverage of structured interviews for Axis I and Axis II disorders and should be considered a standard reference for forensic psychologists and psychiatrists. Because of its superiority with retrospective assessments, this section features the Schedule of Affective Disorders and Schizophrenia (SADS; Spitzer & Endicott, 1978a). To begin this overview, we compare the SADS to other Axis I interviews.

Comparison to Axis I Interviews

A natural assumption of many forensic experts is that the Structured Clinical Interview for DSM-III-R (SCID; Spitzer, Williams, & Gibbon, 1987; Spitzer, Williams, Gibbon, & First, 1990) is a more recent and therefore better validated measure (see Williams et al., 1992). As reported in Table

9.1, this reasoning (i.e., more recent, therefore better validated) is not warranted. While the SCID does provide information about DSM criteria, it lacks information regarding (1) the severity of symptoms, (2) reliability, (3) malingering, and (4) applicability to insanity cases. Table 9.1 provides a comparative overview of the three major Axis I structured interviews (SADS, SCID, and DIS-III-R).

A critical issue in insanity evaluations is the establishment of not only the presence of a key symptoms but their severity. While most Axis I interviews simply categorize symptoms as either "clinical" or "subclinical," the SADS provides an unequaled opportunity to rate the severity of symptoms. Because the SADS focuses on discrete time periods, separate ratings can be accomplished for the time of the offense and the current time. Moreover, the reliability of symptoms is a hallmark of the SADS.

Other advantages of the SADS over the SCID and DIS include initial research on its usefulness in detecting response styles, especially malingering (Rogers, 1997; Ustad, 1996). Efforts were also made with the SADS to reduce the transparency of some questions. For example, the following screening question for delusions is very general and

TABLE 9.1. A Comparison of the SADS, SCID, and DIS-III-R: Relative Merits for Insanity Evaluations

Characteristic	SADS	SCID	DIS-III-R
Current symptoms			
Coverage	Focused/in depth	DSM criteria	DSM criteria
Severity	Gradations	Clinical/ subclinical	Clinical/ subclinical
Retrospective symptoms			
Coverage	Focused/in depth	Partial	Lifetime
Severity	Gradations	Clinical/ subclinical	Clinical/ subclinical
Reliability			
Diagnosis	Good	Variable	Variable
Symptoms	Excellent	Not established	Not established
Response styles			
Transparent inquiries	Variable	Yes	Yes
Potential malingering	Indicators	Unknown	Unknown
Insanity research studies	Yes	No	No

Note. SADS = Schedule of Affective Disorders and Schizophrenia (Spitzer & Endicott, 1978a); SCID = Structured Clinical Interview for DSM-III-R (Spitzer, Williams, Gibbon, & First, 1990); DIS-III-R = Diagnostic Interview Schedule—Version III—Revised (Robins, Helzer, Cottler, & Goldring, 1989).

nonperjorative, "Have you had any ideas that other people might not understand?" (Spitzer & Endicott, 1978a, p. 25). In addition, the SADS is the only Axis I interview on which insanity research has been conducted.

Description of the SADS

The SADS is an extensive semistructured diagnostic interview for the evaluation of Axis I disorders, particularly psychotic and mood disorders. For Part I of the SADS, ratings of individual symptoms are rendered for (1) worst period in the current episode and (2) current time (i.e., typically the preceding week). For purposes of an insanity evaluation, the "worst period" is operationalized as the "time of the alleged offense" (Rogers & Cavanaugh, 1981a). Part II covers past episodes of Axis I disorders as well as histories of alcoholism and antisocial behavior.

The format for SADS administration consists of an informal rapport-building interview, which precedes the formal portion of the SADS. Attorneys should be alert for cases in which the SADS questions were administered without an informal and unstructured introduction; this nonstandardized usage may alienate patients and diminish the validity of the SADS. The SADS questions are administered in a systematic manner and are composed of three types of inquiries (see Rogers, 1995a): (1) "standard questions," which are asked of all patients; (2) "optional probes," structured questions that are asked when further clarification is needed; and (3) "unstructured questions" devised by the interviewer when additional information is needed beyond the standard questions and optional probes. Final ratings of symptoms represent a composite of clinical data; whenever possible, they should not be based solely on the patient's responses.

Reliability and Validity

Rogers (1995a, pp. 89–90) summarized 10 major reliability studies with the SADS.[1] The major findings are summarized below:

- Interrater reliability for symptoms: median reliability coefficient of .82.
- Test–retest reliability for symptoms: median reliability coefficient of .72.
- Interrater reliability for diagnosis: median reliability coefficient of .82.
- Test–retest reliability for diagnosis: median reliability coefficient of .57.

The reliability of symptoms is particularly impressive and unprecedented in diagnostic studies. In addition, the diagnostic reliability is very robust and superior to that for the SCID and the DIS. In contrast, test–retest reliability is much more variable and appeared to be affected by the setting and the interval between the testing and retesting.

Diagnostic validity is essentially a bootstrapping operation whereby new methods attempt to improve on the current methods. Rogers (1995a) provided a comprehensive summary of recent developments in the validation of the SADS. The key findings are summarized below:

♦ Original studies demonstrated the expected relationships between the SADS and the Research Diagnostic Criteria (RDC; Spitzer, Endicott, & Robbins, 1978).
♦ Genetic and familial correlates have been studied with some success for establishing differences between disorders.
♦ Mixed but generally positive results have been established in comparisons of the SADS with other psychological measures.

The challenge of establishing diagnostic validity is that DSM diagnoses are used as "ground truth." From this perspective, validity is considered the fidelity between SADS inquiries and the DSM inclusion criteria. While sharing similar content, the critical question remains unexamined, "Does the wording of questions influence the likelihood of an accurate response?" Beyond this issue, the SADS appears to be moderately successful in achieving a convergence with other measures and correlates with familial and background variables.

Applicability to Insanity Evaluations

Forensic Studies

Rogers and his colleagues (Rogers & Cavanaugh, 1981a; Rogers, Thatcher, & Cavanaugh, 1984) examined the usefulness of the SADS in assessments of criminal responsibilities.[2] Combining across the two samples, they found significant differences between defendants evaluated clinically as sane and insane. These differences were particularly salient for psychotic symptoms: delusions, hallucinations, and formal thought disorder. Other differences were observed for manic symptoms and associated features of depression. As expected, the Global Assessment Scale of the SADS evidenced pronounced differences in rated impairment; sane evaluatees evidenced mild to moderate impairment ($M = 64.1$; $SD = 9.3$), while insane evaluatees manifested severe to pervasive impairment (M = 30.4; SD = 13.5). Insane defendants had approximately twice as many symptoms in the clinical range (insane, M = 10.7, SD = 5.5; sane, M = 4.8, SD = 2.1). The two studies underscore the importance of psychotic symptoms and overall impairment in the determination of criminal responsibility. Pertinent to the subsequent discussion of malingering, most defendants clinically evaluated as insane tended to have a circumscribed number of symptoms in the clinical range.

Rogers, Gillis, et al. (1990) investigated command hallucinations and other psychotic symptoms with the SADS in a sample of 65 forensic inpatients who had been court-referred for pretrial evaluations. The sample was composed primarily of schizophrenic disorders (51, or 78.5%) with smaller representations of other psychotic disorders (5, or 7.7%) and mood disorders (9, or 13.8%).

Rogers, Gillis, et al. (1990)[3] found a wide assortment of delusions: delusions of reference (50.8%), delusions of control (40.0%), delusions of mind reading (32.3%), delusions of thought broadcasting (23.1%), delusions of thought insertion (13.8%), delusions of thought extraction (4.6%), persecutory delusions (63.1%), delusions of jealousy (3.1%), delusions of guilt (1.5%), grandiose delusions (38.5%), and somatic delusions (13.8%). For a substantial number (21, or 32.3%), these delusions had a major impact on the defendant's behavior.

Rogers, Gillis, et al. (1990) also found substantial representation of various hallucinations: auditory (70.8%), visual (23.1%), olfactory (15.4%), and somatic (15.4%). Auditory hallucinations frequently involved a running commentary on the defendant's behavior (27.7%) or several voices conversing with each other (33.8%). Unlike delusions, hallucinations had a major impact on the defendant's behavior in only a small number of cases (10, or 15.4%).

As summarized in Chapter 5, Rogers (1997) provided data on the usefulness of the SADS for the detection of potential malingering. He combined data from 104 forensic evaluatees and 90 schizophrenic patients in a partial hospitalization unit to establish what symptom patterns were typical among bona fide patients. Patients who far exceeded the expected patterns were suspected of feigning. In addition, he summarized data from Ustad (1997) on SADS that were administered to 50 genuine patients and 22 suspected malingerers from a metropolitan jail setting.

Rogers (1997) concluded that several strategies appeared robust in the detection of potential malingerers: Contradictory Symptoms (68.2% of feigners), Symptom Combinations (81.8% of feigners), and Indiscriminant Symptom Endorsement (54.5% of feigners). As reported in Chapter 5, these strategies require independent confirmation by established methods (e.g., SIRS) prior to any definite conclusions regarding feigning.

Use of SADS Insanity Cases

The administration of the SADS for a criminal responsibility evaluation (see Rogers & Cavanaugh, 1981a) typically requires 2 to 4 hours, often spread over two separate time periods. In addition to the administration of the SADS proper, the expert must gather an unstructured self-report from the patient regarding his or her emotions, thoughts, and behavior at the time of the alleged offense. This unstructured information provides the expert with a general baseline for examining the accuracy and honesty of further statements elicited during the SADS interview. An adaptation of the SADS for criminal responsibility evaluations that has been found helpful is to score the last episode for the time of the alleged offense and the present time for the defendant's current psychological functioning. This modification allows the clinician to make systematic comparisons of the defendant's present impairment and reported impairment at the time of the crime.

The SADS is also helpful in developing a highly specific account for the time of the offense and quantification of the defendant's psychological symptoms. The clinician often supplements the SADS with detailed probes to establish the presence of specific symptomatology and its relevance to the criminal behavior. For example, with a defendant reporting hallucinations, it is important to establish whether hallucinatory activity was present during the commission of the criminal behavior and what impact, if any, it had on the defendant's willingness and deliberateness in engaging in such behavior.

The SADS's extensive format facilitates the clinician's identification of malingering and deception. It is difficult for a defendant to present a consistent and psychologically plausible report of symptomatology across several hundred clinical inquiries and over different evaluation periods without becoming either inconsistent or confused. Given the complexity of the SADS evaluation, dissimulating defendants frequently fall into a pattern of endorsing many symptoms at a severe level. Thus, by taking comprehensive notes and making specific ratings, the clinician has an extensive data base to address the honesty and completeness of a defendant's self-report.

The forensic expert must follow through carefully on his or her quantification of SADS symptoms. This procedure frequently involves rechecking critical symptoms from one interview to the next and integrating information from other sources, such as collateral interviews and previous mental health records. Practical guidelines for the administration of the SADS in criminal responsibility evaluations include the following:

1. The clinician must make a thorough evaluation of all symptoms regardless of their potential role in criminal responsibility. This standardization provides a comprehensive baseline for comparing the presentation of symptoms against corroborative information. Similar care must also be taken in Part 2 of the SADS, which examines previous episodes of mental disorders. This detailed interviewing may provide additional evidence of malingering or deception, as in the case of one defendant who reported 300 to 400 episodes of major depression in contradiction to corroborative information.

2. The relationship of individual symptoms to the criminal behavior must be assessed. More specifically, the forensic clinician must determine the potential impairment on the basis of key symptoms and the effects of the concomitant disorder on the defendant's ability to qualify for the pertinent insanity standard. Toward this end, the clinician must typically focus on the onset and the duration of critical symptoms as well as their degree of severity.

3. Symptoms that are critical to the diagnosis and opinion must be verified with repeated and thorough probes at different evaluation times, compared with unstructured clinical data, and corroborated with other clinical data. In complicated insanity evaluations, the clinician may wish to employ a multiple SADS evaluation. This procedure (described by Rogers & Cunnien, 1986) involves both the administration of the SADS to the defendant and corroborative SADS interviews in which witnesses or significant others are independently administered portions of the SADS with the focus on the defendant's symptomatology.

4. As described in Chapter 5, the clinician should closely evaluate the reported symptoms for evidence of feigning, based on the type, range, and severity of symptomatology.

In summary, the SADS presents a systematic and comprehensive approach to diagnosis. It allows the forensic clinician to quantify important symptoms at discrete time periods, including the time of the crime, and provides the basis for opinions regarding retrospective diagnosis and concomitant impairment in the assessment of criminal responsibility.

Daubert Standard

The SADS is a well-validated semistructured interview that has been studied in forensic populations, including defendants assessed for criminal responsibility. While the SADS has not been frequently employed by forensic experts (2% of forensic psychologists and 0% of forensic psychiatrists; Borum & Grisso, 1995), this finding likely reflects a lack of training in the SADS rather than any questioning of its validity. In this regard, Grisso (1996) has written approvingly of the SADS's potential role in insanity evaluations. Moreover, the SADS meets the scientific standards for establishing the reliability and validity of structured interviews (Rogers, 1995a). The following guidelines are provided with reference to the *Daubert* standard:

1. *Retrospective assessment of symptoms at the time of the offense:* supported. The SADS provides a reliable means of evaluating both the presence and severity of symptoms at discrete periods of time.

2. *Assessment of potential malingering:* partially supported. The SADS is useful in identifying persons for whom feigning is suspected in their presentation of current and prior symptoms. Importantly, the comparison group of forensic patients includes a substantial number of evaluatees being assessed for past legally relevant events (e.g., insanity and personal injury).

3. *Current and retrospective diagnoses:* partially supported. Data on the SADS indicate its usefulness in establishing both present and lifetime diagnoses. However, the SADS is limited by its use of RDC to establish diagnoses. Fortunately, the SADS covers nearly all Axis I symptoms necessary to render DSM-IV diagnoses.

Mental State at the Time
of the Offense Screening Evaluation

Overview

Melton and his colleagues (Melton et al., 1987; Slobogin, Melton, & Showalter, 1984) developed the Mental State at the Time of the Offense Screening Evaluation (MSE–Offense[4]). The MSE–Offense is composed of three main sections: (1) Historical Information, (2) Offense Information, and (3) a Present Mental Status Examination. These sections are described and critiqued individually.

The pivotal issue of the Historical Information section is the presence of "bizarre behavior." Unfortunately the definition of "bizarre behavior" does not remain consistent across the measure. For prolonged and episodic bizarre behavior, the criteria are "delusions, hallucinations, looseness of association of ideas (thought process incoherent and illogical), disturbance of affect (behavior disorganized, aggressive, intensely negativistic or withdrawn)" (Slobogin et al., 1984, p. 319). For "uncharacteristic" bizarre behavior, the definition changes to "delusions, hallucinations, sudden alterations in consciousness or motor functioning, sudden aggressive affectual discharge" (p. 319). If the defendant does not qualify for bizarre behavior and does not have a history of mental retardation or convulsive disorder, Slobogin et al. (1984) assert that "there is probably no evidence of 'significant mental abnormality' approaching legal relevance" (p. 319).

The Historical Information section is problematic because of its use of syndromes and symptoms incompatible with DSM. Given the MSE–Offense's reliance on DSM, many facets of its decision tree are both imprecise and inconsonant with DSM. As outlined in Table 9.2, several key symptoms (bizarre behavior, disturbance of affect, and loose associations) are conceptualized inaccurately. Inexplicably, mood disorders are subsumed under psychoses, a categorization antithethical with DSM-III and its subsequent revisions. In addition, its decision tree is less than comprehensive; missing diagnoses include (1) severe Axis II disorders (e.g., borderline and schizotypal) are discounted entirely and (2) dissociative disorders do not include dissociative identity disorder. Even more disturbing, the key characteristics for excluding disorders do not adequately cover the intended disorders. For the assessment of mood disorders, clinicians are directed to evaluate affect that is "aggressive, intensely negativistic, or withdrawn" (Slobogin et al., 1984, p. 319). Astoundingly, no characteristics are provided for depression or manic episodes.

TABLE 9.2. Incompatibility of the MSE–Offense with DSM-III and Subsequent Revisions

---

The MSE–Offense endorsed the use of the DSM diagnosis but conceptualized syndromes and symptoms in a manner incompatible with DSM.

1. Hallucinations and delusions are listed as "bizarre behavior."
2. Disorganized behavior is included as a "disturbance of affect."
3. Disturbances of affect for assessment of mood disorders do not include depressed or elevated moods.
4. Mood disorders are limited arbitrarily to "prolonged" periods.
5. Looseness of association is linked with incoherence.[a]
6. Mood disorders are subsumed under psychotic disorders.
7. Sudden alterations of consciousness are subsumed under "bizarre behavior."
8. Delirium can be excluded diagnostically without an assessment of consciousness.

---

[a]See "Derailment" (American Psychiatric Association, 1994, p. 766), which differentiates loose associations from incoherence.

The Offense Information section, unlike Historical Information, does not provide a decision tree. Instead, key issues are simply enumerated. In general, the outline appears to serve as a useful checklist of items to be covered. However, it offers no guidance in how this information is to be evaluated or critical decisions are to be rendered. In addition, its idiosyncratic use of key terms would concern most forensic experts: (1) delusions and hallucinations are considered "evidence of intrapsychic stressors" (p. 320); (2) "fear or panic stimulants" (p. 320) are presented without explanation; (3) the only examples of altered states of consciousness are either alcohol- or drug-induced; and (4) assessment of amnesia appears biased by consideration of only *claimed* amnesia—amnesia is often observed by clinicians rather than "claimed" by defendants. Despite these fundamental concerns, this section remains unchanged (see Melton et al., 1997, p. 240, Table 8.6).

The Present Mental Status Examination section indicates that a "typical" mental status evaluation is administered. Rogers (1995b) conducted a comprehensive review of mental status evaluations and found that the most commonly used are cognitive MSEs, especially the Mini-Mental Status Examination (MMSE; Folstein, Folstein, & McHugh, 1975). Measures, such as the MMSE, are typically useful in identifying moderate to severe dementias, but have limited applicability to psychopathology (Rogers, 1995b).

Reliability

Although the original study was completed more than 14 years ago, the reliability of the MSE–Offense has yet to be established. More specifically, reliability estimates must be considered at three conceptual levels:

- ◆ Reliability of the clinical observations: unknown
- ◆ Reliability of the decision tree: unknown
- ◆ Reliability of the conclusory opinion: unknown

Validity

The sole validity study was composed of 24 mental health professionals, predominantly psychologists and social workers, who completed a 30-hour training course that involved theory and practice in the application of the MSE–Offense. Nonrandomly assigned pairs of clinicians administered the MSE–Offense to a total of 36 inpatients at a forensic hospital.

The goal of the MSE–Offense was to develop a brief screening measure for possible mental disorder defense (i.e., insanity, diminished capacity, and automatism) for outpatient use. While the chief goal was screening out defendants for whom a mental disorder defense does not warrant further examination, it may also be used to "detect the obviously insane individual[5] for whom a more comprehensive evaluation is unnecessary" (Melton et al., 1997, p. 235). However, two fundamental design flaws greatly limit its attainment of these goals.

1. *No data are available on the use of the MSE–Offense as an initial screen.* Because all participants were prescreened in the community, the sample (i.e., only those court-referred to a pretrial inpatient forensic unit) is not representative of outpatient referrals. In addition, their repeated exposure to assessment process (i.e., prescreening, and inpatient admission and other assessment procedures) limits the applicability of these data to initial outpatient assessments. Compounding this problem, five participants were previously administered the MSE–Offense (see Slobogin et al., 1984, p. 311, footnote 19) prior to their involvement in the study.

2. *No data are available on the use of the MSE–Offense by individual evaluators.* Jointly conducted interviews are relatively uncommon in outpatient forensic assessments. Because of the design, these research findings are inapplicable to individual evaluators.

An additional design flaw is the study's attempted simulation of outpatient assessments. Although the MSE–Offense was designed for community screenings, evaluators conducted their interviews with forensic inpatients in a maximum security hospital. Because of the patient population and the setting, evaluators were aware of the substantial likelihood that participants would be severely impaired and warranted diagnosis of Axis I disorders. This awareness erodes our confidence in Slobogin et al.'s (1984) basic conclusion, namely, that their measure will not eliminate defendants with possible mental disorder defenses (i.e., false-negatives). An alternative explanation is that evaluators responded to the demand characteristics of the study (Jung, 1971) and evaluated psychopathology and its relevance to the alleged crime very differently than they would in the community. Needless to say, any facile generalization of assessment data from involuntary inpatients in a maximum security hospital to community screenings is unwarranted.

Results of the 36 cases were compared to inpatient assessments and legal verdicts. The agreement with inpatient assessment was moderate, at 72.2%, with a moderate kappa of .59. Excluding the 8 cases where no verdicts were available (*nolle prosequi*), agreement for a criminal responsibility defense was very modest (2 of 13, cases or 15.4%), while excellent agreement was achieved regarding those found guilty (15 of 15, or 100%). Slobogin et al. (1984) neglected to report the kappa coefficient between the MSE–Offense and the subsequent verdicts. Remedying this oversight, we calculated the kappa coefficient, which proved to be disappointing (kappa = .26). As a statistically nonsignificant finding ($p >$ .10), forensic experts must exercise care in not misrepresenting this finding of concordance to the court.

Applicability to Insanity Evaluations

According to Melton et al. (1997, p. 235), the MSE–Offense has two distinct purposes: (1) to screen out defendants without a possible mental disorder defense and (2) to identify obviously insane individuals. These very different purposes will be addressed separately.

MSE–Offense as a Screen for Insanity

One major constraint on the use of the MSE–Offense is its preoccupation with conclusory opinions. Although the MSE–Offense includes three level of data (clinical observations, decision-tree data, and conclusory opinions), validation has focused entirely on conclusory opinion (i.e., potential legal defense: yes or no). The validation of the MSE–Offense appears incompatible with Melton et al.'s (1997) basic admonition: Conclusory opinions unsubstantiated by clinical data should not be permitted. Not a scintilla of data is presented on symptoms, syndromes, diagnosis, or level of impairment. This point has been overlooked in past reviews (Grisso, 1986; Roesch & Golding, 1987; Rogers, 1986): *the validation of the MSE–Offense relies exclusively on conclusory opinion.*

The MSE–Offense is a psychometrically unproven measure. It lacks rudimentary data on reliability. More explicitly, we do not know whether forensic experts using the MSE–Offense agree on clinical observations, the subsequent decision tree, or the final conclusory opinion. The paucity of research data is striking; the only published study uses one research site, 36 defendants, and 28 verdicts. Convergent validity with inpatient evaluations is encouraging (72.2%) but not sufficient ($N = 36$). Concordance with subsequent verdicts is modest (65.4%) and statistically nonsignificant (kappa = .26; $p = .17$)) Methodological constraints militate against the use of these data with individual evaluators in community settings.

MSE–Offense and the Determination of Insanity

Given the MSE–Offense's sole emphasis on conclusory opinions and its lack of established validity, the findings by Borum and Grisso (1995) are not surprising. They found that 0% of forensic psychologists and 2% of forensic psychiatrists employ the MSE–Offense in criminal responsibility assessments.

The statement by Melton et al. (1997, p. 235) deserves further scrutiny; they assert that the MSE–Offense may be able to be used to "detect the obviously insane individual for whom a more comprehensive evaluation is unnecessary." The designation "obviously insane individual" is predicated on a forensic expert rendering an ultimate opinion. For different reasons, both Melton et al. (1987, 1997) and Rogers and Ewing (1989) find this use of ultimate opinion to be patently unacceptable:

- ♦ Melton et al.'s (1987, 1997) position explicitly prohibits ultimate opinions because they are categorically beyond the expertise of mental health professionals.
- ♦ Rogers and Ewing's (1989) position is that ultimate opinions should not be provided when they are *not* clearly substantiated by reliable clinical data.

Equally disturbing, Melton et al. (1997, p. 235) asserted that this ultimate opinion determination could rest solely on the MSE–Offense with the phrase "for whom a more comprehensive evaluation is unnecessary." This assertion that a brief interview (i.e., 30 minutes; Melton et al., 1997, p. 234) of questionable validity is sufficient for a complex insanity evaluation is indefensible.

The MSE–Offense does not meet the *Daubert* standard for conclusions regarding criminal responsibility. The one published study is marginal at best in meeting the peer-reviewed criterion. The error rates are both poor and insufficiently established. The MSE–Offense is almost never accurate regarding insane defendants (estimated error rate of 84.6%) and is based on an inadequate sample (for total verdicts, $n = 28$). Finally, a close examination of the MSE–Offense finds that it does not meet even the most rudimentary standards for general acceptance as a validated test (e.g., no reliability data).

Rogers Criminal Responsibility Assessment Scales

Rogers (1984) developed the Rogers Criminal Responsibility Assessment Scales (R-CRAS) as a method of standardizing data for use in insanity evaluations. As described by Rogers (1984, p. 1), the R-CRAS is intended to "quantify essential psychological and situational variables at the time of the crime and to implement criterion-based decision models for criminal responsibility." Reviews of the R-CRAS range widely from highly laudatory to caustically negative. This section of the chapter is organized into two components. First, the R-CRAS's validation is described and its applicability to insanity evaluations is considered. Second, the criticisms of the R-CRAS are examined in detail.

Overview

Traditionally, insanity evaluations have been largely an idiosyncratic process, reflecting the propensities and proclivities of the clinician. Substantive differences in forensic conclusions may result from disparities in (1) the organization and quantification of key symptomatology, (2) applications of the insanity standard, or (3) data from the defendant. The development of the R-CRAS was undertaken to address both (1) and (2). Toward this end, Rogers convened a study group composed of four forensic psychologists and three forensic psychiatrists to conceptualize and operationalize the key constructs to be investigated in assessments of criminal responsibility. The study group consulted with Barbara Weiner, JD, a colleague and well-known mental health–law attorney. Further refinements were undertaken after an initial pilot study. The final R-CRAS was the result of an extensive collaborative process with input from seven research sites and a second legal review by Roger Adelman, JD, U.S. Attorney's Office, Washington, DC.

The R-CRAS is composed of 30 variables that are typically rated on a 5- or 6-point scale: "0" for no information, "1" for not present, "2" for clinically insignificant, and "3" through "6" for increasing gradations of clinically relevant symptoms. One consideration in the test development was creating identical scoring (e.g., six corresponding gradations) for each R-CRAS item. While this uniformity would be advantageous statistically, pilot research suggested that requiring six gradations resulted in specious distinctions for some items.

The primary focus of the R-CRAS is the assessment of criminal responsibility with the use of the ALI standard. Subsequent research by Rogers, Seman, and Clark (1986) suggests that the R-CRAS may be applicable to the *M'Naghten* standard with very robust classification rates based on a two-stage discriminant model.

Reliability

The first important consideration is the reliability of the R-CRAS. Although described in the test manual (Rogers, 1984) as "interrater reliability," the tests of its reliability are much more stringent than most interrater reliability studies. In the typical interrater reliability study, one evaluator and one observer are present during and rate the same evaluation. In the case of the R-CRAS, evaluators conducted entirely independent evaluations and completed their R-CRAS ratings based on those independent evaluations. Moreover, the R-CRAS evaluations were not conducted at the same time; the average interval between evaluations was 2.7 weeks. This period is longer than what is typically used on structured interviews for establishing test–retest reliabilities (Rogers, 1995a). The subsequent review of reliability estimates must be evaluated in light of this unprecedented rigor for insanity evaluations.

Reliability estimates for the R-CRAS items were generally successful. For 23 primary items,[6] 12 achieved high correlations ($rs \geq .60$) for individual variables in a test–retest format. An additional 8 items had reliability coefficients in the expected range ($rs > .40$ and $< .60$) for this research paradigm. The remaining 3 items had modest correlations ($rs < .40$).

In Table 9.3, decision rules for the R-CRAS are organized into three general categories: diagnostic, components of insanity, and conclusory opinion. As summarized in Table 9.3, the R-CRAS decision rules are robust across these three categories.[7] The rationale for this organization is that forensic experts may wish to utilize the R-CRAS according to

TABLE 9.3. Reliability of R-CRAS Decision Variables

General category	Decision variables	Kappa	Agreement
Diagnostic variables	Malingering	.48	85%
	Organic mental disorder	1.00	100%
	Major mental disorder	.79	88%
Components of insanity	Loss of cognitive control	.75	87%
	Loss of behavioral control	.80	89%
Conclusory opinion	ALI standard	.94	97%

Note. Data in this table are distilled from Rogers (1994).

Melton's et al. (1997) schema and address diagnostic/impairment considerations alone or venture further to examine components of the insanity standard or the conclusory opinion itself.

Validity

Validation of any psycholegal construct is an imperfect process under less-than-ideal circumstances (see Grisso, 1986). The obstacles to validity are twofold: (1) psycholegal constructs represent social constructions of reality for which external validity (e.g., biological markers) are virtually unattainable, and (2) the evolving nature of case law continues to contribute nuances to the operationalization of insanity standards. Because of these obstacles, standardized methods will never result in a perfect match with legal standards, but they can provide a useful framework for its application.

The *de facto* recommendation of Melton et al. (1997) is to forgo the standardization offered by the R-CRAS in favor of entirely idiographic approaches. This interesting argument could be applied to the validity of all psycholegal constructs: *Because the nomothetic approach to psycholegal constructs is imprecise, perhaps even rudimentary, we should eschew its standardization in favor of no standardization at all, adopting an exclusively idiosyncratic approach.* The legal system is unabashedly pragmatic (Haney, 1980), and expects experts to apply the best available methods. Simply put, verdicts must be rendered today, based on today's knowledge. Invoking the best-available-method perspective, we argue vigorously for the use of less-than-perfect nomothetic measures rather than a reversion to unstandardized evaluations.

The validation of the R-CRAS involved an adaptation of Loevinger's (1957) model. Her model of construct validity is composed of three major parts: substantive, structural, and external. *Substantive validity* requires that the items of a test must address pertinent elements of the construct. Interestingly, even the R-CRAS's most enduring critics (Melton et al., 1987, 1997) do not appear to take issue with its substantive validity.[8]

Structural Validity

For structural validity, a series of a priori hypotheses were constructed and tested. Persons evaluated as insane should demonstrate a relative absence of malingering, more severe psychological impairment, and a greater loss of cognitive and/or behavioral control than those assessed as criminally responsible. Three separate studies combining data from five forensic centers produced remarkably similar patterns (see Rogers, 1984, pp. 15–16) consistent with these hypotheses. Unfortunately, these results have been dismissed as "tautological and relatively trivial" (Melton et al., 1997, p. 233) because clinicians would be pressed to reach these conclusions in addressing the insanity standard. An alternative perspective is that the structural relationship of these three constructs (i.e., malingering, psychological impairment, and loss of control) to insanity is pellucid and compelling.

The "tautological and relatively trivial" reproof deserves closer scrutiny. Are Melton et al. (1987, 1997) correct when they claim that these ratings are trivial and tautological? Several important patterns emerge as countervailing evidence against this charge.

1. An inverse relationship was postulated between voluntary (e.g., malingering) and invol untary (e.g., alcoholic blackout) influences on self-reporting. This relationship was documented (Rogers, 1984, p. 59); calculated for the purposes of this chapter, Cohen's d is .66 for voluntary influences (sane defendants higher) and .99 for involuntary influences (insane defendants higher).

2. The clinical literature indicates the predominance of psychotic symptoms in persons found insane. To test whether psychotic symptoms played a similarly predominant role for the R-CRAS, we calculated effect sizes for psychopathology.

   ♦ As expected, psychotic symptoms evidenced very large effect sizes (M Cohen's d = 2.49) for bizarre behavior (Cohen's d = 1.93), delusions (Cohen's d = 3.42), and hallucinations (Cohen's d = 2.13).
   ♦ As expected, nonpsychotic symptoms had only moderate effect sizes (M Cohen's d = .81).

3. Parallel items were developed to estimate the patients' reported control over their criminal behavior (#23) versus examiners' assessment of this control (#24). Parallel questions were employed because of concerns that sane defendants might overrate their loss of control.

   ♦ As expected, sane defendants tended to *overestimate* their loss of control when items 23 and 24 are compared (Cohen's d = .60).
   ♦ As expected, insane defendants did not overestimate their loss of control. On the contrary, they tended to *underestimate* this loss of control when items 23 and 24 are compared (Cohen's d = .60).

Forensic experts must decide for themselves whether the general findings (i.e., malingering, psychological impairment, and loss of control), as well as these specific findings, deserve the opprobrious terms "tautological" and "trivial." The structural relationship between these variables was also assessed via two-stage discriminant analysis. The individual variables were organized into five scales (Patient Reliability, Organicity, Psychopathology, Cognitive Control, and Behavioral Control) so that the relationship of these constructs to insanity could be tested formally. Rogers (1984) found that persons evaluated as sane and insane were highly discriminable, with hit rates of 97.2% for the calibration and 92.5% for the cross-validation samples. Relevant to structural validity, each summary scale made a substantial and unique contribution to the final classification.

The issue of structural validity can also be addressed by separate discriminant analyses for each component of the R-CRAS decision model. Rogers and Sewell (1999) using combined sample of 413 insanity cases, addressed whether discernible and theoretically relevant patterns would be observed. They established highly discriminating patterns (M hit rates of 94.3%) and accounted for a substantial proportion of the variance ($M = 63.7\%$). As a specific example, the decision point "loss of cognitive control" was strongly associated with awareness of criminality ($r = .68$), delusions ($r = .61$), and bizarre behavior ($r = .63$), but essentially unrelated to mood symptoms ($rs < .30$). These data provide support for the structural validity of the R-CRAS decision model.

External Validity

The external validity of the R-CRAS is difficult to establish in the absence of any gold standard. Although the legal outcome of insanity cases appears to be the most logical option, other factors incidental to the insanity determination may affect the legal outcome (e.g., heinousness of the crime and tenacity of the defense counsel). Bearing this caveat in mind, Rogers (1984) examined the concordance of R-CRAS conclusions with legal verdict. The overall level of agreement was high, at 88.3% (phi coefficient = .72). Given the challenges of mounting a successful insanity defense, it is not surprising that the concordance rate was lower for those evaluated as insane (73.3%) than for those evaluated as sane (95.2%).

We have been unable to unearth any insanity studies in which the clinical method was entirely separate from the legal criterion. Typically, clinical measures used in the insanity evaluation and forming a basis of the court report are compared to the subsequent verdict (e.g., Kurlychek & Jordan, 1980). As noted by Rogers and Ewing (1992), the R-CRAS sought to minimize potential contamination. Because the R-CRAS was a research effort, the triers of fact were not informed that the R-CRAS had even been administered. Obviously, any results (quantitative or narrative) from the R-CRAS were not disclosed to the judge or jury. The design for examining the R-CRAS's validity can be viewed from two different perspectives:

♦ The lack of complete independence between the R-CRAS and subsequent verdict is a potential confound to interpreting the results (Golding & Roesch, 1988).

♦ Because of the efforts to minimize potential confounds, the R-CRAS is the most rigorous evaluation of a specific measure against the verdict of insanity.

An analysis by Rogers, Cavanaugh, et al. (1984) addresses indirectly the R-CRAS's structural validity. Cases of agreement that defendants were *insane* had the most elevated scores on Psychopathology, Cognitive Control, and Behavioral Control. Cases of agreement that defendants were *sane* had the lowest scores on Psychopathology, Cognitive Control, and Behavioral Control. Cases of disagreement constituted a middle group. With reference to structural validity, the clear-cut cases on R-CRAS were very likely to result in a concordant verdict.

Generalizability

Beyond the R-CRAS, no other measures of insanity have systematically addressed the extent to which extraneous defendant characteristics may affect insanity evaluations. As noted in Chapter 1, research is essential to address whether sociodemographic backgrounds affect insanity evaluations. Although univariate differences were observed for education and race,[9] no significant differences were found for age, race, sex, or education when these variables were entered into a discriminant model with the R-CRAS summary scales. Other background variables, including prior juvenile and adult arrests and prior psychiatric treatment, were also nonsignificant.

A second critical issue with generalizability is whether the R-CRAS performs differently depending on the forensic center or the profession of the examiner. Employing a discriminant model, neither the location nor the training provided a unique contribution to the clinical evaluation of sanity. Only an experimental design, which is obviously impractical in actual insanity evaluations, would provide conclusive evidence; these results suggest that examiners are not unduly influenced by their location or training.

Major Criticisms of the R-CRAS

In the previous sections on Reliability and Validity, we alluded to several criticisms levied at the R-CRAS. In this brief section, we systematically delineate the major criticisms and provide a commentary. A more extended discussion regarding the admissibility of the R-CRAS is readily available (Rogers & Ewing, 1992). Consistent with previous analysis, the basic assumption of this commentary is that forensic experts should employ the *best-available methods*. This important concern should not be overlooked:

- Most criticisms of the R-CRAS are based on an absolutistic notion that a certain psychometric standard has not been achieved.
- Our response to these criticisms is based on a relativistic notion that the R-CRAS is superior to the alternative methods.

We firmly believe that very few forensic experts are willing to embrace this absolutistic perspective. The criticisms of the R-CRAS also apply to less standardized approaches. Stated baldly, experts who reject the R-CRAS as insufficiently validated must also accept the invalidity of their own idiosyncratic evaluations.

Table 9.4 summarizes the major criticisms of the R-CRAS as a psychometric measure. In addition, commentators (e.g., Goldstein, 1992a; Melton et al., 1987, 1997; Ogloff, Roberts, & Roesch, 1993) have deprecated the R-CRAS for its use of ultimate opinion testimony. Because the ultimate opinion issue was previously addressed in Chapter 2, only its application to the R-CRAS will be addressed in this section.

Psychometric Issues

Ordinal Measurement

Melton et al. (1987, 1997) castigated the R-CRAS for its use of ordinal rather than interval measurement.[10] This criticism is entirely misplaced because nearly all clinical assessment is ordinal. As an example, the Wechsler Adult Intelligence Scale—Revised (WAIS-R; Wechsler, 1987) was generally held as the best measure for quantifying intellectual functioning.[11] Does its assignment of IQ points really represent intervals? The answer is obvious to forensic experts: a 15-point difference on the WAIS-R does not represent the same quantum of intelligence. The difference in IQ between 70 and 85 bears no resemblance to the differ-

TABLE 9.4. A Comparison of the R-CRAS to the Alternative Methods

Psychometric issues	R-CRAS	MSE–Offense	Traditional methods
Type of measurement	Ordinal	Nominal	Nominal
Interrater reliability			
Clinical variables (r)	.58	Unknown	Unknown
Decision model (kappa)	.81	Unknown	Unknown
Conclusory opinion (kappa)	.94	Unknown	Unknown
Construct validity			
Consistent with hypotheses	Supported	Supported[a]	Unknown
Discriminant models			
ALI	92.5%	Unknown	Unknown
M'Naghten	96.7%	Unknown	Unknown
External validity			
Verdicts (%)	88.3%	65.4%[b]	Unknown
Verdicts (kappa)	.72	.26[c]	Unknown
Generalizability			
Defendant characteristics	Supported	Unknown	Unknown
Expert/setting characteristics	Supported	Unknown	Unknown

[a]For convergent validity, Slobogin et al. (1984) hypothesized agreement between MSE–Offense and comprehensive inpatient assessments. They appeared satisfied with a concordance of 72.2%.

[b]MSE–Offense entails a mental disorder defense (i.e., insanity, diminished capacity, or automatism). For legal outcomes, no cases of diminished capacity or automatism were reported. The concordance for "likely meets a mental disorder defense" was 2 of 13; for such defense the concordance was 15 of 15. In 8 cases, the charges were not pursued and cannot be included in these percentages of agreement.

[c]Nonsignificant ($p = .17$).

ence in IQ between 115 and 130 (Rogers & Ewing, 1992, p. 118). Similar arguments can easily be presented for multiscale inventories and structured interviews. It is simply disingenuous to derogate the R-CRAS by holding it to a higher standard than what has been achieved by the best-validated and most-established psychometric tests.

Reliability

Reliability is the sine qua non of diagnostic validity. Invoking the best-available method, the R-CRAS's reliability is clearly superior to the MSE–Offense and traditional interviews. With respect to symptoms, the SADS would be an excellent alternative to the R-CRAS. For the relationship of symptoms to criminal responsibility, the R-CRAS is unrivaled.

Validity

Despite the criticisms of Melton et al. (1997), the R-CRAS has the most extensive data on construct validity. With reference to external validity, verdicts from insanity trials form a less-than-ideal criterion. In comparing the R-CRAS to the MSE–Offense, the percentages speak for themselves (88.3% vs. 60.7%).

Generalizability

While the data on the R-CRAS are not definitive, they provide evidence that the R-CRAS is generalizable across defendants and examiners. Both the MSE–Offense and traditional measures have unknown generalizability.

Ultimate Opinion Testimony

As acknowledged by Rogers and Ewing (1992), the R-CRAS may be employed with or without conclusory opinions. Perhaps the most judicious use of the R-CRAS would be to apply its decision model for both diagnostic (malingering, organicity, and psychopathology) and impairment (loss of cognitive control and loss of behavioral control) opinions, but to eschew the conclusory opinion. Our reasoning is pragmatic. If the furor over the conclusory opinion detracts from the implementation of the R-CRAS, then less furor and greater standardization is preferable.

Applicability to Insanity Evaluations

The R-CRAS can be employed as either a general template for insanity evaluations or as a specific measure with psychometric properties. Based on informal discussions with forensic experts, we suspect that the R-CRAS is more often used as a template than as a specific measure.

The R-CRAS as a Template

The R-CRAS can be utilized as an organizing model or template for assessments of criminal responsibility. From this perspective, the R-CRAS provides (1) key issues to address, (2) severity ratings to be considered, and (3) a framework for integrating the clinical data. Senior clinicians may also use the R-CRAS within this perspective as a teaching model for how to approach insanity evaluations and frame the critical decision points. The template use of the R-CRAS deemphasizes individual ratings. In addition, forensic reports typically do not describe the R-CRAS, since it was not employed as a psychometric measure.

The R-CRAS as a Psychological Measure

The R-CRAS provides a method of standardizing the evaluation and ensuring that critical issues are not overlooked. The R-CRAS is not a formal psychological test; it is not administered to the defendant. Rather, the R-CRAS is a protocol for organizing and quantifying key symptomatology. Ratings of severity are keyed to the time of the offense and related to the alleged criminal behavior. Perhaps our greatest concern about the use of the R-CRAS is that forensic experts may abridge the assessment process and substitute "either plausible suppositions or theoretical inferences" (Rogers, 1984, p. 23) for clinical and corroborative data. The R-CRAS test manual (Rogers, 1984) is explicit in stating that R-CRAS ratings should (1) be based on a thorough review of all available clinical records and police-investigative reports and (2) be completed immediately following the final clinical interview. We recommend that attorneys question closely the data base for R-CRAS ratings to ensure that forensic experts were thorough in their multiple interviews and record reviews.

Application of the *Daubert* Standard

Borum and Grisso (1996) surveyed forensic psychologists' and psychiatrists' use of forensic instruments in insanity evaluations. They found significant differences based on professional training. Substantial numbers of forensic psychologists (41%) have used the R-CRAS, which was the predominant forensic instrument employed for insanity assessments (78% for the R-CRAS vs. 22% for all others). In contrast, relatively few forensic psychiatrists utilized any forensic instrument more than 10% of the time. Again, the R-CRAS was the most commonly used measure.

The application of *Daubert* to forensic measures is especially challenging. The best-available criterion for establishing error rates is a comparison to the subsequent verdict. When utilized in this manner, the R-CRAS appears to have a knowable error rate (overall = 11.7%; sane = 4.8%; insane = 26.7%). While less than ideal, these percentages are respectable and clearly superior to its alternative (MSE–Offense, overall error rate = 34.6%).

In terms of general acceptance, the R-CRAS is utilized by substantial numbers of forensic experts who conduct insanity evaluations. In terms of critical reviews, commentators have ranged from very positive (Meloy, 1986; Meyer & Deitsch, 1996) to very negative (Goldstein, 1992a). Most reviews (e.g., Grisso, 1986; Melton et al., 1987, 1997; Ogloff et al., 1993) have acknowledged both strengths and limitations of the R-CRAS. Earlier sections of this chapter provide an excellent framework for readers to evaluate the empirical basis of the R-CRAS and the acceptability of its clinical research for insanity evaluations. Acknowledging the vehemence expressed toward the R-CRAS regarding the ultimate opinion and our pragmatic alternative, we hope that this issue does not overshadow the other components of the R-CRAS. Because Rogers is both the author of the R-CRAS and an author of this book, we believe the best course of action is to ask the reader to draw her or his own conclusions on the matter of general acceptance.

Advantages of the R-CRAS for Expert Testimony

The greater standardization offered by the R-CRAS over alternative methods may facilitate the flow of testimony on both direct and cross-examination. For cross-examination, sample questions and corresponding responses are presented in Table 9.5. The primary advantage of this standardization is to avoid the nettlesome questions regarding the frailties of clinical judgment and subjectivity of forensic opinions (Ziskin, 1995).

Conclusion

The SADS and R-CRAS have respective strengths that argue for their integrated use in insanity evaluations. The SADS offers a comprehensive review of psychotic and mood symptoms. It can be implemented reliably for discrete time periods and has valuable data for the identification of potential malingering. In contrast, the R-CRAS is focused on important psychological and situational variables at the time of the offense. It provides forensic psychologists and psychiatrists with a template for organizing and integrating data regarding criminal responsibility. The comprehensiveness of the SADS is complemented by the focus of the R-CRAS.

The MSE–Offense has failed to expand beyond its modest research efforts of 1984. In the absence of (1) fundamental research on reliability and (2) large-scale studies with sound methodology, its authors (Melton et al., 1997) continue to promote its use. Moreover, the authors now recommend its use not only as a screen but for the final determina-

TABLE 9.5. Use of the R-CRAS to Address Cross-Examination

1. Isn't is true Doctor, that your opinion is based on unvalidated hunches and unstandardized observations?

   ♦ While not a formal psychological test, the R-CRAS provides a standardized method of assessing critical symptoms at the time of the offense.

2. Would you agree, Doctor, that unreliable testimony should not be offered in court? [assuming an affirmative response] Cite one study that suggests that your testimony is reliable.

   ♦ By use of the R-CRAS, Rogers (1984) was able to demonstrate that different experts evaluating the same defendant at different times were moderately reliable.

3. Isn't it true that you might be influenced by your general perceptions of the defendant [e.g., her race and background] in making your observations and formulating your opinions?

   ♦ Available research on the R-CRAS did not find any significant influences due to the age, race, sex, or criminal background of the defendant.

4. Would you concede that different doctors from different settings are likely to reach different opinions regarding insanity?

   ♦ That depends on whether standardized or unstandardized methods are used. When the R-CRAS is employed as a standardized method, doctors agree most of the time.

5. What do you mean, "They agree most of the time"?

   ♦ Let me be specific.
   With respect to malingering, experts agree 85% of the time.
   With respect to the presence of a major mental disorder, they agree 88% of the time.
   With respect to whether the defendant was cognitively aware of his/her crime, they agree 87% of the time.
   With respect to whether the defendant was able to control his/her criminal behavior, they agree 89% of the time.

tion in "obviously insane" cases. The result is an egregious example of bad science and unsubstantiated ultimate opinions.

Without the MSE–Offense, forensic experts want to make use of a reliable and valid screen for criminal responsibility. An interesting possibility is the use of an abbreviated SADS, namely, the SADS–Change Version (SADS–C; Spitzer & Endicott, 1978b) which assesses 45 key symptoms. Importantly, the SADS-C is highly reliable in its evaluation of symptoms (median ICC = .88) and has been used with forensic patients, including postacquittal NGRI patients (Rogers, Harris, & Wasyliw, 1983). Recently, the SADS-C has been employed effectively as a screen for mentally disordered offenders (Rogers, Sewell, et al., 1995; Rogers, Ustad, & Salekin, 1998). In addition, data support the usefulness of the SADS-C as a potential screen for malingering (Ustad, 1997).

Notes

1. As a general estimate, we calculated median reliability coefficients across studies. Small differences would likely have occurred if each study were decomposed and a grand median was computed.

2. As with nearly all clinical studies of criminal responsibility, the target measure (i.e., the SADS) was not independent of the full evaluation.

3. The presented data are a reanalysis that was performed especially for this chapter.

4. Although originally abbreviated by its authors as MSE, this abbreviation is generally applied to general mental status examinations (see Rogers, 1995a). To avoid confusion, we have designated this measure as the MSE–Offense.

5. The use of ultimate opinion language by an ardent opponent to ultimate opinions suggests the inescapability of conclusory opinions.

6. A total of 25 variables were included in most validity studies; however, one variable (# 5) had insufficient data and a second variable (#17) was categorical.

7. High kappa coefficients are very difficult to achieve with infrequent categories; this explains the high percentage of agreement for malingering (85%) and the moderate kappa (.48).

8. Referring to the strengths of the R-CRAS, Melton et al. (1997, p. 233) declared, "Rogers has identified and presented in an organized fashion many of the factors that an examiner must consider in an insanity evaluation."

9. Defendants more likely than others to be judged sane were whites and persons with less than a high school education.

10. For those unfamiliar with these terms, an *interval* scale indicates the measurement is uniform across the whole scale. By contrast, an *ordinal* scale indicates "greater than" or "less than" relationships but the measurement is not uniform.

11. The same argument applies to the most recent version, Wechsler Adult Intelligence Scale—Third Edition (WAIS-III; Wechsler, 1997) and the Stanford–Binet (Thorndike, Hagen, & Sattler, 1986).

Chapter 10

Laboratory and Specialized Assessment Techniques: Issues and Methods

Overview

Forensic experts are faced with an array of specialized assessment methods, which have varying degrees of applicability to insanity evaluations. For example, substance abuse assessments are frequently germane with insanity evaluatees in determining the effects of alcohol and drugs on the alleged criminal behavior. In contrast, forensic hypnosis is likely to be peripheral to these evaluations because of its limited validity for enhancing and verifying a defendant's account of the time of the offense. The purpose of this chapter is to provide a summary of laboratory and other specialized methods, with a focus on their forensic applications. Given the technical and scientific nature of most procedures, both attorneys and forensic experts will need to consult and rely on specialists for most cases.

The chapter is organized into two major sections addressing *accuracy of self-report data* and *diagnostic correlates*. Within the accuracy of self-report domain, five measures are reviewed: (1) laboratory methods with sex offenders, (2) polygraph techniques and integrity testing, (3) forensic hypnosis, (4) drug-assisted interviews, and (5) measures of alcohol and drug abuse. For diagnostic correlates, a constellation of procedures and one syndrome are considered: EEG and diagnostic imaging, and the special case of episodic dyscontrol syndrome. For most measures, the format will include a description of the procedures and their forensic relevance.

ACCURACY OF SELF-REPORT DATA

Specialized Methods with Sex Offenders

A pervasive problem in the clinical assessment of sex offenders is obtaining an accurate and complete appraisal of deviant sexual behavior. Understandably, sex offenders are often less than forthcoming about the parameters of their sexual deviance. In addition, sex offenders sometimes attempt to reduce their culpability by externalizing responsibility through claims of intoxication or specific mental states (e.g., dissociation). Forensic experts attempt to rely on several standardized methods to assess deviant arousal and accuracy of self-report. These methods include penile plethysmography (PPG), Abel's Screen (Abel, 1995), and the Multiphasic Sexual Inventory (MSI; Nichols & Molinder, 1984). For more comprehensive coverage of assessment methods with sex offenders, see Ward, McCormack, Hudson, and Polaschek (1997) and Sewell and Cruise (1997). For a review of largely unsuccessful MMPI methods, see Langevin, Wright, and Handy (1990).

Penile Plethysmography

Description

The PPG provides a direct physiological measure of penile tumescence in response to sexual and nonsexual stimuli. It is important to observed that the PPG is not a specific method but a diverse assortment of methods that vary in their instrumentation, stimuli, and use of indices:

 ♦ *Instrumentation* is composed of two major types: (1) circumferential, a linear measurement of tumescence at the base of the penis;

and (2) volumetric, a measure of total displacement due to tumescence. According to Langevin (1988), the circumferential measure is less precise because changes in circumference do not always reflect changes in arousal.

◆ *Stimuli* vary widely across laboratories. Therefore, the stability of deviant findings is open to question because such findings may be limited to a particular set of stimuli. In addition, many clinical settings utilize material that produces only slight levels of arousal. The rationale for this limitation is solely the convenience of the examiner. By keeping the stimuli relatively unarousing, the time needed for detumescence is reduced. However, the clinical meaningfulness of a nonerection (e.g., 10% arousal) is widely assumed rather than rigorously tested.

◆ *Use of indices* is also variable across settings. Abel, Barlow, Blanchard, and Guild (1977) proposed several indices based on comparative arousals to consenting sex, nonconsenting sex, and nonsexual violence depictions. Research has questioned, however, whether these indices can be manipulated (Murphy, Krisak, Stalgaitis, & Anderson, 1984) and their accuracy at identifying rapists (Ward et al., 1997). In the minority of cases where arousal is substantially greater to violent rape than consensual sex, most clinicians would (1) conclude that the individual evidences a pattern of deviant sexual arousal, but (2) would offer no conclusions about deviant sexual behavior

◆ *Any deviant arousal is clinically significant.* In actual practice, some clinicians appear to adopt the untenable position that any degree of arousal to deviant stimuli should be interpreted as a sexual deviation. The adoption of this extreme position is likely to result in unacceptable numbers of false-positives. Most nondeviant males, especially when deprived of sexual outlets via detention, are likely to evidence at least slight arousal patterns to deviant stimuli (Langevin, 1988). Moreover, Harris, Rice, Quinsey, Chaplin, and Earls (1992) found that nonoffenders had *more* arousal that rapists to audiotaped depictions of violent rape.

Efficacy

Sewell and Cruise (1997) provided a comprehensive summary of the PPG and its efficacy at detecting paraphiliac behavior. They summarized two recent meta-analysis (Hall, Shondrich, & Hirschman, 1993; Lalumiére & Quinsey, 1994) that demonstrated moderate effect sizes from .71 to .82. However, effect sizes do not translate into accurate classification. Beyond the variability noted above, several findings raise important questions about the accuracy of PPG assessments:

1. *Reliability of findings.* According to Ward et al. (1997), PPG findings are unlikely to be reliable unless the examinee achieves at least a 75% erection. As noted, many procedures attempt to avoid substantial erections to reduce detumescence time.

2. *Applicability to nonadmitters.* Sewell and Cruise (1997) demonstrated that the bulk of PPG research addresses the wrong issue, namely, the usefulness of PPG indices with sex offenders who acknowledge their deviant behavior. The relevant issue, PPG detection in persons denying deviant behavior versus persons falsely accused, has received little empirical attention. The questionable applicability to research findings on sex offenders to nonadmitters has not escaped judicial notice with reference to the *Daubert* standard. The Supreme Court of New Hampshire found testimony on sex offender profiling inadmissible in part because existing data focused on admitting rather than denying sex offenders (*State v. Cavaliere,* 1995).

Applicability to Insanity Cases

Both in courts applying *Daubert* and those applying alternative tests of evidentiary reliability, across the spectrum of different cases, penile plethysmography generally has been regarded as insufficiently reliable to justify admissibility (*United States v. Powers,* 1995; *Lile v. Mckune,* 1998; *State v. Spencer,* 1995; *In re A.V.,* 1993). In light of these appellate decisions, forensic experts should avoid the use of PPG data in insanity cases unless specific case law permits its use in a particular jurisdiction. Of critical importance, the PPG results should never be used as a "sexual lie detector" with indefensible conclusions regarding a defendant's veracity. Typically, insanity cases do not hinge on whether a paraphilia exists. Clinically, most sex offenders exhibit some control over their deviant behavior and engage in behaviors to reduce the likelihood of apprehension. Strategically, attorneys are likely to have difficulties mounting a successful insanity defense in the absence of severe mental disorder or impairment.[1]

Forensic experts must weigh the potential benefits and drawbacks of using PPG assessments in insanity cases. At best, occasional cases may occur where a denying defendant manifests a strong preferential arousal to deviant stimuli with a sufficient erection (> 75%) to produce reliable results. In such cases, a nonpsychotic motivation for the deviant behavior may be considered. However, paraphilias do not preclude psychosis or other severe psychopathology. The potential drawbacks were described previously and may include overinterpretation of equivocal findings in the absence of a well-defined preference or sufficient erection.

Abel's Screen

Description and Efficacy

To avoid the intrusiveness of PPG assessments, Abel (1995) devised the Abel's Screen, which is composed of a detailed questionnaire and a device that purports to be a "psychophysiological hand monitor." The examinee reports subjective reactions to different visual stimuli including various levels of nudity while staying in physical contact with the purported monitor.

With a total sample of 185 pedophiles, Abel (1995) performed a series of discriminant analyses that produced classification rates generally in excess of 80%. Many of the specific groups of pedophiles were relatively small (e.g., 25 offenders with prepubescent male victims). No cross-validation studies are reported.

Applicability to Insanity Cases

Abel's Screen should not be used in insanity cases for the reasons enumerated below:

1. At present, Abel's Screen lacks sufficient cross-validation to be used in forensic cases. Discriminant analysis without cross-validation can produce a substantial overfitting of the data, resulting in spuriously high classification rates.

2. No appellate decisions were found that addressed Abel's Screen. However, our review of Abel's Screen indicates that it does not meet the admissibility criteria set forth in *Daubert*. Its potential error rate has yet to be established. Moreover, its validation has neither been subjected to peer review nor has it gained general acceptance within the relevant scientific community.

3. Abel's Screen has questionable standing with respect to professional ethics. Its purpose is to deceive clients by deliberately misrepresenting a computer mouse as a psychophysiological measure. Forensic experts must grapple with the ethical problems of modeling deception to persons suspected of deceiving. This blatant deception allows the computer program to calculate a simple covert measurement. In addition, once the simple measurement is discovered via the trial process, the potential usefulness of Abel's Screen is further vitiated.

Multiphasic Sexual Inventory

Description

The Multiphasic Sexual Inventory (MSI; Nichols & Molinder, 1984) is a 300-item true–false questionnaire that is organized into 20 scales and a sexual history. The primary validation of the MSI is content validity derived from the ratings of 11 experts on sex offenders. Based on 200 items from the 1983 version, the authors established a high level of concordance (i.e., at least 9 of 11 experts in agreement) for 78.5% of the items. Given the deletion and modification of items from the 1983 version plus the addition of items in the 1984 version, validation studies with the 1983 version have only marginal relevance to the 1984 version. More specifically, less than 60% of the items in the 1984 version appear unchanged from the 1983 version.

Efficacy and Applicability to Insanity Evaluations

Validation studies have demonstrated group differences between offender and nonoffender populations. The critical issue is discriminant validity. For instance, does an elevation on the Voyeurism Scale correspond to voyeuristic behavior? This issue remains largely unaddressed. Although Schlank (1995) was able to establish MSI clusters, they do not appear to be associated by age (child or adult), gender, or relationship (familial or nonfamilial) of the victim. Moreover, the usefulness of the MSI with persons denying paraphiliac behavior requires empirical investigation. At present, the Lie scales presume that evaluated persons did engage in sexually deviant behavior. Therefore, their utility in distinguishing between denying and falsely accused defendants remains to be investigated.

The MSI does not appear to meet the *Daubert* standard. While studies have examined its correlates with other scales, major concerns have been raised regarding its face validity and vulnerability to response styles (Kalichman, Henderson, Shealy, & Dwyer, 1992; Schlank, 1995). Of critical importance, its usefulness in classifying specific paraphilias among nonadmitting sex offenders remains to be established. Without such data, its error rate is unknown. With reference to case law, *State v. Cavaliere* (1995) held that a sexual profile based in part on the MSI was not admissible under *Daubert*. However, the opinion focused on the MMPI-2 and MCMI-II and only mentioned the MSI briefly.

Polygraph Techniques

Description

The conceptual basis for polygraphs is very simple. An individual's reactivity to specific questions is measured in terms of physiological arousal. As noted by Lykken (1974), these measurements typically entail degree of sweating (galvanic skin response, or GSR), cardiovascular responses (pulse and blood pressure), and breathing (rate and volume of respiration). Despite maintaining the measurements across the last 4 decades, the sophistication of these measurements have increased significantly with the capacity of field polygraphs to provide digitized readings (Patrick & Iacono, 1991). Given this standardized measurement, why are polygraphs not accorded the same status as psychological tests and other procedures? An inherent problem with the current use of polygraphs is that the *output* (i.e., physiological data) is standardized but the *input* (i.e., questions asked by the polygrapher) is not. As an analogue, the value of psychological testing would likely be questioned if each person received a standard answer sheet but his/her own idiosyncratic test items.

The polygraph refers to a constellation of assessment methods that are based not on the technology but the type of questions and comparisons employed (for a thorough review, see Iacono & Patrick, 1997). Briefly, the polygraph methods are comprised of the following:

♦ *Relevant–Irrelevant Test (RIT).* This procedure involves the simple comparison of arousal levels to pertinent questions (e.g., "Were you involved in the armed robbery of *XYZ* liquor store?) to immaterial inquiries (e.g., "Did you drive your car to this appointment?"). Because many innocent persons are reactive to queries that implicitly question their criminal involvement (Iacono & Patrick, 1997), the RIT may produce many false-positives.

♦ *Control Question Test (CQT).* This constellation of procedures was developed in part to redress the problems with the RIT. A control question is an inquiry that is likely to be upsetting to an honest individual because it asks about either common transgressions (e.g., "Have you ever cheated on a test?") or specific mishaps in the person's past. Presumably, an honest individual would be more upset at lying or admitting to his/her misconduct than to responding honestly about their noninvolvement in a specific crime. The controversy surrounding the CQT will be discussed below.

♦ *Guilty Knowledge Test (GKT)*. This method employs questions with a multiple-choice format with information likely to be known only by the perpetrator (e.g., type of weapon used) presented as one of the alternatives. When sufficient information is available, the complicity of an accused can be established with a high degree of probability with very little risk of false-positives.

Several variations of the CQT are available, although not commonly employed in polygraph investigations. For example, the "directed lie" is a variant of the control question for which the subject is instructed to lie and actively think about that lie during the questioning. A second variant, "guilty complex" questions, addresses the subject's responses to a fictitious crime. While these methods may serve to standardize the control question, their validity remains to be established.

Efficacy and Applicability to Insanity Evaluations

The CQT is the predominant method in forensic cases. Unfortunately, scientific opinion regarding the merits of the CQT is highly polarized. Raskin and his colleagues (e.g., Raskin, 1989; Raskin, Honts, & Kircher, 1996) have touted its accuracy. Others (Iacono & Patrick, 1997; Szucko & Kleinmuntz, 1985) have insisted that only studies with rigorous designs be considered; they found no more than moderate levels of accuracy achieved largely at the expense of honest/innocent individuals. Proponents of the CQT often include field studies in which confessions to the polygraph examiner are used as an "independent" criterion; this approach is likely to inflate accuracy estimates. Iacono and Patrick (1997) have argued for blind interpretations of polygraph protocols. When this rigor is introduced into the research design, close to half (i.e., 44%; see Iacono & Partick, 1997) of honest/innocent individuals are likely to be falsely accused.

The GKT, in contrast to the CQT, can establish with a high level of confidence the likelihood whether an individual is knowledgeable of information he or she is denying. Examiners can establish the likelihood of differential arousal to the "guilty" or denied knowledge. Two constraints of the GKT include (1) the reluctance of police investigators to make unpublicized crime details available, and (2) the possibility of implicit learning of crime details through prior interrogation.

An important issue for attorneys is whether standards of professional practice were upheld in the administration of the polygraph. According to Szucko and Kleimuntz (1985), many polygraphers have very modest credentials and training. In addition, deceptive practices are apparently quite common among polygraphers. The types of deception (see Iacono & Patrick, 1987; Szucko & Kleinmuntz, 1985) include (1) the Stimulation Test or "Stim Test" as a demonstration of the polygraph's accuracy (i.e., a ruse in which the polygrapher "detects" a requested lie through a ploy, such as marked cards), (2) claims of infallibility known to be inaccurate by polygraphers, and (3) posttest interrogation of an unscored polygraph, falsely implying evidence of deception. Attorneys may wish to consider as a potential safeguard a requirement that the entire polygraph examination (i.e., interview, testing, and posttest interrogation) be videotaped.

The admissibility of polygraph evidence remains an unsettled issue. Because the subject matter of the *Frye* (*Frye v. United States*, 1923) decision was polygraph evidence, some federal courts have interpreted *Daubert*'s overruling of *Frye* as the test for admissibility of scientific evidence under the Federal Rules of Evidence as reopening the admissibility of polygraph evidence. This interpretation has led these courts to take a more pragmatic, case-by-case approach to the admissibility of polygraph evidence in criminal cases, rejecting their former per se rule against admissibility (see *United States v. Posado*, 1995; *United States v. Cordoba*, 1997). Other federal courts have affirmed their rejection of polygraph evidence (see *United States v. Sanchez*, 1997). Similarly, the majority of state courts continue to apply their per se rule against the admissibility of polygraph evidence (see, e.g., *State v. Porter*, 1995; *People v. Gard*, 1994); *In re Odell*, 1996; and *Perkins v. State*, 1995). Interestingly, the Supreme Court recently grappled with a per se rule against the admissibility of polygraph testimony in *United States v. Scheffer* (1998). The Court upheld the prohibition of polygraph testimony in military courts, citing its uncertain scientific status and the likelihood of significant error rates. Despite the ruling in *Scheffer*, trial courts are obliged to apply *Daubert* or its state counterpart to insanity cases. In cases with sufficient information, the GKT can yield data with high probabilities, especially regarding noninvolvement in the offense.[2] We are concerned about the use of the CQT in light of the enduring controversies regarding its scientific method and potential for misclassifying honest individuals.

Integrity Testing

Description and Efficacy

Iacono and Patrick (1997) provided a masterful review of integrity testing, its validation, and applications. The virtual elimination of polygraphs for employment purposes spawned an industry promoting self-report measures of honesty/integrity. These measures can be grouped as "open integrity" (i.e., questions about honesty and past involvement in illegal behaviors) and "personality-oriented" (e.g., personality correlates related to dependability, conventionality, and lack of impulsivity).

As summarized by Iacono and Patrick (1997), meta-analyses and major reviews have found modest-to-moderate effect validity coefficients for integrity tests. As opposed to measuring integrity per se, most studies have examined work-related behavior. Importantly, classification rates remain problematic; forensic experts would have great difficulty in defending the accuracy of individual cut scores and their relationship to honesty.

Applicability to Insanity Evaluations

Despite its widespread use in work settings, integrity testing should not be used in forensic evaluations. Unlike polygraphs that attempt to examine specific lies (e.g., involvement in a crime), integrity testing is intended as a general measure of honesty and related traits (e.g., trustworthiness and agreeableness). Therefore, it lacks the circumscribed focus of polygraphs. In addition, the external criteria tend to extend beyond honesty to productive and counterproductive behaviors in an employment setting. For these reasons, integrity testing is simply inapplicable to establishing the veracity of a defendant's retrospective account of the offense. In summary, integrity testing should be categorically excluded from assessments of criminal responsibility.

Forensic Hypnosis

Description and Efficacy

Although there is a consensus that hypnosis produces an altered state of consciousness, controversy continues to simmer over the nature of hypnosis and the psychological mechanisms that produce a hypnotic state (Kirsch & Lynn, 1995; Miller & Stava, 1997). Despite this controversy, the early view that hypnosis provides direct access to unconscious material has been largely discredited. Current perspectives posit that hypnotized persons have (1) conscious control over the hypnotic state and (2) the ability to edit and modify material while hypnotized.

Most practitioners agree that hypnosis does occur, and many affirm its treatment potential. For forensic applications, however, the critical issue is whether hypnosis provides any assurance that hypnotically recalled material is more accurate or more complete that other inter-view-based material. To assess the accuracy of hypnotically recalled material, Miller and Stava (1997) delineate the critical issues:

1. Can experienced clinicians reliably distinguish true and simu-lated trances? If a trance can be simulated without detection, then the value of hypnotically recalled material is undermined. Research sug-gests that clinicians cannot detect simulated trances.

2. Can hypnotized persons lie? Research suggests that a hypnotic state does not prevent deception.

3. Can hypnosis distort recall? Because of increased suggestibility, hypnosis may produce effects opposite its intended purpose. For ex-ample, distortions in a person's memory and recall may result in "pseudomemories" (Orne, 1979).

4. Does hypnosis enhance the recall of "forgotten" materials? The issue of hypnotically enhanced memory is highly controversial in light of the recent debates over recovered memories. Despite the potential value of recovered memories, researchers have yet to grapple with the critical issue, namely, a standardized method of distinguishing hypnoti-cally enhanced true memories from false or distorted memories.

The first three issues (simulated trances, lying, and pseudo-memories) argue against the use of forensic hypnosis. If forensic ex-perts cannot establish whether a defendant in an insanity case is hypno-tized, any derived information cannot be accorded special significance. Moreover, the ability to deceive under hypnosis would appear to defeat the primary purpose of forensic hypnosis. Equally concerning, hypno-sis could "deceive" the hypnotized by producing pseudomemories via heightened suggestibility. Without entering the recovered-memories versus false-memory debates (see Loftus, 1998; Ofshe & Singer, 1994; Pope, 1996), these three issues argue against the use of hypnosis in insanity trials. Beyond the three obstacles to forensic hypnosis (simu-lated trances, lying, and pseudomemories), studies (see Loftus, 1998) have amply demonstrated that false memories can easily be implanted and that hypnosis may facilitate this implantation (Spanos, 1996).

Applicability to Insanity Evaluations

In *Rock v. Arkansas* (1987), the Supreme Court held that a state per se rule, which prohibited the admission of the defendant's hypnotically refreshed testimony, violated the defendant's constitutional right to offer evidence on his own behalf. Since *Rock*, many state and federal courts have adopted pragmatic tests for the admissibility of hypnotically in-duced testimony. These rules address concerns with posthypnotic sug-gestion, the qualifications of the hypnotist, the role of the hypnotist in relation to the parties, records of contacts between the hypnotist and the subject, presence of third persons during the hypnosis, the hypnotic tech-niques used, and corroboration of the hypnotically induced memories (*Zani v. State*, 1989). Beyond these rulings, we maintain that forensic hyp-nosis should not be used to determine the veracity of a defendant's ac-count because it is not possible to rule out simulated trances or prevarica-tions under hypnosis. Moreover, insanity evaluations are retrospective assessments entailing accounts of events months or possibly years in the past. The effects of time and the demand characteristics of insanity evaluations add further barriers to the use of forensic hypnosis.

Drug-Assisted Interviews

Description and Efficacy

"Drug-assisted interviews" refers to any assessment method in which recall is apparently facilitated through the administration of medica-tions, primarily barbiturates. The most commonly used drug is sodium amytal (amobarbital). In insanity cases, a several-hour procedure typi-cally is scheduled for reviewing the defendant's thoughts, feelings, and actions at the time of the offense. As a precaution against pseudo-memories, care is taken to ask open-ended questions in an effort to elicit the defendant's account. Often the defendant is asked to recount the details of the offense more than one time.

A comprehensive review (Dysken, Chang, Casper, & Davis, 1979) revealed that most early research lacked experimental rigor. However, more recent studies have employed double-blind procedures and ran-dom assignment of research participants. Two areas of research are es-pecially relevant to insanity evaluations: they address the usefulness of drug-assisted interviews for (1) "desuppression" (i.e., recall of previ-ously forgotten or suppressed material) and (2) veracity of a patient's account. A third issue is whether amytal interviews result in pseudo-memories that distort the defendant's subsequent recall and thereby complicate the assessment of criminal responsibility.

Desuppression

For defendants with incomplete recall, the question arises whether bar-biturates can facilitate the suppressed memories. In this regard, Hain,

Smith, and Stevenson (1966) investigated the usefulness of several medications (i.e., an amphetamine and an anesthetic) in addition to amobarbital in producing desuppression. They did not find an advantage to these drugs in recalling suppressed material. However, these findings must be tempered by two considerations: (1) all patients were administered a conservative dosage of medications that was not titrated to their clinical status and (2) patients were not selected because they were suspected of suppressing highly significant material. Suffering from similar limitations, other controlled studies (see Rogers & Wettstein, 1997) have produced similar findings. As a general observation, controlled research on desuppression has produced disappointing results. In contrast, uncontrolled case studies of suppressed/repressed material sometimes report highly positive results.

Woodruff (1966) studied an issue related to desuppression, namely, whether drug-assisted interviews would elicit more symptoms from patient groups. Interestingly, he found no differences in patients with mood disorders, but did discover that a small number of patients with schizophrenia revealed previously undisclosed delusions and hallucinations. This finding raises the interesting hypothesis of whether drug-assisted interviews could be used with patients minimizing their psychotic symptoms (i.e., those with a defensive response style).

Veracity

The use of drug-assisted interviews to evaluate a defendant's veracity is predicated on the fact that he/she is actually experiencing the effects of sodium amytal. Unlike forensic hypnosis, sodium amytal produces pharmacological effects including nystagmus, thickening and slurring of speech, and errors in counting (Piper, 1993). While this issue has not been formally studied, it would likely be difficult for patients to simulate these features because (1) features, such as involuntary eye movements, would be difficult to feign; and (2) timing would be difficult (i.e., these features only appear at higher dosages; their sudden appearance at lower dosages might reveal deception). As noted by Rogers and Wettstein (1997), some practitioners prefer sodium brevital (a shorter acting barbiturate) because dosages can be closely titrated to ensure that the patient is experiencing the effects of the barbiturate.[3]

Because of the evocative misnomer "truth serum," a common misperception is that sodium amytal interviews provide a safeguard against deception. Interestingly, this matter has received scant research attention. Redlich, Ravitz, and Dession (1951) conducted the only study of sodium amytal to address veracity directly. Only seven participants provided guilt-producing stories which they related to one researcher. In a drug-assisted interview, they attempted not to disclose these stories to a second researcher. Of the seven participants, three were completely successful, two made partial admissions, and two made complete admissions. Because of the limited sample size, any conclusions are tentative. However, the results appear to suggest (1) that some participants can lie during drug-assisted interviews, and (2) others disclose material about which they did not want to be forthcoming. The results do not apply directly to insanity evaluations for two reasons. First, the consequences of revealing contradictory information are much greater in insanity evaluations. Second, forensic experts typically have knowledge about the pivotal issue (the alleged crime), while the Redlich et al. (1951) study presupposed that something important was being withheld.

On a related matter, Dysken, Steinberg, and Davis (1979) studied whether mental health professionals could continue to feign symptoms during an amytal interview. Although all nine mental health staff were successful, these results have only circumscribed relevance. The feigning involved a catatonic stupor. Therefore, its results have little relevance to whether an insanity defendant could maintain an elaborate version of fabricated symptoms.

Pseudomemories

Rogers and Wettstein (1997) summarized cases brought against health care providers for alleged sexual assaults while under sedation. In many cases, it is hypothesized that patients' memories were distorted by the sedation. In addition, many mental health professionals believe that hypersuggestiblity is possible with drug-assisted interviews (Piper, 1995). We recommend that forensic experts take similar precautions to those utilized with forensic hypnosis and refrain from leading questions.

Application to Insanity Evaluations

In clinical settings, drug-assisted interviews are selectively used (1) to assess mute or catatonic patients (Kaplan & Sadock, 1988) and (2) to establish differential diagnosis with certain amnesias (Cercey, Brandt, & Schretlen, 1997). With reference to forensic evaluations, its role is very circumscribed, based on the paucity of relevant studies and dearth of positive findings. Well-designed studies impose methodological constraints that militate against positive findings: (1) random selection of patients, including many for whom issues such as desuppression may not be relevant, and (2) standardization of dosages so that patients often receive less than clinically indicated. Nevertheless, forensic experts cannot use these limitations as a justification for using drug-assisted interviews.[4]

Beyond the clinical applications (e.g., elective mutism and catatonia), drug-assisted interviews should be viewed as a "last-resort method" when faced with several vexing diagnostic issues for three reasons. First, the research on drug-assisted interviews is relatively weak and marginally relevant. Second, drug-assisted interviews may produced hyper-suggestibility and distort subsequent accounts. Third, drug-assisted interviews carry nontrivial risks of medical complications (Kaplan & Sadock, 1988). Given these limitations, what vexing diagnostic problems warrant its occasional use in insanity evaluations?

♦ *Dissociative amnesia.* When clinical data indicate a strong likelihood that the defendant has dissociated his/her memory of the offense, the use of drug-assisted interviews might be considered. The forensic expert has the choice of attempting to elicit dissociated memories via drug-assisted interviews or making inferences about the defendant's behavior based on others' observations. Depending on the individual case, the forensic expert may decide the frailties of amytal recollections potentially outweigh the uncertainties of inferences.

♦ *Deception.* For the purposes of assessing deception, drug-assisted interviews are best viewed as a challenge test. In other words, if the defendant *spontaneously* changes his/her account, such changes may be evidence of deception. However, amytal interviews cannot be used to prove honesty because some individuals are capable of lying while sedated.

The courts generally have not found sodium amytal evidence admissible in the guilt phase of criminal proceedings (see *State v. Jeffers,* 1983; *State v. Pitts,* 1989; *Cain v. State,* 1977). We have not found appellate decisions addressing its admissibility since the *Daubert* decision. In light of the enduring problems with drug-assisted interviews, any conclusions in insanity evaluations, based on drug-assisted interviews, should meet the following two guidelines: (1) conclusions should only be presented if supported by other clinical data; and (2) forensic experts should be explicit about the limitations of drug-assisted interviews in their court reports and subsequent testimony. Drug-assisted interviews should not be used as the sole or primary basis of an expert opinion. Its validation as a measure of veracity does not meet the *Daubert* standard in terms of known-error rate or general acceptance.

Measures of Alcohol and Drug Abuse

Salekin and Rogers (in press) reviewed studies regarding the assessment and treatment of NGRI patients. Although substance abuse was rarely the primary diagnosis, they found that approximately two-thirds of defendants found NGRI had documented substance abuse histories. The role of alcohol and other drugs in the commission of the index offenses is essential to the determination of criminal responsibility. In examining the R-CRAS data base, we found that intoxication at time of the offense is common for both sane and insane defendants. For the time of the crime, the following percentages were found:

♦ Any use of alcohol or drugs: 22.6% of insane and 54.9% of sane defendants
♦ Moderate to severe use of alcohol or drugs: 6.4% of insane and 36.8% of sane defendants
♦ Alcohol or drug-related hallucinosis/delusional syndrome: 2.2% of insane and 0.0% of sane defendants

Straightforward assessment of substance abuse is thwarted by multiple factors that influence the accurate appraisal of substance abuse and the accuracy of reporting. Table 10.1 summarizes important variables influencing defendants' self-reporting; they include defendants' (1) actual knowledge of the type and amount of the substance ingested and (2) motivation to mislead the forensic expert. Extrapolating from adolescent studies of substance abuse (see Rogers & Kelly, 1997), roughly one-half of those evaluated minimized their drug use. Although often overlooked, small percentages likely invented some, if not all, of their drug abuse.

An additional pitfall in forensic cases is the misguided attempt to apply any metric to laboratory findings. As summarized by Rogers and Mitchell (1991), efforts to equate blood alcohol levels with impaired functioning describe only modal response patterns of persons without substantial tolerance. As they noted, clinical cases have been reported with blood alcohol levels exceeding .35 for patients who appear relatively sober.

Structured interviews, described in Chapter 9, often provide the best data for assessments of criminal responsibility. When substance abuse is a central issue to insanity, collateral interviews on substance abuse and its effects have proven valuable. Despite certain psychometric limitations (see Rogers, 1995a), the SCID substance abuse module

TABLE 10.1. Factors Influencing the Appraisal of Substance Abuse in Insanity Cases

Accuracy of defendant's recall

1. Even when motivated, intoxicated persons are often notoriously unreliable in their recall.
2. With the use of illicit drugs, persons are often unaware of the substances ingested or their potency.

Motivation to deceive

1. Particularly with minor offenses, defendants may be motivated to minimize or deny their drug use in order to avoid further criminal charges.
2. With major offenses, an unknown number of defendants may be motivated to exaggerate their drug use and especially its effects on their criminal behavior

Drug levels and criminal behavior

1. Similar serum levels reflect markedly different levels of intoxication among substance abusers.
2. While many defendants have ingested alcohol or drugs at the time of the offense, the amounts (and presumably their blood levels) are often comparable to the amounts typically used by defendents when not committing offenses.

may be helpful for systematically assessing symptoms associated with eight major drug classes (see SCID Module). For insanity evaluations, forensic experts are interested in drug usage and its effects on function preceding both criminal and noncriminal behavior. Therefore, a detailed history of recent substance abuse should focus on the months leading to the index offense.

Do psychometric scales and laboratory findings assist in the detection of substance abuse, especially denied substance abuse? Given the multitude of measures, the answer is necessarily complex. This section will provide a distillation of measures and their usefulness. For more extensive coverage of substance abuse and response styles, see Rogers and Kelly (1997).

Psychometric Measures of Substance Abuse

Screens

The use of screens for substance abuse is debatable in insanity evaluations. While screens are useful in determining whether a more comprehensive evaluation is needed, insanity evaluations should always examine closely substance abuse and its likely role in affecting the criminal behavior in question. However, the use of screens for cross-checking may have limited value.

Rogers and Kelly (1997) identified nine scales used in clinical settings for *screening* potential substance abuse. Several common characteristics of these screens can be observed: (1) face-valid items that are easily recognizable as addressing substance abuse problems, and (2) lack of validity indicators to determine minimized substance abuse. As summarized in Table 10.2, two of the most commonly used screens are the MAST and DAST. These measures are very straightforward in their content and are likely to be useful in screening for *acknowledged* substance abuse. In reviewing these screens, we found no real advantage among them in terms of content and discriminant validity. Therefore, we would recommend the use of the MAST based on its (1) extensive validation with acknowledged alcohol abuse and (2) ready availability. With drug abuse, no screen stands out with respect to validation.

Specialized Measures

Table 10.2 provides a description for three specialized measures of substance abuse: the CDP, the PEI, and the SASSI. Of these three measures, the CDP appears to be the most applicable to insanity evaluations, given its detailed recording of alcohol use and corroboration via an informant. The CDP is likely to be less applicable with the passage of time because it is intended as a contemporaneous measure of alcohol abuse. Also helpful with the CDP is its attempt to establish patterns of use (e.g., drinking alone or drinking to alleviate depression), which provides useful reference points in assessing criminal responsibility for a specific time period.

The PEI and the SASSI have limited usefulness in determinations of substance abuse for insanity evaluations. The PEI is intended for use with adolescents and focuses on the severity of substance abuse rather than on the use of specific drugs and their effects. As such, its information may have peripheral use with adolescents evaluated for insanity. The PEI is one of the few measures to address systematically potential response styles, although much more research needs to be conducted regarding minimized drug abuse. The SASSI is unlikely to provide data to address denied or minimized drug abuse. Because many of its items appear to capitalize on antisocial content, often associated with substance abuse, its discriminability is thwarted. Put simply, most defendants have some antisocial background; therefore, the use of antisocial content is likely to identify both abusers and nonabusers.

TABLE 10.2. A Summary of Psychometric Measures of Substance Abuse

Common screening measures

MAST. The Michigan Alcoholism Screening Test (MAST; Selzer, 1971) is the most widely used screen for alcohol abuse. Its high face validity makes the measure vulnerable to faking (Otto & Hall, 1988; Otto, Lang, Megargee, & Rosenblatt, 1988).

DAST. The Drug Abuse Screening Test (DAST; Skinner, 1982) parallels the MAST for illicit substance abuse. Data suggest that the DAST is vulnerable to defensiveness.

Specialized measures

CDP. The Comprehensive Drinker Profile (CDP; Miller & Marlatt, 1987) is a highly detailed interview for assessing alcohol abuse, impairment, and treatment potential. The CDP includes an elaborate format for quantifying reported alcohol abuse across a week period; potentially, this format could be applied to the time of the index crime. Its structure lends itself to corroboration from informants. Given its extensive validation (for a review, see Rogers, 1995a), the CDP should be considered as a potentially useful measure for criminal responsibility assessments, especially when corroborative interviews are feasible.

PEI. The Personal Experience Inventory (PEI; Winters & Henly, 1989) is an adolescent inventory of substance abuse. Extensive research has documented its usefulness in assessing the *severity* of rather than the *type* of drug abuse. It includes two scales to measure feigned drug use and social desirability. Most notably, the denial of drug abuse is not evaluated. With its extensive delinquent literature, the PEI might be considered in the evaluation of adolescent defendants.

SASSI. The Substance Abuse Subtle Screening Inventory (SASSI; Miller, 1985) was designed to measure substance abuse, whether acknowledged or not. An initial study suggested that elaborate decision rules might identify most defensive substance abusers (Miller, 1985). Although these decision rules were categorized appropriately as provisional, they continue to be used in clinical practice. As a critical oversight, the two more recent versions, SASSI-II (Miller, 1994) and SASSI-III (Lazowski, Miller, Boye, & Miller, 1998) do not have data on defensive substance abusers. A second major concern for the SASSI is its accuracy. Svanum and McGrew (1995) found that the SASSI was less effective than the MAST at detecting substance abuse. In addition, Rogers, Cashel, Johansen, Sewell, and Gonzalez (1997) studied the adolescent version of the SASSI (i.e., SASSI-A) with conduct-disordered youth. They concluded that it produced an unacceptably high percentage of false-positives (i.e., nonabusers classified as abusers). Because of the content of the SASSI and the SASSI-A appears to capitalize on antisocial attitudes and behavior, its use with forensic populations appears to be very limited.

Specific scales on multiscale inventories

MAC. The MMPI MacAndrew scale (MAC; MacAndrew, 1965) was intended to differentiate between alcoholic and nonalcoholic outpatients. A review of 74 studies

(cont.)

TABLE 10.2 (*cont.*)

by Gottesman and Prescott (1989) questioned its clinical usefulness. With the publication of MMPI-2, the MAC was modified slightly to form the MAC-R; however, the revised scale appears to be comparable to the original MAC (see Greene, 1991). When instructed to do so, nearly one-half of alcoholics can successfully deny their abuse of the MAC (Otto et al., 1988).

AAS. The MMPI-2 Addiction Acknowledgment Scale (AAS; Weed, Butcher, McKenna, & Ben-Porath, 1992) is a face-valid measure of substance abuse. Among Hispanic American patients, Fantoni-Salvador and Rogers (1997) found the AAS to be the best scale for persons openly acknowledging substance abuse. Given its face-valid nature, denying substance abuse should be relatively easy to accomplish.

APS. The MMPI-2 Addiction Potential Scale (APS; Weed et al., 1992) is composed of items, which are not face-valid for substance abuse, that may differentiate users and nonusers. Unfortunately, studies (Greene, Weed, Butcher, Arrendondo, & Davis, 1992; Weed et al., 1992) have found only modest differences between criterion groups, thereby calling into question the clinical usefulness of the APS.

Scales B and T. The MCMI Scales B (Alcohol Abuse Scale) and T (Substance Abuse Scale) are designed to assess alcohol and drug abuse. They are considered together because of their substantial item overlap. A review (Craig & Weinberg, 1992) of 16 MCMI studies calls into question the clinical utility of these scales. Over 50% of substance abusers are able to conceal their abuse on the MCMI (Craig, Kuncel, & Olson, 1994). Finally, these scales have been substantially modified on MCMI-II and MCMI-III; therefore, data from the original MCMI is inapplicable to later versions.[a]

ALC. The PAI Alcoholism (ALC; Morey, 1991) scale addresses problems with alcohol abuse and dependence. Fantoni-Salvador and Rogers (1997) found a remarkably high correlation (.80) between alcohol dependence and ALC with Hispanic patients. Because of its face-valid content, denial of alcohol abuse would appear to be readily achievable. As part of an ingenious attempt to estimated minimized alcohol abuse, Morey (1996) devised a regression equation to estimate the "true" ALC score. A potential limitation of the regression equation is that it emphasizes antisocial and aggressive content; persons denying alcoholism may also deny other undesirable activities (i.e., antisocial and aggressive behavior).

DRG. The PAI Drug Abuse (DRG; Morey, 1991) scale addresses the problems and consequences of drug abuse. Similar to the ALC, the DRG items are face-valid and easily recognizable. Morey (1991) developed a second regression equation for denied drug abuse, which appears to have some merit when applied to drug abusers. It has the same limitation as the ALC regression equation, namely, an emphasis on antisocial and aggressive content.

[a]Given the dramatic modifications between MCMI-II and MCMI-III, studies from MCMI-II cannot be extrapolated to MCMI-III (see Rogers, Salekin, & Sewell, 1997).

Specific Scales on Multiscale Inventories

In Table 10.2, we summarize the principal scales for examining substance abuse on three major multiscale inventories: MMPI-2, MCMI-II, and PAI. As a general observation, these scales should only be used for screening purposes (i.e., raising the issue of substance abuse for further evaluation). Attorneys should take great care that forensic experts comply with the following admonition: *Elevations on "substance abuse" scales cannot be equated with any substance abuse diagnosis.* Moreover, elevations on these scales do not provide incremental validity (i.e., make a diagnosis more certain). The reasons for this admonition are compelling:

♦ Scale elevations do not adequately cover DSM symptoms, their severity, or duration. Therefore, the diagnostic basis for establishing a substance abuse disorder is not available.
♦ "Clinically significant" elevations often lack specificity. In other words, nonabusing patients are likely to have scale elevations.
♦ The lack of scale elevations is also not determinative because many substance-abusing patients are either (1) not identified by these specialized scales or (2) are able to suppress their scale elevations.

What are the differences among scales on multiscale inventories in screening purposes for substance abuse? A few critical distinctions are possible:

1. The AAS is likely to be the best screen among MMPI-2 scales for *acknowledged* substance abuse. No recommendations can be offered regarding denied substance abuse.
2. The overlapping Scales B and T of the MCMI-II appear to lack sufficient discriminability to be used in forensic practice.
3. The PAI ALC and PAI DRG scales appear to be useful screens for acknowledged substance abuse. In addition, regression models have some potential to detect denied substance abuse, although their potential to be foiled by persons denying aggressive and antisocial behavior has yet to be fully investigated.

SCID Module

In the above review, an obvious shortcoming is the lack of comprehensive evaluation of illicit drug abuse. One alternative is the administration of the Psychoactive Substance Use Disorders module of the Structured Clinical Interview for DSM-III-R (SCID; Spitzer, Williams, Gibbon, & First, 1990). This module provides exhaustive coverage of drug abuse which is organized into eight drug classes. One limitation of the SCID for forensic evaluations is its variable interrater reliability. More specifically, Williams et al. (1992) found only moderate reliability (median kappa for clinical samples of .59), with marked variations across clinical sites.

The SCID module provides exhaustive coverage of DSM-III-R drug abuse symptoms. Given its face validity, defendants may easily distort the amount and type of drug use. Therefore, the best use of this module is in conjunction with clinical records, laboratory results, and informant interviews. The SCID module provides a comprehensive template for organizing these data.

Laboratory Methods with Substance Abuse

Laboratory procedures for drug abuse vary widely in their window of detection: immediate (e.g., breathalyzer), short term (e.g., urinalysis), and long term (e.g., hair analysis). The purpose of this subsection is to provide a general overview of laboratory methods. In complex cases where laboratory results play a potentially pivotal role, attorneys should contact medical specialists in substance abuse for their expert testimony.

Breathalyzer

Most commonly used with auto-related charges, the breathalyzer provides an accurate estimate of blood alcohol level. Breathalyzer results are best viewed as a "snapshot" of intoxication because blood alcohol levels both peak and diminish at very different rates across individuals (see, e.g., O'Neill, Williams, & Dubowski, 1983). In other words, an arrest several hours after the commission of the offense provides only vague data on alcohol level for purposes of establishing the role of intoxication.

Several cautions are offered regarding the use of breathalyzer data for insanity evaluations:

1. *Legal* intoxication under Driving While Intoxicated statutes should not be confused with *clinical* intoxication. Legal intoxication sets an arbitrary standard regulating when judgment and reaction time may be affected in some drivers. In contrast, clinical intoxication for the purposes of insanity evaluations considers major impairments, based on an individual's perception, thinking, judgment, and behavior at the time of the offense.

2. Blood alcohol levels, as previously noted, cannot be translated by any metric into levels of impairment. Individuals without histories of alcohol dependence manifest markedly different levels of intoxication. The presence of alcohol dependence may increase this variability.

3. Breathalyzer results taken immediately after drinking may be spuriously high. To reduce the likelihood of residual alcohol vapor in the mouth, an interval of at least 20 minutes is recommended.

Urinalysis

Urinalysis is a relatively effective method of detecting drug abuse, typically within a relatively narrow window of detection (i.e., 24–72 hours). A major exception is cannabis, which may be detected weeks after ingestion. According to Kapur (1994), three basic types of urinalysis are commonly used with suspected substance abuse: immunoassay, chromatographic, or chromatography/mass spectrometry methods. Of these, immunoassay should only be used for screening purposes. When positive findings occur with immunoassay, confirmation is required with either chromatographic or chromatography/mass spectrometry methods (Rogers & Kelly, 1997).

Urinanalysis provides a wider window than the breathalyzer, increasing its potential applicability to insanity evaluations. However, forensic experts must be concerned with drug ingestion that occurred after the alleged involvement in the index crime; such use might obscure the findings and their relevance to criminal responsibility. For urinalysis, the following issues must be considered:

1. False-positives (i.e., misclassification as using drugs) may occur as a result of over the counter medications or the ingestion of poppy seeds.
2. False-negatives (i.e., misclassification as *not* using drugs) may occur as a result of contamination (e.g., if not continuously observed during the sample collection, it may be adulterated with toilet water) or flushing (drinking large amounts of water prior to testing).

The most useful application of urinalysis to insanity evaluations is as an independent source to corroborate the defendant's account of substance abuse. When a defendant claims that substantial drug ingestion impaired his/her awareness of the crime, urinalysis may provide independent verification. Equally important, when a defendant claims that his/her erratic behavior was the result of a mental disorder and not intoxication, urinalysis provides valuable data about drug use. However, urinalysis will not be an issue in most insanity cases. Unless medical interventions were required at the time of arrest, most criminal defendants are not subjected to urinalysis.

Hair Analysis

Kelly and Rogers (1996) provide a recent summary of hair analysis as a method of detecting drug abuse. Briefly, drug metabolites become embedded in the core of hair shafts. Because scalp hair grows at a relatively constant rate (i.e., approximately 1/2 inch every 30 days), hair samples can document drug use across different time intervals. Like urinalysis, hair analysis typically involves two procedures: radioimmunoassay of hair (RIAH) to determine the presence of drugs, and gas chromatography/mass spectrometry (GC/MS) to confirm its presence and possibly estimate the amount of drug use.

Hair analysis offers a unique perspective to insanity evaluations. Unlike the breathalyzer or urinalysis, hair analysis is truly a retrospective measure. Months following the index crime, hair samples can often be examined to provide a general timeline about drug use. Therefore, significant drug use in the month surrounding the offense can be evaluated independent of the defendant's account. Unlike urinalysis, questions about a particular sample (e.g., misidentification or contamination) can be circumvented by repeat testing at different laboratories. In addition to repeat testing, hair analysis offers several advantages over urinalysis: (1) not susceptible to countermeasures, (2) negligible false-positives, and (3) applicable to a wider range of drugs.

In our experience, hair analysis is not routinely used in insanity evaluations. Its chief limitation is the imprecision of its timeline. No statements can be offered about the defendant's drug use on the day of the index crime. Nevertheless, the defendant's general drug use during this period can be evaluated. Given its expense, forensic experts may wish to use hair analysis selectively in insanity evaluations. One possibility is to restrict its use to cases in which the defendant (1) was severely impaired and (2) has a past history of substance abuse.

Commentary Concerning Substance Abuse Measures

The previous review of psychometric and laboratory methods clearly outlines their potential accuracy in detecting past substance abuse. As a general rule, there is an inverse relationship between degree of precision and extended time framework. For example, specialized scales on multiscale inventories have the least precision and the broadest time period; they attempt to measure either past experiences with an unspecified time period or future propensities. In contrast, the breathalyzer is highly accurate for a very limited time period. Simply put, inconsistent findings across dissimilar measures may reflect differences in evaluated time periods and the accuracy associated with these periods.

One observation is inescapable in this review of substance abuse measures: *impairment due to drug abuse is poorly measured.* Although clinical correlates (i.e., psychometric methods) and biological measurement (i.e., laboratory methods) of substance abuse can achieve acceptable levels of accuracy, they do not address impairment. Use of the CDP and unstructured interviews with the defendant and informants are likely to be the best sources of clinical data on impairment.

How does the *Daubert* standard apply to substance abuse measures? Given the dozens of measures and procedures, only general guidelines are provided:

♦ Determination of substance abuse by questionnaires and inventories? *Not supported.* Most psychometric methods should be viewed as valuable screens but not as independent sources of data regarding the presence of substance abuse or its diagnosis.

♦ Determination of substance abuse by laboratory methods? *Supported.* In the determination of substance abuse at the time of testing, laboratory methods may provide well-established tests with known accuracies.

♦ Determination of substance abuse by structured interviews? *Supported.* In the determination of substance abuse diagnoses, structured interviews (e.g., SCID module and CDP) may furnish acceptable data, provided that informants corroborate the defendant's account. In light of *Daubert*, the severity of a substance abuse disorder can be described generally in terms of symptoms and frequency of symptoms.

♦ Determination of impairment on tests and laboratory methods? *Not supported.* The degree of impairment on these standardized measures is not sufficiently established. Testimony attempting to link substance abuse measures to impairment would not pass muster under the *Daubert* standard.

DIAGNOSTIC CORRELATES

The second major section of this chapter provides an overview of specialized laboratory procedures that are primarily used to evaluate brain pathology and genetic abnormalities. This section is entitled Diagnostic Correlates to emphasize the importance of these procedures in clarifying diagnostic and etiological questions. Rarely do these procedures shed direct light on the complex interrelations between abnormal findings and the emergence of criminal behavior. Therefore, the focus in this section will be on providing a nontechnical overview rather than a detailed analysis of their relevance to criminal responsibility.

Attorneys will find that the great majority of forensic psychologists and psychiatrists are not sufficiently trained as to offer expert testimony on the specific findings from these specialized procedures. Instead, forensic experts typically rely on consultative reports from neurologists and radiologists, and integrate these findings into their final reports. If data from these procedures appear pivotal to a particular insanity case, attorneys must seek the appropriate specialists from neurology, neuroradiology, and neurosciences. Within these fields, subspecialization is often required for state-of-the-art knowledge.

This section begins with an overview of radiologic and imaging methods. The techniques and their primary applications are described. The section also includes a synopsis of episodic dyscontrol syndrome because of its potential relevance to insanity evaluations.

The EEG and Diagnostic Imaging

Electrodiagnostic Techniques

Neylan, Reynolds, and Kupfer (1997) provide a useful summary of electroencephalography (EEG) and quantitative electroencephalography (QEEG). As a review for attorneys, the following outline introduces the specific methods and their customary applications:

1. *EEG* measures the electrical activity of the brain through a standard array of electrodes. It provides a nonspecific indicator of cerebral functioning. It is primarily used in the diagnosis of seizure disorders but may also be useful in assessing dementias.

2. *QEEG* provides a computer-based synthesis of EEG data and can provide a topographic map of electrical activity. The QEEG has been used in research to detect brain ischemia and different mental disorders. According to Neylan et al. (1997), the sensitivity and specificity of the QEEG have yet to be firmly established.

3. *Evoked potentials* utilize a standard EEG that is supplemented with a standard sensory stimulus. Research has demonstrated group

differences, often between schizophrenic and nonschizophrenic patients.

Langevin, Ben-Aron, Wortzman, Dickey, and Handy (1987) reviewed the early literature on abnormal EEGs in violent offenders. They were critical of the methodology used in these studies: (1) offenders were often preselected because of neurological concerns; (2) vague criteria were used to determine brain abnormalities; and (3) EEG interpretations were not checked for reliability. Langevin et al. (1987) conducted their own research and found abnormal EEGs at a comparable rate for violent and nonviolent offenders, although homicidal defendants had the greatest proportion of temporal lobe abnormalities. Drake (1990) provided a different framework for the EEG–violence relationship; he summarized research that suggests personality disorders may be a mediating factor. In other words, the abnormal EEGs may be associated with certain personality disorders (e.g., antisocial personality disorder and borderline personality disorder) and that these personality disorders have a higher incidence of aggressive behavior.

Scarpa and Raine (1997) summarized more recent research on EEG abnormalities and criminal behavior. Like earlier researchers, they found a high proportion (25–50%) of abnormal EEGs for violent recidivating offenders. Surprisingly, results were less consistent for psychopathic offenders. As a complicating feature, Rogers (1986) observed that abnormal EEGs are also associated with schizophrenia and other mental disorders. In this vein, Krakowski, Convit, Jaeger, Lin, and Volavka (1989) found the following percentages of abnormal EEGs among psychiatric inpatients: persistently violent (29.4%), transiently violent (26.5%), and nonviolent (24.3%). Likewise, Wong, Lumsden, Fenton, and Fenwick (1994) examined EEG data on 262 forensic patients. The percentage of abnormal EEGs for patients with low (26.2%) and moderate (24.1%) violence was comparable; highly violent patients had a higher proportion of abnormal EEGs (42.7%) and temporal abnormalities (20.0%). By itself, abnormal EEGs provide little specific information about causative factors contributing to a defendant's criminal behavior.

A study by Shah (1992) highlights the difficulty in establishing a relationship between abnormal EEGs and aggression. Limiting his study to mentally retarded patients on a special locked unit, Shah found 7 of 18 violent patients (38.9%) had abnormal EEGs. The explanation of the abnormal EEGs appeared problematic in light of (1) self-injurious behavior and (2) encephalitis and other medical conditions. The explanation of violent behavior in relation to the abnormal EEGs appeared problematic in light of (1) mental retardation and other comorbid conditions, (2) the variable and sporadic nature of the violence, (3) environmental conditions (e.g., 97% in the daytime), and (4) highly selected sampling of long-term problematic inpatients.

EEGs provide an imprecise measure of seizure activity and epilepsy. According to Tucker and McDavid (1997), EEG results are (1) normal in 20% of epileptic patients, (2) less able to detect nonsurface seizures, and (3) often misinterpreted. In addition, 2% of nonepileptic patients will mimic the spike and wave formations that are characteristic of epilepsy.

Seizure disorders are common in incarcerated populations. While epilepsy was once linked in the popular mind to violence, this relationship is far from simple. In his classic studies, Gunn (Gunn & Fenton, 1969; Gunn & Bonn, 1971) established that epilepsy was more prevalent in prison than in general populations. What accounted for this difference? According to Gunn, four nonexclusive factors are likely responsible: (1) inmates may have greater disturbances of personality and behavior, (2) some epileptics may react to social isolation and rejection with antisocial behavior, (3) deprived early environments represent a risk factor for both criminality and epilepsy, and (4) criminally prone individuals are likely to take more risks, increasing the likelihood of injury-based epilepsy. He also found that the epileptic inmates were involved in *less* violent behavior than their nonepileptic counterparts. In nonincarcerated populations, Devinsky and Valquez (1993) suggested that aggression among epileptic patients might be accounted for by multiple factors beyond neurologic lesions: exposure to violence as a child, adverse social factors, and drug use.

A critical issue is whether the presence of epilepsy per se signals a greater likelihood of aggressive behavior. Under the aegis of the Epilepsy Foundation of American, Delgardo-Esceuta et al. (1981) conducted a monumental study of 5,400 epileptics and found only 19 that engaged in aggressive behavior. The aggressive behavior was undirected, fragmentary, and unsustained (average of 29 seconds).

The presence of temporal lobe epilepsy has been implicated as a correlate to aggression. Interestingly, this term has been officially discarded because of its anatomical focus (Tucker & McDavid, 1997). As noted in the Lagevin et al. (1987) study, temporal lobe abnormalities have been observed in violent offenders (see also Tonkonogy, 1991). Charkasky and Hollander (1997) reported that the primary clinical concern with temporal lobe epilepsy is not seizure-related violence, but violence that occurs between seizures (i.e., interictal aggression). In his review of temporal lobe epilepsy and aggression, Elliot (1992) found marked variations in prevalence rates from 4.8% to 50% for interictal attacks. Elliot concluded that most temporal lobe epileptics are not violent; he speculated whether the aggression was due to a process separate from the epilepsy. However, this focus on interictal aggression greatly complicates seizure-based inferences of causality.

Hillbrand, Foster, and Hirt (1988) provide a counterperspective on temporal lobe abnormalities and aggression. In a sample of 85 forensic inpatients remanded for presentencing evaluations, they examined variables associated with violence. Using a stepwise multiple regression, they found that the presence of temporal lobe abnormality played a small but significant role in *decreasing* the likelihood of violence. The Hillbrand et al. study highlights the problems in attempting to establish causal links, either positive or negative, between temporal lobe epilepsy and violent behavior.

Specialized Use of EEGs: The Episodic Dyscontrol Syndrome

The pioneering work of Mark and Ervin (1970) attempted to establish one neurological basis for violent behavior. With the use of depth electrodes, they attempted to map abnormal EEGs in the limbic and temporal lobe regions of impulsive persons with histories of aggression. Changes in EEGs recordings appeared to precede aggressive behavior. Armed with these data, Mark and Erwin (1970, p. 126) described the episodic dyscontrol syndrome with four cardinal symptoms: (1) history of physical assault; (2) pathological intoxication marked by "senseless brutality; (3) history of impulsive sexual behavior, sometimes including sexual aggression; and (4) traffic violations and accidents. An apparent limitation of this seminal work was the potential circularity between the study population (impulsively aggressive persons, many with criminal histories) and the resulting symptoms (aggression and impulsivity).

The primary advantage of Mark and Erwin's work was their exploration of subcortical EEGs recordings via telemetry. This procedure allowed the investigators to establish EEG patterns and relate these patterns to affective responses and aggression. Unfortunately, a lawsuit from a dissatisfied patient caused sufficient concern regarding liability to terminate their research efforts.

In the absence of subcortical studies, researchers have attempted to establish clinical correlates to episodic dyscontrol. For example, Monroe (1970) attempted to link MMPI and history data to standard EEG findings. However, the magnitude of the correlations was generally small, thereby precluding their clinical applicability. Interest in the episodic dyscontrol syndrome has dwindled; it was recently subsumed under intermittent explosive personality disorder (American Psychiatric Association, 1980). Horvath (1988) provided a cogent summary of recent thinking on episodic dyscontrol syndrome: "The diagnosis is entertained far more often than proved, and the common real findings behind episodes of explosion are excessive but understated alcohol intake and/or a well-disguised antisocial personality" (p. 12). According to DSM-IV, intermittent personality disorder should only be considered after antisocial personality disorder, borderline personality disorder, psychotic disorders, manic episodes, substance abuse, and other disorders are ruled out (American Psychiatric Association, 1994, p. 610).

Ratner and Shapiro (1978) argued for the selective use of episodic dyscontrol syndrome in insanity cases. They contended that "faulty equipment" (p. 429) could sufficiently impair an individual's ability to control his/her criminal behavior. Before the "faulty equipment" argument can be advanced, several issues must be considered:

1. Can the effects of Axis II disorders (antisocial and borderline personality disorders) be ruled out?
2. Can the effects of substance abuse be ruled out?
3. Was the criminal behavior initiated without regard to the consequences? For example, were no precautions taken to avoid arrest?
4. Can a predictable pattern of noninstrumental aggression be established?

Research on episodic dyscontrol syndrome does not necessarily espouse faulty equipment as the primary explanation. In a study of episodic dyscontrol among 130 violent patients, Bach-Y-Rita, Lion, Climent, and Ervin (1971) concluded that an interplay of dynamic issues (e.g., hypermasculinity and inadequate ego defenses) and organic features were responsible for their aggression.

Imaging Methods

A constellation of imaging techniques have been developed in the last 2 decades. This section provides a basic review of anatomical and functional brain images. This review is followed by a synopsis of recent research on brain abnormalities and violence. According to Hurley, Herrick, and Hayman (1997), the two types of anatomical imaging are computerized tomography (CT) and magnetic resonance imaging (MRI). The salient features of these methods are summarized:

- *CT scans* measure tissue density and are used to assess calcified lesions, acute hemorrhage, and screening for other potential problems.
- *MRI Scans* measure the magnetic properties of tissue and are used to assess lesions that are often less accessible to CT scans (e.g., brain stem and subcortical structures). They are sometimes successful at differentiating atrophy from the normal aging process.

Kotrla (1997) summarized the functional scans that include positron emission tomography (PET), single photon emission computed tomography (SPECT), functional magnetic resonance imaging (fMRI), and magnetic resonance spectroscopy (MRS). The salient characteristics of these imaging methods are distilled below:

- *PET scans* measure radioactive isotopes injected into the patient and are used to assess blood flow, cerebral metabolism, and neurotransmitters. Availability is limited to major research centers.
- *SPECT scans* are similar to PET scans but produce only one photon per disintegration. The SPECT is used to study cerebral blood flow and neuroreceptors; it is a less precise tool than the PET.
- *fMRI scans* measure both the structure of the typical MRI and fluctuations in hydrogen nuclei within brain fluids. The latter allows for the assessment of brain activity via changes in oxygen levels. The fMRI is still in its developmental stages.
- *MRS scans* is based on the same technology as fMRI. It alters the parameters of the MRI to measure the response of atoms and subatomic particles. The MRS is used to study the concentration of brain metabolites and their relevance to clinical conditions.

Swayze, Yates, and Andreasen (1987) provided an early yet impressive summary of imaging methods and their role in diagnosing mental disorders. Swayze et al. concluded that group differences among clinical populations are readily apparent, but that the diagnostic implications of these findings have yet to be fully realized. More recent reviews (Hurley et al., 1997; Kotrla, 1997), despite great advances in technology, appear to echo this viewpoint. However, data from Ananth, Gamal, Miller, Wohl, and Wandewater (1993) raise concerns regarding the effectiveness of CT scans for routine evaluations of psychiatric patients.

Forensic experts are unlikely to have the expertise to use these sophisticated imaging methods or to explicate their potential role in insanity evaluations. Therefore, they must rely on neurologists and neuroscientists who specialize in imaging methods. As an important caution, the purpose of these consultations are primarily diagnostic in nature. *Unless specially trained in forensic evaluations of mentally disordered defendants, such consultants should refrain from addressing the relationship of abnormal findings to criminal responsibility.* Given the understandable excitement over new imaging methods, the expert's temptation to capitalize on new technology can be appreciated. However, great care must be taken that group differences (e.g., violent vs. nonviolent patients) on imaging methods are not equated with causality.

Raine and her colleagues (Raine, Buchsbaum, & LaCasse, 1997; Raine, Buchsbaum, et al., 1997; Raine et al., 1998) have performed pioneering work on subcortical functioning of violent offenders via PET scans. In parallel studies of forensic patients charged with murder or attempted murder, they found no differences based on whether planning, sexual assault, or an argument was implicated in the homicidal behavior. Group differences were observed between affective ("hot-blooded") and predatory ("cold-blooded") aggression. In particular, affective murderers had lower prefrontal and higher subcortical activity than normal comparisons. In a sample of murderers referred for forensic assessments, they also found reduced glucose metabolism and abnormal asymmetries in several brain regions. Their conclusions about these findings are especially relevant: "These data do not demonstrate that murderers pleading NGRI are not responsible for their actions, nor do they demonstrate that PET can be used as a diagnostic technique" (Raine, Buchsbaum, & LaCasse, 1997, p. 505).

Wong et al. (1997) examined the PET scans of 31 offenders with schizophrenia or schizoaffective disorders. They found that repetitively violent patients had reduced uptake in the anterior inferior temporal regions. Interpretation of the results is complicated by several issues: the patients were currently (1) not violent, (2) clinically stable, and (3) receiving antipsychotic medications. However, an interesting observation was that 3 of the original 39 (7.7%) offenders had undiagnosed "gross brain pathology" (p. 115).

Frierson, Schwartz-Watts, Morgan, and Malone (1998) examined 54 murderers referred for pretrial forensic evaluations. As a retrospective study conducted following convictions, the study excluded defendants found NGRI. However, nearly one-half of the participants had a past psychiatric history. In this group, abnormal CT/MRI scans were relatively uncommon, occurring in just 9.3% of the cases. Clearly, abnormal scans were not equated with exculpation, but were relatively rare (5.6%) in cases receiving the death penalty.

Two important observations emerge from the above studies. When research is limited to predominantly violent offenders, then abnormal brain scans are likely to be "associated" with violence. This "association" is not a finding but a methodological artifact. In other clinical populations, the incidence of violence is relatively low (see Diaz, 1995). Second, brain abnormalities do not form a consistent pattern across studies of violent offenders.

The admissibility of brain scan evidence is decided on a case-by-case basis. In general, the courts have found no abuse of discretion in trial court decisions excluding scan evidence under *Daubert* and its state court counterparts (*Penney v. Praxair, Inc.*, 1997) or in admitting it (*Hose v. Chicago Northwestern Transp. Co.*, 1995). With reference to insanity evaluations, the critical issue is not structural abnormalities of the brain. Rather, it is the relationship of these generally stable brain abnormalities[5] to what is typically an isolated instance of complex behavior. Because criminal behavior is generally isolated, experts face the heavy burden of addressing the interaction of brain abnormalities with interpersonal and environmental characteristics.

Ciccone (1992; see also Fenwick, 1993) advocated a "neurological defense" to support an insanity plea. He described three cases in which the insanity defense was asserted and CT scans suggested substantial brain pathology. In one of the three cases, the defendant was acquitted, based on the volitional prong of the ALI test. While Ciccone emphasized the neurological findings in the case, the more salient features appear to be the defendant's well-documented paranoid ideation and severe dementia. In other words, the neurological findings were useful in confirming the diagnosis, but the clinical presentation and its pervasive impairment was the most relevant evidence in establishing criminal responsibility. In contrast, to Ciccone, Restak (1993) questions the neurological defense: "In *individual* instances, even the most skilled of neurologists can only speculate about what *might* be the case" (p. 870; emphases in the original).

Conclusion

The watchwords for laboratory procedures are "precision" and "relevance." *Precision* reflects the accuracy of measurement across settings. *Relevance* considers the applicability of the data to retrospective evaluations of criminal responsibility. Conclusions are organized into three sections.

Accuracy of Self-Report Regarding Criminal Behavior

1. PPG methods often lack precision (i.e., they exhibit variability across settings in stimuli, measurement, and indexes) and have limited relevance to *unacknowledged* sexual deviance. At best, PPG methods measure deviant sexual interest but not paraphiliac behavior.

2. Polygraph methods have variable precision. The CQT has only moderate precision, with variability across polygraph examiners. The GKT has moderately high precision. The relevance to insanity evaluations is limited by the research designs. Studies have focused on criminal involvement rather than symptoms and motives at the time of the crime.

3. Integrity testing has poor precision and negligible relevance to insanity evaluations.

4. Forensic hypnosis has very poor precision. Current problems with precision limit its relevance.

5. Drug-assisted interviews lack substantial precision. Their relevance is limited to the role of a challenge test.

Accuracy of Self-Report Regarding Substance Abuse

1. Psychometric screens have moderately high precision. Because of face validity, their relevance is very circumscribed for *unacknowledged* substance abuse.

2. Specialized measures vary substantially in their precision and relevance. The CDP has good precision and moderate relevance. With the use of an informant, the CDP can be tailored to a specific period. The precision of the SASSI is diminished in criminal populations; its relevance is limited by its precision.

3. Scales from multiscale inventories have generally poor precision, although PAI scales have moderate precision. The relevance of MMPI-2 and MCMI-II scales are severely limited by their precision. PAI has modest relevance because its scales measure history/propensity of substance abuse.

4. Breathalyzer has a high level of precision. Its relevance depends on whether it was administered immediately following the crime.

5. Urinalysis has a moderately high level of precision, although its results can be confounded by false-positives and false-negatives.

6. Hair analysis has a high level of precision. Its results have moderate relevance in retrospectively establishing drug abuse for the general period of the crime but not the day of the offense.

EEG and Imaging Methods

1. The EEG has a moderate level of precision with both false-positives and false-negatives. Its results have moderately high relevance for establishing certain disorders but marginal relevance for criminal responsibility.

2. The CT, MRI, and PET scans have high levels of precision. They appear to have moderate relevance for several disorders. Their relevance to criminal responsibility has yet to be established. Although Tancredi and Volkow (1988) have argued that specific abnormalities found on brain scan (e.g., limbic lesions) can be linked with the insanity standard (e.g., second prong of the ALI standard), this putative association is highly speculative.

Notes

1. A small study by Beck, Borenstein, and Dreyfus (1986) suggests that the courts may be reluctant to convict in nonviolent sexual offenses. If true, this finding may have an important bearing on whether the defense should consider an insanity defense, even with a grossly psychotic defendant.

2. The effects of "leaked information" during the interrogation on producing false-positives requires further investigation. For example, asking repeated questions about a particular weapon during the interrogation might result in greater arousal levels for that weapon in comparison to other alternatives.

3. The concern with sodium amytal is that higher dosages may produce several hours of sleep, thereby discontinuing the drug-assisted interview.

4. Although studies with negative findings can often be attacked, the fundamental issue is whether sound research exists to warrant the use of a particular method.

5. Less commonly, brain abnormalities are viewed as fluctuating (e.g., variable results on PET scans). However, establishing the retrospective presence of a fluctuating finding for the specific time of the offense would appear unattainable.

Chapter 11

Clinical Synthesis

Overview
Decision-Making Models
Components of Forensic Decision Making
Application of Statistical Models
Contradictory and Discrepant Findings
"No Opinion" Conclusions
Conclusion

Overview

This chapter examines the process of integrating the psychological information gathered in the formulation of retrospective diagnoses and the concomitant opinion on criminal responsibility. Prior to integration and synthesis, the forensic expert must address the requisite question, "When is the insanity evaluation complete?" This judgment is not rendered in isolation; the diagnostic process and decisions about the completeness of data are clearly intertwined.

One of the most troubling criticisms by Ziskin (1995) questioned the ability of forensic experts to collect reliable clinical data, given their idiosyncratic approaches and subjective methods. The force of this criticism could be blunted by a critique of Ziskin's sources and extrapolations. Nevertheless, his point regarding the quality and completeness of clinical data should not be overlooked. With respect to interview data, we recommend that forensic experts address both Axis I and Axis II disorders, with an emphasis on standardization and reliability. As summarized in Table 11.1, *sole* reliance on traditional interviews is very open to criticism because of their idiosyncratic nature and lack of reliability (see Chapter 7). As a standard for forensic practice, experts should use standardized measures with established reliabilities whenever feasible (see Table 11.1). We do not wish to be misunderstood: we believe that traditional interviews form a necessary and critical component of insanity evaluations. However, we also believe that the sole reliance on traditional interviews jeopardizes the completeness and the reliability of the forensic assessment.

The chapter is organized into four major components. First, we examine different models of diagnostic and forensic decision making. Second, we grapple with the current controversies over the use of statistical models to augment forensic decision making. Third, we examine how forensic experts should handle discrepant and contradictory data. Fourth, we consider the ubiquitously unpopular alternative of rendering a "no opinion."

Decision-Making Models

Forensic experts have come under a barrage of criticism for their ability to integrate clinical and forensic data. The most strident criticism was levied by Stephen Morse, a law professor who argues in favor of curtailing expert testimony to circumscribed clinical observations. Morse (1978, p. 396) concluded that "mental health professionals should not testify about diagnoses or report conclusions about mental illness or even abnormality." While Melton et al. (1997) attempted to appear more moderate, their position is similarly condemnatory toward forensic experts. In a convoluted presentation, Melton et al. (1997) admit that they "share Morse's uneasiness about the state of art in mental health assessment" (p. 18) but would reluctantly allow testimony to the diag-

TABLE 11.1. Quality of Diagnostic Data on Axis I and Axis II Disorders

	Quality of Data		
	Unstandardized	Standardized	Standardized and reliable
Axis I	Traditional	CASH	SADS and DIS[a]
Axis II	Traditional	SCID-II	SIDP and PDE

Note. For Axis I disorders: CASH = Comprehensive Assessment of Symptoms and History; SADS = Schedule of Affective Disorders and Schizophrenia; DIS = Diagnostic Interview Schedule. For Axis II disorders: SCID-II = Structured Clinical Interview for DSM-III-R—Axis II Disorders; SIDP = Structured Interview for DSM-III Personality Disorders; PDE = Personality Disorder Examination. For a comprehensive review of these measures, see Rogers (1995).
[a]The SCID (Structured Clinical Interview of DSM-III-R Disorders) might also be considered, but its reliability is open to criticism.

nosis and formulation, "even if these formulations are at times mere 'stories'" (p. 19).

Mental health professionals need to recognize the sources of expert-bashing and their implicit agendas. When held to the standards they seek to impose on others, the archcritics of expert testimony do not fare well (see Rogers & Bagby, 1993; Rogers & Ewing, 1989). But even if the experts at expert-bashing can be dismissed, the issues of systematic assessment and data integration are important and unavoidable.

How do mental health professionals make clinical decisions? We propose two basic models: the hypothesis-testing and the linear best-fit models. Each model is described with its applicability to insanity evaluations.

Hypothesis-Testing Model

The hypothesis-testing model continues to be the most commonly used approach by forensic experts conducting insanity evaluations. Near the beginning of the evaluation, the forensic expert formulates a hypothesis about the defendant's criminal behavior and diagnosis. The hypotheses for the criminal behavior may range from "actions arising from paranoid schizophrenia and systematized delusions" to "actions stemming from a long history of drug abuse and antisocial behavior." The decision process then focuses on confirming or disconfirming a particular hypothesis. If the hypothesis is disconfirmed, a second hypothesis is generated and a similar process is followed. The final decision is reached when a hypothesis is believed to have appreciably greater confirming than disconfirming evidence.

The hypothesis-testing model is economical in that the most likely thesis is examined before alternative explanations are explored. However, this singular focus also makes the hypothesis-testing model vulnerable to biased judgments. As summarized in Chapter 7, experts are susceptible to the following biases:

Anchoring or Primacy Bias

The working hypothesis (i.e., anchoring bias) is difficult to discard and exerts an undue influence on the final decision. In insanity evaluations, anchoring biases are often coupled with *hindsight biases* (i.e., working from the outcome back to the antecedents). Ross, Lepper, Strack, and Steinmetz (1977) found that knowledge of an outcome (e.g., successful suicide) affected the assessment process. Potential anchoring/hindsight biases in insanity evaluations often involve hypotheses about what motivated the criminal behavior and subsequent clinical presentation. Examples include:

- ◆ The defendant's crime is so disgusting and degrading that it could only be perpetuated by a psychopath.
- ◆ The defendant's rash accusations that the victim was persecuting him/her were the result of paranoid delusions.
- ◆ The defendant's repeated attempts to manipulate jail staff probably indicates malingering.
- ◆ The defendant's crime was bizarre and apparently motiveless; it could only be committed by an actively psychotic person.
- ◆ Drugs have been a constant in the defendant's life predating his/her mental disorder; thus, drugs must be the cause of his/her criminal behavior.

These unspoken but deeply held assumptions may influence the expert's inquiries, data gathering, and final opinion. Attorneys are equally susceptible to primacy and hindsight biases. As part of their responsibility to provide vigorous representation, they may influence experts via a process of forensic identification. As described in Chapter 3, experts often adopt implicitly the working hypothesis or theory of attorneys, which may distort their subsequent findings. Experts, especially those employing the hypothesis-testing model, must think for themselves. As recommended by Borum et al. (1993), experts can search for countervailing evidence and attempt to test alternative hypotheses.

Confirmatory Bias

Clinicians tend to overvalue data that supports their working hypothesis and undervalue or even ignore data that is inconsistent with it. One author of this book (Rogers) is frequently consulted by forensic experts on issues of malingering. Occasionally, the heart of the issue is how to "explain away" unexpected results when what is really needed is a reexamination of the working hypothesis. Why do experts sometimes attempt to dismiss unexpected results? We suspect that confirmatory bias plays an instrumental role.

Overreliance on Unique Data

Unique data are often given disproportionate weight. Bizarre (e.g., decapitation of victims or eating human viscera) or dehumanizing (e.g., asking a child to choose how to die) acts cause strong emotional reactions. These behaviors are likely to be overvalued because of these continued reactions. In addition to paying greater attention to unique information, experts also allow these strong affective responses to affect their judgments (Arkes, 1989).

Premature Closure

An implicit assumption of the hypothesis-testing model is that one diagnostic formulation is more effective than others at explaining the defendant's mental condition and criminal responsibility. Blashfield (1992) found that experienced clinicians typically stopped after rendering the first diagnosis. Unfortunately, this practice (i.e., fulfilling the responsibility of testing the diagnostic hypothesis) results in the marked underdiagnosis of mental disorders. In other words, the majority of mental disorders were overlooked by clinicians in the Blashfield study, resulting in premature closure of the assessment process. As a practical example, forensic experts often neglect other Axis II disorders beyond antisocial personality disorder. The sequential nature of the hypothesis-testing model is likely to cause experts to overlook disorders that may have a bearing on the assessment of criminal responsibility.

Linear Best-Fit Model

The linear best-fit model involves the standardized collection of clinically relevant material, irrespective of the expert's clinical hunches or hypotheses. In comparison to the hypothesis-testing approach, the linear best-fit model is composed of two phases: data collection and decision making. The goal of the data-collection phase is to amass comprehensive and relevant data, undistorted by bias and preconceptions. This phase is described as "linear" because the forensic expert makes very few hierarchical decisions while collecting clinical data. The goal of the decision phase is to examine the relative merits of competing hypotheses. This comparative process allows the forensic expert to establish which hypothesis is the "best fit" for the clinical data.

An excellent example of the linear best-fit model is the SADS (see Chapter 9). Forensic experts using the SADS systematically address several hundred potential symptoms/features, irrespective of their preliminary thoughts. Likewise, Axis II interviews, such as the SIDP and the PDE (see Rogers, 1995a) provide systematic coverage, irrespective of initial presentation. As further protection against bias, experts can collect systematic data from multiple sources. In critical cases, the SADS, SIDP, and PDE can be used as informant interviews so that information can be compared across sources on a symptom-by-symptom basis.

A major advantage of the linear best-fit model is that its standardization allows for direct comparisons. Depending on the measure they use, experts can place faith in the reliability of their observations. Through clinical research, the reliability can be established for symptoms, diagnosis, and impairment. With reliable measurement, a defendant's presentation of symptoms can be examined on two separate occasions, as evidence of consistency in self-reporting. For convergent data, an informant's account of the defendant's symptoms can be elicited.

A potential limitation of the linear best-fit model is that it is less efficient than the hypothesis-testing model because much of the information collected is not used directly in the decision process.[1] For example, the SADS evaluation of a criminal defendant, focusing on the crime and the current time, may take 3 to 4 hours to complete. However, only 1 hour may be directly relevant to a particular case. While labor intensive, the importance of insanity evaluations justifies the expenditure of time required by the linear best-fit model.

Components of Forensic Decision Making

The decision-making process in criminal responsibility evaluations is comprised of four primary components involving the defendant's conduct and psychological impairment. The four components include the following:

- ◆ What happened?
- ◆ What was the intended purpose of the criminal behavior?
- ◆ What was the relationship of the intended purpose to psychological impairment?
- ◆ What is the relationship of the intended purpose and impairment to criminal responsibility?

What Happened?

An essential component of every insanity evaluations is that the forensic expert closely focus on the defendant's actions prior to, during, and immediately following the alleged offense. This focus should include an examination of the defendant's interactions with the victim as well as with others. It should also include an exploration of relevant environmental and situational factors in addressing the circumstances of the crime. Sources of information about what occurred encompass data from the defendant, witnesses, and police officers. Although the defendant should be asked to describe what happened in detail on at least two occasions, this perspective should not be the sole basis of assessment. It is critical that the defendant's account be corroborated, when possible, by independent sources. As discussed in Chapter 7, collateral interviews with witnesses or family members, who observed the defendant at the time of the crime, may be invaluable. Police reports are particularly helpful when they include either statements made by the defendant or verbatim reports by witnesses of what the defendant verbalized. In addition, police reports are useful in confirming a defendant's eccentric or bizarre behavior. However, the absence of such observations cannot be construed as the absence of such symptoms. For example, some police officers, for a variety of reasons, may be unaware of or choose not to describe unusual or "crazy" behavior.

What Was the Intended Purpose of the Criminal Behavior?

What did the defendant hope to accomplish by engaging in the criminal behavior? This inquiry entails more than the obvious. While a defendant may rob a bank for financial gain, he/she may have a myriad of goals for engaging in this behavior, ranging from the support of a drug habit to performing covert operations as a CIA operative. Therefore, it is important to assess the defendant's short- and long-range goals for engaging in the criminal behavior. This assessment often involves a heavy reliance on the defendant's self-reporting, although his/her statements to others are often revealing.

Inferences, irrespective of their plausibility, should not be the primary basis of this determination. Many inferences (e.g., the goal of rape is necessarily sexual gratification) are intuitively appealing and yet potentially erroneous. Cases in which criminal responsibility is raised are often atypical and counterintuitive. Insanity cases have been observed in which sexual offenses were "divinely" inspired, delusionally based, or grossly misperceived. As an example of a gross misperception, a young male with a schizophrenic disorder completely misconstrued an elderly woman bending over her garden as an unambiguous invitation for anal intercourse. He was very perplexed when his amorous efforts were repelled immediately by the sharp-edged trowel she was holding. In this example, the assumption of sexual gratification, while true, would provide a superficial and incomplete explanation of his criminal behavior.

The forensic expert must assess the stated goals in conjunction with other data sources. One consideration is whether a definable pattern of criminal behavior has been observed. For example, a forensic expert cannot disregard an extensive arrest history for drug-related charges in assessing the purpose for index offenses (e.g., burglary and subsequent selling of stolen goods). In such cases, the critical issue is establishing whether this criminal behavior is similar/dissimilar to past offense patterns. In all cases, the intended goals should not be confused with culpability. The goals, by themselves, have only marginal relevance to criminal responsibility. Before the goals become germane, the level of psychological impairment must be established.

What Was the Relationship of the Intended Purpose to Psychological Impairment?

The measurement of psychological impairment is most readily achieved via diagnosis. This process involves three facets: (1) rendering a differential diagnosis, (2) establishing the severity of the mental disorder(s), and (3) substantiating the relationship between the intended purpose and the impairment. Increased intervals between the time of the offense and the time of the assessment may greatly complicate the retrospective diagnosis. If the defendant's functioning has changed substantially during the intervening time, the SADS is strongly recommended for the reliable assessment of prior episodes (see Chapter 9). Diagnosis provides useful information about the genuineness of the disorder and its probable onset and course. A combination of structured and unstructured interviews are likely needed to provide sufficient clinical data for differential diagnosis.

Impairment is even more challenging to assess, especially retrospectively. In this regard, the SADS is especially useful in quantifying the severity of symptoms at discrete time periods. The determination of impairment is essential: the mere presence of auditory hallucinations may have little bearing on the defendant's actions, whether criminal or noncriminal. Conversely, command hallucinations that the defendant is compelled to obey may become the basis of criminal behavior. As a caution, attorneys should be alert for forensic experts who improperly attempt to equate extreme elevations on multiscale inventories with severe impairment (see Chapter 8).

Insanity evaluations require that forensic experts address specific impairment related to criminal behavior. Many defendants manifest severe impairment on such imprecise measures as the Global Assessment Function Scale (GAF; American Psychiatric Association, 1994).

While marginally useful, GAF scores provide no specific data about criminal behavior. To assess the effects of impairment on criminal acts, the forensic psychologist must catalogue examples of impairment. For example, the SADS extensively evaluates manic symptoms. In assessing the effects of these manic symptoms, the expert considers examples of impairment from multiple sources. Typically a discernible pattern of behaviors are associated with specific manic symptoms. Without a pattern of impairment, the genuineness of the presentation is brought into question. As observed by Resnick (1997), the sudden manifestation of impairment coincidental with a criminal act (e.g., arrest occurred after the first and only time the defendant obeyed a command hallucination to expose his/her genitals) is unlikely in genuine patients and requires close examination. Most patterns of impairment involve both criminal and noncriminal behavior. In addition, patterns typically are understandable in light of the course of the disorder. For example, gradual deterioration in a male defendant with schizophrenia results in further impairment in personal hygiene, social relations, and capacity for engaging in goal-oriented activities.

What Is the Relationship of the Intended Purpose and Impairment to Criminal Responsibility?

The final component of forensic decision making is relating the earlier findings (intended purpose and impairment) to the relevant standard of insanity. In this regard, some forensic experts may find the R-CRAS (see Chapter 9) to be useful in organizing their data, especially in light of the ALI standard. Clinical decisions at this point are highly dependent on a correct understanding of the relevant insanity standard (see Chapter 4).

Consonant with the R-CRAS, forensic experts should employ explicit decision models in their assessment of criminal responsibility. In examining the relevant insanity standard, the following questions must be addressed:

- ♦ What type of impairment is required by the insanity standard? A common case is a defendant with delusions that, if true, would justify his/her behavior (e.g., self-defense).
- ♦ Is the impairment the result of a mental disorder or defect? A common diagnostic issue is whether the behavior arises from voluntary intoxication or from a mental disorder. While the strong emphasis is on Axis I disorders (e.g., psychotic and mood disorders), Axis II disorders (e.g., borderline personality disorder) cannot be discounted.

♦ Is the reported impairment genuine? The common concern is whether the defendant is feigning either his/her disorder or the apparent impairment.

From a clinical perspective, the forensic expert typically reverses the order of the questions to assess (1) response styles, (2) differential diagnosis, (3) degree and type of general impairment, (4) specific impairment related to criminal behavior, and (5) the relevant standard of insanity. Although some experts refrain from offering ultimate opinions (for a discussion of the merits, see Chapter 2), they should still consider (4) and probably (5) in order to crystallize their forensic decision making.

The primary limitation of forensic decision models is that they do not allow for a numerical or statistical quantification of each component and its relationship to insanity standards. The following section briefly describes statistical models of prediction and their potential application to criminal responsibility evaluations.

Application of Statistical Models

Statistical models applied to the fields of mental health and medicine have included Bayes' theorem and a range of multivariate analyses. Frequently, the purpose of these methods is to assess the likelihood of a specific outcome (e.g., sane or insane) in the context of select variables and certain base rates. Thus, statistical models examine the accuracy of decisions based on the likelihood of occurrence (e.g., probability of defendants being found insane) and the frequency of certain variables (e.g., diagnosis of schizophrenia or past history of criminal behavior).

An important trend in forensic practice is to offer probabilistic statements regarding a classification. Current efforts, often subsumed under the rubric of risk assessment, include dangerousness (e.g., Borum, 1996; Monahan, 1992; Monahan & Steadman, 1996; Mossman, 1994; Schopp, 1996) and malingering (Mossman & Hart, 1996). We strongly caution against the application of risk assessment to insanity evaluations for the following reasons:

1. *Many models of risk assessment employ Bayes' theorem with the fundamental assumption of stable and known base rates* (Rogers & Salekin, 1998). The most comprehensive data on base rates of successful insanity pleas were collected by Cirincione et al. (1995) on 8,138 defendants from seven states. They found dramatic variations in base rates (i.e., percent-

ages found insane) across the seven states, based on the background of defendants (e.g., gender, race, and age) and the type of offense:

- Gender had marked ranges in base rates for both males (12.4–86.0%) and females (19.7–95.2%).
- Racial differences also varied markedly in base rates for both white (11.8–88.9%) and nonwhite (17.3–82.9%) defendants.
- Age varied dramatically both between and within states. In five of seven states, older defendants were more than twice as likely to be acquitted as their younger counterparts.
- Even the gender of the victim evidenced significant variations in success rates; insanity cases with male victims were 32.8% more likely to be acquitted than cases with female victims.
- Type of crime produced highly variable success rates: murder (14.0–64.7%), other violent offenses (18.6–91.6%), and nonviolent crimes (10.1–86.6%)

Other significant differences in insanity success rates were found for education, marital status, prior arrest, prior inprisonment, prior hospitalization, and diagnosis.

What conclusions can be drawn from these data? First and foremost, these data convincingly demonstrate that *the base rates for insanity acquittals fluctuate impressively.* Therefore, any attempt to impose a base rate will introduce substantial error into the classification. Second, these data demonstrate that *base rates even within a jurisdiction are presently unknowable.* What base rates should be used in an evaluation of a young unmarried African American defendant charged with a property offense: age? race? offense? marital status? In each case, the base rates vary significantly. We have no validated method of choosing the "true" base rate.

2. *Current models of risk assessment used in forensic practice are typically incomplete.* As observed by Rogers (1998), risk-assessment models must account for four components: risk and protective factors, and moderator and mediating effects. Current forensic applications tend to focus on risk factors to the exclusion of other important components. Without providing a technical discussion, it is obvious that the neglect of three out of the four components introduces substantial error into the determinations.

3. *Forensic applications of risk assessment are often confounded by pseudoprecision.* Mossman and Hart (1996) attempted to apply precise

probabilities to particular test scores without taking into account the accuracy of the estimate (e.g., standard error of measurement or SEm) and stability of the specific test scores (test–retest reliabilities). Use of ostensibly precise estimates are confounded by variability in the assessment. As a specific example, some forensic practitioners attempt to use a cut score (i.e., ≥30) on the Psychopathy Checklist—Revised (PCL-R; Hare, 1991) to estimate the risks of reoffending in forensic populations. However, when the SEm is considered, only scores ≥37 should be considered as strong evidence of psychopathy (see Rogers, 1995a; Salekin, Rogers, & Sewell, 1996).[2]

Probabilistic models of criminal responsibility are potentially dangerous to insanity trials because of their false promises of accuracy, completeness, and precision. Attorneys can assail attempts to present probabilities in mathematical or statistical terms by focusing on the dramatically fluctuating base rates, incomplete models based on only a few variables, and the imprecision of measurement. As described in Chapter 3, attorneys are most interested in an *idiographic* approach to the case: How will a unique defendant act under the particular circumstances of the crime? Probabilistic models are designed to eliminate these individualistic characteristics that are integral to insanity determinations.

A final and likely fatal flaw of most probabilistic models is their assumption of a verifiable and reproducible outcome criterion. Insanity, as a legal construct applied through multiple social processes (e.g., trial and jury deliberation), cannot be reified. The construct is shaped differently in each insanity trial by the judge's instructions, attorneys' arguments, experts' testimony, and jurors' commonsensical notions. The verdict cannot be equated with the construct because of the extralegal influences on the process. A jury's desire to punish heinous crimes may override the niceties of nonculpability. A jury's sympathy for a battered spouse may sway their verdict toward an NGRI finding. This establishment of "ground truth" for insanity is a problem for all clinical research on criminal responsibility. However, it becomes greatly magnified when attempting to assign mathematical probabilities to a nonreproducible legal construct.

Contradictory and Discrepant Findings

Insanity cases with a fairly consistent picture both from self-report and corroborative data pose much fewer difficulties than cases with contradictory or markedly discrepant findings. In these latter cases, the forensic expert must critically evaluate these inconsistent findings before reaching any diagnostic or forensic conclusions. For the purposes of forensic evaluations, we have operationalized the two terms:

♦ *Discrepant findings* refer to marked inconsistencies in the severity of symptoms. An example is the inconsistency between a mild dysphoria and a pervasive depression.
♦ *Contradictory findings* is reserved for complete disagreements over the presence of an important behavior or symptom. An example is the defendant's report of being extremely provoked and witnesses' statements to the contrary.

Contradictory statements *within* the defendant's self-reporting brings into question the reliability of this information and the possibility of malingering. The ordering of such contradictory findings is also important. In some cases, no particular direction is observed between initial and subsequent interviews regarding the degree of psychopathology. In other cases, the defendant may report discrepant and contradictory findings, with later reports consistently exhibiting greater psychopathology. Particularly in those cases where the defendant suddenly remembers psychotic symptoms, like hallucinations, the forensic expert must address carefully the issues of malingering and deception.

Contradictory findings between the defendant's self-reporting and corroborative interviews pose several additional issues. It cannot be assumed that information from collateral sources is necessarily accurate or complete. In conducting corroborative interviews, a forensic expert must assess the accuracy of the informant's recall as well as his/her motivation. In one unusual case, an obviously disturbed male defendant claimed that the Mafia had murdered the victim and continued to affirm his own mental health (see Rogers & Cunnien, 1986). A corroborative interview with his mother emphasized his psychotic impairment, although her contact with her son had been limited. A second corroborative interview with his schizophrenic girlfriend tended to normalize his bizarre behavior. Neither the defendant nor the two informants were deliberately attempting to distort their accounts, although together they yielded contradictory findings.

Motivations of informants may influence their presentations. A priori assumptions about these motivations may not be accurate with respect to victims, witnesses, or family members. In one case, a female victim of a sexual offense downplayed the violence and brutality of the young offender's act, at least in comparison to medical evidence and her earlier statements to police. Family members may present overly negative or overly positive views. In one forensic case, a superficially caring mother presented an extremely negative view of her adolescent daughter, completely inconsistent with other corroborative data. When a forensic expert concludes which of two contradictory accounts is more accurate, he/she must be able to defend this decision on more ground than simply "clinical judgment." This decision must take into account the memory, recall, and scope of the corroborative information, as well as the honesty and motivation of each interviewee. In some insanity evaluations, the unreliability of both the defendant and corroborative sources will necessitate the rendering of a "no opinion."

Discrepant and contradictory findings may occur between the defendant's account and psychological testing. Discrepancies may occur with information both on response styles (e.g., malingering and defensiveness) and psychopathology. Because of its frequency of use in insanity evaluations, we will focus on MMPI-2 results. Common examples include the following:

1. Interview data suggest that the defendant is not attempting to feign, while MMPI-2 data raise the question of malingering. As noted in Chapter 8, the majority of defendants in insanity cases have elevations on "fake-bad" indices (e.g., Scale F) even though most are not feigning. *Therefore, moderate elevations on MMPI-2 "fake-bad" indices should not be interpreted as contradictory findings.* Only extreme elevations, when other explanations are ruled out, can be considered as contradictory findings.

2. Interview data support the diagnosis of schizophrenia but the MMPI-2 clinical profile does not have the elevations commonly found in schizophrenic samples. This occurrence should not be considered as either a discrepant or a contradictory finding. Although many persons with schizophrenia exhibit certain MMPI-2 profiles, data would suggest that many do not have these profiles and that substantial numbers have no clinical elevations whatsoever.

3. Clinical interpretations are typically based on correlations, although the magnitude of these correlations are often quite modest (rs in the .30–.40 range). Distinguished from the MMPI-2, the PAI appears to have correlations of moderate magnitude including its forensic applications (see Morey, 1991; Rogers, Ustad, & Salekin, 1998). In the absence of high correlations ($rs \geq 80$), the lack of correspondence between interpretations and other clinical data should not be interpreted as an inconsistency.

Elevations on well-validated multiscale inventories (MMPI-2 and PAI) typically provide clinical information about psychopathology and impairment rather than specific diagnosis. However, the opposite is not true. The lack of clinical elevations cannot be interpreted as an absence of psychopathology or impairment.

Contradictions may also be found between self-report and projective results with respect to psychotic material. Forensic cases occasionally occur in which the only evidence of psychotic thinking is found on projective testing. How much weight should be given to these findings? Considering the vulnerability of projective tests to malingering by the defendant and multiple interpretations by the examiner, it is important that these findings be confirmed. While some progress has been made regarding such indices as the SCZI for the Rorschach, it cannot be related to specific psychotic symptoms or their severity. One modest possibility is to replicate the psychotic findings on the Rorschach with a separate measure, such as the Holtzman. More germane to insanity evaluations is the collection of data from informants regarding possible psychotic symptoms.

Contradictory and discrepant findings can also be observed between interview data and laboratory studies. Such discrepancies frequently question the reliability of the defendant's self-reporting. As noted in Chapter 10, marked discrepancies in alcohol consumption may raise questions about reliability, although experts must take into account the considerable variations in individuals' blood alcohol levels in response to standardized amounts of alcohol. Discrepant and contradictory findings are more difficult to interpret with respect to illicit drug use. Because drug users rarely can verify the type and potency of drugs they use, their misreporting may represent their sincere but inaccurate appraisal of what they thought they were purchasing. As a general caution, laboratory procedures measure changes in the body, not changes in behavior. For example, a high blood alcohol level can confirm heavy drinking but does not necessarily corroborate severe intoxication.

Attorneys should be especially alert for the *consistency trap*, in which a forensic expert has "zero-tolerance" for inconsistency and interprets every inconsistency as evidence of malingering or manipulation. For example, experts occasionally scrutinize individual items on multiscale inventories for any inconsistencies with interview data. This zero-tolerance approach ignores the simple fact that any retrospective evaluation is likely to have some inconsistencies. How does the *consistency trap* work?

♦ Any inconsistency is perceived as evidence of feigning or manipulation.
♦ The lack of inconsistency is seen as either (1) a rehearsed or "prepared" defendant attempting to manipulate the evaluation or (2) an unimpaired defendant unlikely to meet the insanity standard.

We refer to this approach as a "trap" because the outcome is inevitably negative, irrespective of the defendant's intentions or presentation. Attorneys should be mindful of the consistency trap, especially when experts begin to present a fine-grained analysis of individual test items. Rebuttal testimony on the consistency of test items (e.g., MMPI-2 readministrations) may be helpful. The crucial distinction is between *any* discrepancies and *marked* discrepancies; obviously, marked discrepancies relevant to criminal responsibility should be considered.

"No Opinion" Conclusions

One of the more difficult decisions facing a forensic expert is the rendering of a "no opinion." Some forensic psychologists and psychiatrists have a feeling of defeat when they are unable to reach an unambiguous conclusion about criminal responsibility. The reasons for competent experts to reach "no opinions" typically involve either incomplete or contradictory information on issues critical to the determination of insanity. "No opinion" testimony should be considered when serious questions remain unanswered regarding (1) what occurred, (2) its intended purpose, (3) the relationship of the intended purpose to psychological impairment, and (4) the relationship of the impairment to the relevant insanity standard. As noted in Chapter 2, testimony should be offered with a reasonable degree of psychological or medical certainty. This standard implies a strong probability that is not satisfied by unsubstantiated inferences.

The decision to render a no-opinion conclusion falls solely in the domain of the forensic expert. Only the expert can decide on his/her degree of certainty and whether an expert opinion can be ethically advanced. This opinion, like other opinions, should not be negotiated with the attorneys. The decision should also not be the product of group discussion among members of an evaluation team. Although individual input from others may be helpful, a group discussion is apt to introduce a host of extraneous issues (e.g., the relationships among team members and their persuasibility) and should be avoided (for an alternative perspective, see Pitt et al., 1997).

Some forensic experts have never rendered no-opinion conclusions, either in their forensic reports or in subsequent testimony. This lack of "no opinions" may result from either a lack of forensic training or the effects of extraneous factors. Alternatively, it could simply be an expression of overconfidence in their clinical abilities. Surprisingly, attorneys rarely question the credibility of expert witnesses based on their unwillingness to render no-opinion conclusions. Carefully prepared cross-examination or rebuttal testimony might raise legitimate doubts about the credibility of overly confident experts.

A no-opinion conclusion must be organized and presented as carefully as any other conclusion. The forensic expert must present the insufficient or contradictory information. He/she must convincingly demonstrate the multiple explanations suggested by the data and why no firm conclusion can be reached. A well-documented and well-reasoned argument may increase the expert's credibility and minimize the antagonism resulting from no-opinion conclusions. As an example of a no-opinion conclusion, one author conducted an insanity evaluation of a psychotic defendant charged with kidnapping. The victim, a young child picked randomly out of a crowd, was too young and traumatized to offer a coherent account. The defendant was too disorganized to offer a coherent account. The expert could not establish what had occurred during the several hours before the child's release or the intended purpose of the alleged kidnapping. No medical evidence or witnesses were found. Although speculations were possible, no firm conclusions could be reached regarding the intended purpose or criminal responsibility.

Conclusion

The clinical synthesis of relevant data is often the most challenging step in completing insanity evaluations. This chapter provides four major components as one template to guide the integration and subsequent decision. The four components include (1) What happened? (2) What was the intended purpose of the criminal behavior? (3) What was the relationship of the intended purpose to psychological impairment? and (4) What is the relationship of the intended purpose and impairment to criminal responsibility? For each component, the expert must assemble and integrate data from diverse sources. The decision-making process is sometimes thwarted by incomplete, discrepant, and contradictory data. When these complications occur, the expert must struggle to reconcile differences and gather additional information. When problems remain unresolved and available sources of data are exhausted, forensic experts should consider the possibility of rendering no-opinion conclusions.

Notes

1. Technically, all information is used to discount other hypotheses. Practically speaking, the coverage of some symptom patterns (e.g., panic attacks) is unnecessarily extensive.

2. An alternative is the use of encompassing categories (see Rice & Harris, 1990); these assume that all members of a category (e.g., schizophrenia) should be considered as comparable or identical.

Chapter 12

Communication of Findings

Disclosure of the Expert's Findings

An important consideration in the communication of findings by a forensic expert is knowing who will have access to those findings and at what time in the trial process. In general, pretrial discovery of experts and their reports is far more limited in criminal than in civil cases. Experts who will testify in civil cases are typically required to provide opposing parties with a written report describing the testimony that the expert expects to provide at trial, including the supporting analysis and its informational basis. The opposing party must also be provided with the expert's qualifications, publications, compensation, and prior cases involving expert testimony. In addition, experts in civil cases may be deposed and required to answer questions orally under oath. In contrast, discovery of experts in criminal cases has generally been far more limited. The use of pretrial depositions of an opponent's experts in criminal cases is allowed in only a few jurisdictions. Moreover, the exchange of information about what the expert expects to testify to at trial has been far more restricted in criminal cases than in civil cases.

The predominant pattern of discovery rules in criminal cases is based on reciprocal discovery: if the defense requests copies of the reports of the government's experts, the defense is required to provide equal access to the defense expert's reports. Because these rules do not typically require the preparation of reports, but only disclosure of existing reports, they provide little incentive for retained experts in criminal cases to provide extensive written reports.

Amendments to the rules that govern federal criminal trials have sought to move criminal discovery closer to civil discovery. They require the parties to disclose, if requested, "a written summary of testimony" that should include witnesses' opinions, [and] the bases and reasons for those opinions, the witnesses' qualifications" (Federal Rules of Criminal Procedure, 1997, rule 16). Still, no provision is included for pretrial deposition in criminal cases, or pretrial disclosure of the witnesses' compensation, publications, or all cases in which the witness has testified as an expert. However, the Federal Rules require, when requested, a written summary of the expert testimony that the party intends to use during its case in chief. "The summary provided under this subdivision shall describe the witnesses' opinions, the bases and the reasons for those opinions, and the witnesses' qualifications" (Federal Rules of Criminal Procedure, 1997, rule 16). Apart from the pretrial discovery set forth in state and federal rules, the Constitution imposes a burden on the state to disclose exculpatory information within its possession to the defendant (*Brady v. Maryland*, 1963).

One potential limitation on the information a criminal defendant may be required to disclose is the law of privilege that may prevent compelled disclosure of confidential communications between a litigant and a forensic expert retained by the litigant's attorney to assist in the representation (Knapp, Vandercreek, & Fulero, 1993). Although communications between a litigant and a forensic expert are not cloaked by a physician–, psychologist–, psychiatrist–, psychotherapist–patient privilege because they are not intended to facilitate mental health care, they are cloaked by the attorney–client or work-product privilege because they are intended to facilitate legal representation. In approximately half of the states that privilege remains in effect unless the retained expert will be called as a witness by the party who retained him/ her. In the other states, that privilege is waived when the litigant asserts as a claim or defense the emotional condition that the forensic evaluator was retained to assess, even if the defendant does not intend to call the forensic evaluator as a witness (Shuman, 1994). If the privilege is waived, then the examiner can be called as a witness by the prosecution and compelled to disclose his/her communications with the defendant and his/her resulting opinion about the defendant's mental capacity at the time of the event, including any forensic report that may have been prepared.

Appendix B summarizes the current appellate cases governing the discoverability of experts in insanity cases. Both federal and state jurisdictions are divided on this issue. Importantly, these cases do not make a distinction between the discovery of clinical records and the discovery of private notes. Experts in jurisdictions waiving attorney–client privilege should realize that all written material, including personal notes, are discoverable.

Reports versus No Written Reports

Court-appointed experts are typically required by court order to produce a written report. Under these circumstances, the expert has no discretion whether to communicate his/her findings orally or in writing. Beyond relationships governed by court orders, experts may have cogent reasons for producing a written report. These reasons include:

♦ The written report provides an important structure for the expert to organize the clinical data and formalize the decision process. Given the complexity of insanity evaluation, this advantage is substantial.

♦ Experts are sometimes influenced by "forensic identification" (see Chapter 3) in which they are swayed by the retaining attorney. A written report minimizes this possibility because the experts' main findings are memorialized in the report.

♦ The written report may expedite the judicial proceedings by informing the parties of the expert's conclusions. In some jurisdictions, many insanity cases are addressed through plea arrangements.

In summary, the forensic expert has several important advantages to producing a written report, with few disadvantages. With a written report, the experts' inconsistencies or lack of thoroughness will be readily apparent. Experts may be divided on whether this exposure to critical review is a disadvantage. On the one hand, no expert likes the weaknesses of his/her report to be exploited. On the other hand, experts may consider the judicial goals (e.g., a just verdict) at least as important as their own discomfort.

Unlike experts, attorneys may have compelling reasons for not wanting a written report. Especially in jurisdictions that treat the attorney–

client or work-product privilege for all evaluations as waived if an insanity defense is raised, defense counsel may be reluctant to request the expert to produce a written report. However, it is unclear whether the lack of a written report provides any real protection because the expert's clinical data and notes are still available. Beyond the waiver issue, attorneys unfamiliar with an expert may feel more comfortable with requesting oral preliminary findings before requesting a written full report.

Experts should establish their own written policies about written reports. Such policies may obviate misunderstandings about the expert's production of a written report. The decision about a written report is best documented at the time the expert becomes involved in the case. Experts are vulnerable to cross-examination if they accept the conditional approach: "Let's see what your opinion is before you write a report." Cross-examination questions about writing only a "favorable" report create an impression, whether or not justified, that the expert is unduly partisan. Obviously, any attempt to destroy or deny the existence of a forensic report entails serious ethical and legal consequences.

Forensic Reports

A forensic report describes the clinical data and its synthesis that results in the expert's conclusions. It serves not only to communicate how the forensic expert reached his/her conclusions but also as a heuristic to verify that the data were appropriately integrated. A complete report should include the referral issue, description of the evaluation, the defendant's behavior at the time of the offense, clinical description of the defendant, consultations with other professionals, conclusions, and expert opinions regarding criminal responsibility.

Referral

A clear description at the beginning of the forensic report of both the referral source (i.e., who requested the evaluation) and its purpose (i.e., what questions the expert was requested to address) grounds the report and guides both its author and its reader. By articulating the source of the referral, the expert is encouraged to address any relevant court orders, consents, or waivers (e.g., *Miranda*-like warnings) that bear on the propriety of conducting the assessment. In addition, such information provides a valuable context to persons beyond the referral source. By articulating the purpose of the referral, the expert includes the specific language used to identify the legal question. In particular, the forensic expert is also encouraged to describe not only the type of evaluation (e.g., insanity) but to define the relevant test (e.g., ALI) and its specific language. This section motivates the expert to address the specific referral questions in the report and assures the reader of the report's relevance.

Forensic experts are sometimes asked to address multiple referral issues, extending beyond criminal responsibility. Insanity is sometimes coupled with competency to stand trial, capacity to understand *Miranda* warnings, and sentencing issues. We strongly recommend that issues beyond criminal responsibility be addressed in a separate report. Information germane to other issues may have a biasing effect on triers of fact. Therefore, a final issue in addressing the referral question is to ensure that the forensic report is focused on one major issue (e.g., insanity) facing the court.

Description of the Evaluation

The twin purposes of forensic reports are communication and persuasion. These purposes are best achieved when legal and mental health professionals have a clear understanding of the evaluation and its conclusions. In this regard, it is important to describe the evaluation process in meticulous detail. The description should include all tests and procedures utilized, as well as the rationale for their use. It is also advisable to provide a nontechnical explanation of any unfamiliar measures. This thorough description of the evaluation achieves two goals:

♦ It may assist the expert to identify and integrate all of the sources of information that he/she used in the evaluation. Given the complexity and retrospective nature of insanity evaluations, experts must account for all the relevant data and its sources.

♦ It may assist the court and counsel in understanding the evaluation process and assessing its quality. A coherent explanation of what methods were conducted and the purposes of such methods explains the logic and organization of the insanity evaluation. In a noncondescending manner, this section also educates legal professionals about the relevant measures.

♦ It may assist the courts in focusing the legal debate about the comparative validity of particular tests or procedures and their potential contributions to insanity evaluations.

An insanity report based solely on an evaluation of the defendant lacks a firm foundation and is vulnerable to rigorous cross-examination.

To build the necessary foundation, the forensic expert must integrate clinical data from multiple sources. To demonstrate the thoroughness of this integration, other sources of data should be described in detail. Four common sources of information used in many reports are listed below:

1. Review of police investigative reports is delineated, including the arrest reports, witnesses' statements, and any statements made by the defendant. Other information about prior arrests and behavior during detention is likely to be relevant.
2. Review of clinical records is described, including previous hospitalization, evaluations, and outpatient treatment.
3. Collateral interviews with witnesses and family members are outlined.
4. Consultative reports, requested by the forensic expert, are provided, with a rationale for their inclusion.

The Defendant's Behavior at the Time of the Crime

The forensic expert should attempt a thorough description of the defendant's behavior immediately before, during, and following the offense. This information provides the critical framework for later considerations of psychological impairment and criminal responsibility. Unless the descriptions of the defendant's behavior are highly consistent, each source of information should be summarized separately. This summary should always include the defendant's self-reporting, with detailed descriptions of his/her thoughts, feelings, perceptions, and behavior. Since this information should be assessed on more than one occasion, the expert should duly note any significant discrepancies in the defendant's account. Separate sections of the report may summarize police reports and statements made by the defendant and witnesses.

Some experts utilize direct quotes from the defendant or witnesses to capture the defendant's thoughts and feelings prior to and during the offense. Careful preparation with key quotes may add realism and credibility to the report. Care must be taken, however, that the quotes are truly representative of the defendant's or witness's thinking. Any omissions of salient quotes supporting a different perspective may bias the report and raise questions about the expert's impartiality.

An important consideration is whether the insanity report should include a description of previous criminal history, especially previously unreported offenses.[1] The relevance of reporting prior criminal history must be decided on a case-by-case basis, although it often has little direct bearing on criminal responsibility. Prior offenses are sometimes included as part of the diagnosis of antisocial personality disorder (APD) or to explain how the crime in question is part of a pattern of criminal behavior. Even in such cases, the prejudicial impact of such information may outweigh its probative value (Rogers, 1987a). For example, when a defendant meets most of the criteria for APD, is it essential to catalogue his/her past offenses? A substantial hurdle must be overcome before unreported offenses[2] are included in insanity reports. In general, forensic experts should discourage defendants from revealing information about unreported offenses because such disclosures often reflect confusion about a treatment versus forensic role (Shuman, 1993). Assuming the defendant was properly advised about the nonconfidentiality of the assessment, the rules of evidence generally do not ordinarily permit the prosecution to introduce evidence of other crimes (known or unreported) to prove that the defendant is more likely to have committed the offense charged (see Federal Rules of Evidence 404). Accordingly, the examiner should be persuaded that past criminal behavior is highly probative of the defendant's mental status at the time of this offense before including it in the report. This requirement will rarely, if ever, be met.

We caution forensic experts not to consider this component of the forensic report as "routine." Attorneys and courts have access to much of the same data and are able to make independent appraisals of the expert's accuracy in summarizing this critical information. If the accounts appear incomplete or one-sided, attorneys are likely to assume that this apparent bias pervades other elements of the report (e.g., diagnosis and impairment) that are less accessible for independent review. One of the easiest grounds on which to discredit an expert's report is its failure to be complete, thorough, and accurate.

Clinical Description

The report should accurately and completely describe the defendant's psychological functioning at the time of the offense and at the current time. These descriptions and the presentation of relevant clinical material facilitate the assessment process and help to explain the continuity or discontinuity of the defendant's behavior from the time of the offense to the time of trial. Presentation of clinical material for both time periods facilitates the assessment process and underscores the importance of not making unwarranted inferences about the time of the offense from the defendant's current functioning.

The clinical description typically includes the defendant's mental status along with a clear delineation of his/her past and present symptomatology. As discussed in Chapter 7, important benchmarks of impairment include the defendant's interpersonal functioning and capacity for goal-directed behavior (e.g., work or school). In listing symptoms and their resulting impairment, forensic experts often neglect to provide a complete description. An insanity report that simply mentions a defendant's auditory hallucinations has only marginal relevance to the determination of criminal responsibility. In contrast, an insanity report that details the type of auditory hallucination (e.g., command hallucination), its source (e.g., an oracle of God), its content (e.g., suicidal messages), and its effect (e.g., unquestioned obedience) is likely to be highly relevant to criminal responsibility. In addition, many clinical terms may be misunderstood by legal professionals and jurors. For example, the term "depression" has a multitude of meanings even among mental health professionals. By describing the depression, forensic experts are able to clarify its meaning in their forensic reports. For example, some defendants experienced mild dysphoria with recurrent feelings of sadness and emptiness. Other defendants have pervasive depression with severe intensity accompanied by periods of crying and unremitting hopelessness. Examples and detailed descriptions provide the basis for the accurate and convincing presentation of clinical material.

Consultations

Forensic experts are divided in their presentation of consultative reports. The three basic options include (1) a summary of the findings with the report appended, (2) a thorough summary of the findings, and (3) a highly selective summary emphasizing points consistent with the forensic expert. Although few experts would openly endorse the final option, it does occur with some regularity in forensic reports. A commonly encountered example of selective reporting is frequently observed with the use of MMPI-2, MCMI-III, or PAI computerized reports. Although computerized interpretations should be avoided because of their overinterpretation (see the discussion of the MMPI-2 in Chapter 8), the selective reporting of only certain clinical correlates raises additional questions about impartiality and credibility. In general, selective reporting renders the expert vulnerable to devastating cross-examination.

The first option (summary with appended report) is preferable for two reasons. First, the availability of the report minimizes redundancy and allows the expert to briefly describe the most salient issues. Second, the appended report serves as a potential safeguard against the temptation to omit a troubling aspect of the consultant's report. Because competent attorneys will subpoena the consultant's records and reports, access to the report cannot be prevented. By providing a copy, the expert simplifies the process of obtaining the consultant's report and achieves the above objectives.

Forensic experts should not expect perfect agreement between their findings and consultants' reports. Although this statement may be self-evident, some experts appear to have trouble with disagreements among members of their team. We have encountered cases in which forensic experts were reluctant to use consulting psychologists for fear that their results may be troubling to explain.[3] Some disagreements should be expected in every insanity evaluation. Indeed, attorneys should be alert for expert and consultant reports that appear as a seamless "united front." The litmus test of professional collusion is how much communication and possible negotiation occurred *prior* to writing reports.

Disagreements should be presented in a matter-of-fact manner. Efforts to minimize differences or to discount the consultant are readily transparent to attorneys. Instead, the differences between expert and consultant should be stated directly and the reasons for these disagreements articulated. This forthrightness heightens the expert's objectivity and credibility and avoids the unnecessary pitfalls of perceived partisanship.

Clinical Conclusions

The forensic report should present information about the defendant's diagnosis at the time of the offense and at the time of the evaluation. In augmenting the diagnostic picture, clinical data on onset, course, and duration of the disorder are often helpful. Despite their limitations, the DSM diagnoses are the most widely accepted in North America and should be the basis of the diagnosis.[4] The diagnosis per se provides only general information. For insanity reports to be complete, they should delineate the inclusion criteria (i.e., symptoms of the disorder) and address any exclusion criteria (i.e., differential diagnosis). Whenever possible, the diagnosis should include statements about the severity of the disorder and its effect on the defendant's functioning.

Some defendants are not easily diagnosed because of their unusual symptoms; they may warrant only a residual diagnosis (NOS, or "not otherwise specified"). It is critical to note that a DSM diagnosis, while desirable, is not necessary to establish insanity. The critical issue is not the diagnostic criteria for a particular disorder but rather the psychopathological process that underlies the diagnosis. Therefore, the diagnosis is a valuable method of organizing symptoms and associated features. It is not intended as a decision point.

Clinical conclusions should also address the relationship of the mental disorders/psychopathology at the time of the offense to the defendant's criminal behavior. It is important to relate the defendant's psychological impairment to how the criminal behavior was conducted and its salient circumstances (e.g., extreme provocation or intoxication). Pollack, Gross, and Weinberger (1982) argue that forensic experts must examine alternative explanations for why the offense occurred. The examination of different explanations is a rigorous standard requiring a degree of organization and thoroughness that is uncommon in clinical and forensic evaluations. When accomplished, the value of insanity reports increases because legal professionals are able to follow a compelling evaluation of competing hypotheses.

Exploration of the potential determinants of criminal behavior involves a careful integration of relevant information from the "The Defendant's Behavior at the Time of the Crime" and "Clinical Description" subsections. It should discuss how the psychological constructs do and do not contribute to the understanding of the defendant's criminal behavior.

Opinions

An opinion that is well grounded in the facts of the case and the relevant law must, finally, apply the clinical data to the relevant criminal responsibility standard. For example, where the applicable standard is *M'Naghten*, the examiner must analyze how the clinical data bear on each of the elements of that test which asks whether the defendant was "laboring under such a defect of reason, from disease of the mind, as not to know the nature and quality of the act he was doing; or if he knew it, that he did not know he was doing what was wrong." As discussed in Chapter 4, this test incorporates four interrelated and conjunctive concepts (Disease of the Mind, Defect of Reason, Knowing, Nature and Quality of the Act) that the forensic expert must address in applying the test. A similar application of the clinical data to the criteria is required for each insanity standard (e.g., ALI and IDRA); these criteria are outlined in Chapter 4. Opinions should address each component of the insanity standard.

As noted in Chapter 2, whether the expert expresses an ultimate opinion about the defendant's criminal responsibility should turn on several considerations. These considerations involve legal, case-specific, and professional issues:

1. *Rules of evidence.* Most states permit experts to express opinions that embrace an ultimate issue, so long as all of the other requirements for admissibility are met. However, the federal rules prohibit "expert witnesses testifying with respect to the mental state or condition of a defendant in a criminal case [to] state an opinion or inference as to whether the defendant did or did not have the mental state or condition constituting an element of the crime charged or of a defense thereto" (Federal Rules of Evidence 704[b]). In federal courts, experts need to confer with the attorney regarding what words and phrases are permissible in offering conclusions (see Shuman, 1994).

2. *Admissibility under* Daubert. Case-specific data must be carefully evaluated by the forensic expert. In cases where critical data are incomplete or contradictory, the expert may conclude that ultimate opinions are not warranted under *Daubert.* Where the reasoning and conclusions do not appear sound, attorneys may also move to exclude testimony.

3. *Professional views.* Forensic experts are divided regarding the advisability of offering ultimate opinions in forensic cases. Chapter 1 rebuts many of the arguments frequently made against offering ultimate opinions. Still, experts must decide for themselves regarding the advisability of offering ultimate or penultimate conclusions.

In summary, this section provides an extensive outline of components that must be considered in insanity evaluations. Experts are given considerable latitude in how these issues are organized into a coherent report. To assist in report writing, Table 12.1 presents a basic checklist of essential issues. Forensic experts may wish to use this checklist to ensure the comprehensiveness of their reports. Criminal attorneys may wish to review the checklist to evaluate the quality and impartiality of forensic experts.

Pretrial Strategic Conferences

No rule of evidence determines when or how often an attorney must meet with his/her retained expert. Ordinarily, however, it will be useful to meet at least once after the forensic expert has completed the assessment. The earlier in the litigation process this meeting occurs, the more flexibility exists to respond to the expert's finding. With sufficient time, the attorney may raise or abandon a defense, investigate other matters, or retain additional experts. In preparing for these meetings, the expert may wish to consider several transcendent issues.

TABLE 12.1. A Basic Checklist for Insanity Reports

Purpose and referral

1. Is the purpose of the evaluation clearly described?
2. Is the relevant insanity standard named and described?
3. Is the referral source made clear?
4. Is the defendant's consent and understanding of the evaluation documented?

Sources of relevant data

1. Are all relevant clinical records delineated?
2. Are all police-investigative reports recorded?
3. Is the report explict about any unobtained or unobtainable records that might be germane to the case?

Nature of the evaluation

1. Does the report provide date, place, and duration for each interview/test?
2. Does the report delineate tests and standardize measures? Are the purposes of these procedures made explicit?
3. Are any constraints (e.g., testing in a noisy jail) on the evaluation acknowledged openly?
4. Are collateral interviews described with sufficient detail (date, place, and duration)?

Description of the offense

1. Does the report include the police's account of the offense?
2. Does the report include the defendant's versions of the offense?
3. When available, does the report include witnesses' accounts of the offense?

Malingering

1. Is the issue of malingering addressed systematically?
2. Are atypical findings comprehensively evaluated for possible malingering?
3. Is the report clear that screening measures cannot be used to determine malingering?
4. Does the report avoid any interpretations of projective measures when malingering is suspected?
5. Is the dictum observed that malingering should never be classified in the absence of standardized data?

Diagnosis

1. Does the report use DSM criteria? If not, is it explicit that it does not use DSM?
2. Are the inclusion and exclusion criteria addressed systematically? Are examples given for key symptoms?
3. Does the report include all DSM Axis I and II diagnoses, not simply the primary diagnosis?
4. Does the report demarcate diagnoses at the time of the crime from the current time?

(cont.)

TABLE 12.1 *(cont.)*

Opinions

1. Are opinions relevant to the insanity standard?
2. Are opinions well reasoned with clinical data and documentation?
3. Does the report openly acknowledge data that are not supportive of specific opinions?
4. Are alternate opinions considered with supportive data?
5. Is the expert's degree of clinical certainty presented unambiguously?

Finality of Testimony

Unlike therapy, where the treatment regime may be expected to change over the course of therapy, the legal system permits the parties only one fair trial. Once a trial occurs, courts are loathe to consider new information that casts doubt on the accuracy of the earlier decision. Thus, the legal system's expectation for forensic experts, even early in the pretrial process where important decisions must often be made, is that the information provided will be complete and accurate. If further information is needed to complete the assessment, the forensic expert must ascertain whether and when that information will be made available, and clarify the role that information may play in the assessment. In addition, experts should avoid theorizing or extrapolating from the data during early meetings with the attorney. Such speculations may mislead the attorney and will only serve to complicate the expert's thinking.

Allegiance

The attorney's overriding responsibility is to provide his/her client a vigorous representation within the bounds of the law. As summarized in Chapter 3, the attorney's purpose is not necessarily to protect the expert or the expert's reputation. Attorneys owe their allegiance to the side (prosecution or defense) they represent. What about the experts' allegiance? The answer is decomposed into procedures and substance. With respect to procedures, the expert's behavior is dictated by the nature of professional relationship and relevant law. With respect to the substance, experts owe their allegiance to the truth in providing a fair and accurate representation of their conclusions. When an expert is required to testify, the expert's honest and fair representation of his/her findings may be advantageous or detrimental to a defendant's stated objectives.

Preparation

Many experts are insufficiently prepared for pretrial conferences. The expert should perceive pretrial conferences as an important and integral component of the trial. He/she should anticipate most of the trial issues, including the strengths and weaknesses of the case, and the strengths and weaknesses of his/her own testimony. Stated rather dogmatically, a flustered expert during a pretrial conference is likely an ill-prepared expert at trial.

Pretrial Focus

Each meeting between the attorney and the expert, however preliminary, is a planning and trial preparation session. In some cases, these sessions will culminate with a formal mock trial during which the attorney will question the expert as if at trial and have an associate cross-examine the expert. Mock trials are an excellent avenue for adequate preparation and critical evaluation of the anticipated testimony. In other cases, this process may be less formal and may be incorporated in other discussions. In no event, however, should the expert or the attorney tolerate a failure to engage in this important part of the pretrial process. Neither experience as an attorney or an expert, nor past experience working together, provides an assurance that the expert knows the questions that will be asked and the attorney knows the answers that will be given to them.

When preparing for pretrial conferences, we recommend that experts and attorneys review the section of Chapter 3 entitled "Domains of Professional Responsibility." A mutual understanding of professional roles is the foundation for good preparation.

Issues Related to Insanity Trials

The field of expert testimony is replete with folklore about the most effective methods responding to direct and cross-examination. Moreover, attorneys often have definite ideas about how they wish to present an insanity case in order to best sway the jurors. The purpose of this brief section is to provide a distillation of research findings that may be instructive to attorneys and experts involved in insanity cases. These research findings are followed by our own sundry observations about experts' roles in insanity trials.

What Issues Influence Jurors?

Social scientists are very limited in their ability to study actual jurors and are generally prohibited from observing jury deliberations. Therefore, laboratory (i.e., analogue) studies provide a systematic albeit artificial method of studying jurors in insanity trials. Alternatively, juror polls are sometimes used to survey their beliefs about what information was the most influential. What evidence appears to influence jurors faced with the issue of insanity? The salient findings from these studies are summarized below:

1. *Lack of planning and bizarreness.* Roberts et al. (1987) found that a lack of planning appeared to be an important determinant of insanity verdicts among psychotic defendants. The bizzareness of the criminal behavior appears to exert some influence in providing for more GBMI than guilty verdicts. In utilizing these findings, experts may wish to emphasize the presence/absence of these constructs in their testimony. Pickel (1998) found that bizarre details (e.g., drawing symbols in mustard on the victim's body) appeared more salient in jurors' judgments on insanity than expert testimony about motives.

2. *Responsible choices.* Research by Finkel (1989, 1990) indicates that the defendant's capacity to make responsible choices may be key to jury decision making in insanity cases. Employing this finding, prosecutors may wish to demonstrate how the defendant made many other responsible choices close to the time of the offense. Conversely, the defense may wish to emphasize a consistent pattern of impaired decisions.

3. *Responsibility for mental condition.* In insanity trials, Finkel and Slobogin (1995) examined the defendant's contribution to his/her psychological impairment by refusing treatment, stopping medication, or abusing alcohol/drugs. They found that the defendant's irresponsibility for his/her mental condition resulted in fewer acquittals. Depending on the case, either prosecution or defense may wish to emphasize the defendant's contributions to his/her impairment.

4. *Severity of the crime.* Research by Bailis, Darley, Waxman, and Robinson (1995) raised the tantalizing hypothesis that jurors apply a more stringent standard for major (e.g., murder) than minor (e.g., shoplifting) offenses. They also found that the defendants' inability to control their behavior appeared more predictive than their cognitive appreciation. Prosecutors may wish to emphasize the severity of the crime in order to invoke a stringent standard for nonculpability.

5. *Influence of GBMI.* Roberts, Sargent, and Chan (1993) found that providing jurors with the GBMI alternative appears to increase the strin-

gency of their standards for NGRI. Prosecutors may wish to consider this finding, especially with insanity cases where the evidence is more equivocal.

6. *Understandability of juror instructions.* Ogloff (1991) found that prospective jurors rarely were able to identify (≥20.0%) the specific criteria associated with a particular insanity standard. Approximately one-half of jurors (i.e., 48.5%) also appeared to have difficulty understanding the standard of evidence. Attorneys on both sides have a vested interest in jurors' understanding of the verdict decision.

7. *Emotional reactivity.* In an informal polling of jurors, Boudouris (1991) found that emotional reactions overrode decision making. The presentation of affectively upsetting material (e.g., mutilated bodies) may provoke anger and a desire for justice/revenge. The prosecution may wish to emphasize the horror of the crime; the defense counsel should strive to limit the visual evidence.

Courtroom Tactics

Courtroom tactics address strategic decisions made about the presentation of the case (e.g., statements and evidence) and the handling of statements and evidence introduced by the opposing counsel. Experienced attorneys often have definite opinions about the successfulness of certain tactics. The purpose of this section is to highlight courtroom tactics that may be overlooked. We provide a brief summary of relevant research on the courtroom process below:

1. *Stealing thunder.* Should attorneys and experts "steal thunder" (i.e., acknowledge an obvious weakness in their own case) from the opposing side? Rogers and Mitchell (1991) recommended that experts acknowledge weaknesses on direct to avoid giving the impression of being a biased expert. In a study of criminal and civil trials, Williams, Bourgeois, and Croyle (1993) found that the strategy of "stealing thunder" increased the attorney's credibility and indirectly affected the verdict. We suspect that experts would be more persuasive if they conceded weaknesses rather than have opposing counsel pounce on them for their less-than-forthright testimony.

2. *Attacking credibility.* Kassin, Williams, and Saunders (1990) investigated the effects of cross-examination questions designed to attack an expert's reputation. Examples include "Isn't it true that your work is poorly regarded by your colleagues?" and "Hasn't your work been sharply criticized in the past?" Kassin et al. found that such questions damaged the expert's credibility irrespective of the response (admission, denial,

or objection). An untested alternative would be for the expert to ask for clarification.[5]

3. *Inoculating jurors.* Sandys and Dillehay (1995) conducted telephone interviews with actual jurors from criminal trials. In most cases (76.8%), criminal defendants were found guilty. When the first ballot was evenly divided, a guilty verdict occurred in 70.8% of the cases; when the majority of first ballots favored conviction, a guilty verdict was almost inevitable (89.7%). Can defense counsel inoculate jurors against this tendency[6] to settle jury disagreements in favor of guilty verdicts? Defense attorneys may wish to grapple with this problem indirectly by addressing presumption of innocence, personal integrity (e.g., not capitulating to others' opinions), and basic assumptions about mankind (e.g., avoiding the impulse to suspect evil in everyone).

4. *Attacking witnesses.* In interviewing 331 jurors from 38 sexual assault trials, Visher (1987) found that attacking the victim's account as implausible appeared to affect the verdict. It is unclear whether this strategy would extend beyond sexual assault cases or be germane to insanity trials. However, attorneys may wish to consider selectively attacking the plausibility of witnesses' accounts.

5. *Examining an attorney's presentation.* Are attorneys accurate in their appraisals of their own communication abilities? Linz, Penrod, and McDonald (1986) examined 477 jurors' perceptions of attorneys from 50 criminal trials. Unlike prosecutors, defense counsel appear to overrate their effectiveness (e.g., articulateness, enthusiasm, and likableness) and underrate negative aspects of their interpersonal style (e.g., arrogance and nervousness). To improve effectiveness, defense counsel may need feedback from other professionals regarding the effectiveness of their communication. Interpersonal skill is likely to be strongly influential regarding an attorney's competency and trustworthiness (Feldman & Wilson, 1981).

Observations about Experts in Insanity Cases

Experts, like attorneys, are often victims of their own success. A particular style of presentation that produced very positive effects is likely to be overvalued and often repeated. We suspect that particular styles or strategies are rarely critical to any case. Instead, the overall strength of the testimony or the comparative weakness of the cross-examination are likely to be important, yet even these are rarely determinative of the verdict. Past successes are inapplicable to most cases because of fundamental differences in fact patterns, criminal charges, clinical findings, attorneys, and triers of fact.

In the general absence of research, the observations in this section are based on our professional experiences. They should not be viewed as necessarily accurate. Rather, these observations are intended as starting points for further consideration and self-appraisals. Salient issues include the following:

1. *Heterogeneity of styles.* Different styles of expert testimony appear to be effective for different experts. Some experts appear passionate about their testimony, others take care to be assiduously objective, and still others are gentle and likable in their demeanor. We believe that the style of expert testimony does matter, especially in hotly contested cases. However, we hypothesize that the important issue with respect to style is the congruence between the expert's personality and his/her style of expert testimony.

2. *Secondary role.* Insanity trials, despite their frequent dependence on experts, are not about experts. Experts represent one, albeit important, component of trial preparation and presentation. We suspect that some experts have problems adjusting to a secondary role on direct examination and extended questioning of their methods and conclusions on cross-examination. Unlike most clinical settings, in court forensic experts are primarily the recipient of questions to which they must respond.

3. *Misplaced allegiance.* As noted earlier in this chapter, experts sometimes wrongly entrust their allegiance to an attorney. It is not the attorney's responsibility to "look after" or protect the expert. In furthering his/her case, the attorney naturally will object to unfair questions and may strongly agree with the expert's conclusions. However, experts must take care of themselves; their integrity and professionalism is tested in every insanity trial. Expert owe attorneys nothing more and nothing less than the truth.

4. *Communication barriers.* Many experts erect barriers between themselves and the triers of fact. A favorite barrier is to use more jargon than most people can tolerate. As a general guideline, when jargon is used more than once in a sentence, many people stop listening. Although diagnosis and technical terms must sometimes be used, great care should be taken to explain their meaning and to give clear examples. A second and more subtle barrier is to provide information clearly but in a condescending manner; it is very difficult to hear a message when the subtext insults the jurors' intelligence and education. A third barrier is the expectation that jurors can effectively hold complex information for sustained periods of time. An egregious example is MMPI configural and scale interpretation without the visual displays.[7] As a general guideline,

all test material should be presented visually to facilitate communication.

5. *Mystery of cross-examination.* We take strong issue with the assumption that cross-examination is a mystery full of unexpected questions. In most communities, experts can develop a good understanding of the opposing attorney's cross-examination style simply by checking with colleagues. Attorneys can greatly facilitate this process by relating their own experiences with the attorney and pulling representative cross-examination questions from past trials. Related to the case, we recommend that the expert and attorney separately generate potential cross-examination questions for purposes of trial preparation.

Resources are readily available to assist experts in preparing for criminal trials. Examples of highly readable books offering practical suggestions include Brodsky (1991) and Shapiro (1984). In preparation for insanity and other forensic mental health issues, Rogers and Mitchell (1991) provide detailed information and sample cross-examination questions. Finally, Ziskin (1995) presents a system of cross-examination based on general principles (see Rogers & Bagby, 1993). Familiarity with Ziskin-type cross-examination may be important in jurisdictions where this format is frequently used.

Multiple Forensic Roles

Experts may play multiple forensic roles in an insanity defense. An expert may help to assess trial strategies, assist in jury selection, prepare lay witnesses, select expert witnesses, prepare cross-examination of opposing expert witnesses, or offer expert testimony. Economic incentives may motivate attorneys to employ experts for multiple forensic roles. However, important considerations militate against these financial considerations in favor of compartmentalizing forensic roles.

Consulting experts, who do not evaluate the defendant and are not expected to testify, are ordinarily not discoverable. These experts can assist with such important functions as strategic case assessment, witness preparation, expert witness selection, preparation of cross-examination for opposing experts, and jury selection. Experts, when performing these functions, are regarded as an assistant of the attorney whose communications with the attorney are cloaked with the attorney–client or work-product privilege. Thus, counsel can reveal even the most harmful information about the case to consulting experts, confident that the opposing party cannot compel discovery of that information, or even discover the existence of these experts.

In contrast with consulting experts, testifying experts are discoverable. Moreover, it is permissible to cross-examine an expert about the information that was made known to the expert before testifying. The obvious risk of utilizing a testifying expert to assist in strategic considerations or jury selection is revealing discoverable information that would otherwise be outside the scope of discovery. Even where funds are limited for payment of additional experts, it is imprudent to mix consulting and testifying roles. An additional consideration is the impartiality of the testifying expert. If the judge allows questions regarding the expert's "other roles," the triers of fact are unlikely to be impressed regarding the expert's impartiality if he/she admits to "gunning" against the other experts or attempting to "stack" the jury.

Rebuttal Experts

The role of a rebuttal expert is unique in expert testimony and bridges our categorization of consulting and testifying experts. Rebuttal experts may or may not have evaluated the defendant. Rebuttal experts are sometimes employed to counter damaging testimony from the other side. Strategically, some attorneys may believe that the *option* of using rebuttal experts will temper the testimony from opposing experts. Alternatively, the foundation of the expected testimony may have fundamental weaknesses. Although these weakness could be covered by experts prior to the testimony being entered into evidence,[8] the value of this strategy is open to question. Therefore, waiting until the weak testimony is offered provides the optimum chance to nullify its effects through rebuttal testimony. However, the risk of waiting is that rebuttal experts are sometimes squandered because the opposing expert does not testify or testifies to circumscribed issues.

Attorneys occasionally desire to use consulting experts as rebuttal experts. This desire sometimes arises when cross-examination failed to have its desired effect on the opposing expert's testimony. When these requests occur at the last minute, consulting experts may experience a range of emotions from pleasure to surprise and even betrayal. To minimize this eventuality, consulting experts may choose to specify their roles in a written contract so that the possibility of any misunderstanding is removed. Any shift from consulting to rebuttal expert brings to the foreground the above issues regarding the discoverability of potentially damaging information.

Conclusion

The greatest challenge for experts in insanity trials is the careful formulation of their opinion. This challenge involves the integration of clinical data from multiple sources, differential diagnosis, and the comparative analysis of competing conclusions. This challenge is best achieved by a comprehensive report. The second greatest challenge is persuasive communication. The foundation of this communication is the written report, buttressed by test data and records. However, the adversarial context of contested insanity trials brings into sharp relief the parameters of expert testimony and the contours of cross-examination.

Notes

1. Reports of insanity evaluations sometimes include *family* histories of criminal and antisocial behavior. We believe this information is highly prejudicial and noncontributory to conclusions regarding criminal responsibility. Therefore, insanity reports should avoid such prejudicial information.

2. We use "unreported offenses" as shorthand for criminal acts perpetrated by the defendant for which he/she has not been questioned or arrested.

3. Several legitimate reservations may occur, including whether the psychologist (a) is trained in forensic matters and (b) is an expert in the tests administered.

4. If alternative diagnostic systems (e.g., ICD or RDC) are used, it is incumbent on the forensic expert to describe this alternative nomenclature and justify its use.

5. For example, "I am unaware of any sharp criticisms; perhaps you could help me to respond by giving the context of your question." However, it is unclear whether jurors will be able to discern cases in which the attorney is bluffing.

6. A similar tendency does not occur when the majority vote "not guilty" on the first ballot (i.e., 38.1% are subsequently found guilty).

7. As a parallel, experts should consider how often attorneys become confused with the verbal presentation of test data. To test the expert's clarity, we suggest asking attorneys to paraphrase back to experts their understanding of the answer.

8. This option is possible when written reports from opposing experts are available.

Data Bases on NGRI Patients and R-CRAS Evaluations

Studies of NGRI Patients Included in Data Base

For U.S. studies, the total number of NGRI patients was 6,479. The availability data from these studies varied dramatically. For example, data on gender were almost always available (96.4%) while data on primary diagnosis was less consistent (85.6%). Listed below were the studies included with information of the states, sample size, and setting.

Study	State(s)	Sample	Setting
Studies in the United States			
Bieber, Pasewark, Bosten, & Steadman (1988)	NY	132	Both
Wettstein & Mulvey (1988)	IL	137	Inpatient
Bogenberger, Paswark, Gudeman, & Beiber (1987)	HA	107	Both
Wiederanders & Choate (1994)[a]	CA	641	Outpatient
Pantle, Pasewark, Steadman (1980)	NY	46	Both
Criss & Racine (1980)	MI	223	Both
Bloom, Williams, Rogers, & Barbur (1986)	OR	161	Both
Callahan, Steadman, McGreevy, & Clark (1991)	8 states[b]	2,565	Both
Linhorst, Hunsucker, & Parker (1998)	MO	842	Both
Scott, Zonana, & Getz (1990)	CT	173	Both
Morrow & Peterson (1966)	MO	44	Outpatient
Seig, Ball, & Menninger (1995)	CO	149	Inpatient
Heilbrun, Griffin-Heilbrun, & Griffin (1988)	FL	41	Inpatient
Rogers & Bloom (1982)	OR	440	Both
Gacono, Meloy, Sheppard, Speth, & Roske (1995)	CA	18	Inpatient
Shah, Greenberg, & Convit (1994)	NJ	62	Inpatient
Steadman (1980)	NY	378	Both
Petrila (1982)	MO	67	Both
Cohen, Spodak, Silver, & Williams (1988)	MD	127	Outpatient
Norwood, Nicholson, Enyart, & Hickey (1991)	OK	61	Inpatient
Cavanaugh & Wasyliw (1985)	IL	44	Outpatient
Heinbecker (1986)	UT	7	Both
Janofksy, Vandewalle, & Rappeport (1989)	MD	14	Both

Study	State(s)	Sample	Setting
Studies in Canada			
Hodgins, Hebert, & Baraldi (1986)	QB	29	Outpatient
Greenland (1980)	ON	88	Both

Note. "Both" = inpatient and outpatient settings.

[a]Study includes a very small number on non-NGRI patients.

[b]States include CA, GA, MT, NJ, NY, OH, WA, and WI.

R-CRAS Data Base

Rogers and Sewell (1999) reanalyzed R-CRAS data on 413 insanity cases, which was utilized in this book as the R-CRAS data base. These data were categorized by clinical opinion into three groups: (a) insane ($n = 95$ or 23.0%), (b) sane ($n = 288$ or 69.7%), and indeterminate ($n = 30$ or 7.3%). The sample is predominantly male (88.6%) and highly variable in age ($M = 29.14$; $SD = 9.53$; range = 17 to 69).

Appellate Decisions on the Discoverability of Expert Opinions in Insanity Cases

The following decisions affirm that raising the insanity defense does not, by itself, waive the attorney–client privilege for retained, non-testifying experts:

Smith v. McCormick, 914 F.2d 1153 (9th Cir 1990)
United States v. Alvarez, 519 P.2d 1036 (3rd Cir 1975)
Houston v. State, 602 P.2d 784 (AK 1979)
People v. Lines, 531 P.2d 793 (CA 1975)
Miller v. District Court 737 P.2d 834 (CO 1987)
People v. Knuckles, 650 N.E. 2d 975 (IL 1995)
State v. Pratt, 398 A.2d 421 (MD 1979)
People v. Hilliker, 185 N.W. 2d 831 (MI App. 1971)
State v. Kociolek, 129 A.2d 417 (NJ 1957)

The following decisions find the privilege waived for the no-testifying expert once the insanity defense is raised.

Lange v. Young, 869 F.2d 1008 (7th Cir), cert denied, 490 U.S. 1094 (1989)
Austin v. Alfred, 788 P.2d 130 (AZ 1980)
State v. Ross, 646 A.2d 1318 (CT 1994), cert denied 115 S.Ct. 1133 (1995)
State v. Schneider, 402 N.W.2d 779 (MN 1987), cert denied 114 S.Ct. 901 (1994)
State v. Carter, 641 S.W.2d 54 (MO 1982), cert denied 461 US 932 (1983)
People v. Edney, 350 N.E.2d 400 (NY 1976)
Haynes v. State, 739 P.2d 497 (NEV 1987)
State v. Hattllt, 994 P.ed 1026 (WA 1997)

Commonly Used Psychological Tests and Their Abbreviations

Multiscale Inventories

MMPI   Minnesota Multiphasic Personality Inventory
MMPI-2   Minnesota Multiphasic Personality Inventory—2
MCMI   Millon Clinical Multiaxial Inventory (also MCMI-II and MCMI-III)
PAI   Personality Assessment Inventory
BPI   Basic Personality Inventory

Projective Measures

Rorschach
Holtzman Inkblot Technique
Human Figure Drawings
Draw-A-Person Test
House–Tree–Person Test
Thematic Apperception Test (TAT)

Structured Interviews

CDP   Comprehensive Drinker Profile
DIS   Diagnostic Interview Schedule
PCL   Psychopathy Checklist (also PCL-R)
PDE   Personality Disorder Examination
SADS   Schedule of Affective Disorders and Schizophrenia
SCID-D   Structured Clinical Interview for DSM-IV Dissociative Disorders

SCID	Structured Clinical Interview for DSM-III-R
SCID-II	Structured Clinical Interview for DSM-III-R—Axis II Disorders
SIDP	Structured Interview for DSM-III Personality Disorders

Forensic Measures

R-CRAS	Rogers Criminal Responsibility Assessment Scales
SIRS	Structured Interview of Reported Symptoms
MSE-Offense	Mental State at the Time of the Offense Screening Evaluation
	M Test

Cognitive Measures

MMSE	Mini-Mental Status Examination
SB	Stanford–Binet
WAIS	Wechsler Adult Intelligence Scale (also WAIS-R and WAIS-III)
HRB	Halstead–Reitan
LNNB	Luria–Nebraska

References

Abel, G. G. (1995). *The comparison of the Abel Assessment with penile plethymography.* Unpublished manuscript, Behavioral Medicine Institute, Altanta, GA.

Abel, G. G., Barlow, D. H., Blanchard, E. B., & Guild, D. (1977). The components of rapists' sexual arousal. *Archives of General Psychiatry, 34,* 895–903.

Adams, J. J., Meloy, J. R., & Moritz, M. S. (1990). Neuropsychological deficits and violent behavior in incarcerated schizophrenics. *Journal of Nervous and Mental Disease, 178,* 253–256.

Allen, L. M.,III, Conder, R. L., Jr., Green, P., & Cox, D. R. (1997). *CARB '97 Computerized Assessment of Response Bias.* Durham, NC: CogniSyst Inc.

American Academy of Psychiatry and the Law. (1991). *Ethical guidelines for the practice of forensic psychiatry.* Bloomington, CT: Author.

American Academy of Psychiatry and the Law. (1995). *Ethical guidelines for the practice of forensic psychiatry.* Bloomington, CT: Author.

American Bar Association (ABA). (1983). *Model code of professional conduct.* Chicago: Author.

American Bar Association (ABA). (1990). *American Bar Association model code of judicial conduct.* Chicago: Author.

American Bar Association Criminal Justice and Mental Health Standards. (1989). Project of the American Bar Association Criminal Justice Standards Committee, Washington, DC.

American Bar Association (ABA) Standards for Criminal Justice. (1993). *Prosecution and defense functions* (3rd ed.). Washington, DC: American Bar Association.

American Law Institute. (1962). *Model penal code: Proposed official draft.* Philadelphia: Author.

American Psychiatric Association. (1980). *Diagnostic and statistical manual of mental disorders.* (3rd ed.). Washington, DC: Author.

American Psychiatric Association. (1983). American Psychiatric Association statement on the insanity defense. *American Journal of Psychiatry, 140,* 681–688.

American Psychiatric Association. (1987). *Diagnostic and statistical manual of mental disorders* (3rd ed., rev.), Washington, DC: Author.

American Psychiatric Association. (1994). *Diagnostic and statistical manual of mental disorders* (4th ed.). Washington, DC: Author.

American Psychological Association (APA). (1984). Text of position on insanity defense. *APA Monitor, 15,* 11.

American Psychological Association (APA). (1985). *Standards for educational and psychological testing.* Washington, DC: Author.

American Psychological Association (APA). (1986). *Amicus curiae on Thornburgh v. American College of Obstretricians and Gynecologists, 106 S. Ct. 2169 (1986).* Washington, DC: Author.

American Psychological Association (APA). (1992). Ethical principles of psychologists and code of conduct. *American Psychologist, 47,* 1597–1611.

American Psychological Association. (APA). (1994). Guidelines for child custody evaluations in divorce proceedings. *American Psychologist, 49,* 677–680.

Ananth, J., Gamal, R., Miller, M., Wohl, M., & Wandewater, S. (1993). Is the routine CT head scan justified for psychiatric patients? A prospective study. *Journal of Psychiatry and Neuroscience, 18,* 69–73.

Anastasi, A. (1988). *Psychological testing* (6th ed.). New York: Macmillan.

Anderson, T., & Dixon, W. E., Jr. (1993). The factor structure of the Rorschach for adolescent inpatients. *Journal of Personality Assessment, 60,* 319–332.

Appelbaum, K. L. (1990). Criminal defendants who desire punishment. *Bulletin of the American Academy of Psychiatry and Law, 18,* 385–391.

Appelbaum, P. S. (1997). A theory of ethics for forensic psychiatry. *Journal of the American Academy of Psychiatry and Law, 25,* 233–247.

Appelbaum, P. S., & Greer, A. (1994). Who's on trial? Multiple personalities and the insanity defense. *Hospital and Community Psychiatry, 45,* 965–966.

Appelbaum, P. S., Jick, R. Z., Grisso, T., Givelber, D., Silver, E., & Steadman, H. J. (1993). Use of post-traumatic stress disorder to support an insanity defense. *American Journal of Psychiatry, 150,* 229–234.

Arbisi, P. A., & Ben-Porath, Y. S. (1998). The ability of the Minnesota Multiphasic Personality Inventory-2 validity scales to detect fake-bad responses in psychiatric inpatients. *Psychological Assessment, 10,* 221–228.

Archer, R. P. (1992). *MMPI-A: Assessing adolescent psychopathology.* Hillsdale, NJ: Erlbaum.

Archer, R. P., Aiduk, R., Griffin, R., & Elkins, D. E. (1996). Incremental validity of the MMPI-2 content scales in a psychiatric sample. *Assessment, 3,* 79–90.

Arkes, H. R. (1989). Principles of judgment/decision making research pertinent to legal proceedings. *Behavioral Sciences and the Law, 7,* 429–456.

Arkes, H. R., Faust, D., Guilmette, T. J., & Hart, K. (1988). Eliminating hindsight bias. *Journal of Applied Psychology, 73,* 305–307.

Austin v. Alfred, 788 P.2d 130 (AZ 1980).

Austin, G. W., Leschied, A. D., Jaffe, P. G., & Sas, L. (1986). Factor structure and construct valdity of the Basic Personality Inventory with juvenile offenders. *Canadian Journal of Behavioral Science, 18,* 238–247.

Bach-Y-Rita, G., Lion, J. R., Climent, C. E., & Ervin, F. R. (1971). Episodic dyscontrol: A study of 130 violent patients. *American Journal of Psychiatry, 127,* 1473–1478.

Baer, R. A., Wetter, M. W., & Berry, D.T.R. (1992). Detection of underreporting of psychopathology on the MMPI: A meta-analysis. *Clinical Psychology Review, 12,* 509–525.

Baer, R. A., Wetter, M. W., & Berry, D.T.R. (1995). Effects of information about validity scales on underreporting of symptoms on the MMPI-2: An analogue investigation. *Assessment, 2,* 189–200.

Bagby, R. M., Buis, T. E., & Nicholson, R. A. (1995). Relative effectiveness of the standard validity scales in detecting fake-good and fake-bad responding: Replication and extension. *Psychological Assessment, 7,* 84–92.

Bagby, R. M., Gillis, J. R., & Dickens, S. (1990). Detection of dissimulation with the new generation of objective personality measures. *Behavioral Sciences and the Law, 8,* 93–102.

Bailis, D. S., Darley, J. M., Waxman, T. L., & Robinson, P. H. (1995). Community standards of criminal liability and the insanity defense. *Law and Human Behavior, 19,* 425–446.

Baldwin, L. J., Menditto, A. A., Beck, N. C., & Smith, S. M. (1993). Factors influencing length of hospitalization for NGRI acquittees in a maximum security facility. *Journal of Psychiatry and Law, 20,* 257–267.

Barth, J. T., Ryan, T. V., & Hawk, G. L. (1992). Forensic neuropsychology: A reply to method skeptics. *Neuropsychology Review, 3,* 251–266.

Bartol, C. R., & Bartol, A. M. (1987). History of forensic psychology. In I. B. Weiner & A. K. Hess (Eds.), *Handbook of forensic psychology* (pp. 3–21). New York: Wiley.

Beadoin, M. N., Hodgins, S., & Lavoie, F. (1993). Homicide, schizophrenia, and substance abuse or dependency. *Canadian Journal of Psychiatry, 38,* 541–546.

Beahrs, J. O. (1994). Dissociative identity disorder: Adaptive deception of self and others. *Bulletin of the American Academy of Psychiatry and Law, 22,* 223–237.

Beck, J. C., Borenstein, N., & Dreyfus, J. (1986). The relationship between verdict, defendant characteristics, and type of crime in sex-related criminal cases. *Bulletin of the American Academy of Psychiatry and Law, 14,* 141–146.

Beetar, J. T., & Williams, J. N. (1995). Malingering response styles on the Memory Assessment Scales and symptom validity tests. *Archives of Clinical Neuropsychology, 10,* 57–72.

Behnke, S. H. (1997). Assessing the criminal responsibility of individuals with multiple personality disorder: Legal cases, legal theory. *Journal of the American Academy of Psychiatry and Law, 25,* 391–399.

Bell v. Evatt, 72 F.3d 421 (4th Cir. 1995).

Ben-Porath, Y. S., Butcher, J. N., & Graham, J. R. (1991). Contribution of the MMPI-2 content scales to the differential diagnosis of schizophrenia and major depression. *Psychological Assessment, 3,* 634–640.

Bernard, L. C. (1990). Prospects of faking believable memory deficits on neuropsychological tests and the use of incentives in simulation research. *Journal of Clinical and Experimental Neuropsychology, 12,* 715–728.

Berry, D. T. R., Baer, R. A., & Harris, M. J. (1991). Detection of malingering on the MMPI: A meta-analytic review. *Clinical Psychology Review, 11,* 585–598.

Berry, D. T. R., Wetter, M. W., Baer, R. A., Widiger, T. A., Sumpter, J. C., Reynolds, S. K., & Hallam, R. A. (1991). Detection of random responding on the MMPI-2: Utility of *F,* back *F,* and *VRIN* scales. *Psychological Assessment: A Journal of Clinical and Consulting Psychology, 3,* 418–423.

Bersoff, D. N., & Hofer, P. J. (1991). Legal issues in computerized psychological testing. In T. B. Gutkin & S. L. Wise (Eds.), *Computer and Decision-Making* (pp. 225–243). Hillsdale, NJ: Erlbaum.

Bieber, S. L., Pasewark, R. A., Bosten, K., & Steadman, H. J. (1988). Predicting criminal recidivism of insanity acquittees. *International Journal of Law and Psychiatry, 11,* 105–112.

Binder, L. M. (1990). Malingering following minor head trauma. *Clinical Neuropsychologist, 4,* 25–36.

Blashfield, R. K. (1992, August). *Are there any prototypical patients with personality disorders?* Paper presented at the American Psychological Association convention, Washington, DC.

Blau, G. I., McGinley, H., & Pasewark, R. (1993). Understanding the use of the insanity defense. *Journal of Clinical Psychology, 49,* 435–440.

Bloom, J. D., Williams, M. H., & Bigelow, D. A. (1991). Monitored conditional release of persons found not guilty by reason of insanity. *American Journal of Psychiatry, 148,* 444–448.

Bloom, J. D., Williams, M. H., Rogers, J. L., & Barbur, P. (1986). Evaluation and treatment of insanity acquittees in the community. *Bulletin of the American Academy of Psychiatry and Law, 14,* 231–244.

Boehnert, C. E. (1985). Psychological and demographic differences associated with individuals using the insanity defense. *Journal of Psychiatry and Law, 13,* 9–31.

Boehnert, C. E. (1987). Characteristics of those evaluated for insanity. *Journal of Psychiatry and Law, 15,* 229–246.

Boehnert, C. E. (1988). Typology of men unsuccessfully raising the insanity defense. *Journal of Psychiatry and Law, 16,* 417–424.

Bogenberger, R. P., Paswark, R. A., Gudeman, H., & Beiber, S. L. (1987). Follow-up of insanity acquittees in Hawaii. *International Journal of Law and Psychiatry, 10,* 283–295.

Bohm, R. M. (1994). Capital punishment in two judicial circuits in Georgia: A description of the key actors and the decision-making process. *Law and Human Behavior, 18,* 319–338.

Bonynge, E. R. (1994). A cluster analysis of the Basic Personality Inventory (BPI) adolescent profiles. *Journal of Clinical Psychology, 50,* 265–272.

Borum, R. (1996). Improving the clinical practice of violence risk assessment. *American Psychologist, 51,* 945–956.

Borum, R., & Grisso, T. (1995). Psychological test use in criminal forensic evaluations. *Professional Psychology: Research and Practice, 26,* 465–473.

Borum, R., Otto, R., & Golding, S. (1993). Improving clinical judgment and decision making in forensic evaluation. *Journal of Psychiatry and Law, 21,* 35–76.

Boudouris, J. (1991). The insanity defense: Case study and jury analysis. *American Journal of Forensic Psychology, 9,* 43–58.

Bourget, D., & Bradford, J. M. W. (1995). Sex offenders who claim amnesia for their alleged offense. *Bulletin of the American Academy of Psychiatry and Law, 23,* 299–307.

Brady v. Maryland, 373 U.S. 83 (1963).

Brewin, C. R. (1998). Commentary: Questionable validity of "dissociative amnesia" in trauma studies. *British Journal of Psychiatry, 172,* 216–217.

Brodsky, S. L. (1991). *Testifying in court: Guidelines and maxims for the expert witness.* Washington, DC: American Psychological Association.

Bromberg, W. (1979). *The uses of psychiatry in the law: A clinical view of forensic psychiatry.* Westport, CT: Quorum Books.

Brooks, A. D. (1974). *Law, psychiatry, and the mental health system.* Boston: Little, Brown.

Buckhout, R. (1974). Eye-witness testimony. *Scientific American, 6,* 23–31.

Bursten, B. (1982). What if antisocial personality is an illness? *Bulletin of the American Academy of Psychiatry and the Law, 10,* 97–102.

Butcher, J. N., Dahlstrom, W. G., Graham, J. R., Archer, R. P., Tellegen, A., Ben-Porath, Y. S., & Kaemmer, B. (1992). *MMPI-A: Manual for administration, scoring, and interpretation.* Minneapolis: University of Minnesota Press.

Butcher, J. N., Dahlstrom, W. G., Graham, J. R., Tellegen, A., & Kaemmer, B. (1989). *Manual for the administration and scoring of the MMPI-2.* Minneapolis: University of Minnesota Press.

Butcher, J. N., & Willams, C. L. (1992). *Essentials of MMPI-2 and MMPI-A interpretation.* Minneapolis: University of Minnesota Press.

Butcher, J. N., Williams, C. L., Graham, J. R., Tellegen, A., & Kaemmer, B. (1989). *MMPI-2: Manual for administration and scoring.* Minneapolis: University of Minnesota Press.

Cain v. State, 549 S.W.2d 707 (Tex. Crim. App.), cert. denied, 434 U.S.845 (1977).

Callahan, L. A., Steadman, H. J., McGreevy, M. A., & Clark , P. C. (1991). The volume and characteristics of insanity defense pleas: An eight-state study. *Bulletin of the American Academy of Psychiatry and Law, 19,* 331–338.

Campbell, W. G., & Hodgins, D. C. (1993). Alcoholic-related blackouts in a medical practice. *American Journal of Drug and Alcohol Abuse, 19,* 369–376.

Canino, G. J., Bird, H. R., Shrout, P. E., Rubio-Stipee, M., Bravo, M., Martinez, R., Sesman, M., Guzman, A., & Guevara, L. M. (1987). The prevalence of specific psychiatric disorders in Puerto Rico. *Archives of General Psychiatry, 44,* 727–735.

Cardena, E., & Spiegel, D. (1998). Diagnostic issues, criteria, and comorbidity of dissociative disorders. In L. K. Michelson & W. J. Ray (Eds.), *Handbook of dissociation: Theoretical, empirical, and clinical perspectives* (pp. 227–250). New York: Plenum Press.

Cashel, M. L., Rogers, R., Sewell, K. W., & Holliman, N. (1998). Preliminary validation of the MMPI-A for a male delinquent sample: An investigation of clinical correlates and discriminant validity. *Journal of Personality Assessment, 71,* 49–69.

Cavanaugh, J. L., & Wasyliw, O. E. (1985). Adjustment of the not guilty by reason of insanity (NGRI) outpatient: An initial report. *Journal of Forensic Sciences, 30,* 24–30.

Center for Forensic Psychiatry. (1974, June). *Evaluation of guilty-but-mentaly ill.* Seminar at Center for Forensic Psychiatry, Ann Arbor, MI.

Cercey, S. P., Schretlen, D. J., & Brandt, J. (1997). Simulated amnesia and the pseudomemory phenomena. In R. Rogers (Ed.), *Clinical assessment of malingering and deception* (2nd ed., pp. 85–107). New York: Guilford Press.

Champagne, A., Shuman, D. W., & Whitaker, E. (1991). An empirical examination of the use of expert witnesses in American courts. *Jurimetrics Journal, 31,* 375–392.

Chapple v. Ganger, 851 F. Supp. 1481 (E. D. Wash, 1994).

Charkasky, S., & Hollander, E. (1997). Neuropsychiatric aspects of impulsivity and aggression. In S. C. Yudofsky, & R. E. Hales (Eds.), *The American Psychiatric Press textbook of neuropsychiatry* (3rd ed., pp. 485–499). Washington, DC: American Psychiatric Press.

Ciccone, J. R. (1992). Murder, insanity, and medical expert witnesses. *Archives of Neurology, 49,* 608–611.

Ciccone, J. R., & Clements, C. (1987). The insanity defense: Asking and answering the ultimate question. *Bulletin of the American Academy of Psychiatry and the Law, 16,* 329–338.

Cirincione, C. (1996). Revisiting the insanity defense: Contested or consensus? *Bulletin of the American Academy of Psychiatry and the Law, 24,* 165–176.

Cirincione, C., Steadman, H. J., & McGreevy, M. A. (1995). Rates of insanity acquittals and the factors associated with successful insanity pleas. *Bulletin of the American Academy of Psychiatry and the Law, 23,* 399–409.

Cohen, M. I., Spodak, M. K., Silver, S. B., & Williams, K. (1988). Predicting outcome of NGRI patients released to the community. *Behavioral Sciences and the Law, 6,* 515–530.

Committee on Ethical Guidelines for Forensic Psychologists. (1991). Speciality guidelines for forensic psychologists. *Law and Human Behavior, 15,* 655–665.

Committee on Psychiatry and Law, Group for the Advancement of Psychiatry. (1991). *Report No. 131: The mental health professional and the legal system.* Unpublished report.

Coram, G. J. (1995). A Rorschach analysis of violent murderers and nonviolent offenders. *European Journal of Psychological Assessment, 11,* 81–88.

Cornell, R. (1996). *Criterion validity of the MMPI-2 in a state hospital setting.* Unpublished doctoral dissertation, University of North Texas.

Cowles, M., & Davis, C. (1982). The origins of the .05 level of statistical significance. *American Psychologist, 37,* 553–558.

Craig, R. J., Kuncel, R., & Olson, R. E. (1994). Ability of drug abusers to avoid detection of substance abuse on the MCMI-II. *Journal of Social Behavior and Personality, 9,* 95–106.

Craig, R. J., & Weinberg, D. (1992). Assessing drug abusers with the Millon Clinical Multiaxial Inventory: A review. *Journal of Substance Abuse Treatment, 9,* 249–255.

Cressen, R. (1975). Artistic quality of drawings and judges' evaluations of the DAP. *Journal of Personality Assessment, 39,* 132–137.

Criss, M. L., & Racine, D. R. (1980). Impact of change in legal standard for those adjudicated not guilty by reason of insanity 1975–1979. *Bulletin of the American Academy of Psychiatry and Law, 8,* 261–71.

Cunnien, A. J. (1986). Alcoholic blackouts: Phenomenology and legal relevance. *Behavioral Sciences and the Law, 4,* 73–85.

Cutler, B. L., Moran, G., & Narby, D. J. (1992). Jury selection in insanity defense cases. *Journal of Research in Personality, 26,* 165–182.

Dahlstrom, W. G. (1992). Comparability of two-point high-point code patterns from original MMPI norms to MMPI-2 norms for the restandardization sample. *Journal of Personality Assessment, 59,* 153–164.

Daniel, A. E., Beck, N. C., Herath, A., Schmitz, M., & Menninger, K. A. (1984). Factors correlated with psychiatric recommendations of incompetency and insanity. *Journal of Psychiatry and Law, 12,* 527–544.

Daubert v. Merrell Dow Pharmaceuticals, Inc., U.S. 113 S.Ct. 2786 (1993).

Davidson, H. A. (1952). *Forensic psychiatry.* New York: Ronald Press.

Davidson, H. A. (1965). *Forensic psychiatry* (2nd ed.). New York: Ronald Press.

Davis v. United States, 165 U.S. 373 (1897).

Dawes, R. M. (1989). Experience and validity of clinical judgment: The illusory correlation. *Behavioral Sciences and the Law, 7,* 457–467.

Deatherage v. State, 948 P.2d 828 (Wa. 1997).

Deffenbacher, K. A., Bothwell, R. K., & Brigham, J. C. (1986, August). *Predicting eyewitness identification from confidence: The optimality hypothesis.* Paper presented at the annual convention of the American Psychological Association, New York.

Delgado-Escueta, A. V., Mattson, R. H., King, L., Goldensohn, E. S., Spiegel, H., Madsen, J., Crandall, P., Dreifuss, F., & Porter, R. J. (1981). The nature of aggression during epileptic seizures. *New England Journal of Medicine, 305,* 711–716.

Denney, R. L. (1996). Symptom validity testing of remote memory in a criminal forensic setting. *Archives of Clinical Neuropsychology, 11,* 589–603.

Devinsky, O., & Valquez, B. (1993). Behavioral changes associated with epilepsy. *Neurology Clinic, 11,* 127–149.

Diaz, F. G. (1995). Traumatic brain injury and criminal behavior. *Medicine and Law, 14,* 131–140.

Dinwiddle, S. H. (1996). Genetics, antisocial personality, and criminal responsibility. *Bulletin of the American Academy of Psychiatry and Law, 24,* 95–102.

Dix, G. E. (1984). Criminal responsibility and mental impairment in American criminal law: Response to the Hinckley acquittal in historical perspective. In D. N. Weisstub (Ed.), *Law and mental health: International perspectives* (pp. 1–44). New York: Pergamon Press.

Doerr, H. O., & Carlin, A. S. (Eds.). (1991). *Forensic neuropsychology: Legal and scientific bases.* New York: Guilford Press.

Drake, M. E., Jr. (1990). Neurophysiologic aspects of personality disorders. *American Journal of EEG Technology, 30,* 117–125.

Dressler, J. (1995). *Understanding criminal law* (2nd ed.). New York: Bender.

Drukteinis, A. M. (1992). Serial murder—The heart of darkness. *Psychiatric Annals, 22,* 532–538.

Durham v. United States, 214 F.2d 862 (D.C. Cir. 1954).

Dysken, M. W., Chang, S. S., Casper, R. C., & Davis, J. M. (1979). Barbiturate-facilitated interviewing. *Biological Psychiatry, 14,* 421–432.

Dysken, M. W., Steinberg, J., & Davis, J. M. (1979). Sodium amobarbital response during simulated catatonia. *Biological Psychiatry, 14,* 995–1000.

Edwards, D. W., Morrison, T. L., & Weissman, H. N. (1993). The MMPI and MMPI-2 in an outpatient sample: Comparisons of code types, validity scales, and clinical scales. *Journal of Personality Assessment, 61,* 1–18.

Eissler, K. R. (1986). *Freud as an expert witness* (C. Trollope, Trans.). Madison, CT: International University Press. (Original work published 1979)

Elliot, F. A. (1992). Violence: The neurological contribution: An overview. *Archives of Neurology, 49,* 595–603.

Elliot, R. L. (1987). An introduction to organic brain syndromes. *Behavioral Sciences and the Law, 5,* 287–306.

Elliot, R. L., Nelson, E., Fitch, W. L., Scott, R., Woldber, G., & Singh, R. (1993). Informed decision making in persons acquitted not guilty by reason of insanity. *Bulletin of the American Academy of Psychiatry and Law, 21,* 309–320.

Emery, P. E., & Emery, O. B. (1984). *A case study of the New Hamsphire rule.* Unpublished manuscript, Dartmouth Medical School, Dartmouth, NH.

Erdberg, P. (1990). Rorschach assessment. In G. Goldstein & M. Hersen (Eds.), *Handbook of psychological assessment* (2nd ed., pp. 387–399). New York: Pergamon Press.

Estelle v. Smith, 451 U.S. 454 (1980).

Ewing, J. A. (1988). Substance abuse: Alcohol. In R. Michels, J. O. Cavenar, H. K. H. Brodie, A. M. Cooper, S. B. Guze, L. L. Judd, G. L. Klerman, & A. J. Solnit (Eds.), *Psychiatry* (Vol. 2, chap. 89). Philadelphia: Lippincott.

Exner, J. E. (1969). *The Rorschach system.* New York: Grune and Stratton.

Exner, J. E. (1974). *The Rorschach: A comprehensive system.* New York: Wiley.

Exner, J. E. (1986). *The Rorschach: A comprehensive system: Vol. 2. Interpretation* (2nd ed.). New York: Wiley.

Exner, J. E. (1991). *The Rorschach: A comprehensive system: Vol. 1. Basic foundations* (2nd ed.). New York: Wiley.

Exner, J. E. (1993). *The Rorschach: A comprehensive system: Vol. 1. Basic foundations* (3rd ed.). New York: Wiley.

Exner, J. E., Jr. (1996). A comment on the Comprehensive System for the Rorschach: A critical examination. *Psychological Science, 7,* 11–13.

Exner, J. E., Jr. (1997). The future of the Rorschach in personality assessment. *Journal of Personality Assessment, 68,* 37–46.

Fantoni-Salvador, P., & Rogers, R. (1997). Spanish versions of the MMPI-2 and PAI: An investigation of concurrent validity with Hispanic patients. *Assessment, 4,* 29–39.

Faust, D. (1995). Neuropsychological (brain damage) assessment. In J. Ziskin (Ed.), *Coping with psychiatric and psychological testimony* (5th ed., vol. 2, pp. 916–1044). Los Angeles: Law and Psychological Press.

Feldman, S., & Wilson, K. (1981). The value of interpersonal skills in lawyering. *Law and Human Behavior, 5,* 311–324.

Fenwick, P. (1987). Somnambulism and the law: A review. *Behavioral Science and the Law, 5,* 343–350.

Fenwick, P. (1990). Automatism, medicine, and the law. *Psychological Medicine Monograph, 17* (whole).

Fenwick, P. (1993). Brain, mind, and behavior: Some medicolegal aspects. *British Journal of Psychiatry, 163,* 565–573.

Fink, W. H. (1995). *The MMPI-2 validity scales in the detection of malingering in criminal forensic groups.* Unpublished doctoral dissertation, Illinois School of Professional Psychology, Rolling Meadows, IL.

Finkel, N. J. (1989). The Insanity Defense Reform Act of 1984: Much ado about nothing. *Behavioral Sciences and the Law, 7,* 403–419.

Finkel, N. J. (1990). De facto departures from insanity instructions: Toward the remaking of common law. *Law and Human Behavior, 14,* 105–122.

Finkel, N. J. (1991). The insanity defense: A comparison of verdict schemas. *Law and Human Behavior, 15,* 533–555.

Finkel, N. J., & Handel, S. F. (1988). Jurors and insanity: Do test instructions instruct? *Forensic Reports, 1,* 65–79.

Finkel, N. J., Shaw, R., Bercaw, S., & Koch, J. (1985). Insanity defenses: From the jurors' perspective. *Law and Psychology Review, 9,* 77–92.

Finkel, N. J., & Slobogin, C. (1995). Insanity, justification, and culpability toward a unifying schema. *Law and Human Behavior, 19,* 447–464.

Fischhoff, B. (1982). Debiasing. In D. Kahneman, P. Slovic, & A. Tversky (Eds.), *Judgment under uncertainty: Heuristics and biases* (pp. 422–444). New York: Cambridge University Press.

Floyd, F. J., & Widaman, K. F. (1995). Factor analysis in the development and refinement of clinical assessment instruments. *Psychological Assessment, 7,* 286–299.

Folstein, M. F., Folstein, S. E., & McHugh, P. R. (1975). Mini-mental state: A practical method of grading cognitive state of patients for the clinician. *Journal of Psychiatric Research, 12,* 189–198.

Fowles, G. P. (1988). Neuropsychologically impaired offenders: Considerations for assessment and treatment. *Psychiatric Annals, 18,* 692–697.

Frank, G. (1976). On the validity of hypotheses derived from the Rorschach: I. The relationship between color and affect. *Perceptual and Motor Skills, 54,* 411–427.

Frederick, R. I., Carter, M., & Powel, J. (1995). Adapting symptom validity testing to evaluate suspicious complaints of amnesia in medicolegal evaluations. *Bulletin of the American Academy of Psychiatry and the Law, 23,* 231–237.

Frederick, R. I., & Foster, H. G. (1991). Multiple measures of malingering on a forced-choice test of cognitive ability. *Psychological Assessment: A Journal of Clinical and Consulting Psychology, 3,* 596–602.

Freedman, L. Z., Guttmacher, M., & Overholser, W. (1961). Mental disease or defect excluding responsibility: A psychiatric view of the American Law Institute's model penal code proposal. *American Journal of Psychiatry, 118,* 32–34.

French, A. P., & Shechmeister, B. R. (1983). The multiple personality syndrome and criminal defense. *Bulletin of the American Academy of Psychiatry and the Law, 11,* 17–25.

Friedlander, M. L., & Stockman, S. J. (1983). Anchoring and publicity effect in clinical judgment. *Journal of Clinical Psychology, 39,* 637–643.

Frierson, R. L., Schwartz-Watts, D. M., Morgan, D. W., & Malone, T. D. (1998). Capital versus noncapital murder. *Journal of the American Academy of Psychiatry and Law, 26,* 403–410.

Frye v. United States, 293 F. 1013 (D.C. Cir. 1923).

Fulero, S. M., & Finkel, N. J. (1991). Barring ultimate issue testimony: An "insane" rule? *Law and Human Behavior, 15,* 495–507.

Fyans, L. J., Jr. (1988). Review of Rogers Criminal Responsibility Assessment Scales. In D. K. Keyser & R. C. Sweetland (Eds.), *Test Critiques* (pp. 463–468). Kansas City, MO: Test Corporation of America.

Gacono, C. B., Meloy, J. R., Sheppard, K., Speth, E., & Roske, A. (1995). A clinical investigation of malingering and psychopathy in hospitalized NGRI patients. *Bulletin of the American Academy of Psychiatry and Law, 23,* 387–397.

Gallucci, N. T. (1990). On the synthesis of information from psychological tests. *Psychological Reports, 67,* 1243–1260.

Ganellen, R. J. (1996). Comparing the diagnostic efficiency of the MMPI, MCMI-II, and the Rorschach: A review. *Journal of Personality Assessment, 67,* 219–243.

Gee, M. M. (1997) Modern status of test of criminal responsibility-state cases. *American Law Reports, 9,* 526–543.

General Electric Company v. Joiner, 118 S.Ct. 512 (1997).

Gier v. Educational Services Unit No. 16, 845 F. Supp. 1342 (D. Neb. 1994), *aff'd,* 66 F.3d 940 (8th Cir. 1995)

Gilbert, J. (1978). *Interpreting psychological test data.* New York: Van Nostrand Reinhold.

Gilmore, M. M., & Kaufman, C. (1988). Dissociative disorders. In R. Michels, J. O. Cavenar, H. K. H. Brodie, A. M. Cooper, S. B. Guze, L. L. Judd, G. L. Klerman, & A. J. Solnit (Eds.), *Psychiatry* (Vol. 1). Philadelphia: Lippincott.

Goebel, R. A. (1983). Detection of faking on the Halstead–Reitan Neuropsychological Test Battery. *Journal of Clinical Psychology, 39,* 731–742.

Golden, C. J., & Grier, C. A. (1998). Detecting malingering on the Luria–Nebraska Neuropsychological Battery. In C. R. Reynolds (Ed.), *Detection of malingering during head injury litigation* (pp. 133–162). New York: Plenum Press.

Golden, C. J., Purisch, A. D., & Hammeke, T. A. (1985). *The Luria–Nebraska battery manual.* Palo Alto, CA: Western Psychological Services.

Golding, S. L. (1983, October). *The assessment, treatment, and community outcome of defendants found not guilty by reason of insanity.* Paper presented at American Psychology and Law Society Conference, Chicago, IL.

Golding, S. L., & Roesch, R. (1988). The assessment of criminal responsibility: A historical approach to a current controversy. In I. B. Weiner & A. K. Hess (Eds.), *Handbook of forensic psychology* (pp. 395–436). New York: Wiley.

Goldstein, A. S. (1967). *The insanity defense.* New Haven, CT: Yale University Press.

Goldstein, G. (1990). Comprehensive neuropsychological assessment batteries. In G. Goldstein & M. Hersen (Eds.), *Handbook of psychological assessment* (2nd ed., pp. 197–227). New York: Pergamon Press.

Goldstein, R. L. (1992a). Dr. Rogers' "insanity detector" and the admissibility of novel scientific evidence. *Medicine and Law, 11,* 441–447.

Goldstein, R. L. (1992b). The Mickey Finn defense: Involuntary intoxication and insanity. *Bulletin of the American Academy of Psychiatry and Law, 20,* 27–31

Goodman, G. S., & Hahn, A. (1987). Evaluating eyewitness testimony. In I. B. Weiner & A. K. Hess (Eds.), *Handbook of forensic psychology* (pp. 258–292). New York: Wiley.

Goodman-Delahunty, J. (1997). Forensic expertise in the wake of *Daubert. Law and Human Behavior, 21,* 121–140.

Goodness, K. (1999). *Retrospective assessment of the malingering: R-SIRS and CT-SIRS.* Unpublished doctoral dissertation, University of North Texas.

Gottesman, I. I., & Prescott, C. A. (1989). Abuses of the MacAndrew MMPI alcoholism scale: A critical review. *Clinical Psychology Review, 9,* 223–258.

Gough, H. G. (1950). The F minus K index for the MMPI. *Journal of Consulting Psychology, 14,* 408–413.

Gough, H. G. (1954). Some common misperceptions about neuroticism. *Journal of Consulting Psychology, 18,* 287–292.

Green, P., Astner, K., & Allen, L. M., III. (1996). *The WordMemory Test: A manual for oral and computer-administered forms.* Durham, NC: CogniSyst Inc.

Greenberg, S., & Shuman, D. (1997). Irreconcilable conflict between therapeutic and forensic roles. *Professional Psychology: Research and Practice, 28,* 50–57.

Greene, R. L. (1991). *The MMPI-2/MMPI: An interpretive manual.* Boston: Allyn and Bacon.

Greene, R. L. (1997). Assessment of malingering and defensiveness on multiscale inventories. In R. Rogers (Ed.), *Clinical assessment of malingering and deception* (2nd ed., pp. 169–207). New York: Guilford Press.

Greene, R. L., Weed, N. C., Butcher, J. N., Arrendondo, R., & Davis, H. G. (1992). A cross-validation of the MMPI-2 substance abuse scales. *Journal of Personality Assessment, 58,* 405–410.

Greenland, C. (1979). Crime and the insanity defense: An international comparison, Ontario and New York State. *Bulletin of the American Academy of Psychiatry and Law, 7,* 125–137.

Grekin, P. M., Jemelka, R., & Trupin, E. W. (1994). Racial differences in the criminalization of the mentally ill. *Bulletin of the American Academy of Psychiatry and Law, 22,* 411–420.

Griffin, P. A., Steadman, H. J., & Heilbrun, K. (1991). Designing conditional release programs for insanity acquittees. *Journal of Mental Health Administration, 18,* 231–241.

Grisso, T. (1986). *Evaluating competencies: Forensic assessments and instruments.* New York: Plenum Press.

Grisso, T. (1991). A developmental history of the American Psychology–Law Society. *Law and Human Behavior, 15,* 213–231.

Grisso, T. (1993). The differences between forensic psychiatry and psychology. *Bulletin of the American Academy of Psychiatry and Law, 21,* 133–145.

Grisso, T. (1996). Clinical assessments for legal decision-making in criminal cases: Research recommendations. In B. D. Sales & S. A. Shah (Eds.), *Mental health and law: Research, policy, and services* (pp. 109–140). Durham, NC: Carolina Academic Press.

Grisso, T., & Appelbaum, P. S. (1992). Is it unethical to offer predictions of future violence? *Law and Human Behavior, 16,* 621–633.

Groth, A. M. (1979). *Men who rape: The psychology of the offender.* New York: Plenum Press.

Group for the Advancement of Psychiatry. (1983). Criminal responsibility and psychiatric expert testimony. In L. Z. Freedman (Ed.), *By reason of insanity: Essays on psychiatry and the law* (pp. 31–35). Wilmington, DE: Scholarly Resources.

Grudzinskas, A. J., & Appelbaum, K. L. (1998). *General Electric Co. v. Joiner:* Lighting up the post-*Daubert* landscape? *Journal of the American Academy of Psychiatry and Law, 26,* 497–503.

Gunn, J., & Bonn, J. (1971). Criminality and violence in epileptic prisoners. *British Journal of Psychiatry 118,* 337–343.

Gunn, J., & Fenton, G. (1969). Epilepsy in prisons: A diagnostic survey. *British Medical Journal, 4,* 226–328.

Gutheil, T. G., & Appelbaum, P. S. (1982). *Clinical handbook of psychiatry and the law.* New York: McGraw-Hill.

Hagan, W. A. (1997). *Whores of the courtroom: The fraud of psychiatric testimony and the rape of American justice.* New York: HarperCollins.

Hain, J. D., Smith, B. M., & Stevenson, I. (1966). Effectiveness and processes of interviewing with drugs. *Journal of Psychiatric Research, 4,* 95–106.

Hall, G. C., Shondrick, D. D., & Hirschman, R. (1993). The role of sexual arousal in sexually aggressive behavior: A meta-analysis. *Journal of Consulting and Clinical Psychology, 61,* 1091–1095.

Hall, H. V., & McNinch, D. (1988). Linking crime-specific behavior to neuropsychological impairment. *International Journal of Clinical Neuropsychology, 10,* 113–122.

Halleck, S. L. (1992). Clinical assessment of the voluntariness of behavior. *Bulletin of the American Academy of Psychiatry and Law, 20,* 221–236.

Halpern, A. L. (1992). Misuse of post-acquittal hospitalization for punitive purposes. *Psychiatric Annals, 22,* 561–656.

Haney, C. (1980). Psychology and legal change: On the limits of factual jurisprudence. *Law and Human Behavior, 4,* 147–200.

Hans, V. P. (1986). An analysis of public attitudes toward the insanity defense. *Criminology, 4,* 393–415.

Hans, V. P., & Slater, D. (1983). John Hinckley Jr. and the insanity defense: The public's verdict. *Public Opinion Quarterly, 47,* 202–212.

Hare, R. D. (1991). *Manual for the revised psychopathy checklist.* Toronto: Multi-Health Systems.

Harris, G. T., Rice, M. E., Quinsey, V. L., Chaplin, T. C., & Earls, C. (1992). Maximizing the discriminant validity of phallometric assessment data. *Psychological Assessment, 4,* 502–511.

Hartlage, L. C. (1998). Clinical detection of malingering. In C. R. Reynolds (Ed.), *Detection of malingering during head injury litigation* (pp. 239–260). New York: Plenum Press.

Hathaway, S. R., & McKinley, J. C. (1951). *The Minnesota Multiphasic Personality Inventory Manual.* New York: Psychological Corporation.

Haynes v. State, 739 P.2d 497 (NEV. 1987).

Heaton, R. K., Grant, I., & Mathews, C. G. (1991). *Comprehensive norms for an expanded Halstead–Reitan battery: Demographic corrections, research findings, and clinical applications.* Odessa, FL: PAR.

Heaton, R. K., Smith, H. H., Jr., Lehman, R. A. W., & Vogt, A. J. (1978). Prospects for faking believable deficits on neuropsychological testing. *Journal of Consulting and Clinical Psychology, 46,* 892–900.

Heilbrun, A. B., Jr. & Heilbrun, M. R. (1989). Dangerousness and legal insanity. *Journal of Law and Psychiatry, 11,* 39–53.

Heilbrun, K. (1992). The role of psychological testing in forensic assessment. *Law and Human Behavior, 16,* 257–272.

Heilbrun, K. (1995). Child custody evaluations: Critically assessing mental health experts and psychological tests. *Family Law Quarterly, 29,* 63–78.

Heilbrun, K., & Collins, S. (1995). Evaluations of trial competency and mental state at time of offense: Report characteristics. *Professional Psychology: Research and Practice, 26,* 61–67.

Heilbrun, K., & Griffin, P. A. (1993). Community-based forensic treatment of insanity acquittees. *International Journal of Law and Psychiatry, 16,* 133–150.

Heilbrun, K., Griffin-Heilbrun, P. A., & Griffin, N. (1988). Comparing females acquitted by reason of insanity, convicted, and civilly committed in Florida, 1977–1984. *Law and Human Behavior, 12,* 295–311.

Heinbecker, P. (1986). Two years experience under Utah's mens rea insanity law. *Bulletin of the American Academy of Psychiatry and Law, 14,* 185–191.

Helmes, E., & Holden, R. R. (1986). Response styles and faking on the Basis Personality Inventory. *Journal of Consulting and Clinical Psychology, 54,* 853–859.

Henrichs, R. W. (1990). Current and emergent applications of neuropsychological assessment: Problems of validity and utility. *Professional Psychology: Research and Practice, 21,* 171–176.

Herald v. Hood, C.A. No. 15986, 1993 Ohio App. LEXIS 3688 (Ohio Ct. App. July 21, 1993).

Herman, J. L. (1995). Crime and memory. *Bulletin of the American Academy of Psychiatry and Law, 23,* 5–17.

Hermann, D. H. J. (1986). Criminal defenses and pleas in mitigation based on amnesia. *Behavioral Sciences and the Law, 4,* 5–26.

Hersh, K., & Borum, R. (1998). Command hallucinations, compliance, and risk assessment. *Journal of the American Academy of Psychiatry and Law, 26,* 353–359.

Hillbrand, M., Foster, H. G., Jr., & Hirt, M. (1988). Variables associated with violence in a forensic population. *Journal of Interpersonal Violence, 3,* 371–380.

Hiscock, C. K., Rustemier, P. J., & Hiscock, M. (1993). Determinatin of criminal responsibility: Application of the two-alternative forced-choice strategem. *Criminal Justice and Behavior, 20,* 391–405.

Hodges, J. R., & Warlow, C. P. (1990). Syndromes of transient amnesia: Towards a classification. A study of 153 cases. *Journal of Neurology, Neurosurgery, and Psychiatry, 53,* 534–543.

Hodgins, S., Hebert, J., & Baraldi, R. (1986). Women declared insane: A follow-up study. *International Journal of Law and Psychiatry, 8,* 203–216.

Holtzman, W. H. (1984a, September). *Clinical applications in personality assessment and psychodiagnosis.* Paper presented at the 23rd International Congress of Psychology, Acapulco, Mexico.

Holtzman, W. H. (1984b). *Clinical uses of the HIT with adolescents.* Unpublished manuscript, University of Texas at Austin.

Homant, R. J., & Kennedy, D. B. (1986). Judgment of legal insanity as a function of attitude toward the insanity defense. *International Journal of Law and Psychiatry, 8,* 67–81.

Horton, K. D., Smith, S. A., Barghout, N. K., & Connolly, D. A. (1992). The use of indirect memory tests to assess malingered amnesia: A study of metamemory. *Journal of Experimental Psychology: General, 121,* 326–351.

Horvath, T. B. (1988). Organic brain syndromes. In R. Michels, J. O. Cavenar, H. K. H. Brodie, A. M. Cooper, S. B. Guze, L. L. Judd, G. L. Klerman, & A. J. Solnit (Eds.), *Psychiatry* (Vol. 2). Philadelphia: Lippincott.

Hose v. Chicago Northwestern Transp. Co., 70 F.3d 968 (8th Cir 1995).

Houston v. State, 602 P.2d 784 (Alaska, 1979).

Howard, R. C., & Clark, C. R. (1985). When courts and experts disagree: Discordance between insanity recommendations and adjudications. *Law and Human Behavior, 9,* 385–394.

Huckabee, H. M. (1980). *Lawyers, psychiatrists, and criminal law: Cooperation or chaos?* Springfield, IL: Thomas.

Hurley, R. A., Herrick, R. C., & Hayman, L. A. (1997). Clinical imaging in neuropsychiatry. In S. C. Yudofsky & R. E. Hales (Eds.), *The American Psychiatric Press textbook of neuropsychiatry* (3rd ed., pp. 205–237). Washington, DC: American Psychiatric Press.

Iacono, W. G., & Patrick, C. J. (1987). What psychologists should know about lie detection. In I. B. Weiner & A. K. Hess (Eds.), *Handbook of forensic psychology* (pp. 460–489). New York: Wiley

Iacono, W. G., & Patrick, C. J. (1997). Polygraph and integrity testing. In R. Rogers (Ed.), *Clinical assessment of malingering and deception* (2nd ed., pp. 252–281). New York: Guilford Press.

In re A.V., 849 S.W.2d 393 (Tex.App. 1993).

In re Odell, 672 A.2d 457, 459 (RI 1996).

Insanity Defense Reform Act of 1984, Pub. L. No. 98-473, secs. 401, 402, 20 (1984).

Insanity Defense Work Group. (1983). American Psychiatric Association statement on the insanity defense. *American Journal of Psychiatry, 140,* 681–688.

Isely v. Capuchin Province, 877 F. Supp. 1055 (E.D. Mich. 1995).

Iverson, G. L. (1995). Qualitative aspects of malingered memory deficits. *Brain Injury, 9*, 35–40.

Iverson, G. L., & Franzen, M. D. (1996). Using multiple objective memory procedures to detect simulated malingering. *Journal of Clinical and Experimental Neuropsychology, 18*, 38-51.

Iverson, G. L., Franzen, M. D., Demarest, D. S., & Hammond, J. A. (1993). Neuropsychological screening in correctional settings. *Criminal Justice and Behavior, 20*, 347–358.

Iverson, G. L., Franzen, M. D., & McCracken, L. M. (1991). Evaluation of an objective assessment technique for the detection of malingered memory deficits. *Law and Human Behavior, 15*, 667–676.

Iverson, G. L., Franzen, M. D., & McCracken, L. M. (1994). Application of a forced-choice memory procedure designed to detect experimental malingering. *Archives of Clinical Neuropsychology, 9*, 437–450.

Jackson, D. N. (1987). *Basic Personality Inventory manual* (preliminary version). Port Huron, MI: Sigma Assessment Systems.

Jackson, D. N. (1989). *Basic Personality Inventory manual.* Port Huron, MI: Sigma Assessment Systems.

Jackson, D. N., Fraboni, M., & Helmes, E. (1997). MMPI-2 content scales: How much content do they measure? *Assessment, 4*, 111–117.

Jackson, M. W. (1988). Lay and professional perceptions of dangerousness and other forensic issues. *Canadian Journal of Criminology, 30*, 215–229.

Janofksy, J. S., Vandewalle, M. B., & Rappeport, J. R. (1989). Defendants pleading insanity: An analysis of outcome. *Bulletin of the American Academy of Psychiatry and Law, 17*, 203–211.

Jeffrey, R. W., & Pasewark, R. A. (1983). Altering opinions about the insanity plea. *Journal of Psychiatry and Law, 6*, 39–40.

Jenkins v. United States, 307 F2d 637 (DC Cir 1962).

Jennison, K. M., & Johnson, K. A. (1994). Drinking-induced blackouts among young adults: Results from a national longitudinal study. *International Journal of Addictions, 29*, 23-51.

Joiner, T. E., Jr., & Schmidt, K. L. (1998). Drawing conclusions—or not—from drawings. *Journal of Personality Assessment, 69*, 476–481.

Jung, C. G. (1957). On simulated insanity. In C. G. Jung, *Psychiatric studies: Collected works* (2nd ed., pp. 159–205; R.F.C. Hull, trans.). Princeton, NJ: Princeton University Press. (Originally published in 1903.)

Jung, J. (1971). *The experimenter's dilemma.* New York: Harper & Row.

Kahneman, D., & Tversky, A. (1982). Intuitive prediction: Biases and corrective procedures. In D. Kahneman, P. Slovic, & A. Tversky (Eds.), *Judgment under uncertainty: Heuristics and biases* (pp. 414–421). New York: Cambridge University Press.

Kalichman, S. C. (1993). *Mandated reporting of suspected child abuse.* Washington, DC: American Psychological Association.

Kalichman, S. C., Henderson, M. C., Shealy, L. S., & Dwyer, M. (1992). Psychometric properties of the Multiphasic Sex Inventory in assessing sex offenders. *Criminal Justice and Behavior, 19*, 384–396.

Kaplan, H. I., & Sadock, B. I. (1988). *Synopsis of psychiatry, behavioral sciences, clinical psychiatry* (5th ed.). Baltimore: William & Wilkins.

Kapur, B. (1994). Drug testing methods and interpretations of test results. In S. MacDonald & P. Roman (Eds.), *Drug testing in the workplace* (pp. 103–120). New York: Plenum Press.

Kasper, M. E., Rogers, R., & Adams, P. (1996). Dangerousness and command hallucinations: An investigation of psychotic inpatients. *Bulletin of the American Academy of Psychiatry and Law, 24,* 219–224.

Kassin, S. M., Williams, L. N., & Saunders, C. L. (1990). Dirty tricks of cross-examination: The influence of conjectural evidence on the jury. *Law and Human Behavior, 14,* 373–384.

Keilitz, I. (1984). *The guilty but mentally ill verdict: An empirical study* (Working paper). Williamsburg, VA: Institute on Mental Disability and the Law, National Center for State Courts.

Keilitz, I. (1985). *Researching the insanity defense.* Williamsburg, VA: National Center for State Courts.

Keilitz, I., & Fulton, J. P. (1983). *The insanity defense and its alternatives: A guide to policy makers.* Williamsburg, VA: National Center for State Courts.

Kelly, K., & Rogers, R. (1996). Detection of misreported drug use in forensic populations: An overview of hair analysis. *Bulletin of the American Academy of Psychiatry and Law, 24,* 85–94.

Kenley v. Armontrout, 937 F.2d 1298 (8th Cir.), cert. denied, 502 U.S. (1991).

Kirby v. State, 410 SE2d 333 (Ga App 1991).

Kirsch, I., & Lynn, S. J. (1995). The altered state of hypnosis: Changes in the theoretical landscape. *American Psychologist, 50,* 846–858.

Klinge, V., & Dorsey, J. (1993). Correlates of the Woodcock–Johnson Reading Comprehension and Kaufman Brief Intelligence Test in a forensic psychiatric population. *Journal of Clinical Psychology, 49,* 593–598.

Knapp, S., Vandercreek, L., & Fulero, S. M. (1993). The attorney-psychologist-client privilege in judicial proceedings. *Psychotherapy in Private Practice, 12,* 1–15.

Kopelman, M. D. (1987). Crime and amnesia: A review. *Behavioral Sciences and the Law, 5,* 323–342.

Kopelman, M. D., Green, R. E. A., Guinan, E. M., Lewis, P. D. R., & Stanhope, N. (1994). The case of the amnesic intelligence officer. *Psychological Medicine, 24,* 1037–1045.

Kopelman, M. D., & Stanhope, N. (1997). Rates of forgetting in organic amnesia following temporal lobe, diecephalic, or frontal lesions. *Neuropsychology, 11,* 343–356.

Kopelman, M. D., Wilson, B. A., & Baddeley, A. D. (1989). The Autobiographical Memory Interview: A new assessment of autobiographical and personal semantic memory in amnestic patients. *Journal of Clinical and Experimental Neuropsychology, 11,* 724–744.

Kopelman, M. D., Wilson, B. A., & Baddeley, A. D. (1990). *The Autobiographical Memory Interview.* Edmunds, U.K.: Thames Valley Test Company.

Kotrla, K. J. (1997). Functional neuroimaging in neuropsychiatry. In S. C. Yudofsky, & R. E. Hales (Eds.), *The American Psychiatric Press textbook of neuropsychiatry* (3rd ed., pp. 239–270). Washington, DC: American Psychiatric Press.

Krakowski, M. I., Convit, A., Jaeger, J., Lin, S., & Volavka, J. (1989). Inpatient violence: Trait and state. *Journal of Psychiatric Research, 23,* 57–64.

Kroner, D. G., & Reddon, J. R. (1996). Factor structure of the Basic Personality

Inventory with incarcerated offenders. *Journal of Psychopathology and Behavioral Assessment, 18,* 275–284.

Kroner, D. G., Reddon, J. R., & Beckett, N. (1991). Basic Personality Inventory clinical and validity scales: Stability and internal consistency. *Journal of Psychopathology and Behavioral Assessment, 13,* 147–154.

Kumho Tire Co. v. Carmichael, 119 S. Ct. 1167 (1999).

Kunjukrishnan, R., & Varan, L. R. (1992). Major affective disorders and forensic psychiatry. *Psychiatric Clinics of North America, 15,* 569–574.

Kurlychek, R. T., & Jordan, L. (1980). MMPI profiles and code types of responsible and nonresponsible criminal defendants. *Journal of Clinical Psychology, 36,* 590–593.

Kurtz, R., & Meyer, R. G. (1994, March). *Vulnerability of the MMPI-2, M Test, and SIRS to different strategies of malingering psychosis.* Paper presented at the American Psychology-Law Society, Santa Fe, NM.

Lachar, D., & Wrobel, T. A. (1979). Validating clinicians' hunches: Construction of a new MMPI critical item set. *Journal of Consulting and Clinical Psychology, 47,* 277–284.

Lalumiére, M. L., & Quinsey, V. L. (1994). The discriminability of rapists from non-sex offenders using phallometric measures: A meta-analysis. *Criminal Justice and Behavior, 21,* 150–175.

Lange v. Young, 869 F.2d 1008 (7th Cir), cert denied, 490 U.S. 1094 (1989).

Langevin, R. (1988). Defensiveness in sex offenders. In R. Rogers (Ed.) *Assessment of malingering and deception* (pp. 269–290). New York: Guilford Press.

Langevin, R., Ben-Aron, M., Wortzman, G., Dickey, R., & Handy, L. (1987). Brain damage, diagnosis, and substance abuse among violent offenders. *Behavioral Sciences and the Law, 5,* 77–94.

Langevin, R., Wright, P., & Handy, L. (1990). Use of the MMPI and its derived scales with sex offenders. *Annals of Sex Research, 3,* 453–486.

Laws, D. R., & O'Donohue, W. (Eds.). (1997). *Sexual deviance: Theory, assessment, and treatment.* New York: Guilford Press.

Lazowski, L. E., Miller, F. G., Boye, M. W., & Miller, G. A. (1998). Efficacy of the Substance Abuse Subtle Screening Inventory-3 (SASSI-3) in identifying substance dependence disorders in clinical settings. *Journal of Personality Assessment, 71,* 114–128.

Lees-Haley, P. R. (1992). Psychodiagnostic test usage by forensic psychologists. *American Journal of Forensic Psychology, 10,* 25–30.

Lees-Haley, P. R. (in press). Attorneys influence expert evidence in forensic psychological and neuropsychological cases. *Assessment.*

Lees-Haley, P. R., & Dunn, J. T. (1994). The ability of naive subjects to report symptoms of mild brain injury, post-traumatic stress disorder, major depression, and generalized anxiety disorder. *Journal of Clinical Psychology, 50,* 252–256.

Lees-Haley, P. R., Smith, H. H., Williams, C. W., & Dunn, J. T. (1995). Forensic neuropsychological test usage: An empirical survey. *Archives of Clinical Neuropsychology, 11,* 45–51.

Leong, G. B., Silva, A., & Weinstock, R. (1991). Dangerous mentally disordered criminals: Unresolvable societal fear? *Journal of Forensic Sciences, 36,* 210–218.

Lewis, D. O., & Bard, J. S. (1991). Multiple personality and forensic issues. *Psychiatric Clinics of North America, 14,* 741–756.

Lezak, M. D. (1995). *Neuropsychological assessment* (3rd ed.). New York: Oxford University Press.

Lidz, C. W., Meisel, A., Zerubavel, E., Carter, M., Sestak, R. M., & Roth, L. H. (1984). *Informed consent: A study of decision-making in psychiatry.* New York: Guilford Press.

Lile v. Mckune, 1998 U.S. Dist. LEXIS 15102.

Lindblad, A. D. (1994). Detection of malingered mental illness within a forensic population: An analogue study. *Dissertation Abstracts International, 54-B,* 4395.

Lindemann, J. E., & Matarazzo, J. D. (1990). Assessment of adult intelligence. In G. Goldstein & M. Hersen (Eds.), *Handbook of psychological assessment* (2nd ed., pp. 79–101). New York: Pergamon Press.

Linhorst, D. M., & Dirks-Linhorst, P. A. (1997). The impact of insanity acquittees on Missouri's public mental health system. *Law and Human Behavior, 21,* 327–338.

Linhorst, D. M., Hunsucker, L., & Parker, L. D. (1998). An examination of gender and racial differences among the Missouri insanity acquittees. *Journal of the American Academy of Psychiatry and the Law, 26,* 411–424.

Linz, D., Penrod, S., & McDonald, E. (1986). Attorney communication and impression making in the courtroom: Views from off the bench. *Law and Human Behavior, 10,* 281–302.

Lipkin, R. J. (1990). Free will, responsibility, and the promise of forensic psychiatry. *International Journal of Law and Psychiatry, 13,* 331–359.

Loevinger, J. (1957). Objective tests as instruments of psychological theory. *Psychological Reports, 3,* Monograph Supplement IX, 635–694.

Loftus, E. F. (1979). *Eye-witness testimony.* Cambridge, MA: Harvard University Press.

Loftus, E. F. (1998, March). *Update on the repressed memory controversy.* Paper delivered at the Eighth Annual National Symposium on Mental Health and the Law, Miami, FL.

Loftus, E. F. (1992). When a lie becomes memory's truth: Memory distortion after exposure to misinformation. *Current Directions in Psychological Science, 48,* 121–123.

Loftus, E. F., Miller, D. G., & Burns, H. J. (1987). Semantic integration of verbal information into visual memory. In L. S. Wrightsman, C. E. Willis, & S. M. Kassin (Eds.), *On the witness stand: Controversies in the courtroom* (pp. 157–177). Newbury Park, CA: Sage.

Loftus, E. F., & Palmer, J. C. (1974). Reconstruction of automobile destruction: An example of the interaction between language and memory. *Journal of Verbal Learning and Verbal Behavior, 13,* 585–589.

Long, C. J., & Collins, L. F. (1997). Ecological validity and forensic neuropsychological assessment. In R. J. McCaffrey, A. D. Williams, J. M. Fisher, & L. C. Laing (Eds.), *The practice of forensic neuropsychology: Meeting challenges in the courtroom* (pp. 153–164). New York: Plenum Press.

Low, P. W., Jeffries, J. C., Jr., & Bonnie, R. J. (1986). *The trial of John W. Hincklely Jr.: A scase study in the insanity defense.* Mineola, NY: Foundation Press.

Lowenstein, R. J. (1998). Dissociative amnesia and dissociative fugue. In L. K. Michelson & W. J. Ray (Eds.), *Handbook of dissociation: Theoretical, empirical, and clinical perspectives* (pp. 307–336). New York: Plenum Press.

Lykken, D. T. (1974). Psychology and the lie detector industry. *American Psychologist, 29,* 725–739.

Lynch, B. E., & Bradford, J. W. (1980). Amnesia: Its detection by psychophysiological measures. *Bulletin of the American Academy of Psychiatry and Law, 8,* 288–297.

MacAndrew, C. (1965). The differentiation of male alcoholic outpatients from nonalcoholic psychiatric outpatients by means of the MMPI. *Quarterly Studies of Alcohol, 47,* 161–166.

Machover, K. (1949). *Personality projection in the drawing of the human figure.* Springfield, IL: Thomas.

Madden, D. J., Lion, J. R., & Penna, M. W. (1977). Assaults on psychiatrists by patients. *American Journal of Psychiatry, 133,* 422–429.

Maeder, T. (1985). *Crime and madness: The origins and evolution of the insanity defense.* New York: Harper & Row.

Mark, P. H., & Ervin, F. R. (1970). *Violence and the brain.* New York: Harper & Row.

Martell, D. A. (1992). Forensic neuropsychology and the criminal law. *Law and Human Behavior, 16,* 313–336.

Martell, D. A. (1996). Organic brain dysfunctions and criminal behavior. In L. B. Schlesinger (Ed.), *Explorations in criminal psychopathology: Clinical syndromes with forensic implications* (pp. 170–186). Springfield, IL: Thomas.

Martin, R. C., Franzen, M. D., & Orey, S. (1998). Magnitude of error as a strategy to detect feigned memory impairment. *Clinical Neuropsychologist, 12,* 84–91.

Matarazzo, J. D. (1990). Psychological assessment versus psychological testing: Validation from Binet to the school, clinic, and courtroom. *American Psychologist, 45,* 999–1017.

McCann, J. T., & Dyer, F. J. (1996). *Forensic assessment with the Millon Inventories.* New York: Guilford Press.

McCloskey, K. M., Wible, C. G., & Cohen, N. J. (1988). Is there a special flashbulb memory mechanism? *Journal of Experimental Psychology: General, 117,* 171–181.

McCutcheon, L. E., & McCutcheon, L. E. (1994). Not guilty by reason of insanity: Getting it right or perpetuating myths? *Psychological Reports, 74,* 764–766.

McDonald v. United States, 312 F2d 847 (DC Cir 1962).

McDonald-Scott, P., & Endicott, J. (1984). Informed versus blind: The reliability of cross-sectional ratings of psychopathology. *Psychiatry Research, 12,* 207–217.

McDowell, C., & Acklin, M. W. (1996). Standardizing procedures for calculating Rorschach interrater reliability: Conceptual and empirical foundations. *Journal of Personality Assessment, 66,* 308–320.

McGreevy, M. A., Steadman, H. J., Dvoskin, J. A., & Dollard, N. (1991). New York State's system of managing insanity acquittees in the community. *Hospital and Community Psychiatry, 42,* 512–517.

Meloy, J. R. (1986). Review of Rogers Criminal Responsibility Assessment Scales. *Bulletin of the American Academy of Psychiatry and Law, 14,* 99.

Meloy, J. R. (1992). Voluntary intoxication and the insanity defense. *Journal of Psychiatry and Law, 20,* 439–456.

Meloy, J. R., & Gacono, C. B. (1992). The aggression response and the Rorschach. *Journal of Clinical Psychology, 48,* 104–114.

Meloy, J. R., Hanson, T. L., & Weiner, I. B. (1997). Authority of the Rorschach: Legal citations during the past 50 years. *Journal of Personality Assessment, 69,* 53–62.

Melton, G. B., Petrila, J., Poythress, N. G., & Slobogin, C. (1987). *Psychological evaluations for the courts.* New York: Guilford Press.

Melton, G. B., Petrila, J., Poythress, N. G., & Slobogin, C. (1997). *Psychological evaluations for the courts* (2nd ed.). New York: Guilford Press.

Melton, G. B., & Russo, N. F. (1987). Adolescent abortion: Psychological perspectives on public policy. *American Psychologist, 42,* 69–72.

Menninger, K. A., Jr. (1968). *The crime of punishment.* New York: Viking Press.

Mensch, A. J., & Woods, D. J. (1986). Patterns of feigning brain damage on the LNNB. *International Journal of Clinical Neuropsychology, 8,* 59–63.

Meyer, G. J. (1997a). Assessing reliability: Critical corrections regarding the Rorschach Comprehensive System. *Psychological Assessment, 9,* 480–489.

Meyer, G. J. (1997b). Thinking clearly about reliability: More critical corrections regarding the Rorschach Comprehensive System. *Psychological Assessment, 9,* 495–498.

Meyer, R. G., & Deitsch, S. E. (1996). *The clinician's handbook.* Boston: Allyn & Bacon.

Michigan Stat. Ann. 1975 Mich. Pub. Acts 180 (codified at Mich. Comp. Laws §§§§ 330.1400a, 768.29a(2), 768.36 (1979)).

Miller v. District Court 737 P.2d 834 (Col. 1987).

Miller, G. A. (1985). *The Substance Abuse Subtle Screening Inventory—Revised (SASSI-R) manual.* Bloomington, IN: SASSI Institute.

Miller, G. A. (1994). *The Substance Abuse Subtle Screening Inventory—Revised (SASSI-R) manual.* Bloomington, IN: SASSI Institute.

Miller, H. (1961). Accident neurosis. *British Medical Journal, 1,* 919–925.

Miller, R. D., Olin, J., Beven, G., & Covey, J. (1995). Public evaluations of unrepresented defendants. *Bulletin of the American Academy of Psychiatry and Law, 23,* 93–103.

Miller, R. D., & Stava, L. J. (1997). Hypnosis and dissimulation. In R. Rogers (Ed.), *Clinical assessment of malingering and deception* (2nd ed., pp. 282–300). New York: Guilford Press.

Miller, W. R., & Marlatt, G. A. (1987). *Comprehensive Drinker Profile: Manual supplement.* Odessa, FL: Psychological Assessment Resources.

Millon, T. (1983). *The Millon Clinical Multiaxial Inventory manual* (3rd ed.). Minneapolis: National Computer Systems.

Millon, T. (1987). *Manual for the Millon Clinical Multiaxial Inventory—II* (2nd ed.). Minneapolis: National Computer Systems.

Millon, T. (1993). *Millon Adolescent Clinical Inventory manual.* Minneapolis: National Computer Systems.

Millon, T. (1994). *The Millon Clinical Multiaxial Inventory—III manual.* Minneapolis: National Computer Systems.

Mitchell, C. N. (1988). The intoxicated offender—Refuting the legal and medical myths. *International Journal of Law and Psychiatry, 11,* 77–103.

Mitchell, J., Trent, R., & McArthur, R. (1993). *Human Figure Drawing Test (HFDT).* Los Angeles: Western Psychological Services.

Mittenberg, W., Azrin, R., Millsaps, C., & Heilbronner, R. (1993). Identification of malingered head injury on the Wechsler Memory Scale—Revised. *Psychological Assessment, 5,* 34–40.

Mittenberg, W., D'Attilio, J., Gage, R., & Bass, A. (1990). *Malingered symptoms following mild head trauma: The post-concussion syndrome.* Paper presented at the 18th Meeting of the International Neuropsychological Society, Orlando, FL.

Mittenberg, W., DiGiulio, D. V., Perrin, S., & Bass, A. E. (1989). Symptoms following mild head injury: Expectations as etiology. *Clinical Neuropsychologist, 3,* 297.

Mittenberg, W., Rotholc, A., Russell, E., & Heilbronner, R. (1996). Identification of malingered head injury on the Halstead–Reitan Battery. *Archives of Clinical Neuropsychology, 11,* 271–281.

Mittenberg, W., Theroux-Fichera, S., Zielinski, R. E., & Heilbronner, R. L. (1995). Identification of malingered head injury on the Wechsler Adult Intelligence Scale—Revised. *Professional Psychology: Research and Practice, 26,* 491–498.

M'Naghten's Case (1843). 10 Cl. & Fin. 20., 8 Eng. Rep 718.

Monahan, J. (1992). Mental disorder and violent behavior: Perceptions and evidence. *American Psychologist, 47,* 511–521.

Monahan, J., & Steadman, H. J. (1996). Violent storms and violent people: How meteorology can inform risk communication in mental health law. *American Psychologist, 51,* 931–938.

Monroe, R. R. (1970). *Episodic behavior disorders.* Lexington, MA: Lexington Books.

Moran, R. (1981). *Knowing right from wrong: The insanity defense of Daniel McNaughtan.* London: Collier McMillan.

Morey, L. C. (1991). *Personality Assessment Inventory: Professional manual.* Tampa, FL: Psychological Assessment Resources, Inc.

Morey, L. C. (1996). *An interpretive guide to the Personality Assessment Inventory (PAI).* Tampa, FL: Psychological Assessment Resources, Inc.

Morey, L. C., & Lanier, V. W. (1998). Operating characteristics of six response distortion indicators for the Personality Assessment Inventory. *Assessment, 5,* 203–214.

Morrow, W. R., & Petersen, D. B. (1966). Follow-up on discharged offenders— "Not Guilty by Reason of Insanity" and "Criminal Sexual Psychopaths." *Journal of Criminal Law, Criminology, and Police Science, 57,* 31–34.

Morse, S. J. (1978). Law and mental health professionals: The limits of expertise. *Professional Psychology, 9,* 389–399.

Mossman, D. (1994). Assessing predictions of violence: Being accurate about accuracy. *Journal of Consulting and Clinical Psychology, 62,* 78—792.

Mossman, D., & Hart, K. J. (1996). Presenting evidence of malingering to courts: Insights from decision theory. *Behavioral Sciences and the Law, 14,* 271–291.

Munley, P. H., Busby, R. M., & Jaynes, G. (1997). MMPI-2 findings in schizophrenia and depression. *Psychological Assessment, 9,* 508–511.

Munsterberg, H. (1908). *On the witness stand: Essays on psychology and punishment.* New York: McClure.

Murphy, W. D., Krisak, J., Stalgaitis, S., & Anderson, K. (1984). The use of penile tumescence measures with incarcerated rapists: Further validity issues. *Archives of Sexual Behavior, 13,* 545–554.

Murray, H. A. (1943). *Thematic Apperception Test manual.* Cambridge, MA: Harvard University Press.

Murstein, B. I. (Ed.). (1965). *Handbook of projective techniques.* New York: Basic Books.

Myers, W. C., & Vondruska, M. A. (1998). Murder, minors selective serotonin reuptake inhibitors, and the involuntary intoxication defense. *Journal of American Academy of Psychiatry and the Law, 26,* 487–496.

Neely v. Newton, 149 F.3d 1074 (10th Cir.1998).

Nestor, P. G., & Haycock, J. (1997). Not guilty by rason of insanity of murder: Clinical and neuropsychological characteristics. *Journal of American Academy of Psychiatry and the Law, 25,* 161–171.

Neylan, T. C., Reynolds, C. F., III, & Kupfer, D. J. (1997). Electrodiagnostic techniques in neuropsychiatry. In S. C. Yudofsky, & R. E. Hales (Eds.), *The American Psychiatric Press textbook of neuropsychiatry* (3rd ed., pp. 165–179). Washington, DC: American Psychiatric Press.

Nichols, H. R., & Molinder, I. (1984). *Multiphasic Sex Inventory.* Tacoma, WA: Author.

Norwood, S., Nicholson, R. A., Enyart, C., & Hickey, M. L. (1991). Characteristics and outcomes of NGRI patients in Oklahoma. *Behavioral Sciences and the Law, 9,* 487–500.

Note. (1987). Resurrection of the ultimate issue rule: Federal rule of evidence 704(b) and the insanity defense. *Cornell Law Review, 72,* 620–640.

Ofshe, R. I., & Singer, M. T. (1994). Recovered-memory therapy and robust repression: Influence and pseudomemories. *International Journal of Clinical and Experimental Hypnosis, 42,* 391–410.

Ogloff, J. R. P. (1991). A comparison of insanity defense standards on juror decision making. *Law and Human Behavior, 15,* 509–521.

Ogloff, J. R. P., Roberts, C. F., & Roesch, R. (1993). The insanity defense: Legal standards and clinical assessment. *Applied and Preventive Psychology, 2,* 163–178.

O'Neill, B., Williams, A. F., & Dubowski, K. M. (1983). Variability in blood alcohol concentrations: Implications for estimating individual results. *Journal of Studies on Alcohol, 44,* 222–230.

O'Reilly-Fleming, T. (1992). From beasts to Bedlam: Hadfield, the Regency Crisis, M'Naghten, and the "mad" business in Britain, 1788–1843. *Journal of Psychiatry and Law, 20,* 167–190.

Orne, M. T. (1979). The use and misuse of hypnosis in court. *International Journal of Clinical and Experimental Hypnosis, 27,* 311–341.

Othmer, E., & Othmer, S. C. (1989). *The clinical interview using DSM-III-R.* Washington, DC: American Psychiatric Press.

Otto, R. K. (1989). Bias and expert testimony of mental health professionals in adversarial proceedings: A preliminary investigation. *Behavioral Sciences and the Law, 7,* 267–273.

Otto, R. K., & Hall, J. E. (1988). The utility of the Michigan Alcoholism Screening Test in the detection of alcoholics and problem drinkers. *Journal of Personality Assessment, 52,* 499–505.

Otto, R. K., Lang, A. R., Megargee, E. I., & Rosenblatt, A. I. (1988). Ability of Alcoholics to escape detection by the MMPI. *Journal of Consulting and Clinical Psychology, 56,* 452–457.

Overholser, J. (1962). Criminal responsibility: A psychiatrist's viewpoint. *American Bar Association Journal, 48,* 529–530.

Owens, S. M. (1997). Criminal responsibility and multiple personality defendants. *Mental and Physical Disability Law Reporter, 21,* 133–143.

Pankratz, L. (1988). Malingering on intellectual and neuropsychological measures. In R. Rogers (Ed.), *Clinical assessment of malingering and deception* (pp. 169–192). New York: Guilford Press.

Pankratz, L., & Binder, L. M. (1997). In R. Rogers (Ed.), *Clinical assessment of malingering and deception* (2nd ed., pp. 223–236). New York: Guilford Press.

Pantle, M. L., Pasewark, R. A., & Steadman, H. J. (1980). Comparing institutionalization periods and subsequent arrests of NGRI patients and convicted felons. *Journal of Psychiatry and Law, 8,* 305–316.

Parsons v. State, 2 So. 854 (Ala. 1887).

Parwatikar, S. D., Holcomb, W. R., & Menninger, K. A. (1985). Detection of malingered amnesia in accused murderers. *Bulletin of the American Academy of Psychiatry and the Law, 13,* 97–103.

Pasewark, R. A., & Seidenzahl, D. (1979). Opinions concerning the insanity plea and criminality among mental patients. *Bulletin of the American Academy of Psychiatry and Law, 7,* 199–202.

Patrick, C. J., & Iacono, W. G. (1991). A comparison of field and laboratory polygraphs in the detection of deception. *Psychophysiology, 28,* 632–638.

Pendergrast, M. (1995). *Victims of memory: Incest accusations and shattered lives.* Hinesburg, VT: Upper Access, Inc.

Penney v. Praxair, Inc., 116 F.3d 330 (8th Cir 1997).

Pennsylvania, 18 Pa. Cons. Stat. Ann. § 314 (1997).

Penrod, S. D., Fulero, S., & Cutler, B. L. (1995) Expert psychological testimony on eyewitness reliability before and after Daubert: The state of the law and the science. *Behavioral Sciences and the Law, 13,* 229–259.

People v. Edney, 350 N.E.2d 400 (NY. 1976).

People v. Gard, 158 Ill. 2d 191, 632 N.E.2d 1026 (1994).

People v. Hilliker, 185 N.W. 2d 831 (MI. App. 1971).

People v. Knuckles, 650 N.E. 2d 975 (IL. 1995).

People v. Lines, 531 P.2d 793 (Cal. 1975).

People v. Schmidt, 216 N.Y. 324, 110 N.E. 945 (N.Y. 1915).

People v. Wolff, 394 P.2d 959 (Cal. 1964).

Perkins v. State, 902 S.W. 2d 88 (Tex. Ct. App. 1995).

Perlin, M. L. (1994). *The jurisprudence of the insanity defense.* Durham, NC: Carolina Academic Press.

Perlin, M. L. (1996). The insanity defense: Deconstructing the myths and reconstructing the jurisprudence. In B. D. Sales & D. W. Shuman (Eds.), *Law, mental health, and mental disorder* (pp. 341–359). Pacific Grove, CA: Brooks/Cole.

Perlman, M. D., & Kaufman, A. S. (1990). Assessment of child intelligence. In G. Goldstein & M Hersen (Eds.), *Handbook of psychological assessment* (2nd ed., pp. 59–78). New York: Pergamon Press.

Perr, I. N. (1991). Crime and multiple personality disorder: A case history and discussion. *Bulletin of the American Academy of Psychiatry and the Law, 19,* 203–214.

Petrila, J. (1982). The insanity defense and other mental health dispositions in Missouri. *International Journal of Law and Psychiatry, 5,* 81–101.

Pickel, K. L. (1998). The effects of motive information and crime unusualness on jurors' judgments in insanity cases. *Law and Human Behavior, 22,* 571–584.

Piper, A. (1993). "Truth serum" and "recovered memories" of sexual abuse: A review of the evidence. *Journal of Psychiatry and Law, 21,* 447–471.

Pitt, S. E., Brandt, J. D., Tellefsen, C., Janofsky, J. S., Cohen, M. E., Bettis, E. D., & Rappeport, J. R. (1997). Group dynamics in forensic pretrial decision-making. *Journal of the American Academy of Psychiatry and Law, 25,* 95–104.

Pollack, S. (1976). The insanity defense as defined by the proposed Federal Criminal Code. *Bulletin of the American Academy of Psychiatry and Law, 4,* 11–23.

Pollack, S., Gross, B. H., & Weinberger, L. E. (1982). Principles of forensic psychiatry for reaching psychiatric–legal opinions. In B. H. Gross & L. E. Weinberger (Eds.), *The mental health professional and the legal system* (pp. 25–44). San Francisco: Jossey-Bass.

Pope, H. G., Jr., Hudson, J. I., Bodkin, J. A., & Oliva, P. (1998). Questionable validity of "dissociative amnesia" in trauma victims: Evidence from prospective studies. *British Journal of Psychiatry, 172*, 210–215.

Pope, K. S. (1996). Memory, abuse, and science: Questioning claims about false memory syndrome epidemic. *American Psychologist, 51*, 957-974.

Pope, K. S., Butcher, J. N., & Seelen, J. (1993). *The MMPI, MMPI-2, and MMPI-A in court: A practical guide for expert witnesses and attorneys.* Washington, DC: American Psychological Association.

Popper, K. (1959). *The logic of scientific discovery.* New York: Basic Books.

Prandoni, J. R., & Swartz, C. P. (1978). Rorschach protocols for three diagnostic categories of adult offenders: Normative data. *Journal of Personality Assessment, 42*, 115–120.

Prentice, S. E. (1995). A history of subspecialization in forensic psychiatry. *Bulletin of the American Academy of Psychiatry and Law, 23*, 195–203.

Psychiatric Security Review Board. (1991). A model for management and treatment of insanity acquittees. *Hospital and Community Psychiatry, 45*, 1127–1131.

Psychological Corporation. (1997). *WAIS-III and WMS-II technical manual.* San Antonio, TX: Author.

Quen, J. M. (1978). Isaac Ray and Charles Doe: Responsibility and justice. In W. E. Barton and C. J. Sanborn (Eds.), *Law and the mental health professions* (pp. 235–250). New York: International Universities Press.

Quen, J. M. (1981). Anglo American concepts of criminal responsibility. In S. J. Hucker, C. D. Webster, & M. H. Ben-Aron (Eds.), *Mental disorder and criminal responsibility* (pp. 1–10). Toronto: Butterworth.

Rachlin, S., Halpern, A. L., & Portnow, S. L. (1984). The volitional rule, personality disorders and the insanity defense. *Psychiatric Annals, 14*, 139–147.

Radwin, J. O. (1991). The multiple personality disorder: Has this trendy alibi lost its way? *Law and Psychology Review, 15*, 351–373.

Raine, A., Buchsbaum, M. S., & LaCasse, L. (1997). Brain abnormalities in murderers indicated by positron emission tomography. *Biological Psychiatry, 42*, 498–507.

Raine, A., Buchsbaum, M. S., Stanley, J., Lottenberg, S., Abel, L., & Stoddard, J. (1997). Selective reductions in prefrontal glucose metabolism in murderers. *Biological Psychiatry, 36*, 365–373.

Raine, A., Meloy, J. R., Bihrle, S., Stoddard, J., LaCasse, L., & Buchsbaum M. S. (1998). Reduced prefrontal and increased subcortical brain functioning assessed using positron emission tomography in predatory and affective murderers. *Behavioral Sciences and the Law, 16*, 319–332.

Raskin, D. C. (1989). *Psychological methods in criminal investigation.* New York: Springer.

Raskin, D. C., Honts, C. R., & Kircher, J. C. (1996). The scientific status of research on polygraph techniques: The case for polygraph tests. In D. L. Faigman (Ed.), *The West companion to scientific evidence.* Minneapolis: West Publishing.

Ratner, R. A., & Shapiro, D. (1978). The episodic dyscontrol syndrome and criminal responsibility. *Bulletin of the American Academy of Psychiatry and the Law, 7*, 422–431.

Redlich, F. C., Ravitz, L. J., & Dession, G. H. (1951). Narcoanalysis and truth. *American Journal of Psychiatry, 106*, 586–593.

Reed, J. E. (1996) Fixed vs. flexible neuropsychological test batteries under the Daubert standard for the admissibility of scientific evidence. *Behavioral Sciences and the Law, 14*, 315–322.

Rees, L. M., Tombaugh, T. N., Gansler, D. A., & Moczynski, N. P. (1998). Five validation experiments of the Test of Memory Malingering (TOMM). *Psychological Assessment, 10,* 10–20.

Reichlin, S. M., Bloom, J. D., & Williams, M. H. (1993). Excluding personality disorders from the insanity defense—A follow-up study. *Bulletin of the American Academy of Psychiatry and Law, 21,* 91–100.

Reitan, R. M., & Wolfson, D. (1993). *The Halstead–Reitan Neuropsychological Test Battery: Theory and clinical interpretation.* Tuscon, AZ: Neuropsychological Press.

Reitan, R. M., & Wolfson, D. (1996). The question of validity of neuropsychological test scores among head-injured litigants: Development of a dissimulation index. *Archives of Clinical Neuropsychology, 11,* 573–580.

Reitan, R. M., & Wolfson, D. (1998). Detection of malingering and invalid test results using the Halstead–Reitan Battery. In C. R. Reynolds (Ed.), *Detection of malingering during head injury litigation* (pp. 163–208). New York: Plenum Press.

Resnick, P. J. (1997). Malingered psychosis. In R. Rogers (Ed.), *Clinical assessment of malingering and deception* (2nd ed., pp. 47–67). New York: Guilford Press.

Restak, R. (1993). The neurological defense of violent crime: "Insanity defense" retooled. *Archives of Neurology, 50,* 869–871.

Retzlaff, P. (1996). MCMI–III validity: Bad test or bad validity? *Journal of Personality Assessment, 66,* 431–437.

Retzlaff, P., Sheehan, E., & Fiel, A. (1991). MCMI–II report style and bias: Profile and validity scale analyses. *Journal of Personality Assessment, 56,* 466–477.

Rice, M. E., & Harris, G. T. (1990). The predictors of insanity acquittal. *International Journal of Law and Psychiatry, 13,* 217–224.

Rice, M. E., Harris, G. T., Lang, C., & Bell, V. (1990). Recidivism among male insanity acquittees. *Journal of Psychiatry and Law, 18,* 379–403.

Richardson, J. T., Ginsburg, G. P., Gatowski, S., & Dobbin, S. (1995). The problems of applying *Daubert* to psychological syndrome evidence. *Judicature, 79,* 10–16.

Riethmiller, R. J., & Handler, L. (1998). Problematic methods and unwarranted conclusions in DAP research: Suggestions for improved research practices. *Journal of Personality Assessment, 69,* 459–475.

Roback, H. B. (1968). Human figure drawings: Their utility in the clinical psychologist's armamentarium for personality assessment. *Psychological Bulletin, 70,* 1–19.

Roberts, C. F., Golding, S. L., Fincham, F. D. (1987). Implicit theories of criminal responsibility: Decision making and the insanity defense. *Law and Human Behavior, 11,* 207–232.

Roberts, C. F., Sargent, E. L., & Chan, A. S. (1993). Verdict selection processes in insanity cases. *Law and Human Behavior, 17,* 261–275.

Robey, A. (1978). Guilty but mentally ill. *Bulletin of the American Academy of Psychiatry, 6,* 374–381.

Robins, L. N., Helzer, J. E., Cottler, L. B., & Goldring, E. (1989). *NIMH Diagnostic Interview Schedule, Version III—Revised.* St. Louis, MO: Washington University School of Medicine.

Robins, L. N., Helzer, J. E., Weissman, M. M., Orvaschel, H., Gruenberg, E., Burke, J. D., Jr., & Regier, D. A. (1984). Lifetime prevalence of specific psychiatric disorders in three sites. *Archives of General Psychiatry, 41,* 949–958.

Robitscher, J. B. (1966). *Pursuit of agreement: Psychiatry and the law.* Philadelphia: Lippincott.

Rock v. Arkansas, 483 U.S. 44 (1987).

Roesch, R., & Golding, S. L. (1980). *Competency to stand trial.* Chicago: University of Illinois Press.

Roesch, R., & Golding, S. L. (1987). The assessment of criminal responsibility: A historical approach to a current controversy. In I. B. Weiner & A. K. Hess (Eds.), *Handbook of forensic psychology* (pp. 395–436). New York: Wiley.

Rogers, J. L., & Bloom, J. D. (1982). Characteristics of persons committed to Oregon's Psychiatric Security Review. *Bulletin of the American Academy of Psychiatry and the Law, 10,* 15–164.

Rogers, J. L., & Bloom, J. D. (1985). The insanity sentence: Oregon's Psychiatric Security Review Board. *Behavioral Sciences and the Law, 3,* 69–84.

Rogers, R. (1984). *Rogers Criminal Responsibility Assessment Scales (RCRAS) and test manual.* Odessa, FL: Psychological Assessment Resources.

Rogers, R. (1986). *Conducting insanity evaluations.* New York: Van Nostrand Reinhold.

Rogers, R. (1987a). Ethical dilemmas in forensic evaluations. *Behavioral Sciences and the Law, 5,* 149–160.

Rogers, R. (1987b). The APA position on the insanity defense: Empiricism vs. emotionalism. *American Psychologist, 42,* 840–848.

Rogers, R. (Ed.). (1988). *Clinical assessment of malingering and deception.* New York: Guilford Press.

Rogers, R. (1990a). Development of a new classificatory model of malingering. *Bulletin of the American Academy of Psychiatry and Law, 18,* 323–333.

Rogers, R. (1990b). Models of feigned mental illness. *Professional Psychology, 21,* 182–188.

Rogers, R. (1992). *Structured Interview of Reported Symptoms (SIRS).* Odessa, FL: Psychological Assessment Resources.

Rogers, R. (1995a). *Diagnostic and structured interviewing: A handbook for psychologists.* Odessa, FL: Psychological Assessment Resources.

Rogers, R. (1995b). Mental status examinations. In R. Rogers, *Diagnostic and structured interviewing: A handbook for psychologists* (pp. 31–61). Odessa, FL: Psychological Assessment Resources.

Rogers, R. (Ed.) (1997). *Clinical assessment of malingering and deception* (2nd ed.). New York: Guilford Press.

Rogers, R., & Bagby, R. M. (1993). Can Ziskin withstand his own criticisms? *Behavioral Sciences and the Law, 11,* 223–233.

Rogers, R., Bagby, R. M., & Chakraborty, D. (1993). Faking schizophrenic disorders on the MMPI—2: Detection of coached simulators. *Journal of Personality Assessment, 60,* 215–226.

Rogers, R., Bagby, R. M., Crouch, M., & Cutler, B. (1990). Effects of ultimate opinions on juror perceptions of insanity. *International Journal of Law and Psychiatry, 13,* 225–232.

Rogers, R., Bagby, R. M., & Dickens, S. E. (1992). *Structured Interview of Reported Symptoms (SIRS) and professional manual.* Odessa, FL: Psychological Assessment Resources.

Rogers, R., Cashel, M. L., Johansen, J., Sewell, K. W., & Gonzalez, C. (1997). Evaluation of adolescent offenders with substance abuse: Validation of the SASSI with conduct-disordered youth. *Criminal Justice and Behavior, 24,* 114–128.

Rogers, R., & Cavanaugh, J. L. (1981a). Application of the SADS diagnostic interview to forensic psychiatry. *Journal of Psychiatry and Law, 9,* 329–344.

Rogers, R., Cavanaugh, J. L., Seman, W., & Harris, M. (1984). Legal outcome and clinical findings: A study of insanity. *Bulletin of the American Academy of Psychiatry, 12,* 75–83.

Rogers, R., & Clark, C. C. (1985, October). *Diogenes revisited: Another search for the ultimate NGRI standard.* Paper presented at the annual meeting of the American Academy of Psychiatry and Law, Albuquerque, NM.

Rogers, R., & Cruise, K. R. (1998). Assessment of malingering with simulation designs: Threats to external validity. *Law and Human Behavior, 22,* 273–285.

Rogers, R., & Cunnien, A. J. (1986). Multiple SADS evaluation in the assessment of criminal defendants. *Journal of Forensic Sciences, 30,* 222–230.

Rogers, R., & Dickey, R. (1991). Denial and mimimization among sex offenders: A review of competing models of deception. *Annals of Sex Research, 4,* 49–63.

Rogers, R., & Ewing, C. P. (1989). Proscribing ultimate opinions: A quick and cosmetic fix. *Law and Human Behavior, 13,* 357–374.

Rogers, R., & Ewing, C. P. (1992). The measurement of insanity: Debating the merits of the R-CRAS and its alternatives. *International Journal of Law and Psychiatry, 15,* 113–123.

Rogers, R., Gillis, J. R., Turner, R. E., & Frise-Smith, T. (1990). The clinical presentation of command hallucinations. *American Journal of Psychiatry, 147,* 1304–1307.

Rogers, R., Harrell, E. H., & Liff, C. D. (1993). Feigning neuropsychological impairment: A critical review of methodological and clinical considerations. *Clinical Psychology Review, 13,* 255–274.

Rogers, R., Harris, M., & Wasyliw, O. E. (1983). Observed and self-reported psychopathology in NGRI acquittees in court-mandated outpatient treatment. *International Journal of Offender Therapy and Comparative Criminology, 27,* 143–149.

Rogers, R., Hinds, J. D., & Sewell, K. W. (1996). Feigning psychopathology among adolescent offenders: Validation of the SIRS, MMPI-A, and SIMS. *Journal of Personality Assessment, 67,* 244–257.

Rogers, R., & Kelly, K. S. (1997). Denial and misreporting of substance abuse. In R. Rogers (Ed.), *Clinical assessment of malingering and deception* (2nd ed., pp. 108–129). New York: Guilford Press.

Rogers, R., & McKee, G. R. (1995). Use of the MMPI-2 in the assessment of criminal responsibility. In Y. S. Ben-Porath, J. R. Graham, G.C.N. Hall, R. D. Hirschman, & M. S. Zaragoza (Eds.), *Forensic applications of the MMPI-2* (pp.103–126). Newbury Park, CA: Sage.

Rogers, R., & Mitchell, C. N. (1991). *Mental health experts and the criminal courts: A handbook for lawyers and clinicians.* Toronto: Carswell.

Rogers, R., & Nussbaum, D. (1991). Interpreting response styles of inconsistent MMPI profiles. *Forensic Reports, 4,* 361–366.

Rogers, R., Nussbaum, D. N., & Gillis, J. R. (1988). Command hallucinations and criminality: A clinical quandary. *Bulletin of the American Academy of Psychiatry and Law, 16,* 251–258.

Rogers, R., & Reinhardt, V. (1998). Conceptualization and assessment of secondary gain. In G. P. Koocher, J. C., Norcross, & S. S. Hill, III (Eds.), *Psychologist's desk reference* (pp. 57–62). New York: Oxford University Press.

Rogers, R., & Salekin, R. T. (1998). Beguiled by Bayes: A re-analysis of Mossman and Hart's estimates of malingering. *Behavioral Sciences and the Law, 16,* 147–153.

Rogers, R., Salekin, R. T., & Sewell, K. W. (1997, August). *Meta-analysis of the MCMI:*

Clinical usefulness for Axis II disorders. Paper presented at the American Psychological Association Convention, Chicago.

Rogers, R., Salekin, R. T., & Sewell, K. W. (1999). Validation of the Millon Clinical Multiaxial Inventory for Axis II disorders: Does it meet the Daubert standard? *Law and Human Behavior, 23,* 425–443.

Rogers, R., Salekin, R. T., Sewell, K. W., Goldstein, A., & Leonard, K. (1998). A comparison of forensic and nonforensic malingerers: A prototypical analysis of explanatory models. *Law and Human Behavior, 22,* 353–367.

Rogers, R., & Seman, W. (1983). Murder and criminal responsibility: An examination of MMPI profiles. *Behavioral Sciences and the Law, 1,* 89–95.

Rogers, R., Seman, W., & Clark, C. C. (1986). Assessment of criminal responsibility: Initial validation of the R-CRAS with the M'Naghten and GBMI standards. *International Journal of Law and Psychiatry, 9,* 67–75.

Rogers, R., Seman, W., & Stampley, J. (1984). A study of sociodemographic characteristics of individuals evaluated for insanity. *International Journal of Offender Therapy and Comparative Criminology, 28,* 3–10.

Rogers, R., & Sewell, K. W. (1998). *Test of Cognitive Abilities: Preliminary test manual.* Unpublished test.

Rogers, R., & Sewell, K. W. (1999). The R-CRAS and insanity evaluations: A reexamination of construct validity. *Behavioral Sciences and the Law, 17,* 181–194.

Rogers, R., Sewell, K. W., Cruise, K. R., Wang, E. W., & Ustad, K. L. (1998). The PAI and feigning: A cautionary note on its use in forensic-correctional settings. *Assessment, 5,* 399–405.

Rogers, R., Sewell, K. W., & Goldstein, A. (1994). Explanatory models of malingering: A prototypical analysis. *Law and Human Behavior, 18,* 543–552.

Rogers, R., Sewell, K. W., Morey, L. C., & Ustad, K. L. (1996). Detection of feigned mental disorders on the Personality Assessment Inventory: A discriminant analysis. *Journal of Personality Assessment, 67,* 629–640.

Rogers, R., Sewell, K. W., & Salekin, R. (1994). A meta-analysis of malingering on the MMPI-2. *Assessment, 1,* 227–237.

Rogers, R., Sewell, K. W., & Ustad, K. L. (1995). Feigning among chronic outpatients on the MMPI-2: An analogue study. *Assessment, 2,* 81–89.

Rogers, R., Sewell, K. W., Ustad, K. L., Reinhardt, V., & Edwards, W. (1995). The Referral Decision Scale in a Jail Sample of Disordered Offenders. *Law and Human Behavior, 19,* 481–492.

Rogers, R., Thatcher, A. A., & Cavanaugh, J. L. (1984). Use of the SADS diagnostic interview in evaluating legal insanity. *Journal of Clinical Psychology, 40,* 1538–1541.

Rogers, R., & Turner, R. E. (1987). Understanding of insanity: National survey of forensic psychiatrists and psychologists. *Health Law in Canada, 7,* 71–75.

Rogers, R., Turner, R. E., Helfield, R., & Dickens, S. E. (1988). Forensic psychiatrists' and psychologists' understanding of insanity: Misguided expertise? *Canadian Journal of Psychiatry, 33,* 691–695.

Rogers, R., Ustad, K. L., & Salekin, R. T. (1998). Convergent validity of the Personality Assessment Inventory: A study of emergency referrals in a correctional setting. *Assessment 5,* 3–12.

Rogers, R., & Wettstein, R. M. (1985). Relapse in NGRI outpatients: An empirical study. *Journal of Offender Therapy, 29,* 227–236.

Rogers, R., & Wettstein, R. M. (1997). Drug-assisted interviews to detect malingering and deception. In R. Rogers (Ed.), *Clinical assessment of malingering and deception* (2nd ed., pp. 239–251). New York: Guilford Press.

Ross, C. A. (1991). Epidemiology of multiple personality disorder and dissociation. *Psychiatric Clinics of North America, 14*, 503–518.

Ross, C. A. (1998). History, phenomenology, and epidemiology of dissociation. In L. K. Michelson & W. J. Ray (Eds.), *Handbook of dissociation: Theoretical, empirical, and clinical perspectives* (pp. 3–24). New York: Plenum Press.

Ross, C. A., Heber, S., Norton, G. R., Anderson, G., Anderson, D., & Barchet, P. (1989). The Dissociative Disorders Interview Schedule: A structured interview. *Dissociation, 2*, 169–189.

Ross, L., Lepper, M. R., Strack, F., & Steinmetz, J. (1977). Social explanation and social expectation: Effects of real and hypothetical explanations of subjective likelihood. *Journal of Personality and Social Psychology, 35*, 817–829.

Rotgers, F., & Barrett, D. (1996). *Daubert v. Merrell Dow* and expert testimony by clinical psychologists: Implications and recommendations for practice. *Professional Psychology: Research and Practice, 27*, 467–474.

Rotter, M., & Goodman, W. (1993). The relationship between insight and control in obsessive-compulsive disorder: Implicatios for thc insanity defense. *Bulletin of the American Academy of Psychiatry and Law, 21*, 245–252.

Rubinsky, E. W., & Brandt, J. (1986). Amnesia and criminal law: A clinical overview. *Behavioral Sciences and the Law, 4*, 27–46.

Sackeim, H. A., & Stern, Y. (1997). Neuropsychiatric aspects of memory and amnesia. In S. C. Yudofsky, & R. E. Hales (Eds.), *The American Psychiatric Press textbook of neuropsychiatry* (3rd ed., pp. 501–518). Washington, DC: American Psychiatric Press.

Saks, E. R. (1995). The criminal responsibility of people with multiple personality disorder. *Psychiatric Quarterly, 66*, 119–131.

Saks, E. R. (1997). *Multiple personality disorder and criminal law.* New York: New York University Press.

Salekin, R. T., & Rogers, R. (in press). Toward effective treatment and release of NGRI patients: Current knowledge and future directions. In J. B. Ashford, B. Sales, & W. H. Reid (Eds.), *Treating adult and juvenile offenders with special needs.* Washington, DC: American Psychological Association.

Salekin, R. T., Rogers, R., & Sewell, K. W. (1996). A review and meta-analysis of the Psychopathy Checklist and Psychopathy Checklist—Revised: Predictive validity. *Clinical Psychology: Science and Practice, 3*, 203–315.

Sales, B., Shuman, D. W., & O'Connor, M. (1994) In a dim light: Admissibility of child sexual abuse memories. *Applied Cognitive Psychology, 8*, 399–406.

Sandys, M., & Dillehay, R. C. (1995). First-ballot votes, predeliberation dispositions, and final verdicts in jury trials. *Law and Human Behavior, 19*, 175–195.

Sauer, R. H., & Mullens, P. M. (1976). The insanity defense: M'Naghten vs. ALI. *Bulletin of the American Academy of Psychiatry and the Law, 4*, 73–75.

Scarpa, A., & Raine, A. (1997). Psychophysiology of anger and violent behavior. *Psychiatric Clinics of North America, 20*, 375–394.

Schacter, D. L. (1986a). Amnesia and crime: How much do we really know? *American Psychologist, 41*, 286–295.

Schacter, D. L. (1986b). Feeling-of-knowing ratings distinguish between genuine and simulated forgetting. *Journal of Experimental Psychology: Learning, Memory, and Cognition, 12*, 30–41.

Schinka, J. A., & Borum, R. (1993). Readability of the adult psychopathology inventories. *Psychological Assessment, 5,* 384–386.

Schlank, A. M. (1995). The utility of the MMPI and the MSI for identifying sexual offender typology. *Sexual Abuse: A Journal of Research and Treatment, 7,* 185–194.

Schopp, R. F. (1991). *Automatism, insanity, and the psychology of criminal responsibility.* New York: Cambridge University Press.

Schopp, R. F. (1996). Communicating risk assessments: Accuracy, efficacy, and responsibility. *American Psychologist, 51,* 939–944.

Schretlen, D. J. (1997). Dissimulation on the Rorschach and other projective measures. In R. Rogers (Ed.), *Clinical assessment of malingering and deception* (2nd ed., pp. 208–222). New York: Guilford Press.

Scott, D. C., Zonana, H. V., & Getz, M. A. (1990). Monitering insanity acquittees: Connecticut's psychiatric security board. *Hospital and Community Psychiatry, 41,* 980–984.

Sechrest, L. (1963). Incremental validity: A recommendation. *Educational and Psychological Measurement, 23,* 153–158.

Seig, A., Ball, F., & Menninger, K. A. (1995). A comparison of female versus male insanity acquittees in Colorado. *Bulletin of the American Academy of Psychiatry and Law, 23,* 523–532.

Selzer, M. L. (1971). Michigan Alcoholism Screening Test: The quest for a new diagnostic instrument. *American Journal of Psychiatry, 127,* 1653–1658.

Sewell, K. W., & Cruise, K. R. (1997). Understanding and detecting dissimulation in sex offenders. In R. Rogers (Ed.), *Clinical assessment of malingering and deception* (2nd ed., pp. 328–350). New York: Guilford Press.

Shah, A. K. (1992). Violence, death, and associated features on a mental handicap ward. *Journal of Intellectual Disability Research, 36,* 229–239.

Shah, S. A. (1986). Criminal responsibility. In W. J. Curran, A. L. McGarry, & S. A. Shah (Eds.), *Forensic psychiatry and psychology: Perspectives and standards for interdisciplinary practice* (pp. 167–208). Philadelphia: Davis.

Shah, P. J., Greenberg, W. M., & Convit, A. (1994). Hospitalized insanity acquittees' level of functioning. *Bulletin of the American Academy of Psychiatry and Law, 22,* 85–93.

Shahzade v. Gregory, 923 F. Supp. 286 (D. Mass. 1996).

Shapiro, D. L. (1984). *Psychological evaluation and expert testimony.* New York: Van Nostrand Reinhold.

Shuman, D. W. (1993). The use of empathy in forensic examinations. *Ethics and Behavior, 3,* 289–302.

Shuman, D. W. (1994). *Psychiatric and psychological evidence* (2nd ed.). Colorado Springs, CO: Shepherds/McGraw-Hill

Shuman, D. W. (1996). *Psychiatric and psychological evidence* (2nd ed., rev.). Colorado Springs, CO: Shepherds/McGraw-Hill

Shuman, D. W., & Greenberg, S. A. (1998). The role of ethical norms in the admissibility of expert testimony. *ABA Judges Journal, 37,* 4–43.

Shuman, D. W., & Sales, B. D. (1998). The admissibility of expert testimony based on clinical judgment and scientific research. *Psychology, Public Policy, and Law, 4,* 1–27.

Silver, E. (1995). Punishment or treatment: Comparing the lengths of confinement of successful and unsuccessful insanity defendants. *Law and Human Behavior, 19,* 375–388.

Silver, E., Cirincione, C., & Steadman, H. J. (1994). Demythologizing inaccurate perceptions of the insanity defense. *Law and Human Behavior, 18,* 63–70.

Silver, S. B., Cohen, M. I., & Spodak, M. K. (1989). Follow-up after release of insanity acquittees, mentally disordered offenders, and convicted felons. *Bulletin of the American Academy of Psychiatry and Law, 17,* 387–400.

Silver, S. B., & Spodak, M. K. (1983). Dissection of the prongs of ALI: A retrospective assessment of criminal responsibility by the psychiatric staff of the Clifton T. Perkins Hospital Center. *Bulletin of American Academy of Psychiatry and Law, 11,* 383–387.

Silver, S. B., & Tellefsen, C. (1991). Administrative issues in the follow-up treatment of insanity acquittees. *Journal of Mental Health Administration, 18,* 242–252.

Simon, R. A. (1967). *The jury and the defense of insanity.* Boston: Little, Brown.

Simon, R. J. (1983). The defense of insanity. *Journal of Psychiatry and the Law, 11,* 183–202.

Simon, R. I., & Wettstein, R. M. (1997). Toward the development of guidelines for the conduct of forensic psychiatric examinations. *Journal of the American Academy of Psychiatry and Law, 25,* 17–30.

Slobogin, C. (1985). The guilty but mentally ill verdict: An idea whose time should not have come. *George Washington Law Review, 53,* 49–527.

Slobogin, C., Melton, G. B., & Showalter, C. R. (1984). The feasibility of a brief evaluation of mental state at the time of the offense. *Law and Human Behavior, 8,* 305–320.

Slovenko, R. (1993). The multiple personality and the criminal law. *Medicine and the Law, 12,* 329–340.

Skinner, H. A. (1982). The Drug Abuse Screening Test. *Addictive Behaviors, 7,* 363–371.

Smith v. McCormick, 914 F.2d 1153 (9th Cir 1990).

Smith, G., & Hall, J. (1982). Evaluating Michigan's guilty but mentally ill verdict: An empirical study. *University of Michigan Journal of Law Reform, 16,* 77–114.

Smith, G. P. (1997). Assessment of malingering with self-report measures. In R. Rogers (Ed.), *Clinical assessment of malingering and deception* (2nd ed., pp. 351–370). New York: Guilford Press.

Spanos, N. P. (1996). *Multiple identities and false memories.* Washington, DC: American Psychological Association.

Spiegel, A. D., & Spiegel, M. S. (1991). Not guilty of murder by reason of paroxysmal insanity: The "mad" doctor vs. "common-sense" doctors in an 1865 trial. *Psychiatric Quarterly, 62,* 51–66.

Spitzer, R. L., & Endicott, J. (1978a). *Schedule of affective disorders and schizophrenia* (3rd ed.). New York: Biometrics Research.

Spitzer, R. L., & Endicott, J. (1978b). *Schedule of affective disorders and schizophrenia— Change version.* New York: Biometrics Research.

Spitzer, R. L., Endicott, J., & Robbins, E. (1978). Research diagnostic criteria for the use in psychiatric research. *Archives of General Psychiatry, 35,* 773–782.

Spitzer, R. L., Williams, J. B. W., & Gibbon, M. (1987). *Structured clinical interview for DSM-III-R (SCID).* New York: Biometrics Research.

Spitzer, R. L., Williams, J. B. W., Gibbon, M., & First, M. B. (1990). *Structured clinical interview for DSM-III-R (SCID).* Washington, DC: American Psychiatric Press.

Squire, L. R., & Shimamura, A. P. (1988). Learning and memory. In R. Michels, J. O. Cavenar, A. M. Cooper, S. B. Guze, L. L. Judd, G. L. Klerman, & A. J. Solnit (Eds.), *Psychiatry* (vol. 3). Philadephia: Lippincott.

State v. Alberico, 861 P.2d 192 (N.M. 1993).

State v. Carter, 641 S.W.2d 54 (MO. 1982), cert denied 461 US 932 (1983).

State v. Cavaliere, 663 A.2d 96 (N.H. 1995).

State v. Esser, 16 Wis. 2d 567, 115 N.W. 2d (1962).

State v. Hattllt, 994 P.ed 1026 (WA 1997).

State v. Hungerford, 1995 WL 378571 (N.H. Super. Ct. May 23, 1995).

State v. Jeffers, 135 Ariz. 404; 661 P.2d 1105 (1983).

State v. Kociolek, 129 A.2d 417 (NJ. 1957).

State v. Pike, 49 N.H. 399 (1870).

State v. Pitts, 562 A.2d 1320, 1348 (N.J. 1989).

State v. Plummer, 374 A.2d 413 (N.H. 1977).

State v. Porter, 241 Conn. 57, 698 A.2d 739 (1995).

State v. Pratt, 398 A.2d 421 (MD. 1979).

State v. Rodrigues 679 P.2d 615 (Ha. 1984), cert denied 469 US 1078 (1984).

State v. Ross, 646 A.2d 1318 (CT 1994), cert denied 115 S.Ct. 1133 (1995).

State v. Schneider, 402 N.W.2d 779 (MN, 1987), cert denied 114 S.Ct. 901 (1994).

State v. Searcy 798 P.2d 914 (Idaho 1990).

State v. Solomon, 570 N.E.2d 1118 (Ohio 1991).

State v. Spencer, 119 N.C. App. 662, 459 S.E.2d 812 (N.C. App.), rev. denied, 341 N.C. 655, 462 S.E.2d 524 (1995).

Steadman, H. J. (1980). Insanity acquittals in New York State, 1965–1978. *American Journal of Psychiatry, 137,* 321–326.

Steadman, H. J., McGreevy, M. A., Morrissey, J. P., Callahan, L. A., Robbins, P. C., & Cirincione, C. (1993). *Before and after Hinckley: Evaluating insanity defense reform.* New York: Guilford Press.

Stearns, A. W. (1945). Isaac Ray, psychiatrist and pioneer in forensic psychiatry. *American Journal of Psychiatry, 101,* 573–583.

Stein, L.A.R., Graham, J. R., & Williams, C. L. (1995). Detecting fake-bad MMPI-A profiles. *Journal of Personality Assessment, 65,* 415–427.

Steinberg, M. (1993). *Interviewer's guide to the Structured Clinical Interview for DSM-IV Dissociative Disorders (SCID-D).* Washington, DC: American Psychiatric Press.

Steinberg, M., Bancroft, J., & Buchanan, J. (1993). Multiple personality disorder in criminal law. *Bulletin of the American Academy of Psychiatry and the Law, 21,* 345-356.

Strasburger, L. H., Gutheil, T. G., & Brodsky, A. (1997). On wearing two hats: Role conflict in serving as both psychotherapist and expert witness. *American Journal of Psychiatry, 154,* 448–56.

Strub, R. L., & Black, F. W. (1985). *The mental status examination in neurology* (2nd ed.). Philadelphia: Davis.

Strub, R. L., & Wise, M. G. (1997). Differential diagnosis in neuropsychiatric disorders. In S. C. Yudofsky, & R. E. Hales (Eds.), *The American Psychiatric Press textbook of neuropsychiatry* (3rd ed., pp. 331–346). Washington, DC: American Psychiatric Press.

Subcommittee on Criminal Law of the U.S. Senate Judiciary Committee. (1982).

Hearings on limiting the insanity defense. Washington, DC: U. S. Government Printing Office.

Svanum, S., & McGrew, J. (1995). Prospective screening of substance dependence: The advantages of directness. *Addictive Behaviors, 20,* 205–213.

Swartz, J. D., Reinehr, R. C., & Holtzman, W. H. (1983). *Holtzman Inkblot Technique, 1956–1982: An annotated bibliography.* Austin: University of Texas Press.

Swayze, W. W., II, Yates, W., & Andreasen, N. C. (1987). Brain imaging: Applications in psychiatry. *Behavioral Sciences and the Law, 5,* 233–238.

Swensen, C. H. (1957). Empirical evaluations of human figure drawings. *Psychological Bulletin, 54,* 431–466.

Swensen, C. H. (1968). Empirical evaluations of human figure drawings: 1957-1966 *Psychological Bulletin, 70,* 20–44.

Szucko, J. J., & Kleinmuntz, B. (1985). Psychological methods of truth detection. In C. P. Ewing (Ed.), *Psychology, psychiatry and the law: A clinical and forensic handbook* (pp. 441–466). Sarasota, FL: Professional Research Exchange.

Tanay, E. (1978). Psychodynamic differentiation of homicide. *Bulletin of the American Academy of Psychiatry and Law, 6,* 364–369.

Tancredi, L, & Volkow, N. (1988). Neural substrates of violent behavior: Implications for law and public policy. *International Journal of Law and Psychiatry, 11,* 13–49.

Taylor, S. E. (1982). The availability bias in social perception and interaction. In D. Kahneman, P. Slovic, & A. Tversky (Eds.), *Judgment under uncertainty: Heuristics and biases* (pp. 190–200). New York: Cambridge University Press.

Teplin, L. A., & Voit, E. S. (1996). Criminalizing the seriously mentally ill: Putting the problem into perspective. In B. D. Sales & S. A. Shah (Eds.), *Mental health and law: Research, policy, and services* (pp. 283–318). Durham, NC: Carolina Academic Press.

Terr, L. (1994). *Unchained memories: True stories of traumatic memories, lost and found.* New York: Basic Books.

Thompson, J. S., Stuart, G. L., & Holden, C. E. (1992). Command hallucinations and legal insanity. *Forensic Reports, 5,* 29–43.

Thornburgh v. American College of Obstetricians and Gynecologists, 106 S. Ct. 2169 (1986)

Thorndike, R. L., Hagen, E. P., & Sattler, J. M. (1986). *The Stanford–Binet Intelligence Scale: Fourth Edition.* Chicago: Riverside.

Tombaugh, T. N. (1997). The Test of Memory Malingering (TOMM): Normative data from cognitively intact and cognitively impaired individuals. *Psychological Assessment, 9,* 260–268.

Tonkonogy, J. M. (1991). Violence and temporal lobe leison: Head CT and MRI data. *Journal of Neuropsychiatry, 3,* 189–196.

Towers, T., McGinley, H., & Pasewark, R. A. (1992). Insanity defense: ethnicity of defendants and mock jurors. *Journal of Psychiatry and Law, 20,* 243–256.

Trueblood, W., & Binder, L. M. (1997). Psychologists' accuracy in identifying neuropsychological test protocols of clinical malingerers. *Archives of Clinical Neuropsychology, 12,* 13–27.

Trueblood, W., & Schmidt, M. (1993). Malingering and other validity considerations in the neuropsychological evaluation of mild head injury. *Journal of Clinical and Experimental Neuropsychology, 15,* 578–590.

Tucker, G. J., & McDavid, J. (1997). Neuropsychiatric aspects of seizure disorders. In S. C. Yudofsky & R. E. Hales (Eds.), *The American Psychiatric Press textbook of neuropsychiatry* (3rd ed., pp. 561–582). Washington, DC: American Psychiatric Press.

Tygart, C. (1992). Public acceptance/rejection of insanity—M ental illness legal defenses for defendants in criminal homicide cases. *Journal of Psychiatry and Law, 20*, 375–389.

United States v. Alvarez, 519 P.2d 1036 (3rd Cir 1975).

United States v. Brawner, 471 F.2d 969 (D.C. Cir. 1972).

United States v. Cordoba, 104 F.3d 225 (9th Cir. 1997).

United States v. Currens, 290 F.2d 751 (3d Cir. 1961).

United States v. Freeman, 357 F.2d 606 (2d Cir. 1966).

United States v. Hall, 93 F.3d 1337 (7th Cir. 1996).

United States v. Posado, 57 F.3d 428 (5th Cir. 1995).

United States v. Powers, 59 F.3d 1460 (4th Cir 1995).

United State v. Riker, 869 P.2d 43 (Wash, 1994).

United States v. Rincon, 28 F.3d 921 (9th Cir. 1994), cert. denied 513 U.S. 1029 (1994).

United States v. Rouse, 100 F.3d 560 (8th Cir. 1996).

United States v. Salava, 978 F.2d 320 (7th Cir. 1992).

United States v. Sanchez, 118 F.3d 192 (4th Cir. 1997).

United States v. Scheffer, 118 S.Ct. 1261 (1998).

United States v. Scholl, 959 F. Supp. 1189 (D. Ariz. 1997).

United States v. Shaffer, 2 Fed. 999 (10th Cir. 1993).

United States v. Shay, 57 F.3d 126 (1st Cir. 1995).

Updike, C. E., & Shaw, G. A. (1995). Differences in attitudes toward the temporary insanity and the insanity defense. *American Journal of Forensic Psychiatry, 13*, 59–67.

Ustad, K. L. (1996). *Assessment of malingering on the SADS in a jail referral sample: Screening and comprehensive evaluation.* Unpublished doctoral dissertation, University of North Texas, Denton.

Visher, C. A. (1987). Juror decision making: The importance of evidence. *Law and Human Behavior, 11*, 1–17.

Walters, G. D. (1988). Assessing dissimulation and denial on the MMPI in a sample of maximum security, male inmates. *Journal of Personality Assessment, 52*, 465–474.

Wang, E. W., Rogers, R., Giles, C. L., Diamond, P. M., Herrington-Wang, L. E., & Taylor, E. R. (1997). A pilot study of the Personality Assessment Inventory (PAI) in corrections: Assessment of malingering, suicide risk, and aggression in male inmates. *Behavioral Sciences and the Law, 15*, 469–482.

Ward, T., McCormack, J., Hudson, S. M., & Polaschek, D. (1997). Rape: Assessment and treatment. In D. R. Laws & W. O'Donohue (Eds.), *Sexual deviance: Theory, assessment, and treatment* (pp. 356–393). New York: Guilford Press.

Wechsler, D. (1987). *Wechsler Memory Scale—Revised manual.* San Antonio, TX: Psychological Corporation.

Wechsler, D. (1997). *Wechsler Adult Intelligence Scale—Third edition.* San Antonio, TX: Psychological Corporation.

Wedding, D. (1983). Clinical and statistical prediction in neuropsychology. *Clinical Neuropsychology, 5*, 49–54.

Weed, N. C., Butcher, J. N., McKenna, T., & Ben-Porath, Y. S. (1992). New measures for assessing alcohol and drug abuse with the MMPI-2: The APS and AAS. *Journal of Personality Assessment, 58,* 389–404.

Weiner, B. A. (1980). Not guilty by reason of insanity: A sane approach. *Chicago Kent Law Review, 56,* 1057–1085.

Weiner, B. A. (1985). Insanity evaluation. In S. J. Brakel, J. Parry, & B. A.Weiner (Eds.), *Mentally disabled and the law* (pp. 707–734). Chicago: American Bar Association.

Weiner, I. B. (1995). Methodological considerations in Rorschach research. *Psychological Assessment, 7,* 330–337.

Weiner, I. B. (1997). Current status of the Rorschach inkblot method. *Journal of Personality Assessment, 68,* 5–19.

Weiner, I. B., Exner, J. E., Jr., & Sciara, A. (1996). Is the Rorschach welcome in the courtroom? *Journal of Personality Assessment, 67,* 422–424.

Weinstock, R. (1995). *Opinions by AAPL's Committee on Ethics.* Bloomington, CT: American Academy of Psychiatry and Law.

Weisberg, L. A., Strub, R. L., & Garcia, C. A. (1993). *Decision making in adult neurology* (2nd ed.). Toronto: Decker.

Wells, G. L. (1987). Applied eyewitness-testimony research: System variables and estimator variables. In L. S. Wrightsman, C. E. Willis, & S. M. Kassin (Eds.), *On the witness stand: Controversies in the ourtroom* (pp. 139–156). Newbury Park, CA: Sage.

Wettstein, R. M., & Mulvey, E. (1988). Disposition of insanity acquittees in Illinois. *Bulletin of the American Academy of Psychiatry and Law, 16,* 11–24.

Wettstein, R. M., Mulvey, E., & Rogers, R. (1991). Insanity defense standards: A prospective comparison. *American Journal of Psychiatry, 148,* 21–27.

Whitlock, F. A. (1963). *Criminal responsibility and mental illness.* London: Butterworth.

Wiederanders, M. R., & Choate, P. A. (1994). Beyond recidivism: Measuring community adjustments of conditionally released insanity acquittees. *Psychological Assessment, 6,* 61–66.

Wiener, B. A. (1985). The mentally disabled and the criminal law. In S. J. Brakel, J. Parry, & B. A. Wiener (Eds.), *The mentally disabled and the law* (pp. 693–801). Chicago: American Bar Foundation.

Wiener, D. N. (1948). Subtle and obvious keys for the MMPI. *Journal of Consulting Psychology, 12,* 164–170.

Wigmore, J. (1909). Professor Munsterberg and the psychology of testimony. *Illinois Law Review, 3,* 399–445.

Williams, A. D. (1998). Fixed versus flexible batteries. In R. J. McCaffrey, A. D. Williams, J. M. Fisher, & L. C. Laing (Eds.), *The practice of forensic neuropsychology: Meeting challenges in the courtroom* (pp. 57–70). New York: Plenum Press.

Williams, J. B. W., Gibbon, M., First, M. B., Spitzer, R. L., Davies, M., Borus, J., Howes, M. J., Kane, J., Pope, H. G., Jr., Rounsaville, B., & Wittchen, H. U. (1992). The structured clinical interview for DSM-III-R (SCID): II. Multisite test–retest reliability. *Archives of General Psychiatry, 49,* 630–636.

Williams, J. M. (1998). The malingering of memory disorder. In C. R. Reynolds (Ed.), *Detection of malingering during head injury litigation* (pp. 105–132). New York: Plenum Press.

Williams, K. D., Bourgeois, M. J., & Croyle, R T. (1993). The effects of stealing thunder in criminal and civil trials. *Law and Human Behavior, 17,* 597–609.

Williams, L. M. (1994). Recall of childhood trauma: A prospective study of women's memories of child sexual abuse. *Journal of Consulting and Clinical Psychology, 62,* 1167–1176.

Winters, K. C., & Henly, G. A. (1989). *The Personal Experience Inventory (PEI) test and manual.* Los Angeles: Western Psychological Services.

Wion v. United States, 325 F.2d 420 (10th Cir. 1963), cert. denied, 377 U.S. 946 (1964).

Wong, M. T. H., Fenwick, P. B. C., Lumsden, J., Fenton, G. W., Maisey, M. N., Lewis, P., & Badawi, R. (1997). Positron emission tomography in male violent offenders with schizophrenia. *Psychiatry Research: Neuroimaging Section, 68,* 111–123.

Wong, M. T. H., Lumsden, J., Fenton, G. W., & Fenwick, P. B. C. (1994). Electoencephalography, computed tomography, and violence ratings of male patients in a maximum-security mental hospital. *Acta Psychiatrica Scandanavia, 90,* 97–101.

Wood, J. M., Nezworski, M. T., & Stejskal, W. J. (1996a). The Comprehensive System for the Rorschach: A critical examination. *Psychological Science, 7,* 3–10.

Wood, J. M., Nezworski, M. T., & Stejskal, W. J. (1996b). Thinking critically about the Comprehensive System for the Rorschach: A reply to Exner. *Psychological Science, 7,* 3–10.

Wood, J. M., Nezworski, M. T., & Stejskal, W. J. (1997). The reliability of the Comprehensive System for the Rorschach: A comment of Meyer (1997). *Psychological Assessment, 9,* 490–494.

Woodruff, R. (1966). The diagnostic use of the amylobarbital interview among patients with psychotic illness. *British Journal of Psychiatry, 112,* 727/0732.

Wysocki, J. J., & Sweet, J. J. (1985). Identification of brain damaged, schizophrenic, and nomral medical patients using a brief neuropsychological screening battery. *International Journal of Clinical Neuropsychology, 7,* 40–44.

Yuille, J. C., & Daylen, J. (1998). The impact of traumatic events of eyewitness memory. In C. P. Thompson, D. J. Herrmann, J. R. Read, D. Bruce, D. G. Payne, & M. P. Toglia (Eds.), *Eyewitness memory: Theoretical and applied perspectives* (pp. 155–177). Mahwah, NJ: Erlbaum.

Zachary, R. A. (1986). *Shipley Institute for Living Scale—Revised manual.* Los Angeles: Western Psychological Services.

Zani v. State, 767 S.W.2d 825 (Tex. Civ. App, 1989).

Ziskin, J. (1995). *Coping with psychological and psychiatric testimony* (5th ed., vol. 2). Los Angeles: Law and Psychology Press.

Zonana, H. (1994). *Daubert v. Merrell Dow Pharmaceuticals*: A new stand for scientific evidence in the courts? *Bulletin of the American Academy of Psychiatry and the Law, 22,* 309–325.

Zusman, J., & Simon, J. (1983). Differences in repeated psychiatric examinations of litigants to a lawsuit. *American Journal of Psychiatry, 140,* 1300–1304.

Author Index

Subject Index